EVANSTON
WYOMING

Also available by Dennis J Ottley

Remembering (Korea: 1950-1953)

IZZARD INK PUBLISHING COMPANY
PO Box 522251
Salt Lake City, Utah 84152
www.izzardink.com

LIBRARY OF CONGRESS CONTROL NUMBER: 2018960342

Designed by Alissa Rose Theodor
Cover Design by Andrea Ho
Cover Photograph by Shelly & Deann Horne of Creative Ink Images
Cover Images: Robert Castillo/Shutterstock.com ivangal/Shutterstock.com
monofaction/Shutterstock.com

First Edition January 28, 2019

Contact the author at djottleybooks@gmail.com

Hardback ISBN: 978-1-64228-014-2
Softback ISBN: 978-1-64228-021-0
eBook ISBN: 978-1-64228-022-7

1967 TO 1995

EVANSTON WYOMING

VOLUME FOUR

BOOM-BUST-POLITICS

"IN THE EYES OF A MAYOR"

DENNIS J OTTLEY

IZZARD INK
— PUBLISHING —

CHAPTER 23

1989....1989 wasn't looking too good for Sandy and me because, after selling Uinta Realty, Inc. to my son and his associates, I became just another sales person for the agency. I tried very hard to take care of my obligations to the City of Evanston as mayor while at the same time making an effort to sell property and making a living. Being mayor didn't make it easy, but I did not want to resign because I wanted to make sure everything the city had going on would be completed.

Sandy and I were having a tough time keeping up with our debts, which included the debts I took with me from the agency. I was really concerned about the Union Tank Car Corp., which was under siege. A lot of local folks wanted them to move out of the roundhouse and machine shop, because those same folks wanted the property to go back into the hands of the city for historical reasons. This was a problem that ended up going on for years, and I was afraid that we could lose Union Tank Car before it was over.

The first meeting of the new year was held on January 9th at 7:00 p.m. I called the meeting to order. The first order of business, after roll call, the approval of the minutes and payment of the outstanding bills was the swearing-in ceremony of the Oath of Office. Administered by City Clerk Don Welling, the new council member Jerry Wall and re-elected councilmen, Tom Hutchinson and Clarence Vranish, were sworn in.

The *Uinta County Herald* issue of January 11th reported that: *Tears and mirth were seen at Monday's Evanston City Council meeting with the stepping down of former council member Julie Lehman and the swearing in of the new members of the council.*

I was very proud of Julie for staying on board until after the election and after a replacement was sworn in. When her husband, Judge

Larry Lehman, had been appointed by Governor Mike Sullivan to fill the vacancy of a district judge in Rawlins early last year, Julie had said that she would resign from the city council after school was out in June. At that time I asked her to please stay on until after the election. However, she not only stayed on after the election, she also stayed on until her term was up at the end of the year and I thanked her for that.

The Evanston City Councilmembers and I praised her highly for her outstanding performance as a member of the council, and I presented her with a bouquet of roses, a plaque, and her name tag. She received plenty of hugs before she left her place on the bench. She was very much appreciated and had been a good member of the council, always keeping in mind the best interests of the community.

Also honored was employee Ross Wilson, who was retiring from service. Ross had been a very dedicated employee for many years with excellent work ethics and a record of good service.

Next Allen Kennedy, Superintendent of Operations, was honored for a certification of completion from the California State University for further study in the operation and maintenance of wastewater collection systems.

In congratulating Allen, the council and I thanked him for his outstanding service to the City of Evanston in the past, and hoped this education from the university would assist him in solving any problems that the city may have with the wastewater system.

In other business, Councilmen Tom Hutchinson and Clarence Vranish were nominated for President of the Council. The vote was tied, but after a recess was called and the meeting reconvened, Vranish withdrew his name and Hutchinson was elected as President.

During my annual State of the City address, I praised the accomplishments of the city in the past year, but I also stated that I was very concerned with the continuing budget problems.

The *Uinta County Herald* of January 11th quoted me: *"The accomplishments this past year have been good,"* Ottley stated.

"Sulphur Creek Dam and the pipelines have been completed this year, the project is approximately 10 months ahead of schedule along with nearly $5 million under budget. Thanks to the previous council we will have the

funding to pay the money back." County Road was another project that was completed in the past year. Ottley explained that the city funded the project after the state backed out of it. "The project was completed and the people in the area should be proud of the beautiful road they now have," he continued.

The reason the Wyoming Highway Department backed out of the County Road project was because of change orders that caused the state to exceed their committed funds. They refused to furnish any more funds. Therefore the city had to find additional funds to finish the job, though the project had almost been finished with state funds.

I spoke of the reconstruction of the highway, Harrison Drive, on the west end of Evanston, and commented on how well the Wyoming Highway Department and the contractor had performed in getting the job completed by the deadline date of September 1, 1988.

The *Herald* quoted me: *"Now we have sidewalks on all the main streets in the city."*

I also praised the Uinta County Economic Development Board for encouraging the Job Corps center to locate in the area, and for supporting the Kern River Pipeline project. I said, "If those projects are built they could bring new industry to Evanston and help diversify the economy."

Other projects I spoke of were Depot Square, the Wyoming Centennial Celebration for 1990, the Bear River Rendezvous, and Support Your Community Week. I said I thought these were all good projects and would help bring the community together and boost the economy.

The *Herald* quoted me saying: *"We showed more pride in the city than we have in a long time, we have begun looking at things in a positive manner."*

I spoke of many more projects such as the Bear River State Park, the Sulphur Creek Dam project, and the expansion of the water treatment plant. I spoke of last year's grass fire and how all the folks in the county helped to keep it from spreading and causing more damage and possibly costing lives. It made me feel good to see the people of Uinta County come together to help their fellow citizens. *You couldn't find any action by the public that showed more dedication and positive thinking than how everyone pitched in to help.*

I also praised the city council for all their cooperation and assistance in helping to make the year a success, and I thanked the staff and administration, and all members of the various city boards and commissions. *"You all are the backbone of the city, I'm only the figurehead. You are the folks who have made things happen, you are the ones that have made Evanston a proud community,"* the *Herald* quoted me.

During my annual statement I also spoke of the loss of several of Evanston's outstanding citizens such as Darrell Staley, Phil Mensing, J. P. Hudson, Andy Mullhall, Francis (Pappy) Taylor and Sterling Aanerud, who had all been outstanding citizens who supported the community by getting involved and helping others.

⁓≫⊃

Phil Mensing, 45, was shot and killed at the landfill by Ken Stefanick, 49, an irate neighbor of Phil's brother, Steve Mensing, 43, who was also shot and wounded. His wound was life-threatening, but he did survive. There had been a dispute between Steve Mensing and Stefanick concerning Stefanick's son Michael.

On a Saturday afternoon in April, 1988, when Phil was helping his brother Steve take a load of trash out to the landfill, Stefanick followed them in his van. At approximately 5:00 p.m., while the Mensings were unloading their trash, Stefanick started shooting at them, killing Phil and wounding Steve.

After the shooting, landfill workers telephoned police, and officers were en route to the landfill when they spotted Stefanick driving back to town. Two police cruisers turned around and chased Stefanick into Evanston, where he crashed his van into a brick wall at the Uinta County Sheriff's office, located in the southeast corner of the Courthouse at that time, causing $10,000 to $20,000 in damage. Stefanick smashed his van up pretty bad and got out and started shooting at the officers who had been in pursuit. During the shootout, Stefanick was shot in the head and killed by a city police officer.

Evanston lost a good man in Phil Mensing. Phil ran the movie projector at the Strand Theater, and he was taking care of the Old Town Hall clock in the bell tower, keeping it in service and making sure it sounded the bell at the right time, at no charge. He was also very important to the police department, keeping their radio equipment in operation. He was the sort that would help anyone that needed help. It was a sad day for Evanston, another one of those unfortunate incidents causing the community to lose another good and likeable citizen.

Several months after Mensing's death, Sandy put together a large framed wall plaque titled "Top Cop". The plaque had a photo of the entire Police Department and a statement of what a terrific job the Evanston Police Department was doing and how much we and the city appreciated the protection and quick response to calls to keep the city safe. During her presentation she said, *My heroes have always been cowboys, but cops are now also my heroes.*

The *Uinta County Herald* reported what each city council member had to say during the first meeting in January: *Jon Lunsford praised the department heads and their professionalism and willingness to serve the community, and cautioned the council to remain watchful of the budget in the remaining fiscal year.*

Will Davis stressed his concern for stricter enforcement of drinking while driving laws, economic development importance and more stress put on waste management.

Craig Nelson mentioned his joy of working with the staff and the council. "It is a pleasure to serve the city," he said.

Tom Hutchinson proposed a 24-hour phone system be placed in city hall. He also expressed concern about the city budget.

Clarence Vranish complimented the mayor on a "job well done." He also felt the city employees did a great public service, "they should be allowed dignity in the work place and be left alone to do their job, not held up to ridicule."

I made the appointments of the officials, first reappointing Steve Snyder as Administrative Assistant to the Mayor, Don Welling as City Clerk/Treasurer and his assistant Steve Widmer as Manager of Financing and Accounting, Dennis Harvey as Chief of Police, Brian Honey as City Engineer, Dennis Boal as City Attorney,

John Phillips as City Court Justice, Paul Knopf as Community Development Director and City Planner, and Allen Kennedy as Supervisor of Operations.

All were confirmed by a motion made by Councilman Nelson, seconded by Davis, with 5 yes votes and 1 abstaining (Vranish). Why, I don't recall, but the motion passed with a majority.

I also assigned council members, once again, to act as department liaisons for the city and make their reports at every council meeting. Appointed were Clarence Vranish for streets and alleys; Tom Hutchinson for the water and sewer department; Will Davis for the sanitation department and solid waste; Jon Lunsford for the fire department, to act as liaison between the city and county governments, and to oversee the city shop; Tom Hutchinson and me for the recreation joint powers board; and Jerry Wall for the Urban Renewal Agency and Beautification Committee. I, as mayor, would remain Police Commissioner with Nelson and Wall acting with me on the commission. Also, I would act as liaison to the Evanston Housing Authority, and Vranish would be Evanston's representative to the Lincoln Uinta Association of Governments (LUAG) by attending their meetings and reporting back to the council.

Motion was made by Councilman Davis to confirm all the above appointments, seconded by Nelson, with all voting in favor.

During this meeting I appointed Susan Miller to the Evanston Planning and Zoning Commission. She replaced Don Coleman, who had recently retired from the commission. The city council confirmed the appointment of Susan Miller with a unanimous vote.

Don Coleman and Larry Matthews had both recently submitted their letters of resignation to the council. The council and I accepted their letters and thanked them for their service while serving on the P & Z Commission.

Also during this first meeting of 1989 we unanimously passed, on third reading, an ordinance to change the meeting days to the first and third Thursday of the month at 7:00 p.m.

County Commissioner John Stevens was present at the meeting to report to the Evanston City Council results of a meeting that Steve

Snyder and he had recently attended with the Rich County, Utah Commissioners in Randolph, Utah. The meeting addressed the possibility of seeding the clouds in the Wasatch Front of Utah to try to create more moisture for the area, because in recent years we have had many dry summers.

Stevens told the council that he thought that the Wyoming congressional members should be contacted for their help in passing new legislation or guidelines in Congress. He said he felt that cloud seeding could affect the amount of precipitation in the Bear River watershed.

I didn't know enough about the subject of cloud seeding to really take him seriously, and I sensed that the members of the council felt the same way. I never knew how far Stevens took this proposal, but I know he made an effort for quite some time to get folks to listen to him. There were several articles in the newspaper about it, and I know he talked to the Wyoming delegation in Congress, and I believe he had the Uinta County Commissioners pretty much sold on it. But as far as I know nothing ever became of the program. At end of the day, I didn't feel that anyone took the idea very seriously.

During the meeting Resolution 89-1 was introduced by Councilman Davis to support Salt Lake City, Utah in its bid for the 1998 Winter Olympics. Motion was made by Councilman Hutchinson, seconded by Wall, to adopt Resolution 89-1 with all voting in favor.

Resolution 89-2 was introduced by Councilman Nelson to permit the Evanston Police Department to adopt a "Ride Along" program, based on policies set by the department and approved by the Evanston City Council.

"Ride Along" was a program to give a police officer the right to allow someone of their choice to ride with them while on duty. It was meant for a young person who might be interested in police work to get an idea of what is expected of a police officer and what their duties were in keeping law and order. The ride-along person could be a high school or college student, a relative, or someone else at the officer's discretion, but it must be a responsible person interested in police work.

Motion was made by Councilman Lunsford, seconded by Davis, for the adoption of Resolution 89-2 with all voting in favor.

During the meeting I thanked Councilman Vranish for finding information from the Uinta County Clerk's office concerning the distribution of voters in each of the three Evanston wards during the 1988 election.

He reported the following:

Primary: Ward 1 - 1,234 votes; Ward 2 - 1,112 votes; Ward 3 - 1,142 votes.

General: Ward 1 - 1,383 votes; Ward 2 - 1,418 votes; Ward 3 - 1,304 votes.

I explained that I thought we made a smart move by re-adjusting the ward boundaries because from the election results of 1988 it appeared that the wards were much more equal now than they had been. The council agreed.

During a work session in late January it came to my attention that there was a problem with the Downtown Improvement District. I didn't have enough information on the problem yet, but there appeared to be a question as to what properties and property owners were included in the district. Therefore, as it was a work session and no official action could be taken at this time, I appointed a tentative committee to look into the problem and review it, then report back to the city council later.

The committee was comprised of Dennis Boal, city attorney; Steve Widmer, assistant city treasurer; John Stevens, county commissioner, insurance agent and property owner; Art Monroe, Evanston businessman and property owner; and Jon Lunsford and Clarence Vranish, city council members.

During the regular city council meeting on Monday, January 23rd, the final payments for the completion of the County Road project were paid. The project included the improvement of the roadway and the Bear River Bridge, and was constructed with funds from the Wyoming State Farm Loan Board and the City of Evanston.

The County Road was now improved with two lanes and a center lane for turning, and sidewalks and curbing on both sides of the street, as well as crosswalks for pedestrians crossing the street. It was a big improvement and was much safer for vehicle traffic and pedestrians.

City Engineer Brian Honey said, *Even with the final change orders on the project we came in $6,500 less than the bid amount. All participants, JBP Construction and Uinta Engineering have done an excellent job,* he added.

Honey also reported on the Bear River intake project connecting the pipeline to the Sulphur Creek Reservoir project. He said that although we hadn't planned completion of the intake until April 1989, it looked like they would be finished by the end of February 1989.

The Wyoming Downs horse racing, located just north of Bear River City, had been running for quite some time. Rancher Richard Sims and his associates originally opened the racetrack, but at this time it had been sold to another group. The track had helped the economy of Evanston in some ways, especially in the summertime during the racing season.

During the council meeting Community Development Director and City Planner Paul Knopf reported that Ladbroke Racing would be coming to the Evanston Planning and Zoning Commission to request a conditional use permit to open a horse betting parlor in town and televise races at the Weston Budget Inn (now Day's Inn).

Televised races would mean that we would have off-track betting in certain establishments in town, which would help the economy. It would not only create a few jobs, it would also increase sales tax and other tax revenues for the city and county.

NEW PIN — The chamber of commerce now has a supply of Evanston pins for sale. Pins are also available from many of the town's businesses.

Evanston pin is now for sale

The new "Fresh Air, Freedom and Fun" promotional pins have now arrived and are available at the chamber of commerce offices and many Evanston businesses.

The pins cost $3 and feature the famous Wyoming bucking bronco. The pins will be used to promote Evanston in different parts of the country.

According to Denice Wheeler, chair of the Evanston Visitor and Convention Council, any business interested in selling the pins should contact the chamber at 789-2757.

Uinta County Herald, April 5, 1989.

Also during the January meeting I made more appointments. Donna Bruce was appointed to the Parks and Recreation Board to fill a vacancy left by the resignation of Susan Vanderhoef; Nelle Gerrard was appointed to the Planning and Zoning Commission to fill in the vacancy left by Larry Matthews; and Leon Clyde Pruett, Jodi Deru, Kathy Bauman, Bonnie Phillips, Nelle Gerrard, Julia Davis and Janet Stugelmeyer were all appointed to the Beautification Committee.

Councilman Nelson made a motion to confirm these appointments, seconded by Councilman Davis, with all voting in favor.

The Beautification Committee would be a commission working under the direction of the Urban Renewal Agency, headed by Jim Davis.

City Planner Paul Knopf announced that the new "Fresh Air, Freedom and Fun" pin would be available to the public on March 1st of that year. The Tourist and Convention Committee of the Evanston Chamber of Commerce had selected that motif to go on the official Evanston pin.

The pin will feature the slogan, "Fresh Air, Freedom and Fun," plus the famous Wyoming bucking bronco. It will have three colors with a gold-colored background and will sell for $3.00 each, Knopf said.

It was reported that the economy was looking up, and the school district was losing fewer students than previously. Though this indicated that we were not losing population as we had been, more and more foreclosures were being published in the newspaper each week. To me that was an indication that we were still in a slump and the housing market was getting no better.

During the January 23rd regular meeting, Resolution 89-4 was introduced by Councilman Hutchinson to amend the personnel policy naming the holidays declared by the city as follows:

The City recognizes eleven (11), eight (8) hour holidays each calendar year. The holidays are listed below:

New Year's Day, January 1
President's Day, Third Monday in February
Memorial Day, Last Monday in May

Independence Day, July 4

Labor Day, First Monday in September

Columbus Day, Second Monday in October

Veteran's Day, November 11

Thanksgiving Day, Fourth Thursday in November

Thanksgiving Friday, Day after Thanksgiving

Christmas, December 25 and preceding or succeeding day

Motion was made by Councilman Davis to adopt Resolution 89-4, seconded by Lunsford, with all voting in favor.

✐

On February 2, 1989 Evanston and area had a huge snowstorm and a blinding blizzard, closing Interstate 80 between Evanston and Fort Bridger. During this storm my youngest son, Cody was on his way back from Vernal, Utah when he and his work partner, Russell Foxley, got lost in the storm.

While returning from a job they had been doing for their employer, Ross Rae Electric Company of Evanston, in Vernal, they were stopped just west of the Bingo Truck Stop (TCA Truck Stop at present), and were told they could go no farther because Interstate 80 was closed. Cody called me from the truck stop and told me that Foxley and he decided they would try to get home by using the old U.S. Highway 30 S to County Road 173 and go through Piedmont to State Highway 150 South. He told me that he needed to get home to take his son, Jhett, to Utah for surgery the next day.

When they didn't show up in Evanston, we reported them missing to the Uinta County Sheriff's Office about 8:00 a.m. the next morning. The Sheriff's deputies and other personnel from the office immediately mobilized and went in search of them. They began their search from both sides of the county, Bridger Valley and Evanston, but when the two weren't found they brought in snowcats and focused on the Piedmont area. Ross Rae Electric used its snowcat manned by Deputy Mark Baca and Ralston DeGraw to search the area. They found Foxley in the Piedmont area walking towards Evanston. I was notified immediately of Foxley's rescue, and Foxley told the rescue team that Cody had stayed with the vehicle located to the east. It was located on the Piedmont Road, a mile and a half in from where County Road 173 intersects with the old U.S. 30. They both had stayed in the vehicle overnight.

Cody was found asleep in the vehicle and appeared to be in good condition.

"Thank the Lord he was all right. I want to thank the Sheriff's officers and those who worked so hard trying to find him," the *Uinta County Herald* quoted me.

I also thanked Ross-Rae Electric for offering their assistance and equipment in trying to find the two men.

Our first regular city council meeting of the month was scheduled for that same Thursday night of February 2nd. I went to the meeting, but after calling the meeting to order, I mentioned to those in attendance that I would be leaving the meeting early because my son had been lost in the snowstorm. Therefore, I left after roll call, the approval of the minutes and paying outstanding bills, and after re-appointing Mark Harris and Mildred Palmer to serve another 3-year term on the Urban Renewal Agency, which the council confirmed by a unanimous vote.

There was no one present for public participation and there was no old business to come before the Council. Tom Hutchinson, President of the Council was not in attendance, leaving only Vranish, Councilmen Will Davis and Craig Nelson, and Councilwoman Jerry Wall. Therefore, when I asked to be excused, I turned the meeting over to Councilman Clarence Vranish.

The city council proceeded to act on a few resolutions that were on the agenda, plus Councilman Davis made a motion to go into executive session to discuss water line connections on properties beyond the city limits on Wyoming State Highway 150 South, seconded by Nelson with all voting in favor.

Because the Sulphur Creek Reservoir Dam and Pipeline projects were funded by state and federal money, the City of Evanston could not deny those living outside of Evanston water service if they requested it.

The property owners on Highway 150 South had requested that they be allowed to hook into city water, but a water service line had not been extended that far south of the city; it ended at the city limits. The added distance would be approximately one mile of service line at the expense of the city, but the property owners would be required to pay for hookups and monthly water fees as set by city ordinance.

Therefore, with the city agreeing to run the water service line south of Evanston, Councilman Nelson had made a motion to advertise for bids for the service line project on Highway 150 South. The motion was seconded by Davis with 4 yes votes. The motion passed unanimously.

The *Uinta County Herald* reported that the 27-minute Evanston City Council meeting was one of the shortest ever.

Later, during a regular city council meeting on March 2nd, Councilman Davis made a motion to award the bid on Highway 150 South water line project to the low bidder, Jasco, Inc. for the amount of $15,598.14. The motion was seconded by Councilman Nelson, with all voting in favor.

Evanston City Councilman Will Davis was very enthusiastic about getting a recycling program going. He said he hoped that Evanston would become a leader in the State of Wyoming with a recycling and solid waste management program.

He said that he believed it was time to address solid waste management problems by creating a recycling program. The present landfill was filling up faster than anticipated, he indicated.

According to Davis, in the near future the city would first start an aluminum can recycling program, and that the proceeds from the sale of aluminum would be used to help with the Bear River and Environment Project.

I agreed with Councilman Davis that the City of Evanston should start a recycling program, and that landfills were very expensive to operate and that we should do whatever possible to save room in the landfill. Later on the city purchased a building not too far from the public works building and we decided to turn that into a recycling center to store all materials. Having recycle containers placed in various locations around town made it easier for the folks to dump their recycled materials such as aluminum cans and other metals, paper and cardboard, etc. With this building, the city was able to get into the recycling business full time. We advertised and did whatever was necessary to encourage the public to recycle.

Woodsy came to town

Woodsy the Owl came to Evanston last week to help the city kick off its recycling program. Woodsy is the mascot of the U.S. Forest Service and urges people not to pollute. Shown from left are Mayor Dennis Ottley, Woodsy, and Brian Lowe, president of the Evanston Beautification Committee.

Employee Barry Constantine was appointed to oversee the recycling program by sorting materials and locating buyers for the materials. His office would be in the new recycling building and he would be a full time employee. It turned out to be a very good program. The public helped out an awful lot by using the containers around town, and it saved a lot of garbage from going to the landfill.

In 1980, during my first term as mayor, I happened to be visiting with one of Evanston's native sons, Bill Fields. Bill had lived here all his life, and while serving in the United States Navy during WWll he was wounded, costing him one of his eyes. But Bill was very artistic and a damn good photographer.

Bill was also very intelligent, not very stable or dependable, but likeable. He never held a permanent job; he would just hang out around town being kind of a roustabout, talking to people and frequenting the local bars. I don't think you could describe him as a town drunk, but he did visit the bars often, maybe just to talk to folks but not to drink all that much.

Because he was the way he was, talking to people and being friendly, he seemed to know a lot about what was going on in Evanston, and about Evanston's history. He knew everyone in town and everyone knew him.

Being as artistic as he was, he had designed many of the Labor Day posters for Cowboy Days, and painted many pictures that, I believe, are still hanging in many different locations in town. He was also often hired as the official photographer for the three-day cowboy event. That day in 1980, when I was visiting with Bill, we started talking about the changes in Evanston, and in our conversation the old Oak Tavern saloon came up. The Oak Tavern was located in the building where the F.O.E. Eagles Lodge is now located. But originally, as far as Bill and I knew, the Oak was owned by Glen Mills, also a native of Evanston. Glen was a two- or three-generation member of a family that had resided in Evanston for many, many years.

When gambling became illegal in Wyoming in the early 1950s, ten or so years later Glen Mills lost his business. Why, I had no idea. After the time that Glen owned the tavern, there had been two or three other owners before it became the Eagles' lodge.

Bull rider on downtown Front Street. *Note bullet hole in the bull rider's hat.

Cattle drive on Front Street heading for the railroad stockyards.

During Glen's ownership of the business some of my friends and I often visited his bar; he treated us well and we liked him. Sometimes he would even hold a check for some of the guys who needed help until their payday. While at the bar we often talked about the murals that Glen had on the wall above his work counter. There were two murals, 4 or 5 feet in width and 7 or 8 feet in length. The paintings were of locations, buildings, events and scenes of Evanston, and they seemed to tell a story. But while sitting at the bar, we noticed that there was a small hole at the top of one of the murals. When asked about the hole, Glen told us the story of him and Square Bateman, one of his card dealers. During the time that Evanston had casino gambling going on, the two got to drinking after closing hours and, getting a little tipsy, they got their guns out, horsing around, when one of them shot at the picture and put the hole in it. At first we thought he was just BSing us, but later on we found his story to be true.

While Bill Fields and I were visiting in 1980, he told me that when one of the new owners was remodeling the place they just pulled those murals off the wall and threw them in the garbage can behind the tavern. Bill was walking in the alley at the time they were remodeling and spotted those murals in the garbage. When he went into the tavern he asked the new owner if he could have them, the new owner said sure; they were no good to him. Bill didn't hesitate. He took them home to add to the rest of his relics that he collected around town. They were painted on a sheet of canvas, which helped keep them in one piece when they were pulled off the wall. Bill and I both felt they were priceless.

While talking to him about the Oak Tavern, the subject of those murals came up and I told Bill that it would have been a shame if those paintings had been destroyed. That is when he told me that he had them at his house.

I was surprised and asked what shape they were in. He said that they were in pretty good shape but needed cleaning. He invited me to his house to look at them. His house is next to where The Green-horn floral shop is now located, across Main Street from the new post office. His house is still standing and isn't much to look at. It should probably be torn down, but it has a new owner and for some reason or other they have chosen not to.

When Bill took me to look at those paintings, I noticed a lot of relics and what some people would call junk, but the old saying, *"What is one man's trash, may be another man's treasure,"* certainly seemed to fit Bill perfectly. But he also had some stuff that I thought could be worth a lot of money. I found his house to be quite untidy, but some of the stuff he had in there was pretty damn interesting and well worth saving.

When Bill showed me the murals they were quite dirty and looked a little ragged, but with a little straightening out and cleaning up I felt they would be worth saving. I asked Bill if he wanted to sell them and he said he would, but he wanted $1,100 for both of them. I was quite surprised that he would price them that high, but I really wanted to save them and fix them up with frames. They could be displayed somewhere in town where folks could see them, because I thought they told a good story and people would enjoy the history behind them.

In 1980, at the peak of the boom, Uinta Realty was doing very well financially and I was making pretty good money, and I knew that Bill was basically broke. I had never been one to do much dickering when it came to buying something, so I told him that I would buy them and clean them up and display them in my office.

Carrying the paintings, he came with me to my office, which was also located on Main Street, just a few buildings from his home. My office was on the main floor of the Old Town Hall (the old fire station). While there I wrote him a check for $1,100, and he handed the murals to me. He thanked me for being interested in them and hoped that I could successfully clean them up and display them so Evanston folks could see them. I guess some people would say I was crazy for paying that much for them, but I have never been sorry for purchasing those murals.

After I bought them, I didn't tell anyone how much I paid for them. I actually felt that I did pay way too much for them, but I was glad to have them in my possession and was anxious to display them.

When I showed them to Sandy, she said she could clean them up and straighten them out. So we took the paintings upstairs to one of the vacant offices in the Old Town Hall and laid them out on a long table. She had an old large rolling pin that she used to straighten them out, and then applied some kind of fluid to clean them up without harming the paint.

After Sandy had them clean and looking real good, I showed them to my dad during one of his visits from Orem, Utah, and he told me that I ought to have them framed. I agreed that framing them would make it easier to hang them, because without frames they would have had to be pasted to a wall like they were in the old Oak Tavern.

After telling Dad what I knew about the story behind the pictures, he volunteered to make the frames for me. He was set up at his home in Orem to do a lot of small carpenter work. He measured the paintings and said he would make the two frames so that very little of the picture would be hidden.

When Dad brought the stained frames, perfectly sized, he stapled the paintings to the frame, stretching them out as much as he could, and made the murals look quite good.

With the murals framed and ready to be hung, I first invited Glen Mills to my office to look at them. The next morning he came to my office. Being up there in age, not too healthy, and carrying his cane, he was quite slow getting up those stairs. When he entered the office where the pictures were he appeared to be overly but, I noticed, he had a saddened look.

I got two folding chairs for us to sit on. We sat there for quite some time, him being very teary-eyed, while he told me the history of those paintings.

He told me that the way those painting all came about was that he and his brother, John Mills, owner of the Dunmar "Best Western" Motel at one time, collected a bunch of photos of Evanston and took them to Ogden, Utah to an art studio and had them paint the murals from small photographs that they had collected of Evanston (that is why there are a few places on the murals that are not accurate).

He told me how the bullet hole got in the one mural. The story that I had previously been told was true.

After the art studio finished the paintings, he and his brother John had them pasted to the wall above his back counter and bar in the Oak Tavern. He was quite teary at times while I was talking to him, and after telling him I had to leave for a bit, he asked me if he could just sit there for a while. I told him to take as much time as he liked.

Glen had been sitting in that office staring at those murals for hours after I left him, and when he hobbled down the stairs with his cane, and came into my office I could see that he was pretty blurry-eyed, and had been thinking back and reminiscing all that time.

But he thanked me for saving the murals and asked me what I was going to do with them. I told him that Sandy and I decided to hang them up in the old Beeman-Cashin building now that it had been refurbished, so Evanston folks and others could see them. I told him the story of how Bill got the paintings, and said that he should thank Bill Fields for finding them and saving them. After a few minutes he kind of let out a sigh and left, appearing to be feeling much better.

After getting the murals framed and ready to be hung, I wrote a short summary about the paintings based on what Glen Mills had told me. I also had those framed. They would be displayed on the wall near each painting where folks could read a little history about them. Jim Davis, Director of the Urban Renewal Agency, loved those murals and was very excited about hanging them in the Beeman-Cashin building. Jim was instrumental in getting the B-C building moved and getting it refurbished. He got Gary Bentley, the city's carpenter and maintenance man, to hang the paintings up along with the framed stories. I believe he also had Frankie Workman, the city's custodian, help him.

Not too long after those murals were placed in the B-C building, Glen Mills passed on. Evanston lost another one of our "Old Timers". But those murals are still displayed on the wall of the Beeman-Cashin building where many local folks have looked at them over the years, made comments about them, and even remembered them being on the wall at the old Oak Tavern; and they also remembered both, Glen and John Mills very well.

Another issue was the Job Corps Center in Wyoming. It had been suggested that a Job Corps training center be established somewhere in Wyoming, preferably the Evanston area. Wyoming was one of the few states that did not have a Job Corps Center. Therefore, we were being closely looked at.

However, one objection to Evanston being selected as a site was that the Weber Job Corps Center in Ogden that had been in operation for many years was less than 100 miles from Evanston, causing us a little concern about getting chosen. But that reasoning didn't have much to do with it, because Wyoming wanted the troubled young people of Wyoming to stay in the state instead of being sent to an out-of-state center.

Don Eversole, training representative for the state Job Services agency told us that the Job Corps was a government-sponsored training program to help participants to learn a trade and improve their education.

During this time, the City of Evanston and Uinta County both appeared to want the Job Corps Center located somewhere in Uinta County. Of course the city council and I wanted it located as near to Evanston as possible because we felt it would have a big impact in helping the economy.

In the process of applying for Evanston to be chosen, the city council voted unanimously to submit our application along with a scenario of what the City of Evanston had to offer to the U.S. Forest Service, who was sponsoring the project.

Some of the questions they asked were: Was Evanston financially prepared to support the project? Was Evanston's law enforcement well enough staffed and prepared for possible problems? Will the non-city groups be willing to accept and support the project? In our scenario we submitted positive answers on all their questions.

The Uinta County Commissioners also submitted their application and scenario in favor of Uinta County being selected as the county to locate the Center. All commissioners appeared to be in favor, and helped locate a site for the center.

It was looking good for the City of Evanston, especially after Governor Sullivan and the Wyoming Land Commission approved a site for us. The proposed site was in a section of government-owned land about two miles south of Evanston, across from the Jamison Industrial Park about a few hundred yards to the west off Highway 150. We all felt it would be an excellent location for the new Job Corps Center.

The previous year, in 1988, Councilman Clarence Vranish even wrote a letter to Utah Senator Orrin Hatch requesting his support in selecting Evanston for the site of the Job Corps Center, which I believed helped some.

There had been eight centers authorized by the U.S. Department of Labor, and Wyoming did not have a Job Corps Center, so they definitely wanted to locate a center in Wyoming. Governor Mike Sullivan and the Wyoming Congressional delegation all appeared to be in support of Wyoming being chosen.

Although it was looking really good for Evanston, after the location was selected and accepted by all involved, the issue became quite controversial. The folks residing on Highway 150 complained that they did not want the center out there near their homes. This caused a lot more folks throughout Uinta County to think negatively about locating a Job Corps Center anywhere in the County of Uinta. They had the idea that the young students in the center would just be problem kids and juvenile delinquents, and would cause a lot of problems.

I told the press that Uinta County was in a good position for the Job Corps Center. I told them about the location and that hopefully the final decision would be made sometime mid-April of 1989, but it wasn't, and wouldn't be decided on for quite some time. I stated that the name of the center would officially be "Bear River Job Corps Center," and would create an additional 50 to 60 jobs. But due to several factors it would be a while before any decision about location was definite. I also told the press that Fremont County in central Wyoming was competing for the center, but I felt that the Evanston and

Uinta County group had done their homework and their proposal was far ahead of any others.

I indicated that some of the cost of extending utilities could be covered by the city and county through Economic Development Grants, and the acquisition of the land from the State of Wyoming or the Bureau of Land Management (BLM) could be accomplished in less than a month at no cost to the Job Corps.

However, opposition against the center being located in Uinta County was starting to get hot and heavy. Folks that were living south of Evanston, near the proposed site, were strongly against it, causing others to feel the same way, including some organizations. Also, I was getting worried because some city council members were starting to think differently and I was afraid that all this controversy would be getting back to the U.S. Forest Service and the Department of Labor, having a big effect on their decision. It did.

In a talk with one of the groups opposed to Evanston being the site for the center, I reminded them of a little history: back in the late 1880s, when there was talk about Evanston getting what was at that time referred to as the Insane Asylum, and what is now called the Wyoming State Hospital. I mentioned to them how much, at that time, the citizens of the Town of Evanston opposed having it in Evanston. The people fought hard against it. I told them when I came to Evanston in 1947 it was still referred to as the Insane Asylum. Some folks didn't like it that, so they changed it to the Wyoming State Hospital or the hospital for the mentally ill, and no longer would it be referred to as an insane asylum.

But at any rate, although the townsfolk didn't want it, they still got it. And as far as I know the Community of Evanston had never regretted it, because it had been a great benefit to the economy over all these years. I said to the group, "The Wyoming State Hospital has been an asset to the community and the folks learned to appreciate it, just as you will if we are fortunate enough to be selected for the [Job Corps] Center."

In late spring of 1989, the City of Evanston was notified that neither Evanston nor Uinta County would be selected for the new Job

Corps Center. It was a real disappointment to me, but when some of the council members even turned against it, it had a big effect on the decision, and with all the scuttlebutt going on from the opposition. Over the years it was decided by those in power to locate the Center in Fremont County.

Evanston City Administrator Steve Snyder told the press, *We had the indirect backing of U.S. Congressman Craig Thomas, and thought we would be one of the sites selected.* It was a big disappointment to Snyder and me, and to some of the council members, and it was a big disappointment to many others who were in favor of the center. We all knew it was something that Evanston needed to help boost the economy.

In the meantime, the tentative committee appointed to look into the situation of the Downtown Improvement District had reported on the specific problems. Many property owners within the improvement district were very upset and claimed that some of the promises made to them during the Martin Administration were never kept, so they didn't feel that they should pay their designated share.

The committee reported that the district was formed in 1984 and 1985, when bonds were sold in the amount of $760,000 to finance improvements within the district. The district was formed for the purpose of constructing, acquiring property, razing buildings for the United States Post Office, parking lots at 11th (Harrison) and Center Streets and behind the old federal building (post office) on Center Street, as well as installing paving, curbs, gutters, sidewalks, lighting and landscaping in the downtown core area.

The committee also reported that prepayment of the bonds was set up on a tier system. Those businesses (property owners) nearest the core area would be required to pay more than those on the outside fringe.

The report continued to say that there were 87 participants in the district and, at that time, 18 of those businesses were behind in their payments. Several of those business owners claimed it would be impossible for them to pay off the debt.

One owner of two businesses in the district who refused to pay the assessment, claimed that his original payment was $9,911 in 1985, but with the interest at 12 percent compounded annually plus penalties for not making his payment, that had grown to approximately $20,000. He stated that he was in a "Catch 22" situation, because if a lien was filed by the city, causing him to either pay or face foreclosure, he would be forced into bankruptcy.

After the council had heard all the delinquent property owners' concerns, it was suggested in a work session that a 30- to 60-day waiver of the penalty be offered as an incentive for those businesses that were behind in their payments, but no action could be taken at this time.

During our second regular council meeting on February 16th, Resolution 89-10 was introduced by Councilman Davis to authorize the City of Evanston to obtain a permit from the Army Corps of Engineers to repair and stabilize the existing dike at the Evanston Ice Ponds.

This permit would have enabled the Bear Project Committee to apply for funds to repair the dike controlling the flow from Bear River to the ponds so they could help keep them filled and useful to the public for recreation purposes.

Motion was made by Councilman Vranish to adopt Resolution 89-10, seconded by Nelson with all voting in favor.

The city was successful in obtaining the requested permit from the Corps of Engineers and the committee obtained the funds, and repaired and stabilized the dike, controlling the flow of water into the ponds.

Also during the February meeting, Resolution 89-11 was introduced by Councilman Davis authorizing the City of Evanston to enter into an agreement with the Denver Research Group to provide a study and analysis of the economic benefits of the Kern River Pipeline Project. The study would provide information on economic and other benefits that would enable the city to pursue further action in support of the project with information on how beneficial it would be to the city for economic growth and other effects.

Motion was made by Councilwoman Wall for the adoption of Resolution 89-11, seconded by Vranish, but Councilman Lunsford amended the motion to change the name Kern River Pipeline to Wyoming-California Natural Gas Pipeline, seconded by Wall.

Motion was passed to adopt Resolution 89-11 as amended, with 6 yes votes and 1 no vote from Councilman Hutchinson.

I don't recall why Tom Hutchinson voted against the motion, but I'm sure he had his reasons.

During this meeting I suggested that the Employee's Deferred Compensation Plan go back to being mandatory and put into force at the time of the new fiscal year. During my first term as mayor, I encouraged the council to set this program up. At that time the city council and I felt that full-time city employees deserved and should have a retirement plan, which they never had before. We set the plan up so each employee paid 10 percent of their paycheck into the plan, and the city would match their 10 percent and put that money into the plan. These funds would be put into an interest-bearing account and when an employee quit or retired they would be able to draw out those funds plus whatever interest it had gained. Because of city monies involved, the council felt that the plan should be mandatory. It was a great plan, and the employees overwhelmingly voted in favor of it.

However, when I went out of office and Gene Martin become mayor, sometime during his term some employees complained about the retirement program being mandatory. They wanted it to be paid to them with their paycheck. Therefore, Mayor Martin and the city council removed the mandatory requirement, which in my mind was stupid, because all it did was give those employees that wanted to receive it in the paycheck, including the 10% the city contributed, an immediate 10% increase in pay. It defeated the entire idea of making sure that all employees would have something to look forward to when they retired or quit their employment.

Resolution 89-38 was introduced by Councilman Vranish during the month of June, prior to the budget deadline, making the Employee's Deferred Comprehensive Plan mandatory. Motion was made by Councilwoman Wall for adoption of Resolution 39-38, seconded by Hutchinson, with 5 yes votes, 1 no vote (Nelson), and 1 absent (Lunsford).

I felt that because of city funds being contributed to that plan over and above their paycheck, the plan should be made mandatory, and I told the council that. They agreed with me and in a later meeting the action was taken to do just that. A few employees were upset about it, but most weren't concerned, because most of them remained with the original plan.

During the February meeting Councilwoman Wall made a motion that the City Council meeting of March 2nd begin at 5:00 p.m. instead of 7:00 p.m., and be advertised as such because of the heavy agenda scheduled for that meeting. The motion was seconded by Hutchinson, with all voting in favor.

During the March 2nd meeting Councilman Vranish sponsored and introduced Charter Ordinance 89-1, the first charter ordinance that had been sponsored for a long time. The ordinance was to change our fiscal year for the budget from the present July 1st through June 30th to match the state and federal government fiscal years, October 1st through September 30th.

There was a lot of concern about the ordinance becoming law: Evanston would be the only city or town in the State of Wyoming that had their fiscal year matching that of the state and federal governments. Therefore, during discussion, Steve Widmer, Manager of Financing and Accounting was directed to check into the impact of this Charter Ordinance, but we would pass it on first reading to see where it went.

The reasoning behind the act was to be able to coincide with the state and federal governments, especially when state and federal funds (loans, grants etc.) were included. Some of the council members believed that it would make it easier to prepare a budget if we knew where the state and federal funds were coming from. Though not necessarily in favor, I was willing to give it a chance to see where it went, but I wasn't expecting it to pass on the third and final reading.

Councilwoman Wall made the motion to pass Charter Ordinance 89-1 on first reading, seconded by Davis, with all voting in favor.

Last April, Mr. Joe Dobry entered the city council meeting with a rifle in his hands, trying to make a point, because the local police officers removed a hunting knife from his son while in a local café. His concern was if Section 15-8 of the city code did not include rifles, *why would it be against the law to carry a hunting knife?* This was an old city code that should have probably been amended a long time ago, but apparently was overlooked.

I asked him, why the rifle? He responded that he was just trying to get the council's attention on an old section of the city code that prohibited knifes being carried in public places. Well, he got the council's attention, and he got the council to take action on changing the law.

During the March 2nd council meeting Councilman Davis sponsored Ordinance 89-2, and Councilman Nelson introduced it. The ordinance was to amend Section 15-8 of the Dangerous Weapons Code of the City of Evanston.

After a short discussion, Councilman Hutchinson made the motion to pass Ordinance 89-2 as amended, seconded by Vranish, with all voting in favor. This ordinance went on to be passed on second and third readings by a unanimous vote and became law immediately.

The eighth annual Agri-Business banquet was held on March 2nd of this year at the Weston Lamplighter Inn (Days Inn), sponsored once again by the Uinta County Rural Development Committee. The program was set up to bring the agricultural industry and business entrepreneurs together for better public relations and understanding, and it was also a time to honor those outstanding citizens involved in agriculture and business each year.

This year Evanston's Citizen of the Year award, selected by the Evanston City Council, went to Alma Craig for her volunteer work at the rest home. She also spent many hours weekly at the Regional Hospital, the Senior Citizens Center, and the day care center for children. It was an award well deserved.

The Wyoming State Legislative session had ended and during an interview with the *Uinta County Herald* asking me how I felt about their legislation requesting a long-term solution to municipal finance problems in Wyoming. A long-term solution had not been reached by the 1989 legislature.

My answer was published in the *Uinta County Herald* issue of March 10, 1989:

"A careful and intelligent plan was presented to the legislature by a joint interim legislative committee that would have solved the problems we are facing due to the $55 million per year in state shared revenue of sales tax, mineral royalties, sales and cigarette taxes that has been lost to Wyoming communities," Dennis J. Ottley, Mayor of Evanston said. "Positive and progressive steps were taken in helping communities deal with current municipal finance problems, but the total package which would have been a solution was rejected.

"The cornerstone of the entire package was a bill to share an additional 1/10 of a cent of the state sales tax with cities and towns," Ottley said. "This bill will allow us to continue benefiting at an appropriate level from the state's economic activity. The downside of this bill, which has been signed by the Governor, is the two year sunset amendment that was attached and will discontinue the funding in two years.

"This makes it difficult for long term planning and somewhat defeats the original intention of the joint interim committee for a long-term solution for municipal financing." "The rainy day account will provide for long-term stabilization of revenues through any future boom and bust cycles and the changes the one cent local option sales tax will help us do a better job of budget planning," Ottley said.

"I feel very good about the work of the joint interim committee and bills that were passed by the legislature. We will still have to return to the legislature in two years to pursue our goal of long-term solution to financing public services in Evanston.

"In the meantime we will continue our efforts to provide essential benefits for the people of Evanston."

Ottley added that he felt Uinta County's delegation, Senator John Fanos and Representatives Ron Micheli and Jerry Parker, provided strong leadership and assistance on the community issues.

During the regular city council meeting of March 16th, Sheila Bricher-Wade, Rheba Massey and Fred Chapman, of the Wyoming State Archives, Museum and Historic Department of the State Historic Preservation Office, awarded the City of Evanston two plaques with special emphasis on the Union Pacific Railroad Complex at Depot Square and the Downtown Historic District. The two plaques were to be placed on the historic buildings where they could be seen by the public as determined by the Urban Renewal Agency.

When President of the Urban Renewal Agency, Bob Schuetz presented Ms Bricher-Wade to the council, she said *The first time I came to Evanston it was to view the first church in this community. Things have certainly happened while I've been gone.* She commented that the Evanston Depot and the Union Pacific complex is the largest grouping of U.P.R.R. buildings in the state, *and we will be using Evanston as an example,* she continued.

During the meeting of March 16th some of the property owners involved in the Downtown Improvement District were in attendance, concerned about their delinquent assessment and wanting to express those concerns to the city council.

The minutes of the council meeting quoted me expressing my empathy for the problems they were experiencing; however, I said that it was a legal Improvement District with bonds that had been sold, and there were *bonds and interest that must be paid for.* I suggested that perhaps the penalty that had accrued to this point could be waived if people paid off their assessments or brought the assessments current by June 1, 1989.

Councilman Jon Lunsford asked the people involved not to think of the council as enemies. They were only neighbors and friends that had concern for their problems.

At this time, Resolution 89-15 was introduced by Councilman Vranish, authorizing the waiver of penalty payments for assessed landowners of the Evanston Downtown Improvement District.

Motion was made by Vranish for the adoption of Resolution 89-15, seconded by Lunsford, with 6 votes in favor and 1 abstaining (Councilwoman Wall felt she had a conflict and had left the chambers).

This resolution appeased the property owners. We never heard any more about the improvement district, and it was completely paid off in the next few years.

During the regular city council meeting of April 6th the council members and I gave special recognition to public works employee Dan Martin for his completion of Volume I, Operation and Maintenance of Wastewater Collection Systems School. This course is provided by an educational institute for public employees involved in the operation and maintenance of wastewater treatment plants and services.

We all offered our appreciation and congratulations for the completion of the work related school. Dan Martin was a very loyal and dedicated employee.

Charter Ordinance 89-1 would change the City of Evanston's fiscal year to fit the State of Wyoming and the federal government's fiscal year of October 1st through September 30th. The ordinance passed on first and second readings, but was tabled by motion and seconded because some of the council members requested more time to study the ordinance. It was tabled until the special city council meeting of April 13th was scheduled. The motion to table passed by a unanimous vote.

During the meeting Councilman Craig Nelson reported that the City of Evanston had received a $25,000 grant from the State of Wyoming Recreation Commission to be used towards the improvements of the Bear River Project and Ice Ponds. According to Evanston Planning Director Paul Knopf, who prepared the grant application for the city, there were 40 applications asking for a total of $923,000. "Albert Pilch, member of the state recreation commission, from Evanston really pushed for the funding," said Knopf. "He really went to bat for us. Of the seven projects funded, Evanston was one of five which received all the money it requested," Knopf continued.

He explained that the City of Evanston would match the $25,000 with $50,000 in services, equipment and staff time. The money would be used for site improvements such as grading, land leveling, dredging, debris removal and dike rehabilitation.

Knopf also reported on the Adopt-A-Tree program, and that the City of Evanston was awarded a plaque for their downtown tree planting effort by the Take Pride in America organization.

During the special city council meeting of April 13th, in addition to representatives from the *Uinta County Herald* and the Evanston Broadcasting Company (KEVA Radio), we had a group of young Boy Scouts: Jason Voss, Justin Lunsford, Weston Lunsford and their leaders, Susan Lunsford and Lance Voss.

The special meeting agenda listed Charter Ordinance 89-1 as the only item. After introducing the Scouts, Councilman Jon Lunsford made a motion to remove the charter ordinance from the table for third and final reading, seconded by Nelson, with all voting in favor. Therefore, the charter ordinance was put back on the floor for discussion.

During discussion I first reminded the council that in order to pass a charter ordinance, it must have a two-thirds vote from the entire council, and that it would take five members of the council's vote to come up with the two-thirds. After a short discussion I called for a vote on the motion made and tabled during the last city council meeting, to pass Charter Ordinance 89-1 on third and final reading. A roll call vote was called for: Clarence Vranish, Jerry Wall, and I all voted yes, and Craig Nelson, Will Davis, and Jon Lunsford voted no. Councilman Tom Hutchinson was absent. The motion failed.

I don't know why I voted in favor of the charter ordinance, because I really didn't much care which way it went. I wasn't expecting it to pass from the start, but some of the council members felt it would be very helpful to have the same fiscal year that the state and feds worked from.

During the city council meeting of April 20th I introduced Miss Gina Madia, the beautiful daughter of Dave and Patsy Madia, because she had been recently chosen in Washington, D.C. as the nation's National Cherry Blossom Queen. I asked her to approach the public podium and tell those in attendance how she was chosen and what was required of her in representing our nation.

She explained that she was nominated by Wyoming's delegation to Congress, and between Congress and the President George H. W. Bush, she was selected from dozens of other nominees from other states. She said that it was a real honor to be chosen. She had the opportunity to tour the White House, the nation's Capitol, and the District of Columbia. She also stated that she would be going to Japan, during the Japanese Cherry Blossom celebration, for a two-week tour as a goodwill ambassador, and would represent Wyoming and the United States for the next year during her reign as Queen.

After Gina made her presentation, the City of Evanston gave her a contribution in the amount of $1,000 to assist her in her travel expenses. The funds were from the mayor's contingency fund and all agreed. The entire council congratulated her and said they knew she would be a great ambassador.

Mary Lou Norris, who was in attendance at the April 20th meeting, approached the city council about her concerns about a racist candidate for the U.S. Congress, Daniel Johnson, who was contemplating making the Evanston area his residence. Mrs. Norris was wondering whether any action could be taken to discourage any activity that might be derogatory to our Constitution and whether the city would make an effort to discourage this person from residing in Evanston.

I told her that I had checked on other areas in Wyoming where Mr. Johnson attempted to reside. At the present he lived in Casper, where folks were trying to get rid of him, and I thought that was why he was looking to make Evanston his home. I also told her that we were looking into the idea of a program that would discourage him from moving here or anywhere else near Evanston.

I explained that I investigated the activities that had been conducted in other areas by this group, and I would never welcome this caliber of people to our community. I also reminded everyone that they should all appreciate the freedom of America and stay close to those principles that have made America a great nation.

Elect

DANIEL JOHNSON

Independent Candidate for

U. S. House of Representatives, Wyoming

Election date: Wednesday, 26 April 1989

Daniel Johnson, Lois Johnson, his wife, Geraldine, age 1,
William, age 1 month

The *Uinta County Herald* issue of April 21st ran an article stating that Daniel Johnson had looked at some homes for sale in Evanston. The article was titled, WHITE SUPREMACIST VISITED EVANSTON.

The article read: *Reports that white supremacist Daniel Johnson is looking to relocate to Evanston had Mayor Dennis Ottley's phone ringing off the hook on Wednesday.*

Johnson recently moved to Casper from Southern California and believes that citizenship should be stripped from most non-whites and that they should be deported from the United States. He is also running for the U.S. House of Representatives in the current special election.

The *Herald* article continued: *Ottley said Wednesday, "If Johnson's philosophy is what is being reported, I don't want him here in Evanston.*

"We can't legally stop him from moving here, but would watch him real carefully. If he did anything illegal, he would be arrested."

The *Herald* continued: *Johnson is an international corporate attorney specializing in representing Japanese companies in the international transactions, according to his campaign materials. He is in favor of the Pace Amendment to the United States Constitution which would repeal the 14th Amendment. The 14th Amendment was passed after the Civil War and it protects citizenship rights.*

The Pace Amendment would also take away citizenship from anyone that was more than one-eighth Mongolian, Asian, Asian Minor, Middle Eastern, Semitic, near Eastern American Indian, Malay or other non-European. It would bar all Hispanics and those with any trace of Black ancestry.

The city council in Casper is considering writing a letter in opposition to Johnson.

Ottley said Johnson would probably be discussed by the Evanston City Council.

Barry Coster, with Uinta ERA Realty, confirmed that Johnson was in town and that he showed him some neighborhoods. "We discussed housing costs," said Coster. "But it was just in the way of a potential sales lead. We didn't speak of any specific homes."

"He told me who he was and gave me a brochure. I didn't read it at the time and I didn't realize he was so controversial," Coster added at the conclusion of the article.

Johnson planning to keep 'Pace' office in California

By KATHARINE COLLINS
Southwestern Wyoming bureau

EVANSTON — White supremacist Daniel Johnson says he still plans to move to Wyoming but has changed his mind about relocating his "Pace Amendment" organization headquarters in the state.

Johnson, who ran unsuccessfully as an independent candidate in the recent special election to fill former Rep. Dick Cheney's U.S. House seat said he will not abandon his "newly-adopted state" of Wyoming and plans to be settled in Evanston by the end of June to pursue "business activities."

But Johnson said he decided not to move the headquarters of the League of Pace Amendments from the Los·Angeles area to Evanston. He said he was "so poorly received" by local officials in Helena, Mont., and earlier this year in Casper that he has concluded "public officials (in Montana and Wyoming) do not want the League in their city."

Johnson is the author of the Pace Amendment — a proposed constitutional measure that would strip non-whites of U.S. citizenship.

However, Johnson said that wherever he goes, he takes along assistants who deal with League business, and that Evanston will be no exception.

"But the business enterprises I will be engaged in will be unrelated to the political activity I'm involved in," Johnson said. "I would like to show people that I'm a good guy, a good citizen."

Johnson said he and his family, and associate John Abarr — an organizer for the Ku Klux Klan in Wyoming — are making final preparations to move to Evanston.

"I expect to be in full swing (in Evanston) by the end of this month," Johnson said earlier this week from his law office in Glen-

DANIEL JOHNSON
Hopes to make Evanston home

dale, Calif. "My undertaking in Evanston is going to be primarily ... in business activities to try to help turn the economy around in Evanston and Wyoming."

Johnson's earlier efforts to obtain housing in Evanston aborted when area real estate broker Mel Elson broke off negotiating the purchase of a home for Johnson, saying he found Johnson's racial views "repugnant." An investigator at the Wyoming Real Estate Commission confimed earlier this week that a "verified complaint" against Elson was received by the commission May 17, and that an investigation will be carried out.

Another local broker is helping Johnson locate suitable business space and a residence for Johnson, his wife and two children, and for Abarr, Johnson said, declining to reveal the name of the broker or agency.

Casper Star-Tribune, June 9, 1989.

The brochure that Daniel Johnson was passing around was his campaign pamphlet stating that he was running for Wyoming's vacant seat of Representative Dick Cheney, who was appointed recently by President George H. W. Bush as Secretary of Defense. Johnson stated in his pamphlet that he was running on an independent ticket with the idea of getting the Pace Amendment passed. The special election was held on Wednesday, April 26, 1989, but he lost the election and Craig Thomas was easily elected to fill the seat.

On June 9, 1989 the *Casper Star Tribune* came out with an article stating, *White Supremacist Daniel Johnson says he still plans to move to Wyoming but has changed his mind about relocating his "Pace Amendment" organization headquarters in the state.*

Johnson, who ran unsuccessfully as an independent candidate in the recent special election … said he will not abandon his "newly-adopted state" of Wyoming and plans to be settled in Evanston by the end of June to pursue "business activities."

The *Casper Star* article continued: *But Johnson said he decided not to move the headquarters of the League of Pace Amendment from the Los Angeles area to Evanston. He said he was "so poorly received" by local officials in Helena, Montana, and earlier this year in Casper that he has concluded, "public officials (in Montana and Wyoming) do not want the League in their city."*

Johnson is the author of the Pace Amendment – a proposed constitutional measure that would strip non-whites of U.S. citizenship.

"But the business enterprises I will be engaged in will be unrelated to the political activity I'm involved in," Johnson said. "I would like to show people that I'm a good guy, a good citizen."

Johnson said he and his family, and associate John Abarr – an organizer for the Ku Klux Klan in Wyoming – are making final preparations to move to Evanston, the article continued.

"I expect to be in full swing (in Evanston) by the end of this month [June]," Johnson said earlier this week from his law office in Glendale, California. "My undertaking in Evanston is going to be primarily … in business activities to try to help turn the economy around in Evanston and Wyoming."

Johnson's earlier efforts to obtain housing in Evanston aborted when area real estate broker Mel Elson broke off negotiating the purchase of a home for Johnson, saying he found Johnson's racial views "repugnant." An investigator at the Wyoming Real Estate Commission confirmed earlier this week that a "verified complaint" against Elson was received by the commission May 17, and that an investigation will be carried out.

Another local broker is helping Johnson locate suitable business space and a residence for Johnson, his wife and two children, and for Abarr, Johnson said, declining to reveal the name of the broker or agency, the *Casper Star* concluded.

A Letter to the Editor was sent to the *Casper Star Tribune* by a group of Evanston residents urging Daniel Johnson to relocate elsewhere. The letter said:

Please let it be known that we, as residents of Evanston, do not encourage the relocation of Johnson and his family to our community. Evanston is a family-oriented community. We don't feel that the type of people Johnson attracts would be an asset to our town.

We love our community, our schools, but most of all our children, who definitely don't need such an influence in this town or any other.

Johnson, you are not welcome in this community. We strongly suggest you find another town to relocate.

This letter was signed by 32 of Evanston's residents and was published in both the *Casper Star* of June 9th, and the *Uinta County Herald*. The City of Evanston also received a letter from the City of Casper warning of the Pace Amendment group.

Evanston received dozens of letters from all over the country, encouraging the City of Evanston to do everything they could to discourage those people from settling in our community. There were news articles published statewide for several weeks concerning this group and what they were trying to accomplish.

My understanding was that he finally located in a home in Grass Valley off of Wyoming State Highway 150 South at the edge of Evanston's city limits. I don't recall whether he rented the home or bought it, but now he was a resident of Evanston, which concerned a lot of people.

But after a few council meetings and special meetings it was decided that folks in Evanston were going to organize and come up with a plan for a rally showing the support for *"equality and respect for all people."* The program was planned for sometime in July and a chairman would be selected to spearhead the rally.

During the April 20th meeting we passed several ordinances on the third and final readings concerning uniform fire codes, electrical, plumbing and mechanical codes. We also acted on a flood damage prevention ordinance on third reading. All ordinances passed unanimously.

We adopted Resolution 89-23, authorizing the city to enter into a contract with Forsgren Associates to provide engineering services for the Bear River Park Ice Pond Dike Project; and Resolution 89-24, authorizing the city to enter into a contract with Uinta Engineering and Surveying, Inc. for engineering services for the Sixth Street Sewer Project.

Both resolutions were adopted by a unanimous vote by the council, but Councilwoman Wall abstained from voting on 89-24 because she felt that she had a conflict of interest.

Another first was about to begin in Evanston. Paul Knopf, City Planning Director, with support from Janique Eckman, Executive Director of the Evanston Chamber of Commerce, and the Evanston Parks and Recreation District, planned the first "High Uinta Classic Stage Race." The program would include a 70-mile bicycle race, from Kamas, Utah on State Highway 150 to the Sulphur Creek Reservoir, over the Uinta Mountains. Following the High Uinta Race there would be time trials, and a race through downtown Evanston, all on bicycles. The dates set for this year's event were June 24th and 25th.

Knopf worked hard on this program and hoped the event would be a big success and become annual. He got the Evanston Chamber of Commerce to co-sponsor the event with the city, and Eckman and Knopf would be key in organizing the race. The primary purpose of the event was to bring people to Evanston to help the economy.

They already had bicyclists committed from the Salt Lake City and the Denver areas, and had already gotten approval from the highway departments. *A really important part of this race is safety,* Knopf said to the city council. *We've had excellent response from all of those law enforcement people,* he added.

The event did become an annual event for Evanston and Kamas, and, I might add, it was a very successful event every year during my terms as mayor. Paul Knopf spearheaded the event each year, and through the years there were a few changes made to fit traffic problems and Evanston neighborhood concerns.

SUCCESSFUL EVENT — The first Indian Days were held on Saturday and more than 4,000 attended and saw authentic Native American dancers, mountainmen, and other interesting exhibits. The event was staged by the Uinta County Museum Board to commemorate a significant Indian artifact donation the museum's collection. Chairing the event was Denice Wheeler. Shown from left are Melissa Lee, Wheeler's granddaughter; Wheeler, and Evanston Mayor Dennis Ottley.

Uinta County Herald, May 31, 1989.

This was another dream Paul Knopf had that came true. Paul was a dreamer and a doer. He reminded me of a quote that I once read: *"When you cease to dream you cease to live."* I don't remember who the quote was by, but it fit Paul perfectly.

Another new and successful event that happened in May of this year was Indian Days, a program sponsored by the Uinta County Museum Board with Denice Wheeler, another dreamer and a doer, acting as County Chairperson of Uinta County for the upcoming events of the Wyoming Centennial celebration. This was a fund-raising event to raise money for the 1990 Wyoming celebration.

Denice Wheeler said that the event was a huge success. *More than 4,000 people attended,* she said. She added that Indian Days was to honor Native Americans, and that an Indian artifact collection had been donated to the museum during the ceremony. There were Shoshone Indian dancers and mountain men participating as part of the celebration.

During the regular city council meeting of May 4th Resolution 89-9 came up for adoption, but was tabled because of some unanswered questions. The resolution would authorize the City of Evanston to enter into a memorandum of understanding with the Wyoming Recreation Commission concerning annexation of the Bear River State Park.

After being amended during the next city council meeting of May 18th, Councilman Vranish made a motion to adopt Resolution 89-9 as amended, seconded by Lunsford, with all voting in favor. The Wyoming Bear River State Park would now be a part of the City of Evanston.

Also during the May 18th meeting Ann Bell, Evanston's Chairperson of the Wyoming Centennial celebration stated that in honor of the celebration they would build a replica of the Old Chinese Joss House, a Chinese house of worship, that had been located in old China Town on County Road near the old mill building, now known as the Old Mill and the Painted Lady Restaurant and Bar, and where Dave's Meat Market is at the present.

She pointed out that the Chinese had a big part in the early history of Evanston by working on the railroad and in the Almy mines.

She said that the Evanston Chinese Joss House was one of only three in the United States at that time. The other two were located in San Francisco and New York City, but in the early 1920s the Joss House in Evanston had burned down along with most of old China Town, she explained. The panels of the original building, which were saved from the fire, were in the Wyoming State Museum in Cheyenne, and that the artifacts would be returned to Evanston to be displayed in the new replica of the Joss House when the project was completed.

She pointed out that the city had pledged $15,000 towards the construction, but the committee would need to raise the remainder. Some of the funds would be raised by selling Wyoming Centennial belt buckles, cups and other centennial souvenirs, and there would be hours of in-kind work done by volunteers as a part of the matching funds.

The project date of completion was July 8, 1990 and it would be constructed on Depot Square next to the Beeman-Cashin Building. Bell said that their goal was to have the opening during Railroad Heritage Days in July.

Ann Bell had a great committee comprised of herself, Ester Ben, Ann Pennington, John Bowers, Mike and Janise Davis, Kathy Ball, Glenda Krjeci, Jean Painter Cook, Sandy Ottley, and many others that volunteered their services.

During the May 18th meeting, Resolution 89-30 was introduced by Councilman Will Davis authorizing the City of Evanston to extend an offer to purchase real estate from J. D. Kindler for the purpose of establishing a public park in the Centennial Valley area.

At that time there was no park or recreation area anywhere close to the Centennial Valley Subdivisions. So those residing in the area petitioned the city for a playground for their children. The city took action immediately to obtain the land and proceed to furnish that area with a park. The park, when finished, would be called Centennial Park.

Councilman Lunsford made a motion for the adoption of Resolution 89-30, seconded by Wall with all voting in favor.

Herb Weston, owner of the Weston Budget Inn (at present Day's Inn) approached me about better access from Harrison Drive into his motel. He wanted to open a new road off Harrison to J. B.'s Restaurant and his motel. I told him I would bring this up to the council. I had mentioned this to the city council during a work session and they all agreed to have City Attorney Dennis Boal draw up a resolution to be acted on by the May 18th meeting. Therefore, during the May meeting Councilman Tom Hutchinson introduced Resolution 89-32 supporting the authorization of additional access for the west end businesses from Harrison Drive, but was tabled by motion until the June 1st meeting, because the council thought that we should talk to the highway department first.

In the meantime, I approached the Wyoming Highway Department concerning the access, because it was right on the edge of Interstate 80 system, and I wasn't sure whether or not we had to have their permission. I made arrangements to meet with Leno Menghini, Superintendent of the highway department, and he stated that we did have to receive permission from them, because that area is in the I-80 system district. He told me he had no problem with our request, but would need to talk to the commissioners. He indicated that he would let me know in the near future what the commission determined.

Leno Menghini informed me, in writing, that the Wyoming Highway Commission had given the City of Evanston the go-ahead on the new access into J. B.'s Big Boy Restaurant and the Weston Budget Inn.

After we received the approval from the state, Resolution 89-32 was brought off the table for discussion during the city council meeting on June 1st. In attendance were several west end business people opposing the resolution. They were concerned it would hurt their businesses. The council had been informed that in order to make the access public, the area should be platted. With that consideration, the motion adopt Resolution 89-32 failed by a unanimous vote against.

However, this access would become a reality in the future by Resolution 89-67, introduced by Councilwoman Wall, noting that the street had been platted as suggested by the city council. After a short discussion Councilman Vranish made the motion to adopt Resolution 89-67, seconded by Hutchinson with all voting in favor.

The access was eventually constructed and the street was named Weston Drive. Other programs that went over well in Evanston during the month of June were the Annual Urban Renewal Ball and the Annual Chili Cookoff. Both events were very successful and folks in Evanston went all out in support of both.

June 14th, Flag Day, as I was driving around town checking things out I again noticed the Stars and Stripes flags placed on several locations in Depot Square and all the flags waving while I was driving over the overpass. It reminded me that I needed to send the Veterans of Foreign Legion, Post 4280, a donation for hanging all these beautiful flags.

LETTERS

Flag appreciation

Editor: Each holiday as I see our flag "Old Glory" flying extensively over our community, only due to the efforts of a few patriotic and dedicated veterans, those members of the Veterans of Foreign Wars, I tell myself that someone, sometime has got to tell these brave men and women how much they are appreciated.

It never ceases to amaze me how great a job, for so many years this flag program has been going on with very little said about it. I feel it's time your organization was commended.

This project goes on the entire year, without question, where every holiday, and other special national events, flags are displayed on most all businesses, some residential homes and other locations throughout our community. To see this so often, makes me very proud, and I could never say enough to let you know how a program such as this makes a person feel.

I am a great lover of the American flag, and feel that it could never fly enough. Our flag is a sure sign of the freedom that the American people have enjoyed the past 200 years.

I want to thank you all for your undying spirit, and personal efforts to keep our flag tradition alive.

Dennis Ottley
Mayor

Editor's note: Mayor Ottley shared this letter with the Herald. The original was sent to Commander Dennis Sundberg of the Veterans of Foreign Wars No. 4280 in Evanston.

A story of the *"Stars and Stripes"* that I felt just fit the *"Freedom & Equality Day Rally"* program...

I AM THE FLAG - By Ruth Apperson Rous

I am the FLAG of the UNITED STATES of AMERICA.
I was born on June 14, 1777, in Philadelphia.
There the Continental Congress adopted my stars and strips as the national flag.
My thirteen stripes alternating red and white, with a union of thirteen white stars in a field of blue, represented a new constellation, a new nation dedicated to the personal and religious liberty of mankind.
Today fifty stars signal from my union, one for each of the fifty sovereign states in the greatest constitutional republic the world has ever known.
My colors symbolize the patriotic ideals and spiritual qualities of the citizens of my country.
My red stripes proclaim the fearless courage and integrity of American men and boys and the self-sacrifice and devotion of American mothers and daughters.
My white stripes stand for liberty and equality for all.
My blue is the blue of heaven, loyalty and faith.
I represent these eternal principles: liberty, justice, and humanity.
I embody American freedom: freedom of speech, religion, assembly, the press, and the sanctity of the home.
I typify that indomitable spirit of determination brought to my land by Christopher Columbus and by all my forefathers – the Pilgrims, Puritans, settlers at James town and Plymouth.
I am as old as my nation.
I am a living symbol of my nation's law: the CONSTITUTION of the UNITED STATES and the BILL of RIGHTS.
I voice Abraham Lincoln's philosophy: "A government of the people, by the people, for the people."
I stand guard over my nation's schools, the seedbed of good citizenship and true patriotism.
I am displayed in every schoolroom throughout my nation: every schoolyard has a flagpole for my display.
Daily thousands upon thousands of boys and girls pledge their allegiance to me and my country.

When the new viaduct (overpass) was completed, I met with Dennis Sundberg, Commander of the V.F.W. and some other members about putting flags on the overpass. I told them that the city would make a yearly contribution to them for the flags that they displayed at the city buildings, as well as Depot Square and the overpass.

I thanked them for all their efforts and hard work in putting up hundreds of flags throughout the city on all the days suggested by the National Department of the V.F.W., such as Flag Day and Mother's Day and all official holidays, and many other special days that were recognized. I don't recall everyone involved but I remember some of the older veterans like Lloyd Ball, Junior Anderson, Art Rufi, Tom Dean, Sundberg and many others. I wrote a letter to Commander Sundberg, which was published by the *Uinta County Herald* in a June issue, 1989. The *Herald* titled the letter: *FLAG APPRECIATION.*

The city contributed $2,000 to the V.F.W. each year I was mayor, paid from the mayor's contingency fund.

From the time I had become mayor, the city council always included a Mayor's Contingency Fund of $20,000 in the budget, which I could use as I saw fit as long as it was for the benefit of the city. I mostly used the funds to help schoolchildren who were honored with the opportunity to tour different areas of the country, and such things, but I never used much more than $3,000 or $4,000 of the funds in any one year.

During the June meeting, Resolution 89-36 was introduced by Councilman Craig Nelson, authorizing the City of Evanston to enter into an agreement with Uinta Engineering and Surveying, Inc., to furnish engineering, surveying and project management services for the repair of Main Street. Motion was made by Council Vranish for the adoption of Resolution 89-36, seconded by Hutchinson; motion passed by 5 yes votes, 1 abstention (Wall), and 1 absent (Lunsford).

I must mention that just after I was elected to my second term as mayor, former Councilman David Bills offered to operate the video camera at every city meeting. He said he would volunteer his time, at no charge, and would attend every meeting so that the city would have, in their files, a video copy of the meetings. The city council accepted his offer and he had been operating the camera ever since, not missing a meeting. Before Bills, we had one of the city employees to operate the camera.

During the June 15th city council meeting Councilwoman Jerry Wall, a member of the Centennial Committee, excused herself as a member of the city council and joined her committee in their request for a limited malt beverage permit for the second annual Railroad Heritage Days to be held at Depot Square on July 8, 1989.

Ms Wall explained to the council that all proceeds from the beer sales would go towards funding the construction of the Chinese Joss House replica.

Councilman Will Davis made a motion to approve the Centennial Committee's application for a limited malt beverage permit, seconded by Lunsford. The motion was carried with 5 yes votes, 1 abstention (Wall), and 1 absent (Nelson).

Councilman Tom Hutchinson announced that two city workers, Jeff Martin and Barry Constantine, had recently passed their State Department of Environmental Quality requirements and had received their certificates. The schooling and studying to prepare and pass for receiving the certificates was all on the employees' own time. I, as mayor, gave special commendations to Martin and Constantine for their interest and dedication in obtaining their certificates. I said, "I'm sure this type of training will help you both in your job descriptions."

One day Layton Cottrell of the Crandall Funeral Home met with me and suggested that the city install stop signs at the exits of the downtown alleys. He mentioned that the way some folks came out of those alleys without giving any warning someone was going to get hurt. Apparently, Cottrell had either experienced a problem, or he had witnessed someone almost getting hit. I told him I would mention this to the council, and also the police and city attorney.

I brought the subject up during our next work session and told everyone in attendance what Cottrell had suggested to me. After a short discussion on the matter, everyone seemed to agree, feeling it would be a good safety measure.

Therefore, during the meeting of June 15th, Councilman Clarence Vranish made a motion to place stop signs at the one-way alley exits between Main and Front Streets, entering 10th Street and 11th Street, and between Main and Center Streets entering 9th Street and 10th Street, all in the downtown area. The motion was seconded by Lunsford, with all voting in favor.

During June, an errant herd of buffalo broke out of their enclosure at the Bear River State Park. They got loose and ran freely all over the area when Tom Hutchinson, Director of the State Park called for assistance to help herd the buffalo back into their fenced-in pasture. He noted that it could have been disastrous if the giant beasts had gotten onto the interstate highway.

During the June meeting, Councilman Tom Hutchinson expressed his appreciation to Uinta County Deputy Sheriff Lou Napoli and Under Sheriff Dwain Booth, as well as Bob George with Century Cable TV, Benny Goodwin of the Evanston Fire Department and members of the Evanston Police Department. Tom noted that the entire community responded to help herd the animals back into their pasture.

A special meeting of the Evanston City Council was held on June 20th to hold a public hearing, officially announced earlier, concerning the annual appropriation of funds for the fiscal year of 1989-1990 and consideration for the adoption of Resolution 89-45. Every year, a public hearing was held and recorded to consider input concerning the next budget year.

Councilman Tom Hutchinson introduced Resolution 89-45 to approve the proposed budget.

The total proposed budget for the upcoming fiscal year of 1989-1990 was $8,657,984. The operational budget, which does not reflect capital improvements, grants or loans, was $6,188,738, a decrease of $188,701 from the previous year.

We all commended the departments and administrative staff for their fine work, on the budget. Councilman Hutchinson said, *This is the best budget I've seen in four or five years.*

After a lengthy discussion and some amendments, Councilman Craig Nelson made the motion to adopt Resolution 89-45 as amended, seconded by Vranish with 6 yes votes and 1 absent (Lunsford). During the city council meeting of July 6th, and after the usual business was taken care of, I introduced three Boy Scouts: Vince Pierce, Sterling Pierce, and Tory Morrow, who were in attendance as part of their requirements to achieve their Citizenship Merit Badge. We often had Boy and Girl Scouts in attendance at our meetings to earn various honors required in the scout organizations.

As the first item of new business, Councilwoman Jerry Wall introduced Resolution 89-42, a resolution implementing a Round-up Program to provide additional funds for public improvements and projects.

This program was initially suggested by Councilwoman Wall and as far as I know it is still going on to this day. It was a good idea and I know that, while I was mayor of Evanston, the city raised quite a few funds to help with projects like Depot Square and the Bear Project.

Section 1 of the resolution read: *The City of Evanston, Wyoming, is hereby authorized to implement a "round-up program" whereby citizens will be allowed and encouraged to round-up to the next dollar when paying their water and sewer bills. All monies raised by the "round-up program" shall be used by the City for public improvements and projects as shall be designated by the City Council from time to time by duly adopted motion.*

The motion to adopt Resolution 89-42 was made by Councilman Will Davis, and seconded by Wall. A lengthy discussion followed until I ended debate and called for the vote. The motion passed by a majority with Wall, Davis, Craig Nelson, Jon Lunsford and me voting in favor, and Tom Hutchinson and Clarence Vranish voting against the motion. I was surprised that anyone would vote against something like that, because it was a voluntary program. But then again, I'm sure they had their reasons.

Bids were opened on the construction of the replica of Chinese Joss House. Councilman Will Davis made the motion to award the bid to the low bidder, Southwestern Homes, Inc., in the amount of $31,649, seconded by Lunsford, with all voting in favor.

Bob Schuetz, a partner of Southwestern Homes, Inc. was present to answer any questions, followed by Resolution 89-50, introduced by Councilwoman Wall, authorizing the City of Evanston to enter into a construction contract with Southwestern Homes, Inc.

Councilman Nelson made the motion for the adoption of Resolution 89-50, seconded by Wall, with all voting in favor.

The City of Evanston had been requested to remove the asbestos from the old railroad engine placed at Railroad Park, and the dining car that was set up in Depot Square. The bid on the removal of the asbestos was approximately $10,000, awarded to Keers Environmental, Inc., a company well qualified to handle the removal of asbestos. Keers was the only company to submit a bid, and we needed a company that was familiar with asbestos to do the job.

During this July meeting Councilman Davis made a motion to approve final payment to Keers Environment, Inc. of $10,500.00 for the removal of asbestos, seconded by Wall, with all voting in favor.

In the past there was a lot of discussion in several meetings about the future of the railroad roundhouse property, especially concerning a new lease to the Union Tank Car Company, which had been on a lease since 1974.

During the July 6th city council meeting Mr. Chuck Herzog, representing the Union Tank Car Company, was in attendance to discuss the possibility of a purchase, or of a thirty-year extension on their present lease with the city. The company currently had 20 years left on their present lease. He stated that the railway tank car company was looking to do a $4,000,000 expansion program of their operation that would double the employment they now had. He said that they either needed to purchase the property from the city or needed a long-term lease of at least an additional thirty years, and he was there also to request permission from the city to demolish the old carpenter shop.

Councilman Hutchinson made a motion to authorize the demolition of the carpenter shop, seconded by Lunsford. The motion passed with 6 yes votes and 1 no vote (Wall).

A lengthy discussion took place concerning the sale and/or extended lease of the property, with Charles Demander, Mildred

Palmer, Patsy Madia, and Jim Davis, Director of the Urban Renewal Agency expressing their views.

Councilman Jon Lunsford made a motion, seconded by Councilman Vranish, for the city attorney to prepare a resolution, providing for an extension of an additional thirty years and requiring Union Tank Car Company to show good faith by proceeding to make the $4,000,000 expansion as stated by Mr. Herzog.

Councilman Tom Hutchinson made a motion, seconded by Lunsford, to amend the motion to authorize an appraisal to determine the value of the property. A roll call vote was called for with 4 yes votes (Hutchinson, Nelson, Davis and me), and 3 no votes (Wall, Vranish, and Lunsford). Motion passed.

A roll call vote was also called for on the main motion as amended, with 3 yes votes (Lunsford, Hutchinson, and me), and 4 no votes (Davis, Wall, Vranish, and Nelson). The motion failed.

Following the failure of the previous motion as amended, Councilman Clarence Vranish made a motion to authorize the city attorney to prepare a resolution providing for an extended lease for thirty years if Union Tank Car Company made their estimated $4,000,000 planned improvements. The motion was seconded by Lunsford and passed with 5 yes votes (Lunsford, Vranish, Hutchinson, Nelson, and me), and 2 no votes (Wall and Davis).

This would not be the end of the Union Tank Car Company and the subject of the property of the roundhouse and machine shop. Many folks in Evanston have wanted to shut down the Union Tank Car Company so that the City of Evanston could get back the railroad property for historic reasons.

In one public meeting held for the purpose of discussing the outcome of the roundhouse discussion, one woman in attendance, the wife of a business owner, said, *We don't care about those employees working at the railway car plant; we want to have the roundhouse property given back to the city so we can use it for historic purposes.* She explained why, but her statement pissed me and a lot of other folks off, because as far as I was concerned those 25 or 30 jobs down there were an asset to our community. I went on to explain that the railroad property was given to the city for industrial use when the railroad left Evanston. Most folks could understand that, but there were those that just didn't give a damn about the jobs or the families that were dependent upon the employment.

During this same July meeting, Councilman Tom Hutchinson introduced Resolution 89-51 declaring the intention of the city to vacate a street, which was called at that time Bear River Street, located in the Bear River Subdivision, the business park on Front Street, and changing it to Becker's Circle.

Motion was made by Councilwoman Wall to adopt Resolution 89-51, seconded by Vranish, with all voting in favor.

During the meeting Mr. Steve Wilson and Kathleen Kreiger were in attendance, representing the Walmart development project. They made a presentation that included a sketch plan of a new shopping center, within the Bear River Subdivision, which would include a 66,000 square-foot Walmart store and another 5,000-square-foot building for another business that had not been decided on at the time. A lengthy discussion followed.

The Walmart sketch plan had previously received the approval of the Evanston Planning and Zoning Commission, but not without a lot of public concern.

During the July city council meeting there was a lot of tension among the local downtown business people regarding the proposed Walmart project. At that time, the proposed Walmart site was to be built behind the McDonald's on Becker's Circle, where Murdock's Ranch and Home Supply are at this time, but years later they constructed a much larger store and relocated it to where it is at the present.

Most of the downtown merchants didn't want Walmart coming into Evanston because they were afraid of the competition. And I believe everyone understood that and couldn't blame them, but most of Evanston wanted it because it would help the economy by creating jobs and increasing the city and county tax base. Also, it would keep a lot of folks from driving to the Wasatch Front to do their shopping.

One local downtown merchant Rod McCrimmon, owner of what was then Harrison & Roth Western Store (Serendipity is located there at the present) made a statement printed in the *Uinta County Herald* of July 7, 1989: *...He is very much in favor of the new store. "This town will die if we don't get the store in here. It will bring in business from surrounding towns in Wyoming and the Park City area," he said. "We need the competition, and Walmart is a great store; the finest retail store I've ever seen."*

Other business owners, opposed to the Walmart store, said that the current economy of Evanston isn't strong enough to withstand another type of retail business. They voiced concern over the possibility of losing business, or even closing because of the proposed Walmart.

The Planning and Zoning Commission recommended approval of the Walmart store to the city council, stipulating that more studies of the traffic in that area be taken.

The council will review the sketch plan, and in a best case scenario, the city council could approve the final plat at the July 20 meeting. If all goes as planned, the store could have final approval by the end of August. A tentative opening date is scheduled for Feb. 15, the *Herald* article concluded.

During the same July meeting Councilman Hutchinson made a motion to direct the city attorney to prepare a resolution accepting the Brown School property from Uinta County School District No. 1, seconded by Wall, with all voting in favor.

The city and school district had talked about turning the property of the old Brown School, which the district had already demolished, into a city park. A resolution would be prepared by the city attorney and be ready to act on at the next meeting on July 20th.

Just before adjournment of the July 6th meeting I called for a work session to be held on July 13th, a week before our next regular meeting of July 20th. I explained that there were a few items that the council should discuss prior to our next regular meeting. I reminded everyone that work sessions are open to the public, but the council does not take any action on any issue during the session.

On July 14th I wrote a letter to the League of Pace Amendment Advocates, in Glendale, California that read:

*As Mayor of Evanston, I feel I cannot sit by silently and al-
low anyone to infer that the City of Evanston invites or welcomes
any group or individual with extremist views such as the proposed
Pace Amendment which would deny citizenship to non-whites and
non-Europeans, and in effect repeal our Fourteenth and Fifteenth
Amendments of the United States Constitution.*

*I believe that our nation and our community were built on a
rich and diverse mix of heritage and background. To propose that we
change our constitution and deny citizenship to anyone is both repugnant and out of line with the American way. I believe that racial and
ethnic diversity is what America was built on, and that racial and
ethnic diversity is an asset of our country and our community.*

*The Evanston Community has a rich history of ethnic and racial
diversity, and I'm proud to be a part of it. It is my intention to actively
work to preserve that history and to promote that diversity in our modern
life. Therefore, I do not encourage the location of any activity or program
that would promote the objectives of your proposed Pace Amendment.*

Sincerely,

Dennis J. Ottley,
Mayor

From the time that White-Supremacists Daniel Johnson, Jessie "Jay"
Johnson (no relationship), President of the League of Pace Amendment
Advocates (LPAA), and John Abarr, an organizer for the Ku Klux Klan
(KKK) of Wyoming had all arrived in Evanston, and planned to reside
here, they had distributed their brochures and pamphlets, explaining
what the LPAA stands for, all over town. They set up a booth in downtown Evanston every day, plus they made some home visits and placed
notices on some windows saying such things as, *GET OUT! JEW PIG!*

I was receiving all kinds of letters from different folks, some from out
of town, speaking against the White Supremacists, relating them to the
Neo-Nazi Aryan Nation organization located, at that time, in Hayden
Lake, Idaho. Evanston was getting a lot of attention in other Wyoming
newspapers, as well as some located in the Wasatch Front in Utah.

LETTERS TO THE EDITOR UCH 5/3/89

Take pride

Editor: In Uinta County we pride ourselves on being independent with a philosophy of live and let live. We are tolerant of a variety of lifestyles and beliefs and we're proud of our tolerance. But, because of this very attitude, a storm cloud now looms on our horizon.

Daniel Johnson is leader and spokesman for the league of Pace Amendment Advocates, a white supremacist hate group. Johnson has moved to Evanston and we must object to him importing his organization's bigotry and "hate group" philosophy.

The Wyoming Task Force for Equality has issued a letter warning that the move of white supremacist 'hate" groups to our state is with the avowed purpose of making Wyoming a center for hate group activities.

The so-called "Pace Amendment" calls for repeal of the 14th Amendment to the Constitution which now guarantees citizenship regardless of race or creed. In its place, Pace advocates proposes a Constitutional Amendment wherein "no person shall be a citizen of the United States unless he is a non-hispanic white of the European race, in whom there is no ascertainable trace of Negro blood, nor more than one-eighth Mongolian, Asian, Asian Minor, Middle Eastern, Semitic, Near Eastern, American Indian, Malay or other non-European or nonwhite blood..." and further states, "only citizens shall have the right and privilege to reside permanently in the United States."

The League of Pace Amendment Advocates are actively pursuing the deportation of U.S. citizens whose ancestry falls into these "nonwhite" categories. This is pure bigotry, racism, and facism.

Not only does Johnson and his followers support these ideas, but they have actively promoted Nazi skinhead activities and they openly work with leaders of the Invisible Empire (Ku Klux Klan) and the Aryan Nation. These associates are avowed racists who have no fear of using violence to future their cause.

The citizens of Hayden Lake, Idaho, originally ignored the Aryan Nation when the white supremacists, neo-Nazi group, moved into their community. After suffering violent acts of harrassment and vandalism, this small-town community realized their tolerance was a bad mistake.

Now they urge others to never ignore such groups, warning that hate group activity "grows in the dark."

Johnson has now moved to Evanston because of the outcry in Casper opposing racism and bigotry and re-affirming a passionate belief in equality made the Pace amendment advocate uncomfortable. Remember that tolerance can easily be mistaken for indifference. It is urgent that we voice our community belief in equality, not bigotry.

Now is the time to act. I urge Evanston citizens to talk with their neighbors and friends about what kind of community they want. I urge the clergy to dicuss bigotry with their congregations. I urge teachers and the school board to take steps to reaffirm the concepts of equality and freedom. I urge all community leaders and media to provide us with reasoned leadership in this very nasty situation. A statement of our unbending belief in equality is essential right now.

Lynne D. Fox

Uinta County Herald, May 3, 1989.

Chairperson Lynne Fox and her committee thought that the city better get moving on their plans to counter the LPAA organization's actions. Therefore, during the next city council meeting a resolution was adopted, a proclamation was declared, and Ms Fox gave her report and had named July 26th the day for the *Freedom & Equality Rally.*

I called the city council meeting of July 20th to order at 7:00 p.m. After the usual business, roll call, approval of the minutes, the bills, the acknowledgment of all reports, and the approval of the agenda was completed, I read a letter of resignation from Cindy Shiplet as Community Development Administrative Secretary, effective August 6, 1989.

Councilman Nelson made the motion to accept Miss Shiplet's letter of resignation, seconded by Vranish with all voting in favor. The council and I each thanked Miss Shiplet for her service to the city and wished her well.

Ann Bell, Evanston Centennial Committee Chairman, was in attendance to express her appreciation to her committee members, and others who volunteered their free time to the many projects and special occasions in raising money for Evanston's Centennial project, the Chinese Joss House. She made special mention of all those who attended the groundbreaking ceremony for the Joss House on July 8th.

She also mentioned that her committee and others were very active during Railroad Heritage Days on, trying to raise more funds for the construction of the Joss House, and she announced that they were looking to have the replica in place prior to the Wyoming Centennial celebration in 1990.

I then expressed the city council's and my gratitude to everyone and anyone who gives volunteer help and time to *"make things happen"* for Evanston.

As the first item of old business, Councilman Hutchinson made a motion to authorize an appraisal of the Union Tank Car property, and that the appraisal to be funded from the city council's Contingency Fund. The motion was seconded and the vote was unanimous.

FREEDOM & EQUALITY DAY RALLY !

WEDNESDAY
JULY 26th
7:00 p.m.

DEPOT SQUARE
10th & FRONT STREETS

AN AVOWED WHITE-SUPREMIST HATE GROUP, THE LEAGUE OF PACE AMENDMENT
ADVOCATES, HAS ANNOUNCED PLANS TO MAKE EVANSTON THEIR NATIONAL
HEADQUARTERS!

Newly appointed Pace Amendment spokesman Jessie A. Johnson (former Grand
Dragon of the Ku Klux Klan in Texas) and John Abarr (organizer of the
Wyoming Knights of the Ku Klux Klan) have announced plans to move here to
run the proposed office.

The "Pace Amendment" advocates amending the United States Constitution to
repeal the Fourteenth Amendment and limit American citizenship to white
persons whose ancestral home is the British Isles or northwest Europe!
All other residents will be deported or relocated to "reservations"! Some
of the most violent and active racists and anti-semites in America are
admirers of the Pace Amendment, and its creator is proud of their support.

Facing this possible threat to our community, Mayor Dennis Ottley has
declared July 26th "Freedom and Equality Day".

COME TO THE FREEDOM & EQUALITY DAY RALLY AND PROVE TO THE WORLD that
Evanston supports the traditional values which have built the United
States and Wyoming: equality and respect for ALL people. We support these
values because they are the essence of a free, democratic society.

OUR ECONOMIC STABILITY ALSO REQUIRES US TO SAFEGUARD OUR LIFESTYLE! We
cannot afford a reputation similar to that of the Coeur d'Alene, Idaho
area. New businesses relocate carefully.

Helena and Casper have already let this organization know they find the
Pace Amendment repugnant. Let's add Evanston to the list of places where
bigotry is unwelcome!

Please come and learn more from speakers who are experts in the field of
hate groups. Learn why it is a mistake to ignore this threat. And come
celebrate the cornerstones of our nation - EQUALITY AND FREEDOM FOR ALL
PEOPLE!

CITY OF EVANSTON
1200 Main Street
EVANSTON, WYOMING 82930
(307) 789-9690

1890-1990
WYOMING
CENTENNIAL
A LASTING LEGACY

PROCLAMATION

WHEREAS, The City of Evanston as a democracy is dedicated to the belief that every person, regardless of race, color, creed or gender must be afforded all rights on an equal basis; and

WHEREAS, the pluralism of our society has contributed to the richness of our culture; and

WHEREAS, the City of Evanston is dedicated to the support and development of the worth and dignity of all individuals.

NOW, THEREFORE, I, by virtue of the authority vested in me as Mayor of the City of Evanston, do hereby proclaim Wednesday, July 26, 1989 as;

FREEDOM AND EQUALITY DAY

FURTHER, I urge all residents and citizens of the area to join together in making this a period of rededication to the principles of justice and equality for all people.

Witness my hand and the seal of the City of Evanston this 20th day of July, 1989.

Dennis J. Ottley, Mayor

Under new business Councilwoman Wall introduced Resolution 89-57:

RESOLUTION 89-57
RESOLUTION OF THE CITY OF EVANSTON, WYO-
MING, ENDORSING
DIVERSITY IN CITIZENSHIP, REGARDLESS OF RACE,
COLOR AND CREED.

<u>*Section 1.*</u> *The City of Evanston hereby condemns, deplores and opposes efforts by any group to malign or deprive any citizen of his constitutional rights. Further, the City of Evanston pledges to continue to promote the democratic values of equality and tolerance between people of differing race, color and creed.*
Motion for the adoption of Resolution 89-57 was made by Councilman Nelson, seconded by Wall, with 6 votes in favor and 1 absent (Lunsford).

Following the resolution I proclaimed July 26, 1989 to be Equal Rights Day to coincide with the Freedom & Equality Day Rally. A rally in support of equal rights was planned, according to Committee Chairperson Lynne Fox, at the Beeman-Cashin building at 7:00 p.m.

Chairperson Fox and Ann Bell, Chairperson of the Wyoming State Centennial Committee were both in attendance at the meeting, expressing their views on the importance of equality for all, stating that we should support all programs that are dedicated to freedom and equality for all.

During the meeting there were more resolutions introduced and acted on, with all being adopted unanimously by the council, as well as a report from Patrol Lieutenant Officer Forrest Bright concerning his recent training at the Federal Bureau of Investigation (FBI) Academy in Virginia. Bright expressed his appreciation for the opportunity to attend. He explained that his application had been made in 1981 and that fourteen countries were represented, as well as every state except two, in the United States.

City Engineer Brian Honey and Darryl Alleman from Montgomery Engineering gave an update on the water treatment plant expansion, stating that it looked as though the project would be completed just a bit under budget.

Before adjournment, I called for a work session to be held on Tuesday, July 25th at 5:00 p.m. I also reminded everyone of the Sulphur Creek Dam dedication on July 27th. That there would be a barbecue, a fishing derby, and boat rides planned as part of the events.

I also encouraged everyone to attend the Equality and Freedom Rally on July 26th, and as a reminder, I stated that *everyone interested in freedom should respect not only the American flag, but every flag.*

The July 25th work session was set up primarily to go over plans for the Equality and Freedom Rally, and how it was shaping up. Chairperson Lynne Fox went over her program and indicated that there would be many Evanston citizens of all different nationalities at the rally: Hispanic, Asian, American Indian, African American and many of mixed nationalities, but "All Americans". She also stated that White Supremacist Daniel Johnson, Jessie A. Johnson and John Abarr were planning on setting up a booth just across the street from the Beeman-Cashin building, where the rally would take place. Their booth would be located on 10th Street in front of the Uinta County Museum and Evanston Chamber of Commerce office.

Governor Mike Sullivan was formally invited to the rally, but because of prior commitments, he was unable to attend. He sent a letter that was read at the beginning of the rally.

The letter read: *To the People of Evanston and Uinta County:*

Greetings. I regret that previous commitments prevent me from joining you today at your Freedom and Equality Day Rally, but Jane and I will be with you in spirit.

The citizens of Wyoming, by birthright and by choice, live in a blessed land. We delight in our diversity of origin and take pride in our heritage. We abhor violence and we despise hate, bigotry and racism under all their guises. We declare again today, Wyoming is the Equality State and must remain so.

Thank you for allowing me to add my sentiments to those you express on behalf of all Wyoming.

Yours truly,
Mike Sullivan

On Tuesday, July 25, 1989 the *Casper Star Tribune* ran an article titled, EVANSTON HOPES TO DISCOURAGE SEPARATISTS. The article started out: *Residents and city officials plan to hold a rally Wednesday to discourage a white separatist group from establishing a headquarters in Evanston.*

But a group of Evanston locals, calling itself Uinta County Against Neo-Nazi Terrorism, have organized to oppose the organization, and its founder Daniel Johnson.

"Every community has been doing the same thing to get rid of him (Johnson)," said Evanston Mayor Dennis J. Ottley. *"It worked in other communities, I hope it works here.*

"I don't think that what they believe in and what they're going after is the American way," Ottley said. *"We've been years trying to build a good standard of living in Evanston. We're proud of our community. We don't want anybody to come in and disrupt it."*

The same *Star-Tribune* article quoted Johnson: *"This is very discouraging, so I have to reassess the situation. Do I continue in Evanston or do I just look at a whole different state?"* he asked. *"Even though I'm discouraged, I am not yet turned away. I'm still leaning toward Evanston but not as strongly. I would like to have the opportunity to change people's minds."*

Regardless of Johnson's plans, League members say they will pursue Evanston as a headquarters.

George King, director of education of the League said in a telephone interview from Glendale (CA) that Evanston "is a great little town."

With Evanston as a headquarters, League members would distribute white separatist literature at school yards, grocery stores, after church services – "wherever there's a lot of foot traffic," King said. "When Skinheads come through and have no place to stay, we'll have barracks for them," he added.

Although King says he's aware of local opposition. "We'd love to see the welcome wagon and all the rest of them there [speaking of skinheads]. But every community has got a few liberals and professional white-haters to stir up some people," King said as *the Star-Tribune* article ended.

The *Freedom and Equality Day Rally* was held as planned, on July 26th at 7:00 p.m. on the porch of the Beeman-Cashin Building. Chairperson Lynne Fox and her committee had put on an excellent program with about 1,000 folks from Evanston and Uinta County in attendance. Also in attendance was the press represented by the *Uinta County Herald, Bridger Valley Pioneer, Kemmerer Gazette, Casper Star-Tribune* and the *Salt Lake Tribune*, as well as a representative from KEVA Radio.

The stage setting was flanked by American flags displayed by the Veterans of Foreign Wars (V.F.W.) Post 4280, and dozens of citizens within the county of varied ethnic backgrounds that would fit the description of what the Pace Amendment stood against.

After Chairperson Lynne Fox opened the ceremony, following the invocation, she made her introductions: me as Mayor of Evanston, the members of the Evanston City Council, the Uinta County Commissioners and Uinta County State Legislatures that were in attendance, plus Don Tolin of Casper, Chairman of the Wyoming Advisory Committee for the U.S. Commission on Civil Rights. Ms Fox then welcomed everyone there and spoke about the purpose of the gathering, and stated that the reason we were here was to let Mr. Johnson and Mr. Abarr and their group know that they were not welcome in Evanston or any other city in the State of Wyoming. She told the crowd that the League of Pace Amendment Advocates had been unsuccessful in establishing headquarters in Montana and Wyoming, and that we do not want them locating in Evanston or anywhere in the area. She said, *they are not welcome in this county or state; we are not a prejudiced community.*

After her short introduction she asked me to say a few words in regard to the City of Evanston. After welcoming all those in attendance and expressing my thanks to them I gave a short talk, ending it by saying: *We must take steps to insure the continuation of the values set up by the Bill of Rights and safeguard the equality of life that now exists; One Nation under God, indivisible, with liberty and justice for all.*

Lynne Fox, later in the program, invited anyone of the ethnic group that wished to say a few words to speak. Wyoming State Senator John Fanos, among the ethnic group and of Greek heritage, said very bluntly, "If you think you will be welcome here, think again!"

John Abarr, Grand Knight of the Wyoming Ku Klux Klan, Aaron Phillips, David Speckman, and Lori Arthur, members of the Neo-Nazi Skinheads, were the only visible signs of opposition at the rally.

Given an opportunity to speak and take part in the rally, Speckman said they had come to welcome the League of the Pace Amendment to Wyoming. "We are here to stand up for the rights of the League," said Speckman. "We are not white supremacists. We are white survivalists," Abarr said.

A GESTURE OF EQUALITY — A panel of speakers show their unity and support of equal rights at the Freedom and Equality Day Rally in late July. The rally was estimated to be the largest crowd gathering in Evanston.

CROWD SUPPORT — Approximately 1,000 people attended the Freedom and Equality Day Rally at Depot Square in late July. The rally was organized to oppose the proposed move of the League of Pace Amendment Advocates to Evanston.

Uinta County Herald, January, 2 1990.

Don Tolin, Chairman of the Wyoming Advisory Committee for the U.S. Commission on Civil Rights said that hate groups have a common criminal element. *The thing that concerns all of us in Wyoming is the radical hate groups who have met with the Aryan Nations groups and discussed having a centralized headquarters,* Tolin said. *The League itself may be small in number, but they are well connected.*

The skinheads at the rally said that they like the Evanston location, and that the ideal spot for one of their headquarters would be in the northwest.

The *Salt Lake Tribune* of July 28th said that during the rally, *Protesters chanted, "Go home," and "We beat the Nazis once, we'll do it again," during the Wednesday night confrontation.*

The rally turned hostile when Evanston resident Traci Gilmore asked counterprotesters for a copy of "White Patriot" and then put a match to the national KKK newspaper.

Hundreds gathered around the woman [Gilmore] in Evanston's Depot Square and joined in shouted demands for skinheads to leave the Wyoming-Utah border town. One protester was arrested for trying to grab a Confederate flag unfurled by one of the skinheads, the *Salt Lake Tribune* continued.

Actually the rally went off pretty smoothly. I thought the police and other law enforcement officers held the crowd down without too much trouble, except that one arrest. I had no idea who he was, but he had guts.

The *Uinta County Herald* stated, *At the conclusion of the rally, several people approached the Skinheads and set fire to KKK literature and a swastika flag. The crowd closed in on the Skinheads, and chanted, "Go home," while "escorting" the Skinheads to their car, and out of town.*

There were no other incidents or altercations at the rally.

Mayor Dennis Ottley said that the rally had been a big success. "I think they got the message," the *Herald* article concluded.

At Freedom and Equality Day Rally

Evanston citizens say no to Pace Amendment League

By LAURIE R. QUADE

"If you think you will be welcome here, think again!" said John Fanos, Uinta County state senator, to the white separatists, Ku Klux Klan and skinheads present at the Freedom and Equality Day Rally at Depot Square Wednesday night.

Approximately 1,000 people were in attendance to voice their concern about the selection of Evanston as the national headquarters of the League of Pace Amendment Advocates. The Pace Amendment is a proposal to the United States Constitution that would strip all non-white Americans of their citizenship and deport them to their native homelands. It is based on the book, "Amendment to the Constitution: Averting the Decline and Fall of America," by James O. Pace, a pseudonym used by William Daniel Johnson.

Several speakers, flanked by American flags displayed by the local V.F.W., and representing varied ethnic backgrounds and organizations, spoke out against the League and its affiliated groups. J.L. "Jimmy" Simmons, a member of the Wyoming Task Force for Equality, said "Wyoming is the place where I get along with my fellow man. We will uphold equality."

KKK leader attends rally

John Abarr, Grand Knight of the Wyoming Ku Klux Klan, Aaron Phillips, David Spethman, and Lori Arthur, members of the Skinheads, were the only visible signs of opposition at the rally. Spethman and Phillips were employed by Johnson in his California law office.

The Skinheads are a group of youths that believe in white supremacy. The group, from Casper, said they had come to welcome the League to Wyoming. "We are here to stand up for the rights of the League," said Spethman.

"We are not white supremacists. We are white survivalists," Abarr said. When asked about the significance of the swastikas tatooed on their arms, and displayed on a flag the group car-

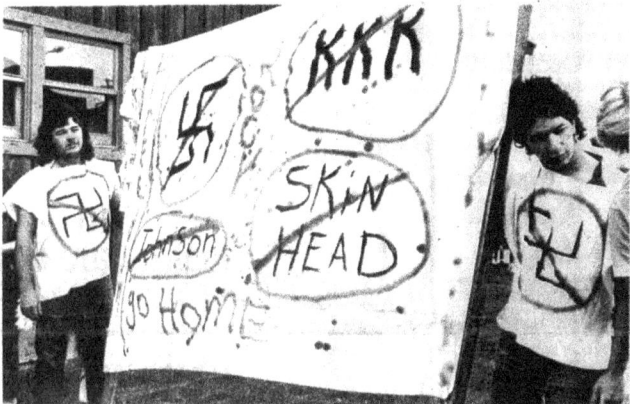

JUST SAY NO — Two local residents made their feelings known with a banner saying no to the swastika, the KKK, Daniel Johnson and the Skinheads during the Freedom and Equality Day rally in downtown Evanston Wednesday evening. See page 10 for a pictorial story of the rally.

ried, Spethman said that the swastika was an ancient symbol dating back to the Viking era. He said that the group did not subscribe to all of Hitler's philosophies.

Self-defense, not violence

When asked about the threat of violence that often accompanies Skinheads and white supremacist groups, the group said that they believe violence to be counterproductive to their cause, but that they did believe in self-defense.

Local youth at the rally said that they didn't care if the League moved to Evanston. "They'll get so bored that they'll leave in a week," one youth said.

Don Tolin, Chairman of the Wyoming Advisory Committee for the U.S. Commission on Civil Rights, said that hate groups have a common criminal element.

"Hate groups grow in the dark," Tolin said after the rally."With light and knowledge, they have no support."

League ties with KKK?

Even though the League claims

no ties with the KKK, Skinheads, and other similar groups, it has very strong ties with those groups, Tolin said. He cited an example of Daniel Johnson's claim that he was not affiliated with the KKK, but, according to Tolin, Johnson and his wife have attended KKK meetings.

"The thing that concerns all of us in Wyoming is the radical hate groups who have met with the Aryan Nations groups and discussed having a centralized headquarters," Tolin said. "The League itself may be small in number, but they are well connected."

The Skinheads at the rally said that they like Evanston because of its near-northwest location, and that the ideal spot for a headquarters would be in the northwest.

Youth soldiers

According to Tolin, the white Aryan youth have been used as soldiers by the League. "It is a fallacy to say that the League is non-violent, when they are responsible for recruiting these youths to do their dirty work," he said.

Tolin said that Spethman had served as treasurer for Johnson's ill-fated Congressional campaign. During that time, a sawed-off shotgun was confiscated in Spethman's house. He was indicted, but charges were dropped because of an illegal search and seizure.

Johnson, who was hoping for more support for his cause, was disappointed with the turnout of the crowd. He did say that there were others at the rally who supported his cause, but declined to say who they were.

At the conclusion of the rally, several people approached the Skinheads and set fire to KKK literature and a swastika flag. The crowd closed in on the Skinheads, and chanted, "Go home," while "escorting" the Skinheads to their car, and out of town.

There were no other incidents or altercations at the rally.

Mayor Dennis Ottley said that the rally had been a big success. "I think they got the message," he said.

Uinta County Herald, July, 28 1989.

1,000 Ralliers Chase Skinheads Out of Evanston

EVANSTON, Wyo. (AP) — About 1,000 people rallying here against a white supremacist's plans to make Evanston a base of operations torched Ku Klux Klan literature and chased Neo-Nazi skinheads out of town.

Protesters chanted, "Go home," and "We beat the Nazis once, we'll do it again" during the Wednesday night confrontation.

The rally turned hostile when Evanston resident Traci Gilmore asked counterprotesters for a copy of "White Patriot" and then put a match to the national KKK newspaper.

Hundreds gathered around the woman in Evanston's Depot Square and joined in shouted demands for skinheads to leave the Wyoming-Utah border town. One protester was arrested for trying to grab a Confederate flag unfurled by one of the skinheads.

The Casper, Wyo., teen-agers, one the founder of the Wyoming Knights of the KKK and the other three members of Casper Aryan Skins, picked up their white supremacist literature, Confederate flags, and banners bearing swastikas, got into a battered orange station wagon and left Evanston through the chanting throng.

Wyoming Knights founder John Abarr had said that he and his group attended Evanston's first Freedom and Equality Day Rally to protest the town's efforts to discourage avowed white supremacist Daniel Johnson from settling in the western Wyoming community.

"We're here to wake up white Aryans and show we're not the neo-Nazi terrorists they think we are," Abarr said. "All these people are here to say he [Johnson] can't move here. We're here to welcome him."

Resident Lynn Fox said Evanston officials organized the event because they feared Johnson, who waged an unsuccessful campaign for the Wyoming U.S. House seat vacated by now-Defense Secretary Dick Cheney, plans to acquire property and live in Evanston.

Johnson, a Brigham Young University graduate authored the John O. Pace Amendment, which sought to limit U.S. citizenship to whites whose ancestral homes are the British Isles or northwestern Europe.

Under the proposed amendment, all other residents would be deported or relocated on special reservations.

Johnson no longer leads the League of Pace Amendment Advocates, a group formed to push passage of the amendment in state legislatures.

However, Jessie A. Johnson, a Texas white supremacist who has taken over leadership of the group, reportedly told Evanston officials he is considering placing the group's headquarters in Evanston. Jessie Johnson and Daniel Johnson are not related.

Salt Lake Tribune, July 29, 1989.

Just after the rally I got hold of Daniel Johnson, the person I first met when they were planning to make Evanston their headquarters, and had a little talk with him and Abarr. Both seemed to be pretty reasonable people, but they told me that they hadn't found a permanent place to live and that I shouldn't worry, because the group had no more interest in locating their headquarters anywhere in Wyoming or Utah. Then they thanked me for at least giving them the opportunity to be heard and then they left, and to the best of my knowledge Evanston never saw any of them again.

"There are those who will say that the liberation of humanity, the freedom of man and mind, is nothing but a dream. They are right. It is the American dream."
Quoted by Archibald MacLeish,
A Continuing Journey

The *Casper Star-Tribune* of August 4th published an article titled, KING HOLIDAY SHOULD BE PUT TO VOTERS: ABARR.

The article started out: *CHEYENNE (AP) – Eager to "stop the Martin Luther King holiday once and for all," a Casper Ku Klux Klan member is considering launching a ballot initiative for Wyoming voters to decide whether to commemorate the slain civil rights leader with a state holiday.*
The article continued: *John Abarr, a member of the white supremacist organization called Wyoming Knights of the KKK, recently requested an application for an initiative from the Secretary of State's office. He said he has been collecting signatures "on and off" but has yet to go "all out."*
"Martin Luther King does not deserve to have a holiday," Abarr said. "He doesn't have the respect that you expect a national hero to have. I don't believe the people of Wyoming believe he's a hero."
The *Star-Tribune* continued: *Gov. Mike Sullivan, while disagreeing with the KKK's political views, said he thinks Abarr's ballot idea is "terrific."*
"Putting the ultimate issue to the vote of the people is a dandy idea," the governor said. "If some guy from the KKK wants to do all the legwork for it that would be great."

Utah Authorities Still Wary of Aryan Influx

The Salt Lake Tribune

Monday Morning—July 31, 1989

Section C — Page 1

OGDEN (AP) — Ogden Police Chief Joe Ritchie says he hasn't let up on gathering information about Idaho's Aryan Nations, even though the white supremacist group apparently has scrapped its plans to put a regional headquarters in this northern Utah community.

Ritchie said his department continues to gather information about the Rev. Richard Butler's Hayden Lake, Idaho-based movement, and monitor the activities of white supremacist groups.

Meanwhile, Utah authorities are focusing on other areas of the state where they fear Butler's followers may be active, and just across the border in Evanston, Wyo., city officials are fighting to stop an avowed white supremacist from making the town his home.

Also, Wendover Police Chief A. June Carter, Utah's only black police chief, says that his department knows of several white supremacists who have moved into the Wendover area, but, "I'd only be speculating if I said what I thought they were doing here."

About a year ago, "There was an individual who was really well into it, and we've since learned that someone took his place after he moved," said Carter. "We had a deal where this one [white supremacist] was watching us and our activities. He'd park across the street and listen to us with a special device."

The federal Bureau of Alcohol, Tobacco and Firearms investigated the incident, and a similar occurrence in Elko County, Nev., authorities said.

Carter said ATF Agent Jimmy Gober went into the man's home with a search warrant and confiscated two firearms and several bugging devices. A judge later ordered authorities to return the items to the man, who has since moved elsewhere.

At Evanston, officials and residents this past week staged an anti-white supremacist rally attended by at least 1,000 people bent on discouraging supremacist Daniel Johnson from settling there.

Don Tolin, chairman of the Wyoming State Advisory Committee for the U.S. Commission on Civil Rights, said Wyoming officials fear Johnson and other white supremacists may be discussing the possibility of making the state a central headquarters for their activities.

Johnson is the author of the John

O. Pace Amendment, which advocates changing the U.S. Constitution to limit American citizenship to whites whose ancestry is either British or northwestern European.

Evanston officials believe Johnson chose their town because of its proximity to the Salt Lake airport and because both he and his wife have relatives in Utah.

In September 1987, Butler announced plans to build a chapter of his church in Ogden because, "We liked the place and we liked the people."

Butler's announcement was met immediately with heated reaction from law enforcement officials, local leaders and representatives of Ogden's black and Hispanic communities.

"He [Butler] would certainly never admit he canceled his plans to

come here because of the pressure we put on him, but we made it very clear they [white supremacists] were not wanted in Ogden," said Ritchie. "I haven't heard a thing about it for at least eight months."

When Butler first announced plans to build a chapter in Ogden, he had just been indicted in Arkansas on federal charges of sedition involving conspiracy to overthrow the U.S. government and financing other activities by armed robbery and counterfeiting.

"He was too busy doing other things to seriously think about extending with a chapter in Utah," Ritchie said.

Butler could not be reached for comment, but a secretary at his headquarters who asked not to be identified said Butler never continued with his Ogden plan because, "Perhaps there were just too many problems."

Ritchie also said he is not pursuing further formal training sessions for his officers to prepare them for incidents that sometimes accompany the insurgence of white supremacists into an area.

In addition, a spokesman for aryanWatch, a group of Utahns organized to oppose racism, said the organization has heard nothing further about Butler's plans.

"We've been quite inactive for the past several months because there's been no activity on the part of the Aryan Nations in Utah," said Gilbert Pacheco, an organizing member of aryanWatch.

Sullivan added he believes the Wyoming voters would pass the measure "*overwhelmingly.*"

"*If he's that confident people don't want it, then let him go ahead and prove it,*" *Sullivan said.*

Should he choose to continue with the initiative, Abarr said he plans to use a copy of the original King Holiday bill sponsored by state Sen. Harriet Elizabeth "Liz" Byrd, D-Laramie, the Star-Tribune article concluded.

After U.S. Congress declared Martin Luther King Day as a national holiday during the month of January of each year, the State of Wyoming was one of the last states to accept it. I think it was because a large population of Wyoming thought it should have been called Civil Rights Day or something different than Martin Luther King day.

I don't think they had a problem so much over the holiday, but when they took the George Washington and Abraham Lincoln birthdays off the calendar and combined them to what they now call President's Day in the month of February it really angered a lot of folks. I'm still upset about that, but what could you do? I think they called it "being politically correct."

Also, after the Martin Luther King Jr. Day was declared a holiday, it was about three years before our local V.F.W. Post 4280 would acknowledge the holiday and they refused to hang the American flag up on that day.

As mayor, in 1992, I wrote a letter to the Commander of Post 4280 requesting them to please acknowledge and accept the holiday as another day to hang the flags. In 1992 they did place all the flags on MLK Day and have ever since.

A few weeks after the Freedom and Equality Day Rally on July 26th, the City of Evanston got read in the *Uinta County Herald* issue of August 16, 1989 this article: PACE AMENDMENT OFFICE HIT BY BOMB. The article went on to read: *A bomb planted in the former headquarters of the League of Pace Amendment Advocates in Glendale, California exploded at approximately 3:00 a.m. August 10.*

The office is the current law office of Daniel Johnson, former leader of the League. Johnson was out of town at the time of the explosion. He was not available for comment.

The bomb, a semi-sophisticated device equivalent to two sticks of dynamite, was placed outside the glass front door. The blast blew out the doors and resulted in an estimate of $5,000 in damages.

According to George King, director of education for the League, the FBI and the Bureau of Alcohol, Tobacco and Firearms are investigating the incident. There are no suspects in the investigation.

At the time of the explosion, a neighbor saw a gray station wagon driving away from the scene. King believes that a leftist or a Jewish terrorist group may be responsible.

John Abarr, Grand Knight of the Wyoming Ku Klux Klan, also believed that the bombing may have been attributed to the Jewish Defense League, a terrorist arm of the New York-based Anti-Defamation League, the *Herald* article added.

⊱✑∽

The next day, Thursday, July 27th, the dedication of the enlargement of Sulphur Creek Dam and Reservoir took place at 3:00 p.m. The project site was approximately 12 miles south of Evanston on Wyoming State Highway 150 South.

The long-term project was completed 10 months ahead of schedule, and came in more than $2 million under budget. The entire project had a total cost under $23 million, and the estimate was $25 million. It was the first major development project undertaken by the Wyoming State Water Development Commission. The state commission paid 75% of the cost through a grant to the City of Evanston, while the city was scheduled to pay the remaining 25% through a low interest (4%) loan with the State Water Commission. Interest on the 25% loan would not accrue for another four years, and first payment would not be due until one year after that.

The dedication of the Sulphur Creek Dam Project was a big success with a large crowd in attendance. Special guests such as Former State Senator and member of the Wyoming Water Development Commission (WWDC) Wes Myers, Director and State Engineer of the WWDC Mike Purcell, State Senator John Fanos, and others were introduced, with each speaking a few words concerning the project.

Following a few words from City Engineer Brian Honey, I spoke of this being a great day for Evanston and welcomed everyone present for taking part in the dedication. I added that, hopefully, our days of rationing water in the City of Evanston would be over, and we would now have enough water to encourage new industry to locate in Evanston and encourage old industry to expand.

I also thanked Councilmen Tom Hutchinson and Clarence Vranish, both in attendance, and members of the previous administration for their interest and dedication in seeing the project through to its completion, and for their time and hard work while serving on the Sulphur Creek Joint Powers Board.

Councilman Tom Hutchinson presented construction photos to all primary contractors and announced the day's agenda:

- Tours of the reservoir, the intake and control room
- Barbecue
- Fish derby and boat rides

It was a fun day for everyone and the City of Evanston was now two-thirds owner of a reservoir and a dam. One-third of the reservoir water would belong to the irrigators. However, with the new addition to the Evanston Water Treatment Plant and the water rights from the Bear River, Evanston should be in good enough shape for water so they would no longer have to depend on the city water wells during the dry seasons, and there should no longer be a need for the rationing of water.

During the regular city council meeting of August 3rd, an announcement was made that the Union Tank Car Company had withdrawn its request for the 30-year extension on their present lease.

Chuck Ferczok, Vice President of Union Tank, told Evanston's Administrative Assistant Steve Snyder that they were putting all previous actions regarding a lease extension on hold.

At this time I told the press that I did not know the reasons for the change of plans. But, though I didn't say anything, I knew exactly why they changed their plans. They were not going to fight with a large group of citizens that didn't want them in Evanston. Those people were more concerned with preserving the history of Evanston than the economy.

But my efforts to keep them in Evanston were not going to stop there. Too many of Evanston's citizens, including me, worked too hard to get the railway car company here, to keep those laid-off employees working, and to get the roundhouse property in operation again.

I had called for a special city council meeting on August 10th to act on Ordinances 89-9, 89-10 and 89-11, all pertaining to corrections to the Bear River Park Subdivision and the Evanston Center Subdivision. Motion was made and seconded, and each ordinance passed on second reading by a vote of 5 yes, 1 abstention (me), and 1 absent (Lunsford). These ordinances passed on third and final reading at the next city council meeting with a vote of 6 yes and 1 abstaining (me). I abstained from the ordinances because of my conflict as a realtor.

During the meeting Resolution 89-62, introduced by Councilman Craig Nelson, was brought up, authorizing the City of Evanston to enter into an agreement with X-It Construction regarding street improvements on Main Street.

Motion was made by Councilman Vranish for the adoption of Resolution 89-62, and seconded by Davis with 5 yes votes, 1 no vote (Hutchinson), and 1 absent (Lunsford).

Before adjourning this meeting, I reminded everyone of a meeting at the Legal Tender Restaurant the next morning, August 11th, from 9:30 a.m. to 11:30 a.m., and that Wyoming's U.S. Senators Alan Simpson and Malcom Wallop would be in attendance to report on the proposed Wyoming-to-California pipeline (the Kern River Pipeline Project). Representatives from WyCal, Kern River, the Federal

Regulatory Commission, and the Wyoming Pipeline Authority were also in attendance.

~~~~

On January 11, 1989 the *Heritage Brief*, a publication of the Wyoming Heritage Foundation of Casper, put out a newsletter stating the following: *For over a year, Governor Sullivan and the Wyoming Natural Gas Pipeline Authority had actively worked to secure a pipeline to take Wyoming's large – but under-utilized – natural gas reserves to the nation's largest new market in southern California.*

In 1988 the Wyoming State Legislature, under bipartisan leadership, had the vision to authorize the Pipeline Authority to negotiate terms for a $250 million, 4% loan with the company that puts together a successful pipeline project – WyCal or Kern River – to move natural gas directly from southwestern Wyoming to California.

The 1988 legislation set definite constraints on the loan. The major ones are:

- *No contract can be signed between the Authority and pipeline company until after April 1, 1989.*
- *The Governor, State Treasurer, and Attorney General must approve the loan.*
- *No money is to be loaned until there are firm contracts for at least 350 Mmcf/d of Wyoming gas and the pipeline is constructed and in operation.*
- *The pipeline company will have to pay higher interest if less than 350 Mmcf/d of Wyoming gas is transported on the line.*
- *The Authority may negotiate a financial agreement with the companies to compensate the state – through actual payments or increased revenue benefits – for lost interest revenue from loaning Permanent Mineral Trust Fund money at 4% instead of the normal investment rate.*

Much of the Authority's attention has been focused on the terms of the financial agreement.

WyCal (CIG Western and Coastal Western Pipeline companies) and Kern River (The Williams Companies and Tenneco, Inc.) are presently the only two proposals to construct a direct natural gas pipeline from Wyoming to California. As the competition for the natural gas market in California heats up, Wyoming's efforts to sell its natural gas become even more important.

An early breakfast in the Director's Room of the Best Western Motel (Dunmar Inn) on August 11th, between 8:15 a.m. and 9:15 a.m. was hosted by the City of Evanston to give the Wyoming Senators an opportunity to meet with panel members prior to the official meeting concerning the natural gas pipeline from Wyoming to California.

At 9:30 a.m. we all convened to the Wyoming Hall area of the Legal Tender Restaurant for the meeting of the Wyoming to California Natural Gas Pipeline, a.k.a. the Kern River Gas Pipeline.

As host mayor, I called the meeting to order and welcomed all those in attendance. I said,

"To our out-of-town visitors, I wish you a good visit and hope you enjoy yourselves and take time out to see this corner of the state. And to you in attendance from Evanston and surrounding areas, I encourage you to use this opportunity to get answers to all of your questions concerning the proposed pipeline.

Thanks to Senator Simpson and Senator Wallop in setting up this meeting so we didn't have to go to the experts for answers, but instead, they brought them to us. This is one of the most important projects for Wyoming that has ever come about. It will impact our community, and all of southwestern Wyoming, and will have far-reaching and long term benefits for our entire state.

I then made my introductions of our special guests; Senator Alan Simpson, Senator Malcom Wallop, and the panel: Ed Boland with the Wyoming Pipeline Authority; Lee Alexander of the Federal Energy Regulatory Commission and Senior Legal Adviser to Commission Chairperson Martha Hesse; Ken O'Connell, Senior Vice President of the WyCal Pipeline; Cuba Wadlington, Executive Vice President of the Kern River Pipeline; Nick Bush, President of the Natural Gas Supply Association; and Steve Rhoads of the California Energy Commission.

Simpson and Wallop both spoke of how the pipeline would benefit the State of Wyoming. Senator Wallop said the State of Wyoming has made a long-term innovative commitment to the proposed pipeline project, and that the market for natural gas will improve and bring stability to the marketplace. Wyoming has the largest supply of natural gas reserves in the nation, with estimates ranging from a 125- to a 167-year supply, he indicated.

Ed Boland of the Wyoming Pipeline Authority said, *The pipeline will be built because California's energy consumption is going to increase.*

The entire panel, including both Senators, agreed that the pipeline would become a reality, but there was one obstacle that delayed the project for several more months. The delay was because of concerns pertaining to the extinction of what they called the *Desert Turtle* in the deserts of Nevada. It was said that the project might not get started until another two years.

UINTA COUNTY HERALD   Wednesday, August 16, 1989

RAPT ATTENTION — A group of interested citizens listened intently to officials from several pipeline corporations and authorities at the Wyoming to California Pipeline meeting in Evanston last Friday.

SENATORIAL ENDORSEMENT — Wyoming Sen. Malcolm Wallop, right, gives a brief history of Wyoming gas production as Sen. Alan Simpson, left, listens. The senators were in Evanston to endorse the Wyoming to California Pipeline at the public meeting held Friday, Aug. 11.

Uinta County Herald, August 16, 1989.

However, the project did finally become a reality with the Kern River Pipeline Company getting the bid. At their expense, they invited City of Evanston officials to the groundbreaking ceremony that would take place approximately 30 miles north of Las Vegas in the Nevada desert, the location and route in which the pipeline was to be constructed. Administrative Assistant Steve Snyder and I both took them up on the invitation. They furnished our flight to Vegas and put us up at one of Las Vegas's finest hotels where we stayed overnight. They then bused us out to the location of the groundbreaking.

It was a nice day and we both enjoyed the trip very much. It was a great honor to be invited to the groundbreaking ceremony of such an important project that would benefit Evanston and Southwestern Wyoming's economy so considerably.

About this time Sandy and I were having some pretty tough times financially. She was still cleaning foreclosed houses, but her business was getting slower and slower. I was trying to sell property, completing a sales contract once in a while, but not enough to keep us going. Being mayor wasn't helping, because many folks, including some of those we considered good friends, just didn't want to deal with someone holding the position of mayor, and the mayor's salary of $1,000 per month wasn't enough to keep us going.

We had already lost several good pieces of property that we had owned free and clear, by mortgaging it to pay off the Lockeroom Etc. debts. It put us too far in debt to keep going, and then when we sold Uinta Realty, Inc., I just became another salesperson.

Also, we had also lost both of our vehicles putting us on foot until we could figure out how we could buy some old used vehicle to get us around town. We were without a vehicle for several weeks and I had no other choice than to use the city administration's car for a while. My secretary at the city, Sharon Constantine said to me, "Denny, as much as you used your own vehicle over the many years you had been on the council and mayor, you shouldn't feel bad about using the city car for your personal use for awhile. You'll get criticized," she continued, "by some loons that wouldn't understand, but as far as I'm concerned I think you ought to use the car and think nothing of it."

I took her advice, and I did get publicly criticized for it, but no one on the city council mentioned it. I got criticized through the "Letters to the Editor" column of the *Uinta County Herald*, and one anonymous letter was sent to the city office.

We never knew who that was but he was telling the truth. I did use the city car quite a bit for my private use for several weeks until Randy, my oldest son, helped me buy a used car from Dave Madia at the Evanston Motor Company with payments low enough that I hoped would be payable.

But by this time we finally had to let everything go back to the banks, except our home. Harry Palmer, President of the Pioneer Bank, gave us a short-term mortgage to try to save our home, but in a couple of years we lost it because the payments were beyond of what we could afford.

Therefore, after talking to City Attorney Dennis Boal we took his advice to file Chapter 13 Bankruptcy, and he also recommended a good bankruptcy attorney who we would make an appointment with. But first I was scheduled that fall to have my left knee operated on.

Dr. Scott Anthony, a new orthopedist in town and recommended by my regular doctor, Dr. Mark Brann, had scheduled me to have an operation on my knee, but was a little doubtful whether or not it would work. I was willing to give the operation a chance, but it didn't fix the problem.

After the operation we made an appointment with the attorney in Cheyenne using the city administrator's car, but buying my own gas. However, while in Cheyenne I also made some necessary visits to the Governor's office, the Secretary of State's office and I got a chance to visit with Leno Menghini, Superintendent of the Wyoming Highway Department, concerning some on-going street projects that the highway department was helping us with.

While visiting our attorney, he told us that he had to have a $6,000 retaining fee before he would consider our case. This put us in a bad situation, but this is the way attorneys operate, and we had no choice but go back home and figure out a way to raise $6,000.

After getting home and explaining to our family our situation our son Dave and his wife, Kerri, said that they would help us. They loaned us the $6,000 with no interest and nothing on paper. They just took a chance that we would pay them back, and we eventually did.

So we went back to Cheyenne and met with the attorney, with me still on crutches from my knee operation, and he took all our information down on who we owed. I told him that I still had some debt from owning Uinta Realty, Inc., and he said we will include all of that. And after appearing before the Cheyenne Judge with our attorney, our bankruptcy had been approved by the courts.

This was a first for Evanston, Wyoming, a mayor filing for bankruptcy while in office. It was a very embarrassing time for my entire family and Sandy and I felt like we had been stripped of everything. It wasn't just embarrassing, it was also very frustrating for us. The Cheyenne attorney kept our bankruptcy as quiet as possible, but the whole town knew because some of our debt was to businesses in Evanston. Although it didn't take long for the public to know about it, there was still no mention in the newspapers or the radio of our misfortune, and we were grateful for that.

Well, as embarrassing as it was, I refused to resign from the position of mayor, as many folks suggested. I only had a little over a year left, and I wasn't about to quit unless I was forced out, but no one appeared to want to do that. I felt that I was a good mayor, regardless of my mishap, and I had done a good job for Evanston and wanted to finish out my term.

During the second city council meeting of August I appointed Tracey Smith to the Evanston Planning and Zoning Commission. Motion was made by Councilman Davis to confirm the appointment, seconded by Nelson, with all voting in favor.

Mike Pexton made a request for help dealing with the problem that was developing with skateboards and the young people using them in areas of Pexton, the Yellow Creek Shopping Center and other shopping areas.

It was also getting to be a problem in the downtown area where the skateboarders used the sidewalks as well as other areas of town.

There had been several pedestrians bumped into by skateboarders, and in some cases actually knocked down. Therefore, the city council requested that City Attorney Boal look into the ordinances and see if there was anything on the books concerning the problem.

Later, reporting back to the city council, Boal said there was nothing except an ordinance concerning bicycles being on sidewalks. He suggested that an ordinance should be looked into concerning skateboards and where they would be allowed. At that time he was directed to prepare an ordinance concerning just that. Also, Recreation Director Dennis Poppinga was asked to look into the possibility of constructing a skateboard rink where the kids could go and do their skateboarding without bothering the pedestrians, and maybe get some help from the state recreation commission.

During the same meeting, Councilman Jon Lunsford made a motion to hold a special meeting on August 24th at 5:00 p.m. to make some changes on the final plat of the Evanston Regional Center so that Walmart and others could get started on construction by the end of the month. The motion was seconded by Nelson with all voting in favor.

Councilwoman Jerry Wall made a motion during the meeting requesting the City of Evanston to prepare a bid for the 1991 Wyoming Association of Municipalities (W.A.M.) annual convention, and a formal presentation to be made at the W.A.M. Board's fall meeting in Kemmerer on September 16th. The motion was seconded and the vote was unanimous.

Also, Councilman Will Davis made a motion for the proceeds from the sale of aluminum cans in one of the bins located at Smith's Food and Drug parking lot be donated to Christopher Staley to help with his liver transplant operation and the proceeds from the other two bins at the parking lot go towards the Depot Square improvements, seconded by Nelson, with all voting in favor.

During the special city council meeting on August 24th, City Attorney Dennis Boal said that all the concerns regarding the four ordinances related to the Bear River Park Subdivision and the Evanston Regional Center Subdivision had been corrected and the ordinances were all ready for third and final readings.

Motions were made separately on each ordinance for passage on third and final reading and seconded. Votes were the same on all four with 4 yes votes (Lunsford, Nelson, Vranish and Wall), 1 abstention (me), and 2 absent (Davis and Hutchinson). Each ordinance had passed on third and final reading.

During the regular city council meeting on September 7th Officer Dean Forman of the Evanston Police Department submitted his letter of resignation, which I read. The letter stated that after 19½ years with the department it was time he retired.

Councilman Nelson made a motion to accept Officer Forman's resignation, seconded by Davis, with all voting in favor.

The council and I all expressed our appreciation for his long term as an officer and wished him well in his retirement. It was also announced that there would be a retirement party for him the following weekend and that we were all invited.

I noted that Dean Forman came on the department during Mayor Bob Burns's administration, when we only had a few full-time police officers and a couple part-time. We had only one car and a budget of less than $400,000. Since that time Forman had seen a lot of changes in the department. He should be proud of his performance, because he had been a good and loyal officer all those years and shown favoritism to no one.

The Water Treatment Plant enlargement project was completed and final payments were made. Our water system now met our expectations and we hoped that the City of Evanston would have no more use for the water wells and that there would be no more rationing water during the summer months.

It was announced that the dedication of the new extended water treatment plant would be at 3:30 p.m. on October 11th and tours would be given by Superintendent Butch Whittaker and his plant crew.

Thanks were due to the Overthrust Industrial Association (O.I.A.) and the Wyoming Water Development Commission (WWDC) for their support and assistance in making it possible for the City of Evanston to enlarge the Sulphur Creek Dam and Pipeline, as well as the new enlargement project n Evanston's Water Treatment Plant.

The Wyoming Centennial Committee entered a float in the Cowboy Days Labor Day parade with Chairman Ann Bell assigning first lady Sandy, Beulah Bowers and Joan Mathson to oversee the project. With the help of City Carpenter Gary Bentley, they built a float displaying a large globe of the world and a large black kettle as a melting-pot with a large spoon, showing that America is a melting pot of nationalities, referencing the previous Freedom and Equality Rally that we had on July 26th.

They had the float decorated in red, white and blue, with signs referring to equality, freedom and unity. After finishing the globe, Gary Bentley said to Sandy, *Look we have built the world.* She laughed, but agreed. The four had fun building that float. It was a beautiful and meaningful sign of America's Constitution, and it took second place in the Civic Floats category, receiving $75.00 which went towards the Joss House project.

During the September 7th meeting Councilman Hutchinson announced that Wastewater Treatment Plant Superintendent Randy Roper had been nominated to receive an award from the Rocky Mountain Region for Water Purification at the plant. "It was because of the efforts of the entire crew at the plant that made these awards possible."

Before adjournment I reminded the council of the W.A.M. Board meeting in Kemmerer September 14th through the 16th at which time we would be making a presentation to the Board for Evanston to host the annual W.A.M. convention in 1991.

On September 21st, during our second regular city council meeting, Mr. Dale Bosworth, Wasatch/Cache National Forest Supervisor presented to City Administrator Steve Snyder and Uinta County Economic Director Ken Klinker plaques for their service, help and expertise in putting together a proposal for a Job Corps Center in the Evanston area.

However, no matter how great a job Snyder and Klinker did, and they did put together a great proposal, our proposal was turned down because of the opposition from some folks in the area.

During this same meeting Councilman Nelson made a motion to approve a monument of the 10 Commandments donated by the

Eagles Lodge (F.O.E.) for placement at Depot Square, contingent upon approval of the Depot Square Committee and the Urban Renewal Agency, seconded by Davis with all voting in favor. However, apparently because of some personal reasons, both the Urban Renewal Agency and the Depot Square Committee turned the project down. There was no further action taken on the matter.

Councilwoman Jerry Wall reported that after Evanston's presentations, made by Steve Snyder, Wall and me, as well as Evanston citizen John Bowers, at the W.A.M. meeting in Kemmerer, Evanston will host the 1991 Wyoming Association of Municipalities annual convention.

It had been over 20 years since Evanston had had the opportunity to host the W.A.M. convention, but Evanston had been very active in W.A.M. activities the past ten or so years which I'm sure helped a lot in getting to, once again, host the event.

I expressed thanks to Councilwoman Wall, Steve Snyder and John Bowers for their success in obtaining the 1991 convention for Evanston. Because of Councilman Wall showing so much interest in W.A.M., she was immediately appointed by me and confirmed by the council to act as chairperson for the event.

Y'all come back now

A colorful and positive statement is made to visitors leaving the town of Evanston — hopefully a statement that will entice them to return. Sponsored by the city Beautification Committee with the support of the Wyoming Highway Department, Evanston was the first community in Wyoming to request the hand painted signs. Pictured with the sign are, from left, Beautification Committee representative Nelle Gerrard, and Mayor Dennis Ottley.

A sign of the times

New Evanston city logo signs were erected Tuesday to help kick-off Support Your Community Week. The signs, located at city entrances on Highway 150, Highway 89, and Bear River Drive and Harrison Drive exits along Interstate 80, were painted by local artist Rick Ludwig. The project was spearheaded by the city Beautification Committee, with the support of the Wyoming Highway Department. Pictured with the new sign are, from left, Evanston City Planner Paul Knopf, Beautification Committee representative Nelle Gerrard, Mayor Dennis Ottley, and City Administrator Steve Snyder.

Uinta County Herald, October 20, 1989.

Prior to adjourning I announced that, although Union Tank Car Company's proposed offer had been withdrawn, there would still be a public meeting concerning the roundhouse on October 5, 1989

In the *Uinta County Herald* issue of September 19th it was announced that Support Your Community Week would be scheduled for October 23rd through the 27th. The program was co-sponsored by the City of Evanston and the Evanston Chamber of Commerce.

"Let's Do Lunch" was the theme of the kick-off on Monday, October 23rd, as Uinta County senior citizens would be recognized at the chamber's membership luncheon to be held at the Weston Super Budget Inn (presently Days Inn), and the annual Citizens Award Banquet would be held on Friday, October 27th at Lotty's Restaurant.

The regular city council meeting of October 5th was conducted by Council President Tom Hutchinson because I was recovering from my recent knee surgery.

Following the roll call, the approval of the minutes, and so on, Council President Hutchinson opened the floor for the public hearing, as previously announced, concerning the roundhouse property and Union Tank Car Company.

There were dozens of citizens in attendance and many were there to make presentations, pro and con, to the council. Frank Swan led the group opposed to the offer, which had already been withdrawn, that U.T.C.C. had previously made to the city concerning the purchase or an extended lease agreement.

Councilman Clarence Vranish checked into the present lease and found an "Escalation Clause" provision stating that the monthly lease amount shall be adjusted based on the Consumer Price Index every January. He pointed out that the commencement date of the lease with Union Tank was in 1979 and the rate of rent was to be adjusted and increased every year in the month of January.

※

In 1972 the Union Pacific Railroad donated 26 acres to the city to be used for industrial purposes, and in 1972 and 1973 former Mayor Bob Burns and I, as a member of the city council, and a couple of others worked very hard and put in a lot of time in getting the railway car company started. The railroad had shut down the roundhouse shops and pulled the dispatch office of the locomotive engineers and firemen out of Evanston, causing the city to lose hundreds of families.

One acre of the property was held back for Time D.C. Trucking to temporarily use for their dispatch (where City Hall now is located); the lot that the Palmers lived on while working for the railroad was sold to the family because of old-time memories; and the rest was leased to the Wyoming Railway Car Company in January of 1974 by Colonel Oliver Shiflet. Former Mayor Burns, Attorney Harry Lee Harris and I went to Ranger, Texas, where the Texas Railway Car Company was located, to talk to Colonel Oliver Shiflet (retired) into coming to Evanston to open up a shop, because we had the facility they would need, and the City of Evanston was in grave need of jobs. At that time there was a big national demand for railway cars to be repaired.

After some very tough years for the former Army colonel, he got the Wyoming Railway Car Company successfully operating and in 1979 he sold out to Lithcote, a Union Tank Car company affiliate. The city gave them a 30-year lease, and now, after 10 years, they have requested a lease extension or possibly to purchase the property.

The original lease with Shiflet and the lease with Union Tank always had the provision that they would pay the property tax as if they were the owners. I never knew what their taxes amounted to, but that would have been up to the County Assessor's office.

Apparently, after 1981 the clause in the lease agreement had been overlooked and the present lease amount had been based on the January 1981 rate adjustment of $1,273.53, which it remained until this time in 1989. But if the escalation clause had been continued as the leased agreement stated, the monthly rate should have been up to $1,778.71 by 1989.

This was an oversight on both former Mayor Martin's Administration and my own. The reason for this oversight was probably because of the changes of personnel in the Treasurer's department over the past several years. It was something that should not have been overlooked by the city or the company, but once Vranish found the escalation provision, Assistant City Treasurer Steve Widmer wrote a letter to Union Tank and the correction was immediately made. I don't believe there was any penalty of any kind charged to the company (lessee), because the city council felt that the city (lessor) had been just as much at fault and just as neglectful as the company.

A more recent photo of the Union Pacific Roundhouse property, owned by the City of Evanston, that was leased to Union Tank Car Company until 1995. Photo courtesy of the Evanston Chamber of Commerce.

Councilman Vranish said in his memo to the council that the city's failure to re-compute the rent increases since 1981 has resulted in a current shortage of approximately $27,000 to date (1989) and over $29,000 by year's end.

This was all spelled out during the public meeting and many comments were made, pro and con, by many in attendance. We had received many letters addressed to the council and me, some against the selling or extending the lease, but most in favor of the sale or lease. The city council was split on the issue, but the majority of the members would have favored the Tank Car Company's proposal. I knew Councilwoman Jerry Wall and Councilman Craig Nelson were against the proposal, but I'm glad that it didn't have to come up for a vote. I think most of the folks, including me, wanted to see a win/win situation, and in the future that was exactly what I would be shooting for.

However, I did write a letter to Mr. Chuck Ferczok asking them to reconsider their offer and that we had received the appraisal, made by Dave Kimball, a local certified appraiser. The appraisal came in at a market approach of $750,000, an income approach of $100,000, and a cost approach of $728,000.

I told him that I thought this appraisal would be a good base to start negotiations with, but he had said the company had already withdrawn their offer and were no longer interested in talking to us concerning either the purchase or the extended lease.

Dave Kimball had his own appraisal service under Western Appraisal Service, but, because he was also a real estate sales agent, several folks accused me of hiring him to do the appraisal of the railroad property because, they claimed, he was a partner of mine with ERA Uinta Realty, Inc.

As far as I could see, the folks claiming that were just trying to stir up trouble because they didn't want Union Tank occupying the property and didn't care about what any appraised value the property would come in at.

In the first place, I was not an owner of ERA Uinta Realty, Inc., and neither was Dave Kimball. We were both just sales agents licensed under ERA. Just as Councilman Lunsford stated in the meeting, *Kimball is well certified and qualified to do appraisals on commercial and industrial properties, and he is local. That is why we selected him to do the job.*

Someone made the statement that there were two other appraisers in Evanston, Hughes Appraisal and Rayo Barker. They were right, but Hughes was not qualified to do appraisals on that type of property, and Barker refused the offer. Both were considered and asked to do the job; we were trying to make sure a local appraiser got the job.

During the public meeting I was also accused of representing Union Tank Car Company as their real estate agent, and was going to make a large commission if the deal came through. Well, U.T.C.C. didn't need an agent for what they were trying to do, they already had their own agent, and the city wasn't in a position to pay a real estate agent for selling any of their property. They didn't do their homework, or they were "judging other people by themselves," but both of these accusations were published in the press. I just couldn't believe that so-called friends could be so deceitful and underhanded. I guess that's *just politics*. President Richard Nixon once said, *"With friends like that, who needs enemies?"*

During the next few years I would be communicating closely with Ferczok trying to make sure Evanston wasn't going to lose U.T.C.C. to Utah, because the rumor was that Union Tank was looking at an Ogden, Utah site and an American Fork, Utah site. I later found out for sure that these were not just rumors, so I got hold of George Peters, District Manager of Upland Industries, Union Pacific Corporation's land company. I had been well acquainted with Mr. Peters, and he had worked with me on several other land deals, public and private.

I approached Mr. Peters with the idea of the city possibly purchasing some of the U.P. property that abutted the roundhouse property to the west. He told me that he would approach his Board of Directors to see what they had to say about it. I told him that we would need 75 to 100 acres, and I told him why. He said they still had about 265 acres on the southwest side of the tracks and approximately

75 acres on the northwest side. He seemed very willing to work with me, but said it could take a while.

I immediately notified Mr. Ferczok of my intentions and he thanked me for trying to do something to keep them in Evanston. He seemed to be very much in favor of remaining in Evanston if we could work something feasible out.

After the public meeting concerning the roundhouse, Administrative Assistant Steve Snyder reported that Western Wyoming College in Rock Springs was considering a truck driving school, and that they would like to locate in Evanston with approximately 200 full-time students.

Councilwoman Wall made a motion for those involved to follow through and that the City of Evanston was definitely in favor of the school being in our city. The motion was seconded by Lunsford, with 6 yes votes and 1 absent (me).

However, this project never got off the ground. Why, I do not know, I think the Western Wyoming College just dropped the whole idea.

Just before adjournment, Councilwoman Wall reported on a seminar the Evanston Police Department had recently conducted concerning hate groups and that there were approximately 110 people in attendance.

Under old business of the regular city council meeting on October 19th, Councilman Vranish made a motion to bring Resolution 89-74, approving and adopting a short term disability payment program for the city employees, off the table. The resolution had been tabled during the last meeting and had been previously introduced by Vranish.

Councilman Vranish made a motion to amend the resolution by changing some wording in it, which was seconded by Lunsford, with 5 votes in favor of the amendment, and 2 absent (Nelson and Davis).

I then called for a vote on the main motion as amended, made by Lunsford at the previous meeting and seconded by Davis. The motion carried with 5 yes votes.

In new business, Councilman Hutchinson introduced and sponsored Ordinance 89-14, establishing uniform requirements and prohibitions for all users discharging into the wastewater collection and treatment system of the City of Evanston. This ordinance amended certain sections of the present ordinance to meet the requirements of the new wastewater treatment plant, and was very necessary. It was passed on all three readings and by unanimous vote in future meetings.

Following new business, Councilman Lunsford made a motion to hold a special meeting on October 26th at 7:00 p.m. to consider and discuss a couple of ordinances, and invite and honor the essay winners of the students participating in the "Evanston the Beautiful" contest sponsored by Evanston's Beautification Committee. The motion was seconded by Hutchinson, with all voting in favor.

Union Pacific Depot to open

RESTORED AND READY — The restored and ready Union Pacific Depot building will be open this week, 'Support Your Community Week,' during the Chamber After-Hours mixer, sponsored by the City of Evanston. The mixer will be held right across the street from the Depot, in the Beeman Cashin building, from 5 to 7 p.m. Wednesday evening, Oct. 25th. Everyone is invited to attend.

THE TICKET CAGE AND BOARD — The nerve center of the depot is always the ticket cage and arrival/departure board. Check the board to see if your train is coming on time, leaving on time or cancelled. It is just like the TV monitors at the airport, now, but that was the equivalent before the technological age hit.

Uinta County Herald, October 24, 1989.

The 3rd annual Support Your Community Week program started off Monday morning of October 23rd with the "Let's Do Lunch" program, where folks were asked to bring their favorite senior citizen(s) and treat them to a lunch. Denice Wheeler was the guest speaker, on the topic of "Preparing for the Golden Years".

Tuesday, October 24th was the Prayer Breakfast sponsored by the Evanston Ambassador's Club and ERA Uinta Realty, Inc. to raise money for the Kristopher Staley liver transplant fund. The $5.00-a-plate breakfast was funded by Lotty's, I.G.A., Smith's, and Curt's Thriftway.

On Wednesday, the City of Evanston hosted the Evanston Chamber of Commerce's monthly mixer in the newly refurbished train depot at Depot Square, and on Thursday the Evanston Beautification Committee sponsored a luncheon at the Beeman-Cashin Building in Depot Square for the essay winners and their parents.

Thursday evening, October 26th, the Evanston City Council held their special city council meeting to honor and announce the student winners who participated in the Beautification Committee-sponsored "Evanston the Beautiful" essay program.

As each student finished reading their essay, they were applauded by the Congregation and presented a green T-shirt inscribed with *Evanston Beautification Committee – Keeping Evanston Spruced Up.*

I, as mayor, expressed appreciation to all present for their participation and for their excellent essays. I also thanked the Wyoming State Hospital staff for the participation and service they had given during the week.

Each member of the council followed up with their appreciation and comments concerning the promotional week.

And to top the week off, one of the biggest events was the Honor Banquet and Appreciation Dinner held on Friday night, October 27th, honoring senior citizens of Evanston who had been active and shown their love and passion by being involved in making Evanston a better place to live. Those named were Elaine Michaelis, Regina

(Butch) Ledgerwood and Archie Willmore, and each was presented a gift to honor them for their services.

Guest speaker for Honor Banquet was Wyoming Congressman Craig Thomas, U.S. Representative.

The 1989 Support Your Community Week once again turned out to be a big success, encouraging Evanston folks of all ages to come together by taking part in the various events. The program also helps the economy by encouraging locals to get involved in the community and setting an example of being a good active citizen. I was very proud of the success of that week.

On November 2nd the first regular city council meeting of the month, I introduced a group of Boy Scouts who were in attendance to fill the requirements for a Merit Badge. The Scouts were Randon Kennedy and Lance Widmer from troop 40; Aaron Morton from troop 30; Mathew Hancock, Jared Davis, Ryan Linford from troop 200; and David Julian from troop 95. I thanked the boys for their attendance and complimented them for their achievements as Scouts, and hoped they would find their presence worthwhile.

Under new business, Councilwoman Wall introduced Resolution 89-78, endorsing an economic development loan to the Evanston Community Development Committee for $16,400. Motion was made by Hutchinson for adoption, seconded by Davis, with all voting in favor, motion passed.

Prior to this meeting, I met with Police Chief Dennis Harvey and told him I would like to have all officers wear a new badge similar to the Old West Marshall's "Star Badge," and that he should order enough for all the officers and for each city council member, including me and some extras, for souvenirs.

He ordered the badges and had received them, and presented each member of the city council and me with the badge during this meeting. The badge was a 6-star badge with *Evanston Police – 1890-1990 – Wyo. Centennial* in the outer circle and *State of Wyoming* in the inner circle, and a bright red Wyoming Cowboy in the center. I thought it was a beautiful symbol to help in the celebration of the Wyoming Statehood Centennial in 1990, and would look good on the uniforms of all Evanston patrol officers. Other police personnel, such as the detectives, would also carry or wear one.

During this meeting City Planner Paul Knopf reported that $30,000 worth of engineering services had been approved for the Bear River Project (ice ponds, etc.) by the Army Corp of Engineers.

Also, Administrative Assistant Steve Snyder reported on the meetings he recently attended in Denver for the National Civic League. He said that cities across the United States were eligible for honorable mention if there were citizen participation in certain projects, and the citizens of Evanston could certainly be proud of their participation in the many projects that have been accomplished, as well as ongoing projects.

Councilman Hutchinson reported that Frank Sheets had recently completed his certification as a Class 4 Operator and Paul Vozakis had completed his Class 2 certification. Both employees were operators at the Wastewater Treatment Plant, and were recognized by the council and me. Hutchinson stated that Evanston had more certified people working in our plants than any other city in the State of Wyoming.

During the Evanston City Council meeting of November 16th, Sandy approached the council with a presentation concerning an endurance race across Wyoming in conjunction with the Wyoming Centennial Celebration and commemorating the renowned "Great Endurance Horse Race" from Evanston to Denver, Colorado in 1908.

She said she would like to have the mayor proclaim May 25, 26 and 27 as the Great Endurance Race Days. She explained she had a committee to assist her on this project and hoped to make it an annual event. However, she mentioned that because of all the fencing and new highways, there would probably be some changes from what they did in 1908. We'd have to talk to a lot of private property owners, the Wyoming Highway Department, BLM and other government agencies to get their permission.

Councilman Hutchinson made a motion to authorize the mayor to declare May 25, 26 and 27, 1990 as the Great Endurance Race Days and to sign a proclamation. The motion was seconded by Nelson with 6 yes votes and 1 absent (Wall).

Under new business, Utah Power and Light Company (presently Rocky Mountain Power) proposed to furnish 35 new street lights on Yellow Creek Road. After some explanation, Councilman Lunsford made a motion to accept the proposal of U.P.& L., seconded by Vranish with 5 yes votes, 1 abstention, and 1 absent (Wall). The motion passed.

I reminded everyone of the Torch Parade on Friday night November 24th, to start at the Presbyterian Church on the corner of 10th and Center to the Beeman-Cashin Building on Depot Square for turning on the city Christmas lights to start off the Noel Season. After the parade, I made a short speech and then I called for the lights to come on. The night was a bit brisk but there was no snow yet that season.

During our first meeting of the month on December 7th we again had a number of Boy Scouts in attendance to earn their merit badges. In introducing the Scouts, I welcomed Neil Stevenson and Les Banks as the Scoutmasters, and Boy Scouts Josh Rasneck, Jeremy Draper, Clinton Stevenson, and Jason Schofield.

I thanked them for their interest in attending the meeting and hoped they not only earned their requirements for their merit badges, but also took this opportunity to learn a little about how the city operates.

After several resolutions were acted on and adopted under new business, General Superintendent Allen Kennedy requested permission to tear down and demolish the old sewage disposal plant at the far end of Sims Lane. He said there had been some vandalism to the property and it could be a danger to any person playing around it.

Councilman Nelson made the motion to direct the Department of Public Works, under the direction of Superintendent Kennedy, to demolish the old sewage disposal plant, seconded by Hutchinson, with all voting in favor.

The topic of the police officers taking intoxicated people home rather than arresting them and taking them to jail was brought up by Police Chief Harvey. The chief said this is getting to be a problem for the department, and city attorney Dennis Boal added that the city could possibly be sued, especially if the officer took them home and then they left again and had an accident.

I believe that all members of the council, including me, felt the same way as Wall and Vranish, but they were very concerned with what the city attorney had reported. I ended the discussion by stating that this should be taken up with the Police Commission and the commission could bring in their recommendation at the next meeting.

The commission, after meeting a few days later, suggested to the council that because of the increase in population, and because things are not like they were 20 years ago, and the reasons mentioned by the city attorney, it was decided that the policy of taking intoxicated people home should no longer be allowed. Officers would be directed to make the arrest and escort the intoxicated person to jail.

One of the reasons that came up was the fact that Evanston was no longer a small community where folks knew everyone and their families. If an intoxicated driver gave the officer the wrong address, or went back out again and had an accident causing someone to be hurt or possibly killed, or causing a lot of property damage, then the city could be liable and would face a lawsuit. Things in Evanston just weren't like they used to be and neither were the laws.

During the December 7th meeting, Councilman Will Davis stated that there had been a request from some of the school officials to fence Anderson Park. I said that I was against fencing any city park, and that Anderson Park does not belong to the school district, it belongs to the public.

As there was no official request from the Uinta County School District No. 1, no further action was taken.

Before adjourning I reminded everyone of the City's annual Christmas Party at 6:00 p.m. on December 8th, the dedication of the new refurbished train depot, also on December 8th, and the special city council meeting scheduled for December 14th.

Months after the City of Evanston had passed the gaming ordinance allowing bingo and pull-tabs to be legal in establishments sponsored by non-profit organizations, the old Cowboy Casino on Overthrust Road would open up Evanston's first Bingo Super Session.

Saturday, December 9th would be their opening day and they would operate under the name of Wyoming Events Center, and would be sponsored by the Evanston Elks Lodge, as reported by the *Uinta County Herald* issue of December 8th.

The *Herald* also mentioned that there would also be five brand new pull-tab machines at the event center, the first pull-tab machines in the State of Wyoming. There was one machine in Cheyenne, but the first five production models of this new type of gaming device would be in Evanston.

Elks Lodge Trustee Ken Williams recently stated that the bigger the crowds, the larger the share for the Elks. He also indicated that the plan was to have at least one Super Session of Bingo per month.

An editorial by G. C. Duerden was published in the December 12th issue of the *Uinta County Herald* concerning a study of the economics of different communities in the west and mid-west states. Evanston was one of those communities.

The editorial stated: *Professor Floyd Harmston's, from the University of Missouri, research on the economics of communities, looking at hundreds of communities in the West and Midwest.*

One thing which showed itself to be an important factor in any community, Harmston said, was the community's attitude.

We have found most of the residents of Evanston are positive in their attitudes. The elected officials are making steps toward a very progressive valley and they have an obvious positive attitude.

Some of the evidence of this positive attitude are the concrete things in the area. The outstanding recreation facility which Evanston can justly boast, the fine school facilities, the new city hall, depot square and the fine historic preservation effort there, new business opening every week ... on and on.

Harmston said the way for a community to survive and grow is to maintain a positive attitude. Evanston has the proper attitude. It has a potential and the growth will occur, the editorial concluded.

I thought the editorial was great and I commended G. C. Duerden for having published it. I said that I felt that it couldn't have described Evanston any better, and that Professor Harmston should also be commended.

On the 8th of December, the city's annual Employees Christmas Dinner was held and turned out to be a lot of fun and enjoyable. I thanked all those in attendance for the support, the assistance, and all the encouragement they had given me, as their mayor, this past year. I told them that it had not been easy, but we needed to keep thinking positive and keep moving forward if we were going to survive as a healthy and lovable community.

I told them: *I once read a quote that went like this: "Even if you fall on your face, you are still moving forward." So that is my goal, even if we fail once in a while, we will continue to keep moving forward. Goals determine what you are going to be,* I added, and that my goals were to do whatever it took to make Evanston a proud community. *With all your help,* I said, *I know we together can and will be successful.*

HAPPY BIRTHDAY

WYOMING

CHAPTER 24

1990....The year of the Wyoming Statehood Centennial Celebration (1890-1990), an election year and another busy year.

A great quote by Nelson Mandela, South African politician: *"The greatest glory in living lies not in never falling, but rising every time we fall."*

I think of that quote often and I firmly believe that in order to be successful in your endeavors, you must keep trying. Through my experience I have found that if something is worth seeking, the best you can do is give it all you can and most likely you will succeed. What the heck; *"We learn to walk by stumbling."*

The 4th day of the new year I opened up our first regular city council meeting. After roll call, approving the minutes and outstanding bills, and accepting all committee reports, I gave my annual State of the City address.

I started: *"As we go into a new year and a new decade I look back to not only the accomplishments the Evanston community has fulfilled the past year of 1989, but also those accomplishments that have come about this past decade.*

"Our community has come through some trying times during the so-called boom/bust period, but now I feel the economy is presently on an upward trend to the point that we can look forward to some good times."

In my speech I mentioned all the projects that we, as a group working together, had accomplished in 1989: projects such as the Sulphur Creek Dam, the expansion of the Water Treatment Plant, all the much-needed improvements to our infrastructure, and water and sewer lines, storm sewers, and street overlays.

I mentioned that without the assistance of the oil and gas industry, the Wyoming State Farm Loan Board, the Wyoming State Recreation Commission, the Wyoming Water Development Commission, the Wyoming Highway Department and others, these projects would never have been successful.

But most of all I spoke of how proud I was of that the folks in Evanston and Uinta County came together during the great Freedom & Equality Day conducted by Uinta County Against Neo-Nazi Terrorists (U.C.A.N.T.), headed by Lynne Fox, Chairman, who put on such a great program that it chased all the White Supremacists, the skinheads and the Pace Amendment believers out of Wyoming and Uinta County, hopefully for good.

I spoke of the progress on the improvements to Depot Square, the Train Depot, and the Downtown Improvement District, and the completion of the new Evanston Post Office. I also spoke of the many events that were so successful such as the Agri-Business Honor Banquet, Railroad Days, Chinese News Year, Veterans Day Memorial, the Chili Cookoff, the Renewal Ball, Cowboy Days, and another successful Support Your Community Week, and other programs that I may have missed.

I said, *"We live in a proud community. We indeed live in a community of fresh air, freedom and fun. And with all the support and cooperation as we have had in the past, this community can only get better."*

I ended my statement by thanking all who had been involved, including members of the city council and all city employees, county commissioners, legislators, city boards and commissions, the chamber of commerce and other organizations that had assisted in helping to make 1989 another great year.

I reminded those in attendance that this year of 1990 will be a big election year for the state, for the county and for the city. This will be election year for all of the top five state officials, almost all county officials, and Evanston's mayor and three city council members.

Following my statement I made the appointments of the city officials: Steve Snyder, Administrative Assistant; Dennis Harvey, Chief of Police; Paul Knopf, Community Development Director; Don Welling, City Clerk/Treasurer; Steve Widmer, Assistant City Clerk/Treasurer; Brian Honey, City Engineer; Allen Kennedy, Supervisor of Operations; John Phillips, City Judge; Dennis Boal, City Attorney;

and Rick Lavery, Assistant City Attorney. Motion was made by Councilman Nelson to confirm the city official appointments, seconded by Wall, with 6 yes votes, motion passed.

I also made board and commission appointments: Brian Patterson, Planning & Zoning (3-year); Debbie Smith, Housing Authority (4-year); Councilman Tom Hutchinson and Georgia Harvey, Public Service Advisory Board (3-year). Motion by Councilman Davis to confirm was seconded by Vranish, with 6 yes votes. The motion passed.

Wyoming Governor Mike Sullivan and Evanston Mayor Dennis Ottley in Cheyenne during the program to kick-off the Wyoming Centennial of 1990.

I continued with 1-year appointments to the Uinta County Emergency Management Board: Paul Knopf and Don Bodine as Co-ordinators to the City. Motion was made by Councilman Davis to confirm these appointments, seconded by Nelson, with all voting in favor. The motion passed.

Kathy Cue, representing the Chinese New Year Committee, gave her report and extended an invitation to the mayor and city council to be in the parade at 12 noon on January 27th.

Before adjournment I reported that Chevron USA was going to present the BEAR Project with a donation at a luncheon at the new improved Train Depot on January 10th.

During our second city council meeting of the month, on January 18th, the council passed on first reading the first ordinance of the year. Ordinance 90-1, introduced by Councilman Tom Hutchinson and sponsored by Councilwoman Jerry Wall, was to vacate a portion of the alley, being used by the city, located within the Snowden Addition to the City of Evanston.

A petition to vacate the described portion of the alley was filed with the City of Evanston by Rose Fessler, owner of record of the property including the described alley. Although the city had always considered that portion of alley as being a part of city property, the city council determined it would be in the best interest of the city to vacate the property.

Ordinance 90-1 was passed on all three readings over the next few council meetings by a unanimous vote on each reading. I, as mayor, and City Clerk Welling executed a quitclaim deed to Rose Fessler conveying the property to her.

During this January meeting the transfer of funds in the budget came up. Due to the shortfall in some departments in which some projects were already in progress and needed to be completed, at this time, it was necessary to take a hard look at the budget and determine where we could transfer funds from, plus possibly cutting out some items that would have to be held back until later dates.

When the economy is soft and revenues are not coming in as expected, sometimes a governmental body must reopen their budget and do some transferring and cutting in areas that can wait. You have to set priorities, but this can be a problem because everyone on the council might have different priorities. Councilperson representing Ward 1 may not have the same priorities as Councilperson in Ward 3 and so on. Each council member was elected to look out for their ward, but the mayor must look out for the entire community. It makes it kind of tough when making those decisions.

Therefore, Resolution 90-3 was introduced by Councilman Vranish, authorizing the transfer of unencumbered and unexpended appropriation balances of the budget for the fiscal year of 1989-1990.

However, Resolution 90-3 was tabled by motion until the next regular city council meeting on February 1st. There were a few unanswered questions and some members of the council wanted more time to check out a few items mentioned in the resolution.

Before adjournment I asked for announcements and reports from the city council members and staff. Councilman Nelson complimented the police department for their recent drug bust, which was a big one. The Evanston Police Department had been well aware of the local drug traffic for quite some time. They were now giving the problem a lot of their attention because it seemed to be getting worse. It was a problem that needed a lot of attention.

Other reports followed: Councilwoman Wall made her report on the W.A.M. winter workshop that she had recently attended in Cheyenne; I read a letter of appreciation from Dr. Mark Brann for the new lighting on the road to the hospital; Councilman Lunsford reported that there would be a public hearing concerning the enhanced 911 emergency calling number on February 6th at the Uinta County Complex; I expressed appreciation to the Chevron Oil Company and Utah Power and Light Company for the recent and generous contributions they made to the BEAR Project and to the construction of the Joss House; and Assistant Treasurer Steve Widmer reported that the figures were in for the yearly inflation rate and that the new monthly payment from Union Tank Car Company would be $1,862.62 for the year of 1990.

The Chinese New Year's event, the "Year of the Horse," held on January 26th and 27th, was another big success. This is an event where everyone could wish everybody *"Gung Hay Fat Choy"* (Happy New Year). Chairperson Kathy Cue reported that the very successful program started off with a torchlight parade at 5:30 p.m. on January 26th and that Evanston had a number of very distinguished out-of-state visitors of Chinese descent attending the event who had distributed many Chinese articles to the committee.

CHINESE DRAGON — One of the favorites of this area was the Chinese Dragon from DMS, which had just returned from a successful trip to Cheyenne and visit with the governor and Washington delegation.

Uinta County Herald.

On the 27th the traditional Ball Drop program was held. Whoever caught the ball would automatically be the "Keeper of the Key" of the Joss House until the next Chinese New Year. Jan Nelson caught the ball this year, so she would be the Keeper of the Key, and she would be responsible for the safety of the Joss House until the next year.

The food festival following the ball drop, the sculpturing contest, the Chinese dinner held at the Evanston Elks Club, and the shooting off of the fireworks by the Evanston Voluntary Firemen to finalize the Chinese New Year program all turned out great, and Kathy thanked the city officials that entered the parade.

During the January meeting a resolution was introduced to change the city council meeting days from the first and third Thursday to the second and fourth Wednesdays. By changing the days it would give more time to the staff to prepare meetings, and make it easier for some of the council members to meet all their schedules. Motion was made and seconded with all voting in favor.

The *Uinta County Herald* of January 2nd published an article saying that in early January 1990 a new owner, Joe Joyce, will close on purchasing the Wyoming Downs. Mr. Joyce had managed the Uinta Downs racetrack during the season of 1989, and had significant experience at big tracks back east, including instituting the first million dollar thoroughbred horse race in the country.

It was great news for the City of Evanston and I, as mayor, congratulated Mr. Joyce in his new venture and hoped we all could look forward to a great season this year for Uinta Downs. There's no doubt that the racetrack going strong would help Evanston's economy.

The *Uinta County Herald* of January 2nd also announced that the Evanston area had been recently selected for a possible location for a petrochemical plant. Evanston was one of three sites being looked at, according to the article. The other locations were in Canada and on the Gulf Coast. However, the announcement apparently had been prematurely brought out in the media in November of 1989, causing a bit of a stir.

Huntsman Chemical Corporation hoped to start operation of the proposed plant by 1992, wherever it was located. It would take natural gas liquid feed stocks and turn them into a type of plastic as well as make a gas additive, the *Herald* continued.

This would have been a great asset to Evanston and Uinta County's economy, and a great location because of the tremendous natural gas reserve of the Overthrust Belt discovery.

But disappointingly, Evanston was not selected for the proposed plant. Why? I had no idea and was never told, plus I'm not sure where it was located or even if it ever happened at all.

The Evanston Chamber of Commerce meeting of January 8th was called primarily for discussion on the proposed Lodging Tax issue that would, hopefully, be put on the ballot for this year's election. All in attendance were in favor of the tax. It was explained that this tax would not come from locals, but from out-of-towners who make reservations for lodging while visiting Uinta County.

David Radar, President of the Wyoming Hotel/Motel Association, who was in attendance, suggesting that proponents of the measure should "make sure the (local) lodging members are behind it. It doesn't hurt the city or county to support it and you must have all those endorsements in your pocket when you go to the voters," he stated.

According to Denice Wheeler, Chairperson of the Tourism and Convention Committee of the chamber, and who conducted the meeting, stated that 90 percent of the State of Wyoming has the lodging tax, "so it won't shock tourists to pay a two percent tax."

It was discussed whether this would be a county-wide tax or just an Evanston tax. Most members were in favor of going county-wide, but that would have to be discussed with the County Commissioners and the Bridger Valley Chamber of Commerce.

During the meeting I stated that I was in favor of the tax and had been for quite some time. I said, *Too bad we didn't have this in place and collecting money for this past year, with all the Centennial events going on.*

In the *Uinta County Herald* issue of January 19th, an editorial by G. C. Duerden read:

"The proposed lodging [tax] is a good idea. The proposed two percent will be on the daily charges of hotels, motels, campground spaces and short term rental of lodging.

On a $35 per day motel room the tax would be 70 cents per day. It will be paid by visitors to our area and will go to promotion of the community.

State law requires 98 percent of the funds be returned to the area which generates it for the use of that area. A locally appointed "Joint Powers Board" will decide on how the money is spent.

The money from the lodging tax will make it possible for Uinta County to market our attractions and events in surrounding states, the region and even reach a national market.

We commend the idea to the voters of the county as sound, useful and needed, the editorial concluded.

Later in January it was announced that Uinta County hotel/motel owners would support the new lodging tax issue.

During January Jim Davis, Director of the Urban Renewal Agency, and Ann Bell, Chairperson of the Wyoming Centennial Commission, announced that there would be a brick-selling program forthcoming. The idea would be to sell bricks inscribed for anyone interested in having their names, company names or quotes, or anything that comes to mind inscribed on the bricks. The cost of the inscribed bricks would be $35 each, or $50 if you wished the inscription to be in gold print.

The bricks would be used as a money-raising program to help with the construction of the Joss House as part of the Centennial celebration. The bricks would be laid above the ground creating a pathway between the Beeman-Cashin Building and the Joss House. The first 800 dog-bone-shaped bricks, donated by Utah Power and Light, would be on sale during this year's Chinese New Year Food Festival at the Beeman-Cashin Building and would be available for purchase through the end of June, 1990.

Sandy and I purchased a brick for ourselves and each of our sons and their families, and felt that the program was a great idea for raising funds for the Centennial celebration. The project took hold and went over very well, and they had to order more bricks after selling the bricks that Utah Power and Light had donated.

During the regular city council meeting of February 1st, I made more appointments. I appointed Laurie Quade, Jan Nelson, and Debbie Bass to the Beautification Committee with a motion by Councilwoman Wall to confirm the appointments, seconded by Davis with all voting in favor.

I also appointed Brian W. Perkins to the Urban Renewal Agency and re-appointed Norwood Sutton and John Doidge to the same board. Motion was made by Councilman Nelson to confirm these appointments, seconded by Davis with all voting in favor.

After months of discussion in city council meetings and work sessions, plus the many hours spent by Paul Knopf, City Planner, and his staff, the City of Evanston finally came up with Ordinance 90-3 during the Thursday meeting of February 15th.

Ordinance 90-3 was introduced and sponsored by a member of the council to provide for changes in the regulation of signage within the City of Evanston. The ordinance was a very lengthy document describing the heights, the widths and the different forms and shapes of signage permitted, and it named distances, locations and other requirements. After City Attorney Dennis Boal read the title of the ordinance a motion was made by Councilwoman Wall to pass Ordinance 90-3 on first reading, seconded by Hutchinson, followed by a lengthy discussion which I finally ended, and called for the vote. It was unanimous, passing the ordinance on first reading.

This ordinance was then published in full by the *Uinta County Herald*, but during the next two meetings there would be more discussion and amendments made, before it was finally passed in March on the second and third readings by a unanimous vote and became law.

Ordinance 90-3 had become a very controversial issue. Some businesspeople felt that it was too strict. Some felt it wasn't strict enough, and over the next few years it would be amended several times, but would probably never be satisfactory to some folks.

During this same meeting a new tree ordinance was introduced by Councilman Hutchinson and sponsored by Councilwoman Wall. The last tree ordinance failed by a unanimous vote, but with a new number, Ordinance 90-4, was back, providing for a Street Tree Advisory Board and the promotion of Street Trees.

There had been a lot of time and discussion put into this ordinance by the Urban Renewal Agency and the Beautification Committee, and after more discussion by the council it was noted that this ordinance was mostly advisory and not so much regulation.

Councilman Davis made a motion to pass Ordinance 90-4 on first reading, seconded by Nelson. With a vote of 5 yes votes and 2 no votes (Hutchinson and Vranish), the motion passed by a majority. During the March meetings the ordinance also passed by a majority vote on second and third readings, making it law.

During the previous year, most of the city council members and their spouses attended the National League of Cities Annual Convention in Boston, Massachusetts. I really wanted to go because I had never been to Boston and I had a Korean War buddy who had been wounded during the war while standing right next to me. I stayed with him and dressed his wound until we could get him to a helicopter that took him to a Mobile Army Surgical Hospital (M.A.S.H.) unit. He lived in Boston and I would have really liked to have had a chance to visit with him, but I wasn't in a position to go.

After Sandy and I had filed for bankruptcy, we just didn't feel like we could afford the trip. Those trips always seemed to end up costing a person a lot of money out of pocket, even though travel expenses such as airfare, car rental, meals, and board were paid by the city. All other expenses would have to be paid by the individual. So we didn't make the trip to Boston.

I had no problem with others going and encouraged it, because I felt that it was good for mayors and other city officials to attend those meetings. I know that I always got a lot out of them, helping me as a council member as well as mayor. The meetings we attended kept us current on city/town problems, and the meeting would give us ideas on how we could help our community. I'm sure that the City of Evanston council members felt the same way. I hoped that those that did go would come back with good ideas to better our community, and reports on legislation in Congress that would affect cities and towns.

During the convention, when most of the members of the council were there with their spouses, Councilman Clarence Vranish, who hadn't made the trip, made a big issue of the city paying for spouses' expenses. This was a surprise to me, because the city had been paying for the spouses' expenses on trips like that for as long as I could remember, and I thought it was always legit as long as it was in the budget. Vranish wasted no time in making the Wyoming State Auditor's office and the news media aware of the issue.

The next day, when I found out that Vranish had made this issue public before talking to me or any of the council members, I was quite upset. Not because it was right or wrong, but because he could have gone about it in a more fair and reasonable way.

That morning, I was in my office visiting with City Engineer Brian about city projects when Councilman Vranish stuck his head in the door and asked if he could come in. Before answering, I looked at him and said, *You Ass!* and then I motioned him to come in. Brian was quite shocked and didn't know what to say. I guess it surprised Brian because he probably didn't think that I would say something like that to a member of the city council. Vranish knew what I was talking about, but making that statement did take him by surprise. I suppose I shouldn't have addressed him like that, but I was quite upset by learning that kind of news through the press. He could have at least waited until the rest of the council returned from the National League of Cities Convention and then talk to them about it first.

Councilman Vranish, I was told, because of his workplace accident and disability income (his injury had apparently been permanent) was unable to be paid for any type of employment, including pay from the city for serving on the city council (he refused to receive any pay for sitting on the council). He was not permitted to receive pay for any type of time he put in volunteering, and was unable to seek any type of employment. I was told he would lose his disability income if he received any type of pay for any type of activity he was involved in.

Also, by receiving disability income there were certain restrictions on what he could do, and traveling a distance was one of them.

He had to be careful of how much strain he put on his back. I may be a bit wrong in what I'm saying, but I think there is something to it. I'm not trying to make issue about him not being able to work, but I am pointing this out because he was making such an issue about other council members being able to travel with their spouses at the city's expense while representing the city.

Apparently, there was a question whether it was legal to pay for spouses even if it had been in the budget, but it appeared that most cities in Wyoming weren't doing it because they thought it was somewhat unethical. One mayor of another community stated that their city policy was that they encouraged the spouses to go and the city did pay for the spouse's registration, but that was all.

The *Uinta County Herald* published the following: *The City of Evanston did have a specific policy regarding the matter: Resolution 83-88 stated in the employee policy manual, Section 5-2 (d) 2, regarding the reimbursement of expenses, that spouse's or family's expenses are not reimbursable by the city.*

However, a disclaimer exempted elected officials, and upper level management positions from this policy.

Another City of Evanston resolution, 85-134, Section 2, states: "All prior personnel policies are hereby repealed." The 1985 resolution would supersede the 1983 resolution.

The *Herald* quoted me as saying, *"I think my wife, as first lady, always actively promotes Evanston, and receives no compensation except an occasional trip."*

The *Herald* also pointed out that I would be issuing a memo to council members requesting a halt on spouses' travel until the audit is complete. *"I'm a pretty ethical type person. I have high ethics, and I expect my employees to have the same,"* Ottley said.

After we had the annual audit, we received a letter from auditors questioning the City of Evanston's policy of allowing spouses of city officials traveling at the city's expense.

The letter indicated that the city was in violation of Wyoming Statute 16-4-124 which, according to the letter, prohibits the payment of expenses for any person unless they are an employee, official, or a representative of the city.

The statute also stated that funds earmarked for such purposes must be accounted for in the budget. In that case, the City of Evanston was within the law because we always had that item budgeted.

The *Casper Star-Tribune* January issue reported that Steve Snyder, Evanston's administrative assistant to the mayor disagreed with the auditors, because the statute was very vague. *"Our stance is essentially we encourage it,"* Snyder said. *"We think they do represent the city. Barbara Bush goes with George Bush and Jane Sullivan goes with [Governor] Mike [Sullivan]. I'm not sure we're any different from those folks,"* Snyder said. *"We think we are 100 percent within the law. Some people are taking issue with it as a matter of policy, but we don't think we have done anything illegal."*

However, my feelings were that as long as we had the funds budgeted, the elected official's spouse should be encouraged to go, even if it's at the city's expense, as long as it was for just travel and necessary expenses, and in the budget. It's an unfair ruling for towns, cities and counties, because after all, state and national elected officials get tax dollars to pay for all of their spouses' expenses.

But after the audit was received, City Attorney Dennis Boal was instructed to draw up a new resolution stating only elected officials and employees, acting in the interest of the city, would be permitted to receive travel expenses. Although the audit claimed that we had been illegal, since we did have it listed as a budgeted item, there were no penalties or paybacks imposed upon us, because we hadn't tried to hide anything from anybody.

The year 1990 was not only the Wyoming Statehood Centennial, but was also the bicentennial year of the Bill of Rights to the Constitution of the United States of America. Some of the events in the coming months would also be a salute to the Bill of Rights' Bicentennial, which also extends into the year of 1991.

During the March 3rd city council meeting, Councilwoman Wall made a motion to change the next regular city council meeting from March 15th to March 22nd, because March 15th might be named as the night of the Agri-Business Banquet. Motion was seconded by Nelson, with all voting in favor.

A discussion was held concerning Fourth Street and the amount of traffic now using the street to come and go to the Evanston Middle School. After a considerable amount of discussion, Councilman Hutchinson made a motion to make Fourth Street a through street and adopt the proper signage (stop signs) on the other streets as requested by the Public Works Department. Motion was seconded by Vranish, but another motion was made to table the motion until the meeting of March 22nd.

During the March 22nd meeting, the motion to make Fourth Street a through street was amended by being more specific about where and what type of signage would be placed. The main motion as amended passed with all voting in favor.

During the March 3rd meeting Councilman Nelson requested streetlights on Straight and Narrow Drive (the location of senior housing run by the housing authority), and Councilman Vranish expressed a desire for street improvements (paving) to be made on the gravel roads in the cemetery. Both requests were granted and the work was completed that summer.

The ninth annual Agri-Business Banquet was held on March 12th, instead of March 15th. Lynne Fox was honored as the Citizen of the Year by the City of Evanston. Lynne had lived in Evanston since 1974 and was a partner in the engineering firm of Uinta Engineering and Surveying. She had been actively involved in the Uinta County League of Women Voters as past president and held the position of State President of the Wyoming Chapter in 1988-1989.

She had also been actively involved in the Sagebrush Theatre Group, the Renewal Ball Committee, the production of "The Nutcracker," and Chairperson of the Committee to Acquire the Strand Theater. But most of all, she was Chairperson of Evanston's Freedom & Equality Day in 1989, when the League of the Pace Amendment advocates such as Daniel Johnson, leader of the group, and advocates of the Ku Klux Klan, skinheads and others threatened to make Evanston their headquarters.

The City of Evanston felt that Lynne's committee put together a great program, a program that chased those Pace Amendment people not only out of Evanston, but completely out of Wyoming and northern Utah.

The award was proudly made by the mayor and city council and was well deserved. Lynne later became Uinta County Clerk until the time she chose to retire.

During the Planning and Zoning Commission meeting of March 5th, the issue of the rezoning of a portion of Front Street came up again. My son, Randy Ottley, Chairman of the Commission, stepped down because Harold W. Holmes, the applicant, had hired Randy as their spokesperson and real estate agent from ERA Uinta Realty, Inc. Therefore, Randy was at the meeting to represent Mr. Holmes, the applicant of the zone change request.

The application was to rezone a portion of Front Street between First and Second Streets from low-density residential to a community business zone, but there was a large group of opponents at the meeting speaking against the application.

Randy Ottley, representing Mr. Holmes, who had plans of constructing a Taco Johns fast food restaurant there, told the commission that there was already a commercial building on the First Street corner of Front Street selling fireworks and paraphernalia, and the empty lots that Mr. Holmes wanted to use were previously Amoco Oil Company's pipeline warehouse. The old metal building of the warehouse was still standing and had been there actively for year, until Amoco decided to move their warehouse to one of the new industrial parks.

Randy explained that Mr. Holmes purchased the property from Amoco since it had already been used as commercial or industrial property and had assumed he would have no problem putting another commercial establishment up on the same lots. He had no idea he would be required to apply for a zone change or face this much opposition.

The *Uinta County Herald* issue of March 9th quoted Randy: *"I feel that we should be concerned with the people living on Front and Main Streets and alleviate the residents' hardship within reason, but the overall picture is this will be an asset to Evanston. It will employee 16 people, bring in tax* revenue, clean up the property and will bring money into the city," Ottley said. "We are allowing a small minority to dictate against the betterment of Evanston."

"Instead of fighting, why don't we [all the factions involved] get together and decide what it will take to see this through?" he asked.

Randy also entered several documents into evidence for the hearing, including a site plan, a map, and a letter of support from the Evanston Chamber of Commerce. However, nothing that was said or presented made any difference to those opposed. Wayne Bell, representing the neighbors and owner of two of the three houses remaining on the block, spoke against the rezoning and complained that, although Randy Ottley had removed himself from the Chair of the Commission, it wasn't legal for Randy to act on behalf of Mr. Holmes.

But City Attorney Dennis Boal explained that this was perfectly legal and the right thing to do. He said Randy, as a real estate agent, has every right to represent whomever he wants to as long as he declares a conflict and excuses himself from any discussion and from voting on the issue.

After a considerable amount of discussion, pro and con, commission member Brian Patterson made the final motion in favor, seconded by commission member Gerrard. A vote resulted in 4 in favor, 3 against, and 1 abstention. The motion passed in favor of Mr. Holmes's application by a majority vote. The next step would be presenting the issue to the Evanston City Council with the Planning and Zoning Commission's recommendation to pass in favor of the zone change.

During the city council meeting on March 22nd, the application to rezone the block from First to Second Streets was presented by Randy Ottley, Real Estate Broker, representing the applicant, Harold W. Holmes from Cheyenne. I opened up the meeting for discussion and declared that I did not have any conflict of interest in this matter, and that just because my son Randy was hired to represent Mr. Holmes as his realtor, it didn't make me have a conflict and I will be voting on the matter.

This issue caused the meeting to get a little hot and heavy with a lot of discussion, some pro and some con. There had also been many Letters to the Editors and to the city council members and me, also both pro and con. In my inquiries throughout the community I found that most folks were either in favor or didn't care one way or another, but very few were against the zone change. Most folks felt that all of Front Street would eventually turn to commercial any way.

The *Uinta County Herald* issue of March 29th quoted me: *"If a public vote were taken, and I have talked to a lot of people, this would pass. We have spent thousands of dollars to revive the economy in the city. Do we really want more jobs and growth or are we just blowing smoke? Are we saying, business can't come in unless we dictate what you do? Do we really want economic development and a higher tax base? We invite business to the area then in the end we don't want them," said [Mayor] Ottley.*

"We need to make a decision about what's going to happen on Front Street and go in that direction. If we don't pass this tonight, we should correct the Comprehensive Plan which would be a big boost to our economy," he said.

Later in the meeting, Planning and Zoning Director Paul Knopf was directed to begin work on changing the Front Street portion of the plan. This would require hearings and input by all those concerned, the *Herald* concluded.

During this meeting the Evanston City Council once again defeated the issue of Front Street by a 4-2 vote against, with Wall and me voting in favor; Hutchinson, Vranish, Nelson, and Davis voting against; and 1 absent (Lunsford). However this issue would come up before the council once again in the near future.

In the *Uinta County Herald* of April 13th, they indicated that Randy Ottley, Chairman of the Evanston Planning and Zoning Commission, expressed his and the commission's agitation at the city council turning down the Front Street zone change proposal, and amending and making changes in the new sign ordinance.

The *Herald* asked me how I felt about the Planning and Zoning Commission being upset because the council didn't go along with their recommendations, and also, how did I feel about my son's comments?

They published the following statement from me: *"I don't always agree with Rand, but he has a mind of his own," said Mayor Dennis Ottley, "but there is no way in hell I'm going to apologize to the Planning and Zoning Commission. This board [speaking of the city council] is the last step for the sign ordinance to get approved, and as a board it is our right to make changes."* But I also pointed out that the Commission was doing a good job and that their members were very much appreciated for their interest and hard work. We were all after the same thing. But as far as the Commission's recommendation on passing the Front Street zone change and the Council's split decision to deny it, that's something that we will all just have to accept for now, and when the time comes it will eventually be zoned properly.

The *Uinta County Herald* of April 6th reported that when the Tourism and Convention Committee of the Evanston Chamber of Commerce, headed by Denice Wheeler, met on April 4th, they had voted 12-4 that the lodging tax issue would be put on the ballot of the next election, but it would only be the City of Evanston collecting the lodging tax. The Bridger Valley Chamber of Commerce had voted against being included.

The *Herald* also stated that Dan Yates of Utah Power and Light would be appointed to head the drive to sell the idea to the citizens, and Brenda Shaffer would be handling the publicity for the election campaign.

During the regular city council meeting of April 5th several liquor license holders, Whirl Inn, Veranda Bar, Lotty's, Legal Tender, Cowboy Joe's, and the Outpost, had applied for a Gaming License.

After a public hearing was held and a lengthy discussion was held, Councilman Vranish made a motion to grant the request of these applicants. This would give them the right to have pull-tabs in their establishments. Motion was second by Wall, with a 4-3 vote (Vranish, Wall, Nelson, and me voting in favor and Lunsford, Davis, and Hutchinson against). Motion passed by a majority.

By state law, a non-profit organization must be a sponsor of gaming license applications, including Bingo, and a big percentage of the profit must go to the organization, to be used for civic programs.

In this case, the Wyoming Liquor Association, a non-profit organization, asked permission for pull-tab machines to be placed in the various facilities in Evanston in hopes of raising money for their scholarship fund.

During the meeting a group of Girl Scouts who were in attendance requested that the collection of aluminum cans from the bins at the IGA Grocery store location be used for funds towards the expenses of the Girl Scouts attending a special camp. Councilman Lunsford made a motion to allow three new bins to be located in various locations for the collection of aluminum for fundraisers, in this case for the Girl Scouts as requested. The motion was seconded by Nelson with all voting in favor.

In the April 5th meeting, Mr. Judd Redden, representing the Lincoln Uinta Association of Governments (LUAG) approached the city council with a request for funds to be put into LUAG's Revolving Loan Fund.

Councilman Will Davis made a motion to commit funds in the amount of $25,000 to LUAG as monies are paid back to the City of Evanston from loans that had already been made, seconded by Vranish, with all voting in favor. LUAG makes low interest loans, which are matched with federal dollars, for start-up capital on businesses, and payments on the city's portion are paid back directly to the city.

Boy Scout Tom Mortenson and his father were in attendance during the April 5th meeting so Tom could fulfill one of his requirements for his scout badge. I asked Tom to introduce himself and his father and told them that they were very welcome to attend this meeting and other meetings in the future. I also wished Tom the best in achieving his Boy Scout requirements and told his father that he should be very proud of Tom.

After a 10-minute recess called by me, Councilman Jon Lunsford introduced Resolution 90-17, authorizing a grant application to the Wyoming State Farm Loan Board for funding water, sewer and street construction projects for Centennial Valley Estates, Washington Street, Sioux Drive, West Main, and downtown street improvements.

Councilwoman Wall made a motion to adopt, seconded by Vranish, with all voting in favor.

Councilwoman Wall made a motion to allow the Wyoming Centennial Committee to have a parade on May 25th to kick off the Centennial celebration, followed by a scheduled rerun of the 1908 Great Endurance Race.

Sandy came up with the idea, and got the approval of the Centennial Committee to duplicate the renowned Great Endurance (horse) Race from Evanston to Denver that took place in 1908 along the Overland Trail through Wyoming and south to Denver. Wall's motion to allow a parade prior to the Great Endurance Race was seconded by Councilman Hutchinson and passed with all voting in favor.

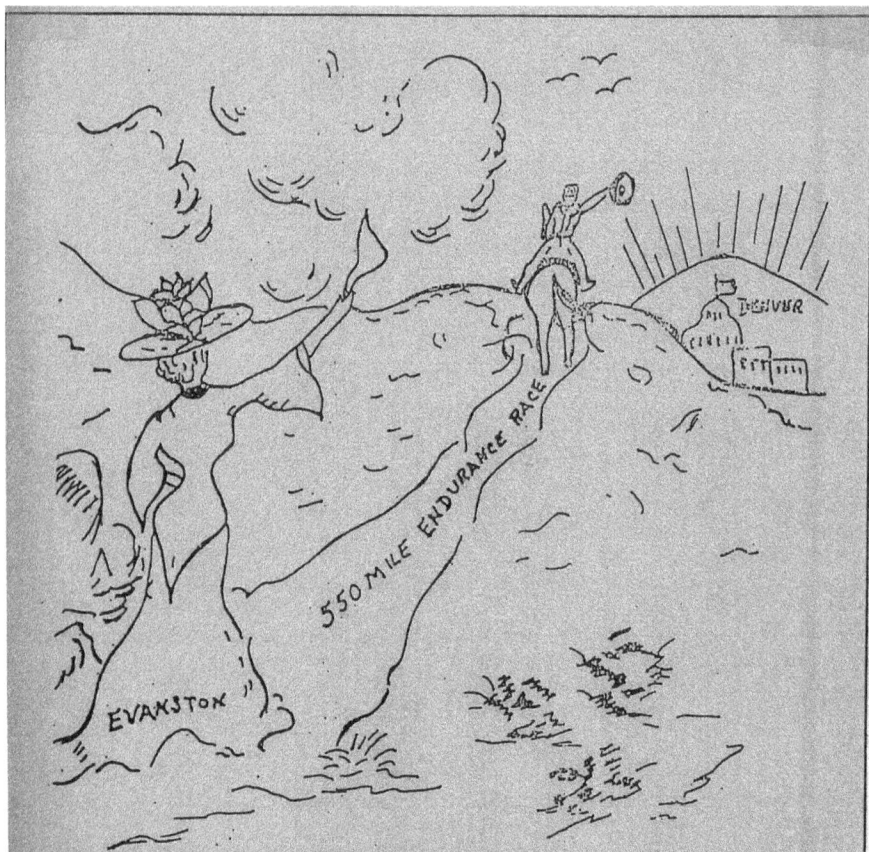

GONE BUT NOT FORGOTTEN!

GREAT ENDURANCE RACE
MAY 1908

taken from the
"WYOMING PRESS" May 30, 1908

Reproduction of original by - Eileen Downs-Jacobs

The *Great Endurance Horse Race* was a book by Jack Schaefer, author of *Shane*, which later became a well-known movie with stars such as Alan Ladd, Jean Arthur, and Van Heflen. Schaefer writes of a race, which took place in 1908. The Great Race, sponsored by the well-known Denver Post, was to start in Evanston, Wyoming on May 30, 1908 and finish on Champa Street in Denver, Colorado.

There was a lot of discussion in the west, with the Denver Post right in the middle of the discussion, about the staying qualities of the Kentucky thoroughbred, the blooded Arabian, the Irish hunter, the French cross-country horse and other varieties of horse famed for their speed and distance.

In January, 1908, the Denver Post issued its challenge, and flatly stated its belief *that the Western bronco could beat them all in the approximately 600 mile race of rugged rolling hills and red desert and up and over the Continental Divide and long stretches of lonely plain and along the edge of the Rockies into the great city of Denver.*

There were twenty five entries in the race, with each man required to ride the same horse all the way. Entrants were from five western states with one from Missouri, and horses were of several breeds from thoroughbreds to the western bronco.

The rider's weight, including equipment, ranged from 160 pounds up to 208 pounds, and the horses ranged from 652 pounds up to 1073 pounds. There was quite a range between weights of riders and horses.

There were six place-prizes paid in dollars, at that time when a dollar was a dollar: 1st place − $500, 2nd place − $250, 3rd place − $200, 4th place − $150, 5th place − $100, and 6th place − $50. Other items were added by individuals and different businesses, such as silver-mounted saddles, a pair of boots, and so on.

Most riders shipped their horses by rail to Evanston, except one cowboy, Charles Workman from Cody, Wyoming who was riding a bronco named Teddy that not long before had been roaming the range. Teddy had been roped in from the range and used as a rodeo bronc, then broken into a saddle horse. Workman rode over 300 miles on Teddy from Cody to Evanston and hand-delivered his entry form. He signed up in a hurry because he wanted to be there early enough to give Teddy a few days' rest before starting the 600 mile race.

"THE GREAT ENDURANCE RACE"
Evanston, Wyoming
May 25 - 28, 1990

Another rider named Frank (Dode) Wykert from Severance, Colorado, stated that he had a horse that would make them all go some to win the race. His name was Samuel (Sam), and his breeding was also a mix bronco.

The race ended up in a tie for first place with Charles Workman from Cody, and Frank (Dode) Wykert from Colorado as winners. Workman's weight, including gear, was 160 lbs., and Teddy, his horse weighed 1025 lbs. Wykert's weight, including gear, was 193 lbs., while Sam, his horse weighed 911 lbs.

It has been said that the movie *Bite the Bullet* was taken from the story of *The Great Endurance Horse Race*.

While reading a book on Evanston and Uinta County history, Evanston's First Lady, Sandy, a devout historian, came across the history of the Great Endurance Race and learned about Jack Schaefer's book, but while trying to find a copy, we found out that only 750 copies of the book were printed, because the type melted after printing, and the only place we could possibly find a copy would be at a store that sold old, rare or used books.

Sandy and I made a trip to Salt Lake City and found a store called Ken Sanders Rare Books. Thinking that there could be a chance that Sanders just might have that book, we ran into some good luck: Mr. Sanders said he just happened to have the book.

When he brought the book to us, it appeared either brand new or very little used It was in great shape and the number of the limited edition was 462. We asked Mr. Sanders the price of the book. Although the book was marked by the publisher at $4.50, we paid far more than that to be able to finally get a good copy, but it was well worth our time.

At this time Sandy had selected her committee: Jake Jacobs and Sandy as Co-Chairs, Bill Hobbs – Trail Master, Mike Fulks – Camp Boss, Jerry Wall – Activities Chair, Jim Davis – Sponsors, Anne Curtis of the *Uinta County Herald* – Photography, John and Kathy Stevens – Awards, Joan Flaherty – Adviser, Dan Killian – Media

Specialist, James D. Bechaver – Race Veterinarian, Blain Blonquist – Timekeeper, Frank Ballentine – Special Exhibits, and Mike Davis, Mike Fulks, Jake Jacobs, and Bill Hobbs as Special Officials.

Also involved were Brian Stokes, John Bowers, Tom and Betsy Wagner, Kathy Ball, Anne Hobbs, Dale Soloman, Lorie Quale, Susan Pierce, Dianne Mills, Barbara Nelson, Ken Hendrix, Chuck Nixon, Phyllis Murphy, Glenda Krejci, Richard and Bob Rosenthal, and Ann Bell, Chairman of Evanston's Wyoming Centennial Committee.

Sandy had put together a large committee and a subcommittee, with all willing to volunteer their time and effort to make the Great Endurance Race of 1990 a big success. The committee was, by law, required to have the race insured.

After studying the original horse race of 1908, and after contacting the Wyoming Highway Department, who was concerned with the traffic on the state and federal highways and freeways, they gave the committee their approval if the race could be made safe from highway traffic.

We met and talked with officials from the U.S. Bureau of Land Management (BLM), the Wyoming and Colorado State Land Commissions and the U.S. Forest Service, and they said that most of their land had been leased to ranchers and others, and it would be a good idea to talk to them first.

The committee met and talked to some of the more local ranchers; some were somewhat belligerent, and some were more willing to cooperate and work with the committee. It seemed almost impossible to run a route from Evanston to Denver similar to the one they ran in 1908.

After meeting and talking things over the committee (although they would have loved to duplicate the original race) agreed that it would be better to keep the race in Uinta County, because of all the new freeways and highways, and because most lands were fenced and there would be too many property owners and entities to get approval from. They decided it would be best to stake a route starting at Evanston by way of Piedmont to Fort Bridger and the same route back to

Evanston by way of Leroy, a three-day race. Entry fees for participants would be set at $20.00 each if in by 10:00 a.m. on May 15th, but
late entries would be $40.00 per rider (there were two late entries),
and the deadline for all entries would be at 5:00 p.m. on May 25th.

All other funding for the event would come from the State of
Wyoming through the Governor's office; many companies, organizations, and individuals agreed to sponsor the event; and monies were
raised by the Centennial Committee through the sale of t-shirts and
other money raising programs.

The committee first marked the trail with ribbons a few days
before the race, but the livestock on the range ate most of them, so
the committee had to remark the route with fluorescent paint so the
cattle wouldn't bother the markers.

The Great Endurance Race for 1990, dedicated to Charles F.
Guild and June Painter Fearn, two well-known local ranchers who
had passed on, would start on Friday, May 25th with a horse parade.
Race participants and any other horse riders who wished to were encouraged to participate in the parade.

There were 28 paying participants, and they were riding horses of various breeds. Each rider would have to ride the same horse
throughout the entire race.

The first leg, a 26-mile route to Piedmont, would start just east of
the Bear River State Park beginning at 9:00 a.m. Saturday morning,
May 26th. Veterinarian checks would be made at the Piedmont stop,
with water and feed for the horses, and lunch would be served to the
riders.

Governor Mike Sullivan and his wife, Wyoming First Lady Jane,
just happened to be in Evanston that weekend. The Governor was
scheduled to give the Evanston High School Commencement Address at the Senior Graduation Ceremony.

While in Evanston, First Lady Jane and the Governor made an
appearance at the Bear River State Park to wish the Great Endurance
Race riders luck and good journey, and they congratulated the committee for their efforts in putting together such a difficult program in
honor of the 1890-1990 Wyoming Centennial.

After a pre-race meeting at the Piedmont stop with the race officials and riders, a Dutch oven supper was served by Skeeter and Jesse
Crompton with all you could eat for $5.50 for adults and $2.50 for
children under 12 years of age.

The second 19.8-mile leg of the race would begin at 9:00 a.m.
on Sunday, May 27th from Piedmont to the Bigelow Road, where
once again the horses would have the vet check and water, and lunch
would be served to riders.

After the one-hour noon stop on Bigelow the riders rode their
horses to the Fort Bridger Rodeo Grounds where a pre-race meeting
was held again, followed by a Buffalo Burger dinner served by the
Fort Bridger Wyoming Centennial Committee, with Linda New-
man-Byers and Mary Aimone acting as Co-Chairs for that portion
of the race.

Ft. Bridger rider wins

CONGRATULATIONS TO THE WINNER—Overall winner Darrel Nielson, Fort Bridger, received a hand shake from Robert "Bob" Alkire and his wife Doris. They came from Pierce, Colo. to be a part of the Great Endurance Horse Race 1990. Alkire's grand uncle was "Dode" Wykert. He and Charles Workman tied for first place in the 1908 race from Evanston to Denver, Colo.

Uinta County Herald, June 5, 1990.

Horses were trucked from Fort Bridger to Leroy via the Bar Hat exit where the third and final 19-mile leg of the race would start at 8:00 a.m. on Monday, May 28th. They would race to Eagle Rock for another vet check and water for the horses, and lunch was again provided for contestants.

The race ended at Bear River State Park with an all-you-can-eat dinner sponsored by the Evanston Lions Club at a cost of $5.00 for adults, $2.50 for ages 12 to 6, and the meal was free to children 6 years and under.

The winner of the race was Darrel Nielson, a cowboy from Fort Bridger riding a mixed bronc named Summer's Joy. He was the great nephew of the original racer from 1890, Dode Wyckert, one of the two who tied for first place.

During the city council meeting of April 19th, Kevin Kallas was appointed to the Evanston Planning and Zoning Commission, with a motion by Councilman Nelson to confirm the appointment, seconded by Hutchinson, with all voting in favor.

I also appointed myself and Councilman Vranish to the Joint Powers Human Service Board. Motion was made by Councilwoman Wall to confirm the appointments, seconded by Lunsford, with all voting in favor.

At this time, I also appointed Councilwoman Jerry Wall as Chairperson of the 1991 W.A.M. convention to be hosted by Evanston. Motion was made by Councilman Nelson to confirm the appointment, seconded by Vranish, with all voting in favor.

Mr. Wayne Bell and a number of residents on Front Street were at the April 19th meeting, requesting a delay of 6 months before the city update the Comprehensive Plan for the future of Front Street.

The *Uinta County Herald* of April 24th had an article titled, FRONT STREET PLAN ALMOST DRAWS FIGHT. The article started out: *Whoever said city council meetings were dull wasn't at the one held April 19th when the issue of reviewing the Comprehensive Plan for Front Street came before the officials.*

Neighborhood spokesman Wayne Bell and a number of residents in the Front Street area arrived unscheduled at the meeting and asked to be placed on the agenda, the *Herald* article continued.

He asked that several favors be given the residents of the neighborhood.

Bell asked the council to delay the hearing on the comprehensive plan for six months.

"There is no way we can sit down right now – we need time to cool off in order to make plans to make it workable for all of us," Bell said.

The other request was to require owner of the Taco John property Harold Holmes to clean up the property.

The article continued: *"I'm not going to promise to hold off on that, not because of the people who live there, but for the economy of Evanston," said Mayor Dennis Ottley.*

The argument quickly escalated after that.

Bell asked, "If you are really interested in the economy, why didn't we try to get the women's and medium security prison here?

Why he didn't mention the Job Corps Center I'll never know, but the article went on: *Ottley returned with the fact that efforts had been made to bring one prison to Evanston. But the other city was also working on getting it.*

Bell then remarked that Ottley and his son Randy (who had been representing Holmes as a real estate agent) *would be making money off the Taco John sale. That was why the proposition was being pushed through so hard,* the *Herald* article continued.

Ottley then asked Bell if he would like to "step outside to the hall."

"I didn't realize you were going to invite me outside," Bell said.

"I didn't realize you were going to make accusations, either, Ottley returned.

The *Herald* didn't quote me correctly. What I said was: *If you are going to make accusations like that about me and my son, maybe we should 'step outside to the hall and discuss it.'* The press always seems to leave out parts of a comment to make it sound worse that it is. I guess what they are really looking for is to create more interest and sell more papers.

The *Herald* article concluded with: *"This situation is really hard on the council, Mayor and the people who live there. But, we have to care about the whole community. There has been a lot of money spent on economic development. We don't want to see you people unhappy, but the change is*

inevitable. It is going to happen, but it is not an easy decision," Councilman
Jon Lunsford *told the crowd.*

After a lengthy discussion, Councilman Vranish made the motion
for any work on the Comprehensive Plan for Front Street be held
back for 6 months, seconded by Nelson, with 4 votes in favor, 2
against the motion (Lunsford and me), and 1 absent (Wall). The
motion passed.

I couldn't believe that any city council would want to hold up
progress for 6 months like that, because by then we would be looking
at winter before we could do any more work on the Comprehensive
Plan. No construction could even get started until the next spring.
Evanston was in need of jobs now, and some of us didn't feel that we
should be losing time by stalling on something that we all knew was
going to happen anyway. When other firms took a look at the city's
actions, causing them to delay their plans, it wouldn't look good for
the city or council, but Lunsford was right: the zone change was inevitable.

During the same meeting Allen Kennedy, Superintendent of Operations, presented Paul Vozakis and Frank Sheets certifications for
completing their training as operators at the new Wastewater Treatment Plant.

The city council and I congratulated them both for their outstanding work and for their success in completing the training.

The Evanston City Council, during the Martin Administration,
exempted certain property from the assessment of the Downtown
Improvement District, and one of those properties was the old federal building (post office) on the corner of 10th and Center Streets. I
don't know why, unless it was because it was government-owned at
the time.

But during this meeting of April 19th, Councilman Tom Hutchinson introduced Resolution 90-13 declaring the intention of the city to
assess properties omitted from the assessment roll of the Downtown
Improvement District, ordering publication and mailing of notices to
the owners. Councilman Vranish made a motion to adopt Resolution
90-13, seconded by Davis. The motion carried with 7 votes.

This included the old federal building that had just been purchased by Rick Sather, who had plans to renovate the interior as
rental space for retail shops and offices.

I had no idea why the property was excluded from the assessment,
but I felt bad for Rick Sather, because it did seem a bit unfair to him,
but he was on the city council when the improvement district was
formed.

The *Uinta County Herald* issue of April 10th quoted Sather: *"When
the downtown plan was made the new post office was included, but no plans
were made for the old one to change,"* he pointed out. *To include the building
in the district took the action by the council,* the Herald stated. *"I think being
included is right, no problem with it, I hope the entire downtown improvement
plans can be achieved, maybe this will help activate that dream,"* Sather concluded.

I had to admire Sather for feeling that way, plus I had to give him
credit for being such a good sport in accepting the assessment. I believe
it encouraged other property owners involved in the district that were
delinquent in paying their assessments to pay without further ado. I
really had a lot of respect for Sather for his stand on the resolution.

⸙

During the month of April, 1990 I had surgery to finally take care of
my left knee after the 1989 operation didn't work out well.

I went back to Dr. Scott Anthony with my left knee and told him
that I was taking his advice to go ahead with a total knee replacement
because my knee was still paining and giving me so much trouble. I
also told him that people were laughing at my leg because it didn't
look like it should. *It's crooked,* I said.

A lot of local folks advised me to go to Utah to get it done, but
when Dr. Marc Brann recommended of Dr. Anthony, I just couldn't
see going out of town, putting my wife and family in a position
where they would have to travel to Salt Lake City or wherever to get
me there and back. Besides, I had all the faith in the world that Dr.
Anthony would do me a good job, and I was right, because after over
27 years I have had very little trouble with the knee.

So during the month of April I was back in the Evanston Regional Hospital getting a total knee replacement, the first type of
operation ever performed in Evanston. But I had a well experienced
orthopedic surgeon that was relatively new to Evanston and I was
damn glad he was here to perform the operation. I was in therapy
and on crutches for several weeks, but it all worked out great. My leg
was straight again.

EVANSTON REGIONAL HOSPITAL •
Community
A BIMONTHLY PUBLICATION   SUMMER 1990

Therapy for
an ex-boxer's "trick knees"

They used to call it "trick knees" when Dennis Ottley was a boxer at age 17. Both knees would often slip from their sockets, a problem that continued to plague him during Korean War combat and later as a businessman and politician. "I guess they just finally wore out," Ottley says.

But ask Denny Ottley today to show off his new knee and the Evanston mayor might lift a pantleg to display his scar. In April 1990, Ottley underwent surgery at IHC Evanston Regional Hospital for a total knee replacement.

Dr. Scott Anthony, orthopaedic surgeon recommended by Ottley's personal physician, Dr. Mark Brann, surgically replaced that worn out joint. Anthony and physical therapist Vic Judd have combined forces to put Dennis

(Continued on page two.)

Evanston Mayor Dennis Ottley, left, recently had a total joint replacement at IHC Evanston Regional Hospital. Helping in the post surgical recovery has been physical therapist Vic Judd.

PAGE ONE

Also during the April council meeting, Councilman Davis introduced Resolution 90-16, to direct the City of Evanston to request that Uinta County submit to the voters of Evanston a proposition to impose a 2% excise tax for lodging services at the next general election, which would be in November, 1990. Motion was made by Councilwoman Wall for adoption, seconded by Nelson, with all voting in favor.

Also Paul Knopf, Community Development Director and City Planner, reported on some of the scheduled annual projects in May for Earth Day and Arbor Day. These projects would include tree planting, city cleanup and several other outdoor celebrations involving mostly young folks of Evanston.

Knopf also reported on the annual High Uintas Classic that would once again be a bike race from Kamas over the high Uintas to Evanston on June 22nd and 24th. He said there would also, once again, be an around-town race in Evanston following the Kamas to Evanston race. He stated that there were 110 racers in last year's program, and expected more for this year.

Just before adjournment of the April 19th meeting I announced that I wouldn't be running for re-election for mayor seat this year due to the fact that Sandy and I were having financial problems. I said "at $12,000 a year there is no way that I could afford to run for mayor again."

This announcement surprised a lot of those in attendance, but there was very little discussion on it, therefore the meeting was adjourned at 10:30 p.m.

The Uinta County Public Health Department requested that I, for this year, proclaim May 7th as National Nurses' Day. Therefore, I signed a proclamation declaring National Nurses' Day with the following in attendance during the signing: Irene Tippits, IHC Evanston Regional Hospital; Kay Hanks, Wyoming State Hospital; Katie Dayton, School Nurse; and Jerry Troshynki, Uinta County Public Health.

Alice Hannahs, RN, who had a distinguished record as both a nurse and administrator in Uinta County, was guest speaker at the dinner event, but Sandy and I were invited as special guests and I was asked to say a few words.

I spoke of my recent visit to the Evanston Regional Hospital, and my experience as a patient during my knee operation and of what great service I received from all the staff, including the doctors, the anesthetists, and a special thank you to all the nursing staff. They were terrific. Due to a conflict with other events going on the day of May 3rd, the regular city council meeting date, the council elected to change the meeting to Thursday, May 10th.

During this meeting I read a letter of resignation from Officer Mike Cole, effective May 12, 1990. Councilman Nelson made the motion to accept the resignation, seconded by Wall, and the motion passed unanimously.

Although, we were losing another good police officer to the Wyoming State Criminal Division, we all wished him good will and success.

It was always a concern when losing a good police officer, because sometimes we had a hard time finding someone, and it is very costly to, by law, send them to Douglas, Wyoming for their police training before they can officially become a cop.

Resolution 90-20 was introduced by Councilman Hutchinson to convey the old Brown School property from the Uinta County School District #1 to the City of Evanston. Councilman Lunsford made the motion to adopt Resolution 90-20, seconded by Davis. A lengthy discussion took place concerning what the city had in mind for the property and where any funding would come for improvements. The schoolhouse had already been demolished by the school district, and it was decided that the city would make an effort to locate funding for another city park.

As the discussion had been going on for some time, I called for the vote on the motion to adopt Resolution 90-20. The motion passed unanimously.

Resolution 90-14-A, which had previously been tabled, was brought off the table with a motion by Councilman Nelson, seconded by Wall, with all voting in favor.

It was a resolution authorizing the City of Evanston to enter into an agreement with the Wyoming Recreation Commission to provide funding in the amount of $25,000 for the BEAR Project. The resolution had the words "in perpetuity" in the body of the resolution, meaning that the property would always be for recreational use, and this seemed to bother most of the council members. Why? I don't know because, as far as I was concerned, I could see no reason the property would be changed in the near future, and even if it was changed to industrial or something 50 or 60 years down the road it could be done by another resolution, but the city would probably be subject to some kind of payback or penalty. I just couldn't see that ever happening.

But after a little more discussion I called for the vote which was 4 no votes (Vranish, Davis, Hutchinson and Lunsford) against 3 yes votes (Wall, Nelson, and me). The motion failed.

Along with Wall and Nelson, I thought that the city council had made a bad move on Resolution 90-14-A, because the BEAR Project was in need of the funding and it was a great project that would benefit the city greatly. This would be brought up by the local press indicating that the city council had made a stupid mistake, and they were probably right. We would just have to wait and see.

Also during this meeting we approved the plat for Shakey's (located where the Front Street Maverik is now). Shakey's shut down a few years later because of the economy, and Maverik purchased the property.

A recent news article in the *Uinta County Star* (a newly published newspaper in Evanston, free to the public with Brian Stokes as an owner) was titled BEAR PROJECT GETS STATE AND FEDERAL ENDORSEMENT. The article went on: *"I am tremendously impressed with what I see going on in Evanston,"* said Chris Brown, National Park representative from Washington, D.C.

Brown, referring to the work done and concepts for the BEAR Project, was in Evanston during the Earth Day celebrations.

The Project is a cooperative effort of the city, county, state, and federal agencies, the *Star* continued.

Governor Mike Sullivan, also in attendance at the BEAR Project luncheon and tree planting ceremony, said he was "tremendously proud of how this project was put together. It takes some vision and patience to stick with a project like this," Sullivan said.

The BEAR *(Better Environment and River) Project, is a plan for river bank stabilization. The project will also incorporate a greenbelt with jogging and biking paths.*

The overall concept of the plan will incorporate the Bear River State Park into the old wastewater treatment plant north of Evanston. (The old treatment plant was located at the far northwest end of Sims Lane.)

The *Uinta County Star*, in their article, stated that during the tree planting celebration, Mickey Corneilson of the Bridger Valley Conservation District presented a check to Governor Sullivan and BEAR Project President Scott Smith for $8,000 to go towards improvement of the BEAR Project.

The *Star* also mentioned a contribution of $30,000 from the Army Corps of Engineers for in-kind services, a contribution of $60,000 of in-kind services from Wyoming Fish and Game, more than $100,000 from the U.S. Geological Survey over the past 4 years, a $50,000 grant from the Wyoming Recreation District, and a $100,000 contribution from Chevron USA.

Other work on the project was provided by Youth Services, who worked off more than $11,000 worth of fines the previous year.

The BEAR Project is ongoing and has been a real asset to the Evanston area, and all those folks that have been involved in making it what it is today should be commended and very proud of what has been accomplished.

The city council meeting of May 17th was the annual Student Government Day meeting. There were about two dozen high school students participating and acting in different positions of city officials.

Naming a few: Geoffrey Phillips acting as Mayor; Bryan Johnson, City Council of Ward 1 (Will Davis); Melissa Buskirk, City Council of Ward 1 (Clarence Vranish); Brady Russell, City Council of Ward 2 (Jon Lunsford); Cyndi Beck, City Council of Ward 2 (Jerry Wall); Brandi Beaty, City Council of Ward 3 (Craig Nelson); and Lorie

Hanks, City Council of Ward 3 (Tom Hutchinson). A number of other students were also appointed to act in place with other official positions of the city.

I felt that the *Student Government Day* was a great program because it not only gave the Seniors of Evanston High an opportunity to see local government in action, but the program also brought their parents and some relatives and friends to the meeting giving them also an opportunity to see the city council in action. I would be willing to say that not for the student program some of those folks would have never attended a city council meeting. Having all those folks in attendance was well worth the program.

STUDENT GOVERNMENT DAY — Evanston High School students spent the day with members of city government learning how local offices and facilities function. Thursday evening the student-members of the city council attended a meeting with their counterparts. They were on hand for decisions on such things as the BEAR Project grant mon rezoning on 7th Street and the school district's decline to fence And son Park playground.

Students learn of city

Evanston High School students and members of the city council blended for a day and the young people learned about government first hand.

Geoff Phillips acted as a counterpart with Mayor Dennis Ottley. Acting for the students on the council were: Melissa Buskirk, Cyndi Beck, Lorie Hanks, Brandy Beaty, Bryan Johnson and Brady Russell.

Todd Thorpe acted in partnership with City Administrator Steve Snyder; Molly Evers, City Planner

Paul Knopf; Rikki Sather, Urban Renewal Director Jim Davis and Rocky Fry, City Attorney Dennis Boal.

Each of the students spent the day with their counterparts learning about their positions, attending city council meeting along with going on tours of the city's facilities.

The elected city council began wondering if it had missed a tourist attraction after almost all of the students commented on the wastewater treatment plant.

Buskirk stated she had learned

a lot, she found it confusing, but valued the experience.

Sather found Davis's activities exciting."Boy, he walks fast, he's a very busy man."

Hanks learned that she was more interested in city government and wanted to get more involved.

The "Student Government Day" is an annual function with students spending the day at city hall.

Uinta County Herald, May 22, 1990.

The May 15th issue of the *Uinta County Herald* had an editorial, I suspected by G. C. Duerden, titled KICKING OUR OWN FOOT. The editorial read, in part: *The BEAR Project was up for a grant from Wyoming Recreation Commission which would be matched with in-kind labor. The Evanston project would get $25,000 in cash for $25,000 worth of time and labor by local volunteers.*

BEAR volunteers have been working, adding up their hours, towards that goal already but the council voted down the grant because of two words, "in perpetuity."

But maybe the council can be reminded of two other words which could change the vote … "election year."

Remember, a vote against the BEAR Project – which will help the area's economy, provide another reason for people to get off I-80 and visit Evanston, spend money, provide sales tax to the coffers of the city and county, enlarge business and improve the environment all in one swoop – could mean a larger vote against those who decide to run for something this year.

Wisdom is seeing the greater good and not just the miserly view, the editorial concluded.

Also, the *Uinta County Star* came out with an article on May 17th concerning the same issue. The article read in part: *At question was the wording "in perpetuity" for the land to be permanently dedicated for recreational usage. The parcel of land in question is located between the Sixth Street overpass and the Super 8 Motel. According to Director of Public Works Allen Kennedy, the area was also a landfill as recently as 30 years ago.*

The area is also a flood plain, Kennedy added.

I might mention that it was also a timber saw mill prior to the overpass being constructed.

The *Herald* article read: *Councilman Tom Hutchinson mentioned the possibility of developing the area into a commercial site at some point in the future.*

"I must have been asleep at the wheel...or it just went by me," said Councilman Jon Lunsford, referring to the council's agreement that the city agree to "in perpetuity" recreational usage of the lot.

The council voted 4-3 against accepting the grant money from the state rec board, the article concluded.

152 DENNIS J OTTLEY

Laurie R. Quaid, in her editorial in the same issue of the *Uinta County Star,* ended it this way: *Twenty-five thousand dollars is a lot of money. The overall concept of the BEAR Project will take a lot of money, and I don't want to hear any of the council members who voted this $25,000 down – Hutchinson, Vranish, Davis, and Jon Lunsford – complain about the money needed to complete the project.*

One does not look a gift horse in the mouth, Ms Quaid's editorial concluded.

During the city council meeting of May 17th, Mr. Ron Fredrickson was invited to present to the council how the one-man garbage truck operated. He showed a video of the truck as it worked and explained to us the benefits of going with the one-truck system.

The council and I have discussed this system many times in various meetings, and are very interested in changing Evanston's present system because it is costly and troublesome for the employees.

During this May 17th meeting Councilman Davis, who voted against the motion to adopt Resolution 90-14-A, made a motion to reconsider the action taken on the resolution at the last meeting, seconded by Hutchinson, who also voted against the resolution. The motion passed by 6 yes votes with 1 absent (Lunsford).

The previous motion to adopt Resolution 90-14-A was made by Councilwoman Wall, seconded by Nelson, and automatically put back on the floor for discussion.

During another lengthy discussion several interested people, present at the meeting, expressed their concerns, mostly in favor of the resolution. When ending discussion I called for the vote, with 5 voting in favor, 1 against (Hutchinson), and 1 absent (Lunsford). Motion passed in favor of the adoption of Resolution 90-14-A.

Reconsidering Resolution 90-14-A, on its second go-around, was proof that the press, plus pressure from the general public can, at times, make a difference in a person's way of thinking, council members in this case, once they have heard more of the facts. Passing this resolution was a great benefit to Evanston. It proved that city officials appreciated the in-kind work that the BEAR Project Committee had obtained from different sources to match funding from the Wyoming Rec Commission of $25,000.

During this meeting of May 17th, Community Development Director Paul Knopf (also City Planner) presented a site plan from McDonald's, which was approved by motion made by Councilman Nelson, seconded by Wall, with all voting in favor.

At the meeting "Woodsie Owl" was in attendance, and announced that there would be a city-wide cleanup day Saturday, May 19th and a picnic held the same day at Martin Park from 12:00 noon to 2:00 p.m. "Woodsie Owl" also asked everyone in attendance to loudly repeat "Give a Hoot, Don't Pollute", they did, very loudly.

I don't recall who was in the Owl Suit, but whoever it was, he or she made a great performance in playing Woodsie, and he or she was very successful in getting Evanston folks involved in the cleanup. Woodsie made a fun project out of it and everyone seemed to enjoy the day.

The Beautification Committee headed the entire cleanup program, working very hard, planting flowers around the trees in downtown Evanston, and painting the front of a building on Front Street that opened up as "Second Hand Rose," owned by Pat Alexander.

Prior to adjourning, Councilman Will Davis announced that he would not be running for re-election for the Ward 1 Councilman seat this upcoming election, and Mr. Jim Williams and his students expressed their appreciation for being able to take part in the meeting as "counterpart to city officials" during this Student Government Day meeting.

The meeting adjourned at 10:30 p.m.

Following my announcement that I would not be running for re-election for mayor, Councilman Jon Lunsford approached me about running again. He indicated that the City of Evanston needed to keep me in as mayor at least another term.

I told him that with Sandy and me being in poor financial condition, I had to get away from the city and try to make a living. "I cannot live off of $1,000 ($12,000 annually) a month, and my wife does not make enough money cleaning foreclosed houses to keep us going," I said.

He asked me, "If I could get the city council to pass a resolution to get the mayor's salary up to $20,000 or $30,000 a year, would you reconsider?"

I said that I would have to talk to my wife and family first, but it would help if you could go for $30,000. Even if I lost the election (and there is a good chance of that because of my bankruptcy), it would still be worth it to whoever got elected, because if you are going to be a good mayor you've got to put a lot of time into it, even though the position isn't considered full time.

So Councilman Lunsford started the ball rolling to raise the city council members' and the mayor's salaries for the next budget year.

The June 5th edition of the *Uinta County Herald* published in the "Letters to the Editor" column a letter from Councilman Jon Lunsford in which he, in part, stated:

During the past 20 years I have in some way been a part of city govern-ment. I have served two separate four-year terms on the city council, and have also been the full-time fire chief for the past 10 years.

I have learned, first-hand through experience, of the demands placed on our elected city officials, their time and their families.

Unless we address this problem soon, only the wealthy or the unemployed will be able to afford to be mayor or on the city council in Evanston.

I know of four self-employed mayors that were financially sound when they went into office and by the time their four-year term was up their busi-nesses were in trouble.

The result has been devastating to their businesses, themselves and, sad but true, to their families. There is no doubt in my mind that if these mayors had spent all the additional hours working at their businesses that they spent serving the city, their businesses would not have been in trouble.

To me this seems too much to expect from our elected officials and their families.

Whenever I have to make a decision about a controversial subject, which this is, I try to base my conclusions on two questions. 1. What is fair? 2. What is right?

If I ask these questions about the compensation paid to our mayor and council, I must answer the compensation is not fair, nor is it right.

Although not the total reason, I am satisfied, this is part of the reason that Mayor Ottley, Councilman Will Davis and myself do not intend to run for reelection.

With only a few days left to file, have you noted how few people have filed for these offices? Is it possible that few are willing to give so much of their time for so little compensation?

It seems to me that a city that will be spending nearly $10 million on next year's budget should be fairer to its elected officials.

I am a firm believer that we get about what we pay for, whether it be cars, clothes, mayors or councils.

This letter was signed by City Councilman Jon Lunsford of Ward 2 and was only printed in part.

The first city council meeting of the next month was held on June 7th with only 3 members of the council present, and the mayor, due to the Wyoming Association of Municipalities (W.A.M.) Annual Convention being held in Casper.

I called the June meeting to order with only three council members present: Tom Hutchinson, Will Davis, and Clarence Vranish. Councilmembers Jerry Wall, Craig Nelson, and Jon Lunsford, and Chief of Police Dennis Harvey, Community Development Director Paul Knopf, Administrative Assistant Steve Snyder, and Urban Renewal Director Jim Davis were all were excused to attend the W.A.M. Convention in Casper.

Due to the lack of council members the meeting kept to a minimum amount of business, but the regular business was taken care of, some reports were made, and some liquor licenses and malt beverage permit hearings were conducted by City Attorney Dennis Boal.

Norman Stephens, Chairman of the Annual Chili Cookoff for 1990 had applied for a malt beverage permit, and reported that the Chili Cookoff would be held on June 16th at the Uinta County Fairgrounds.

After the public hearing and a short discussion Councilman Davis made a motion to approve the Cookoff application, seconded by Vranish. The motion passed by 4 votes in favor, with 3 absent (Wall, Nelson, and Lunsford).

All other liquor license application hearings during the meeting were approved by motion and seconded, passing by a unanimous vote of those present.

Evanston had a large fire at an apartment building located on the corner of 12th Street and Sage Street. The building happened to be vacant at the time, and the fire was considered arson. A life-time Evanston man apparently started the fire and was sent to prison to serve time for starting it and other fires around the area.

But Kay Hanks was present at the June 7th meeting to express her concern about getting the property cleaned up and tearing down what's left of the building. Mrs. Hanks resided at 1237 Sage Street and was a close neighbor of the burned property. She was concerned that the way it was left created a very unsafe situation.

The City Attorney explained that the city had contacted the owner, who resides outside of Evanston, about the potentially dangerous area and a tentative court date had been set for June 26th to hear the matter.

I thanked Mrs. Hanks for her concern and she left the chambers feeling much better about the matter.

Lincoln County had made a bid for the Women's Correctional Center to be built on a site near Sage Junction, west of Kemmerer.

Therefore, Councilman Davis made a motion to direct the mayor to write a letter of support to the Lincoln County Commissioners in their bid to establish the correction center on their proposed site, seconded by Hutchinson with all 4 present voting in favor. The letter was written and sent as directed.

After discussing the idea of running for re-election for mayor with Sandy and family, and considering that Councilman Lunsford was going to introduce a resolution to increase the Mayor's annual salary from $12,000 to $30,000, I thought about maybe running again. Sandy and family all agreed, because I would have to win the election to receive the increase (an active elected official cannot raise their own salary but must be re-elected before receiving it), and if I didn't get re-elected I would be in the same position as if I hadn't run at all.

Lunsford brought up the issue of a raise for the mayor and council members. He felt that a majority of the city council members were in favor of the increases, and I felt that I had enough support from the public that it wouldn't be too costly for me to run again, and it wasn't. The filing date deadline was June 8th and those running for office were as follows: Mayor: Jerry Wall, Tom Hutchinson, Robert Pryor, Willie Cason, and me. City Council candidates: Ward 1 was Nelle Gerrard and Will Davis; Ward 2 was Julie Lehman, Dixie Trout, and Bart Hutchinson; and Ward 3 was David Bills and Craig Nelson.

Although Will Davis had announced earlier along with Council-man Lunsford and me that he wouldn't run for re-election this year, apparently, like me, Davis decided to run again.

The *Uinta County Herald* edition of June 8th headlined: MAYOR RECONSIDERS, WILL RUN FOR ANOTHER TERM. The article stated:

Evanston Mayor Dennis Ottley made the announcement Wednesday he will be re-running for the position.

"I just couldn't afford it, but when Jon Lunsford and Clarence Vranish brought it up and were in favor of raising the wage it opened the door for me to stay with the city," he explained.

"My heart has always been with the city. I understand the budget, and I am concerned about the City of Evanston," he said.

Even if the raise doesn't pass through the city council, Ottley said he will stay in office and remain in the race.

"The mayor's job is full time, but it's not full-time pay. The mayor is always on call, he has to be at functions. Sometimes it's 60 hours a week," he said.

"We need to get the Comprehensive Plan revision going again. We need to move faster on that, we've been putting it off for two years," said Ottley.

"Industry is not the only economic development. It's things like Wyoming Downs and the revitalization of Front Street," he added. "Those give the market for construction."

"I am concerned with Evanston, the county too, but Evanston is my bag. I have no aspirations to go further politically, I'm not a party man," he continued.

Ottley has been involved with city government for 20 years; eight as mayor and 12 as a city councilman, the article continued.

"A number of key people will be retiring in the next four years," he continued, *"and I would like to help replace them with good people. I am glad to see that Will Davis is back in the running. With his involvement in the governor's committee for solid waste and recycling, we want to begin to educate people about recycling,"* Ottley said. *"We want to continue to build with the new one-man, one-truck system of sanitation trucks."*

Some of the projects Ottley hopes to focus his attention on are helping to repair city streets, city-wide cleanup and the east end business district.

"The BEAR Project dike and greenbelt are where they can see the difference," he said.

In the article I talked about the progress that the Evanston Regional Hospital and the Wyoming State Hospital had made, the increase of the school attendance, and how Ehman Industries was growing.

"I think it is the trend with the gas industry," he speculated. *"Everything in the area helps Evanston, he said of Kemmerer's bid for the prison and the valley's growth [talking about Bridger Valley].*

"I don't like to stay stagnant," he laughed. *"I feel I have brought the city through booms and trying times. I hope I can see a time when everyone can make a good living."*

"I've been hurt this past four years, but I should be caught up by the end of summer," he said. *"I have some advantages, I know about the past, as far as the city goes. I've been here 42 years, I'm not a native, but Sandy and the kids are."*

"I think I have done a good job (as mayor) and have a good rapport with people. I listen to the problems and don't shut them out," he claimed.

"Even with the proposed raise, this is not the highest paid employee in the city government. I think the city is big enough for the position to be full time," said Ottley, the article concluded.

According to Evanston Chamber of Commerce Executive Director Janique Eckman's "Chamber Chatter" column in the *Uinta County Herald* of June 8th, the 1990 Renewal Ball, headed by Gerda Robison and Joice Mander was a great success once again. It was held at the Old Post Office building, now owned by Rick Sather, and well over 200 people were in attendance.

On June 19th a special city council meeting was held for the annual public hearing to consider and receive input concerning the 1990-1991 Fiscal Year Budget. City Attorney Dennis Boal was directed to act as Hearing Officer. The hearing was attended by department heads, board and commission members, and a large group of interested citizens.

After the City Attorney closed the lengthy public hearing, in which requests were made for additional funding by several of those present, Councilman Vranish introduced Resolution 90-27, prepared by the Council as follows;

RESOLUTION 90-27
A RESOLUTION PROVIDING INCOME NECESSARY
TO FINANCE THE BUDGET AND PROVIDE FOR AND
AUTHORIZE ANNUAL APPROPRIATION OF FUNDS FOR
THE FISCAL YEAR 1990-1991.

The resolution was quite lengthy, but the total expenditure stated in the resolution was $8,259,496, based on anticipated revenues. This fiscal year budget included a 3% increase to all employees. Motion was made by Councilman Lunsford for the adoption of Resolution 90-27, seconded by Hutchinson.

Councilman Vranish made a motion to make several amendments and adjustments to the resolution, seconded by Hutchinson. After a vote on the main motion as amended, it was adopted with all voting in favor.

The final budget for fiscal year 1990-1991 ended up with a total operating budget of $6,789,463 plus a capital improvement budget of $1,470,033 from July 1, 1990 through June 30, 1991. The final total was $8,259,496, with almost a $300,000 carryover, which would help revenues.

The special city council meeting and public hearing on the budget of fiscal year of 1990-1991 adjourned at 9:20 p.m.

Now that school was out the Evanston Police Department put out notices, as they did every year, warning drivers to take extra caution while driving, because kids would be playing on or near streets and there would be a lot of bicycle traffic.

One program the department set up was called Walk the Circle, to encourage parents with small children to get in the habit of walking around their parked vehicle and checking to make sure there were no children around the area before backing out from wherever they were parked.

The department put out notices in the paper and over the radio plus and posted notices that *Walk the Circle* stickers, to remind people to circle the vehicle before backing out, were available at the police department or at the *Uinta County Herald* office at no cost.

The second regular city council meeting of the month was held on June 21st. One of the first orders of business was my appointment of Ryley Dawson to the Parks and Recreation District Board. The motion was made by Councilman Nelson to confirm the appointment, seconded by Wall. The motion passed with 5 yes votes and 1 absent (Davis).

During this meeting Councilman Lunsford introduced Ordinance 90-13, which read as follows:

ORDINANCE 90-13
ORDINANCE AMENDING AND REENACTING SECTION
2-13.1. Salaries of Mayor and Council Members. OF ARTICLE ll
OF CHAPTER 2 OF THE EVANSTON CITY CODE TO IN-
CREASE THE SALARIES OF THE MAYOR AND COUNCIL
MEMBERS.

Within the body, the ordinance read:

Section 1: The annual salary of City Council Members shall be the sum of Four Thousand Five Hundred Dollars ($4,500.00) to be paid in equal installments every two (2) weeks.

Section 2-13.1. Salaries of Mayor and Council Members.

The annual salary of the Mayor shall be the sum of Twenty Thousand Dollars ($20,000.00) for the first year after the effective date of the salary increase.

The annual salary for the Mayor for the second year and all subsequent years shall be the sum of Thirty Thousand Dollars ($30,000.00). The Mayor's salary shall be paid in equal installments every two (2) weeks.

These salaries shall be paid in addition to any benefits designated by the City Council.

Section 2: The salary increases of this Ordinance shall go into effect after the Mayor and Council Members officially take office after the next election for the Mayor and each Council Member's position.

Councilman Lunsford made a motion to pass Ordinance 90-13 on the first reading, seconded by Nelson.

Councilwoman Wall abstained and excused herself from the Council Chambers.

I couldn't understand why she did that, because if she felt she had a conflict, then every one of the members of the council would have a conflict, including me. Then there would be no one to vote on the ordinance. What she didn't understand was that if she had been against the motion she would have been better off by staying in and voting against it as Councilman Hutchinson did, or voting for it if she chose to.

Wall, Hutchinson and I were all running for the mayor's position and Davis and Nelson are running for re-election, but none of those running would receive the increase in salary unless they happened to win.

The *Uinta County Herald* of June 26th reported Councilman Lunsford as saying; *"I know this is poor timing, this close to election. But, it needs to come up now, I hope it won't affect votes and hurt candidates. But, I have nothing to gain. I'm not running again."*

He claimed only two people had come to him with objections and neither had ever served as elected officials.

Tom Hutchinson quoted figures from other councils around the state. Only Cheyenne and Sheridan were in the same price bracket. Clarence Vranish said he supported the move, basically. "If you want good people to do the job, we need to pay for it," he said. "I don't think passing this after election is up-front or right," he stated.

After a lengthy discussion I called for the vote. There were 4 votes in favor, 1 against (Hutchinson), 1 abstained (Wall), and 1 absent

(Davis). Motion to pass Ordinance 90-13 passed by a majority on first reading. There would be two more readings coming up in the next two meetings.

This meeting of June 21st adjourned at 10:30 p.m.

Because of an important meeting in Cheyenne with state officials, I was absent during the first monthly city council meeting on July; therefore the meeting was conducted by Council President Tom Hutchinson.

During this meeting the city council approved a catering permit to serve malt liquor by Jolly Roger for the Centennial Committee's grand opening of the newly built replica of the original Joss House on Depot Square. The date was set for July 13th with a full day of activities and programs at the Square.

The city council approved also an application for a malt beverage permit for the Mudd Boggs project, also being held in July.

Police Chief Dennis Harvey made a presentation to Officer Doug Matthews and announced to the council that Matthews had been chosen by the Veterans of Foreign Wars as Peace Officer of the Year.

Council President Hutchinson and council members each congratulated and thanked Matthews for his outstanding service as a police officer.

Denice Wheeler, representing the Lodging Tax Committee, which would be coming up as a referendum in the upcoming general election in November, requested funding from the City of Evanston for the committee to promote the 2% Lodging Tax. The additional funds would also help them in their efforts to increase tourism and travel into Evanston.

After a short discussion the council told her that they would take a look at the budget later and get back to her with some funding.

Ordinance 90-13, increasing the mayor and city council members' salaries, came up for second reading. A motion was made by Councilman Lunsford to pass Ordinance 90-13 on second reading, seconded by Davis.

But Councilman Nelson made a motion to amend the ordinance to delete; *"the annual salary of the Mayor shall be Twenty Thousand*

Dollars ($20,000.00) for the first year", and also delete; *"for the second year and all subsequent years,"* and add the words in place; *"the annual salary of the Mayor shall be Thirty Thousand Dollars ($30,000.00)."*

Councilman's Nelson's motion to amend Ordinance 90-13 was seconded by Lunsford with 4 yes votes, 1 no vote (Hutchinson), 1 abstained (Wall), and 1 absent (myself). The motion to amend passed by a majority.

The vote on the main motion to pass Ordinance 90-13 as amended for second reading was the same vote as for the amendment, and passed by a majority.

Other items that came up during the July 5th meeting were: Operations Superintendent Allen Kennedy expressed appreciation from the Public Works Department employees for the recent pay raise.

As mayor, I always tried to give the city employees a pay increase every year when budget was being discussed, because I wanted very much to keep up with the cost of living. During my time as mayor there were very few years that the employees didn't receive a pay raise. I always felt that if you keep the interest of the employees in mind, and try to treat them as fairly as possible, you would get better results out of them, and they would be much more productive. After all, they were the backbone of the community.

Ann Bell, Evanston Chairperson of the Wyoming Centennial Committee, gave a special report during the city council meeting of July 19th, on all of the Centennial activities that had taken place during the celebration.

She said it was a time of heart-swelling pride and tears of joy for the numerous volunteers who worked for two years to make the celebration a success.

She made special mention of the 16 Evanston High School students who traveled to Cheyenne with the dragon they constructed themselves, and how they were involved in Cheyenne's Centennial parade. *Evanston was well represented in Cheyenne,* Ann stated. She told the council that the Chinese Ethnic Group in Cheyenne paid all the expenses for the group of students while they were in Cheyenne.

Ann reported on some of the fundraising projects they have had, such as the inscribed brick project, the T-shirt sales, and sales of other items. She also reported on the Evanston Centennial activities held on July 11 -14.

She mentioned that Evanston's First Lady, Sandy Ottley, gave the highest bid of $125.00 for a picture entitled "A Portrait of a Volunteer." This was a framed shirt worn by Volunteer and Committee Member Eileen Downs-Jacobs when she painted the Joss House and hung the panels. It was to remind all who saw it of the many hours of fun and work which went into the project. Sandy donated that framed shirt to the city to be displayed.

Festivities began on July 11th with a "hanging party" at 7:30 a.m. "It wasn't exactly like it sounds," Ann said. "The event was to celebrate the hanging of the Chinese Panels [which Ann and her committee had received back from Cheyenne] above the doors and at the roof line of the porch of the newly rebuilt Joss House." Depot Square and the entire downtown area was draped with flags and other beautiful decorations to celebrate the Wyoming Centennial.

OFFICIAL PAINTING — A painting of the original Chinese Joss House, a temple of worship, was recently completed by local artist, Eileen Downs-Jacobs. The painting was replicated by studying old photographs of the original Evanston Joss House. Downs-Jacobs said everything in the painting is as authentic as possible, with the vast Wyoming land and sky overwhelming the Chinese gardners. The painting will be on display at local businesses before it is auctioned at the Renewal Ball in June.

Uinta County Herald, January 12, 1990.

She said from July 12th through July 14th there were ongoing activities throughout the Centennial Celebration: fireworks; a parade with a number of floats, some politicians and other participants; and surprisingly, I was chosen to act as Grand Marshall for the parade at the last minute. Also, Bell said, a lot of activity went on at Martin Park, the first Mayor's Centennial Golf Invitational was held at the Purple Sage Golf Course, and there was an art show at the Depot where local artists displayed their beautiful works of art.

There was an Amoco/Chevron Men's Softball Tournament at the Overthrust Ball Park, and a chuck wagon dinner held on Depot Square, catered by the Jolly Roger, followed by a Country Western Dance, Ann added.

The V.F.W. Post 4280 hosted the dedication of the Depot Square flagpole with a community barbecue following the dedication.

We also had a Wyoming Centennial birthday cake for all those in attendance following the barbecue. The cake was baked by Jodi Guild at the main school district cafeteria, Ann reported.

She also reported that the winner of the Centennial Rifle that was raffled off was 17-year-old David Britton. David's Dad signed for it because David was a minor.

On July 14th, the dedication of the newly constructed replica of the Chinese Joss House was held. *This Chinese Joss House, a replica of the original Joss House located across the tracks located near the Jolly Roger Restaurant, is Evanston's "Lasting Legacy" project for the Wyoming Centennial Celebration,* Ann pointed out.

Jesse Hoey, a local businessman of Chinese descent, rang the gong inviting everyone to attend the opening of the new Joss House. Jesse was the owner of the New Gardens Chinese Cafe just across the street from the new structure. He and his wife both helped in the celebration of Evanston's Lasting Legacy.

Taking part in the celebration and dedication of the new Joss House building were also visitors of Chinese descent from Cheyenne and from Old China Town in San Francisco.

Ann reported that while viewing the artifacts within the Joss House, the Chinese Ethnic Group found a few items in the museum that they indicated had no connection to the ancestry or the history of the Chinese people. This seemed to upset a few members of the Chinese group, Ann continued.

Original Joss House panels return home to Evanston

Three of the original panels from Evanston's original Joss House, which burned in 1922, were returned to Evanston from the state museum to be housed in the newly constructed replica

Pete Sixbey and Steve Cotherman delivered the panels to the Joss House Committee.

Cotherman said the panels are "extremely unique objects, literally priceless."

He said several Asian museums were excited about the panels but he also stated they were back where they really belong, in the Evanston Joss House.

Over the years some damage has occurred to the wooden panels, mostly with the delicate high relief carving and gold-leaf on the panels. Sixbey discussed stabilization and cleaning instructions with the Joss House group and Cotherman explained to the group about mounting the panels.

The panels will be housed in the county museum until the Joss House security system in installed.

The panels, drum, gong and other artifacts from the museum will be permanently on display at the Joss House eventually.

Cotherman summed up the feelings of the state museum by stating "we are all very excited about the panels coming back here."

UNVEILING THE PANELS — Ann Bell, Evanston Centennial Committee chairperson, stands with Pete Sixbey and Steve Cotherman, from the state museum, looking over the original panels from Evanston's Joss House, which will be housed in the reconstructed Joss House.

RIBBON CUTTING — Evanston's Chamber of Commerce Red Ribbon Committee helped make the opening of the Joss House with a ribbon cutting, Ann Bell and members of her committee doing the honors.

Uinta County Herald, July 17, 1990.

They were especially upset when they found a photo of a young Asian girl. The committee had been told that it was a photo of Evanston's acclaimed resident, *"China Mary,"* when she was a young prostitute in Park City, Utah. (It was thought by many in Evanston that China Mary had been a prostitute in her younger days, though I had never read or saw any proof of that.)

Apparently the photo wasn't correct, according to the Chinese delegation. The young girl in the photo was not of Chinese descent. They said although they didn't know for sure what nationality she was, her dress appeared to be Japanese.

With the help of the Chinese delegation, Ann Bell and her committee immediately removed all items that had nothing to do with the Chinese or their history. The photo of the young Asian girl was quite an embarrassment to the committee; they had been told by a local historian, who offered the photo to the museum, that it was a photo of young China Mary, which wasn't true. Folks donated items to the Joss House that they honestly thought were Chinese, though apparently some were mistaken.

However, the Chinese delegation was very impressed with the replica of the Joss House and they especially admired the panels that had been in the original House, and were honored to have been invited. Ann told the council that having the Chinese ethnic groups here from out of town added a lot to making the dedication and opening of the Joss House a big success.

Ann Bell expressed her thanks to the mayor and city council for all their support in helping make Evanston's Wyoming Statehood Centennial celebration, and the Lasting Legacy of the Joss House, a big success.

John Bowers, who was the photographer for the Centennial Committee, presented to me a beautiful colored photo in a nice wooden frame of the newly constructed replica of the Joss House. He said, "This is yours, Mr. Mayor, the city already has one. This is yours to keep."

Quite surprised and honored, I thanked him and the committee for the framed picture, and I always have it displayed in a very conspicuous location.

The above is Evanston's project for the Wyoming Statehood Centennial. Recently constructed, this is a replica of the Chinese Jose House, one of only three in the United States during the late 1800s and early 1900s. A part of Evanston history, originally located near what used to be an old mill now known as The Painted Lady Restaurant. The dedication was on July 13, 1990.

I also gave a special thanks to Ann Bell for accepting the chairperson's position, and for her leadership in making the 1990 Wyoming Centennial activities such a big success. I told her that the Joss House will, indeed, be a Lasting Legacy for Evanston in memory of the railroad, Chinese immigrant history, and the Almy coal mines, the beginning of the Town of Evanston.

During the same meeting Mr. Mark Smith, from the United States Geological Survey office, gave a presentation of their studies of the Bear River Project and told of their willingness to work with the Project Committee in accomplishing their goals.

I thanked Mr. Smith for their involvement and said that the Bear River Project Committee was another amazing committee in Evanston that was putting together another great project. I told them I was amazed at how our Evanston committees get outside groups and agencies involved in various Evanston projects.

It reminded me of a quote I once read by Former President Dwight D. Eisenhower: *"Motivation is the art of getting people to do what you want them to do because they want to do it."*

Also during the July 19th meeting Ordinance 90-10, which had been tabled a few meetings back, was voted on by motion to remove from the table.

ORDINANCE 90-10
ORDINANCE APPROVING AND AUTHORIZING A
ZONE CHANGE FOR REAL PROPERTY LOCATED IN
BLOCK 18 OF THE ORIGINAL TOWN OF EVANSTON
AS MORE PARTICULARLY DESCRIBED HEREIN FROM
LOW-DENSITY RESIDENTIAL ESTABLISHED ZONE TO
REGIONAL BUSINESS DEVELOPING PROPERTIES, AND
CURTIS W. ELLINGFORD AND GERALDINE ELLING-
FORD.

This was another controversial ordinance similar to the requested zone change on Front Street between 1st and 2nd Streets, to allow what is in place now on the corner of Center Street and 7th Street (where Westar Printing and Floors & More are now located) to be zoned Regional Business.

Councilwoman Wall made a motion to table Ordinance 90-10 indefinitely, seconded by Davis, with all voting in favor. The motion to table was passed unanimously, but later on Mr. and Mrs. Ellingford's request would come back on the floor again and, like Front Street, would eventually become a reality.

Councilman Davis introduced and sponsored another controversial ordinance, Ordinance 90-14.

ORDINANCE 90-14
ORDINANCE APPROVING AND AUTHORIZING A
ZONE CHANGE FOR REAL PROPERTY LACATED IN
PART OF THE SW ¼ NW ¼ OF SECTION 20, CITY OF
EVANSTON AS MORE PARTICULARLY DESCRIBED
HEREIN FROM LOW-DENSITY RESIDENTIAL ESTAB-
LISHED ZONE TO HIGHWAY BUSINESSE ESTABLISHED
ZONE AS REQUESTED BY LARRY HARVEY.

Councilman Davis made a motion to pass Ordinance 90-14 on first reading, seconded by Hutchinson. During discussion Larry Harvey stated that he was not after a zone change but hoped something could be worked out so he could construct a Miniature Golf Course and retain the present residential zoning.

Lance Voss, a former member of the council who was in attendance, said that he thought the present zoning ordinance could be interpreted to allow this usage. Jon Brown, a resident in the area of the requested zone change, stated that he was opposed to any zone change or a change of usage in their quiet neighborhood.

I spoke up and said, *Zoning is established for a wise and good purpose and no one should try to circumvent the present ordinances for the benefit of anyone. However, we can possibly make an amendment to the ordinance now in place to allow such things as miniature golf courses.* I then ended discussion and called for the vote on the motion by Davis to pass Ordinance 90-14 on first reading. Vote was 5 against, causing the motion to fail by a unanimous vote. There were 2 members absent. Prior to adjournment, I asked for any announcements or comments from the staff.

Community Development Director Paul Knopf made everyone aware of articles about the Bear River Project in some nationally published magazines. Once again, Evanston was getting national publicity.

I explained to those who were in attendance representing the Lodging Tax Committee that any funds that the city gave to them for promoting the tax referendum would have to be channeled through the Evanston Chamber of Commerce, because the committee is not officially organized by state law.

On August 1st the new Walmart store had their grand opening and Evanston lost a few stores, I guess because of it. Pamida, a food and drug market on Yellow Creek closed their doors a few weeks prior to Walmart opening, and Cornets Variety Store, which had been in Evanston since the 1940s, closed their doors just after the opening of the Walmart supermarket. They had been located in downtown Evanston on Main Street.

However, most of the citizens were glad to see a Walmart store in Evanston. It provided a lot of jobs and it kept a lot of folks from going out of town to do their shopping. Having a Walmart store in Evanston would benefit the community much more than it would harm it.

During the August 2nd regular city council meeting, Ordinance 90-13, increasing the salaries of the mayor and city council members, came up for third and final reading. The ordinance had already passed on first and second readings, and was now up for third reading as amended.

Councilman Vranish made a motion to pass Ordinance 90-13 on third and final reading as amended, seconded by Davis. After a short discussion I called for the vote, which ended up 4 in favor (Vranish, Davis, Nelson, and me), 1 against (Hutchinson), 1 abstaining (Wall), and 1 absent (Lunsford). The motion passed by a majority.

Other business to come before the council included the bids on the Centennial Valley utility and street repairs project. There were three bids: Snyder Construction (no relation to Administrative Assistant Steve Snyder), $348,194.20; X-it Construction, $299,019.50; and Jasco, $286, 095.50.

Councilman Nelson introduced Resolution 90-34 and made a motion to award the Centennial Valley project bid to the low bidder Jasco in the amount of $286,095.50, and adopt Resolution 90-34 entering into an agreement with Jasco for the construction of Centennial Valley water, sewer and street improvements. The motion was seconded by Davis with all voting in favor.

It was voted on by resolution that Forsgren Associates oversee the engineering of the construction of the Centennial Valley utility and street project on the City of Evanston's behalf. The council vote was unanimous. And it was voted on by resolution to enter into a contract with Uinta Engineering and Surveying, Inc. to provide engineering services for construction of the downtown street lighting project, and the West Main Street improvements. This also had the unanimous vote of the council.

Prior to adjourning the meeting of August 2nd, I announced that I would be on hand, as I had every year, to support the upcoming Uinta County Fair and the Rich County Fair in Randolph, Utah at the Stock Sale. Evanston would be participating in the Stock Sale.

During the regular meeting of the city council on August 16th, former city council member David Bills brought up the overhead power lines on the west side of Yellow Creek Road from the I-80 underpass to where the lines cross Yellow Creek Road just south of Rocky Mountain Rest Home and Health Care.

His request to the city council was to check with Utah Power and Light (at the present Rocky Mountain Power) about putting the lines underground. I mentioned to Bills that I thought everyone on the city council, including me, thought it was a good idea and I thanked him for bringing it up.

At that time Dan Yates, a representative of Utah P & L, was in attendance to present to the mayor the company's Franchise Check in the amount of $12,671.29 for the second quarter of 1990. While thanking him for the check, I asked Yates to follow up on Mr. Bills request and he indicated that he would and would get back to us.

Prior to adjournment I made a report on the city's participation in both the Uinta County Fair and the Rich County Fair and Rodeo in Randolph, Utah. I told the council that I had made a stock purchase at both fairs and the stock was given back to the young participants to keep or sell again, as they choose.

The City of Evanston had participated in both fairs as long as I had been on the council. I had always felt that it was good publicity for the City of Evanston to show their appreciation to both Uinta and

Rich Counties, because the folks of Rich County and Bridger Valley have always done a lot of their shopping and banking in Evanston. The *Uinta County Herald* issue of August 21st reported: *Evanston Mayor Dennis Ottley and his wife Sandy recently received a letter from the Chinese Historical Society of America inviting them to attend their annual dinner.*

"On behalf of the Society, we wish to thank you and your city for the warm welcome and hope someday to extend our hospitality to you in San Francisco as you have in Evanston to us," the letter read.

"Our annual dinner this coming year will be on the second Saturday in January, 1991 and everyone is invited. Please mark your calendar to come to San Francisco during that period.

"Again thank you, Mrs. Ottley, for looking after the elderly (Chinese) *lady, and looking forward to meeting again one day," according to the letter.*

The elderly Chinese lady the letter was talking about was Lu Shee "Lucy" Yee, former owner of the Ranch Café, located where Bon Rico Restaurant is at this time.

Ottley stated no plans had been made to reciprocate at this time. He stated that "I'll talk to Evanston Centennial Chairperson Ann Bell about sending someone to represent our city," the Herald concluded.

It would depend a lot on the election for Sandy and me to go, and it would depend on the funds the Centennial Committee had left over from the celebration for them to send anyone, but it would be nice publicity if someone representing the city and/or the committee to could go. We'd just have to wait and see. The Primary Election held on Tuesday, August 21st was held with the following results:

Mayoral race: Willie Cason 203, Tom Hutchinson 838, Robert Pryor 69, Jerry Wall 459, and me 900. City Council: Ward 1 – Will Davis 441, Nelle Gerrard 288, and Dick Stocks 126. Ward 2 – David E. Bills 128, Bart Hutchinson 126, Julie Lehman 351, and Dixie Lynn Trout 138. Ward 3 – Byron Martinez 225, Craig Nelson 454, and Jeffrey Shaffer 110.

For the General Election in November for Mayor of Evanston it would be Tom Hutchinson and me, the two highest receivers of votes. Running in the General for Ward 1 would be Will Davis and

Nelle Gerrard; Ward 2 would be Julie Lehman and Dixie Lynn Trout; and Ward 3 would be Byron Martinez and Craig Nelson.

Surprisingly, I received the highest amount of votes, though not beating Hutchinson by much, but I called Tom and congratulated him on his successful election and told him I'd see him in the General. But I did wish him luck.

I was really surprised to win in the Primary because of my bankruptcy and the action in getting the mayor's salary increased. I knew I was going to have to work really hard to beat Tom with the Primary having been that close. I only hoped for a good clean election, because I have always thought a lot of Tom and his family.

On August 31st the City of Evanston sponsored an appreciation dinner to honor D. A. "Swanny" and Verda Kerby of the Bar T Rodeo Contractors at the Legal Tender Restaurant. The Kerbys had furnished stock for the Evanston Cowboy Days Rodeo for approximately 37 years.

"This being the year of the Wyoming Centennial, the City of Evanston wishes to show their appreciation to the longest ongoing program in the city's history, the Evanston Cowboy Days on Labor Day weekend. This is a lasting legacy," the *Uinta County Herald* quoted me.

Swanny and Verda were great people and always gave Evanston a great rodeo. They were the contractors in 1963 when I was Cowboy Days Committee Chairman, and they did me a whale of a job.

There were only four members of the city council, including the mayor, in attendance at the September 6th regular city council meeting. Councilmembers Jerry Wall, Craig Nelson and Will Davis were attending the Wyoming Association of Municipalities (W.A.M.) meeting.

With four members in attendance, Councilmen Hutchinson, Vranish, Lunsford, and me, we did have a quorum. But with three members of the council being absent we did table some of the pending business until the next regular meeting, which would be on September 20th.

During the meeting we held a public hearing on all liquor licenses which came up for renewal on October 1st. City Attorney Dennis Boal opened the hearing for public comments and stated that all liquor licenses in the City of Evanston became due as of October 1st of each year, and the hearing was held early to give the public the opportunity to express their comments and complaints, if any, that they might have concerning any business that was a holder of a liquor license.

During the hearing there wasn't anyone present with complaints, but some of the liquor licensees had a few concerns, and Councilman Vranish had a question concerning folks that were holding licenses that were not in use; there were two or three in that category.

After Attorney Boal closed the public hearing, a motion was made and seconded to approve the renewal of all liquor licenses, but Councilman Vranish made an amendment to the motion requiring all license holders with inactive licenses to furnish to City Clerk Welling proof of purchasing at least $250 worth of alcoholic beverages, as required by law, to continue to hold a license. Vranish's amendment was seconded by Lunsford, passing unanimously with 4 votes. The main motion for the approval of the licenses as amended also passed by a unanimous vote.

Resolution 90-44-A was introduced by Councilman Vranish, to enter into an agreement with Flare Construction Company for the construction of a parking lot at Depot Square.

This was the parking lot on the corner of Front Street and 9th Street next to the newly constructed replica of the old Joss House. Councilman Lunsford made the motion to adopt Resolution 90-44-A, seconded by Vranish. The motion passed with 4 votes and 3 absent (Wall, Nelson, and Davis).

I then brought up a petition presented by a number of citizens, some downtown business people and some other concerned citizens. The petition requested that the City of Evanston eliminate the 2-hour parking enforcement in the downtown area.

This petition was quite a surprise to the council, because we were under the impression that the downtown businesses wanted the 2-hour parking enforcement.

Councilman Lunsford made a motion to honor the request of the petition and directed the city attorney to prepare an amendment to the parking ordinance for the next meeting. The motion was seconded and the vote was called for with 2 yes votes (Hutchinson and Lunsford), and 2 no votes (Vranish and me), and 3 absent. The motion ended up tied, which caused the motion to fail. Therefore the 2-hour parking ordinance would stay enforceable.

Administrative Assistant Steve Snyder reported that the preliminary census figures for 1990 showed a decrease in population for the City of Evanston, and that the City had 15 days to document any errors and make a protest.

Assistant Treasurer Steve Widmer and Community Development Director Paul Knopf were instructed to meet with County Planner Dennis Farley to check into the possibility of any errors or miscalculations in the census count.

An article in the *Uinta County Herald* of September 7th stated that the census showed total population for Evanston was 10,690, declining from the 1986 special census figure by just over 1,500 people.

The article quoted Paul Knopf saying the Census Bureau sent him a letter in January estimating 5070 housing units, but the preliminary count of the census showed only 4,332 housing units, and in 1986 there were 4,855 housing units.

The preliminary count of housing units which are vacant were numbered 825, within the City of Evanston. This compares to 870 vacant units in 1986, the *Herald* read.

Widmer, Knopf and Farley performed a study and found that the preliminary census numbers appeared to be off, and would address specific problems in correspondence with the Census Bureau during the 15-day period.

Prior to adjourning the September 6th council meeting, I read two Letters of Commendations to the following Police Officers: Sergeant Mitch Allmaras from the Clearfield, Utah Police Department, for the assistance he provided in a pending situation; and Lieutenant Paul Dean and Officer Colleen Millburg from the Federal Bureau of Investigation (FBI) for their outstanding performance in their FBI training class.

The city council and I congratulated them on their Letters of Commendation, and expressed our appreciation for doing such a good job as Evanston Police Officers.

During the September 20th city council meeting Ordinance 90-17 was introduced by Councilman Craig Nelson and sponsored by me, to amend the zoning ordinance to conditionally allow commercial outdoor recreation on property contiguous to a Highway Business Commercial District Zone and to better define the permissible zoning districts for golf courses.

This ordinance would allow private outdoor recreation and amusement including miniature golf courses, golf driving ranges, water slides and similar, under a C4 Permit (conditional review use on property located contiguous to a Highway Business Commercial District).

Motion was made by Councilman Hutchinson to pass Ordinance 90-17 on first reading, seconded by Davis with 6 voting for approval and 1 absent (Wall). The motion passed.

Ordinance 90-17 was passed on second and third readings as amended. This ordinance allowed Larry Harvey to proceed with his miniature golf course under a C-4 permit as approved through the Evanston Planning and Zoning Commission. The amendments were word corrections and had no bearing on the meaning of the ordinance. The ordinance was passed by a unanimous vote on all three readings.

Some folks wanted to circumvent the previous ordinance and allow the permit for a miniature golf course before the ordinance was amended, but that was something I was always against. Anyone that attempts to go around an ordinance, in the Evanston Book of Codes, for any purpose is wrong. I think amending any ordinance in question is, by far, the cleanest way of proceeding when a change is necessary, even if it takes a few months longer. The council did the right thing.

During a recent hearing of the Evanston Planning and Zoning Commission, Ottley Enterprises, Inc., owner of Flying J Travel Plaza, requested a permit to put up another high-rise sign, which would be a read-out pole-sign advertising their fuel prices.

Dr. Dean Holt, a close neighbor living next to the Travel Plaza, was the only one in attendance that had any issue with the Flying J's request. However, his complaints had nothing to do with the sign. His concerns were about the noise from the trucks parked in the back of the Plaza, and the garbage that blew towards his home.

After a considerable amount of discussion the Commission voted 4 to 3 against the Flying J's request.

After the P & Z Commission turned his request down, Robert "Bob" Ottley, my brother and the owner of Ottley Enterprises, Inc., appealed his request to the City Council by former City Attorney Dennis Lancaster, who was representing Ottley and the Flying J at this time.

Lancaster told City Attorney Dennis Boal that because the vote of the commission was so close he felt that consideration by the city council was warranted, and requested that the appeal be brought up during the city council meeting of September20th.

When the appeal came up during the meeting, Lancaster explained that he felt that Flying J's request was legitimate and explained to the council about the meeting of the Planning and Zoning Commission, and explained about Dr. Holt's concern. He told the council that the doctor's complaints had nothing to do with the request in question. He explained that Dr. Holt's were about the noise from the trucks and the trash that blew over near his home, though my brother Bob did have the area fenced, which caught most of the trash.

Kevin Kallas, a member of the P & Z Commission, voted against the Conditional Use Permit when the Flying J first requested to be allowed to put up the sign. Kallas was in attendance during the appeal with the city council, and said that he felt misled by information presented to the commission, because he now realized that Dr. Holt's concerns had nothing to do with Ottley's request. He stated that he felt that the doctor's concerns did sway his vote and that he now felt that the sign issue should stand on its own merits, and said he wished he could change his vote.

Bob Ottley, owner of Flying J, said he understood Dr. Holt's concerns and would work out whatever solutions he could to eliminate the doctor's concerns.

Prior to the appeal I announced that I would excuse myself from any discussion and from the chambers. Because Bob was my brother I felt that I should declare a conflict of interest and leave, and I did.

After the appeal was over Councilman Vranish made a motion to override the commission's decision and grant the Conditional Use Permit to the Flying J, seconded by Lunsford. The motion passed with 5 yes votes, 1 absent (Wall), and 1 abstention (me).

There were some folks who had attended the city council meetings that seemed to misunderstand the difference between "Private" and "Public" in the city ordinances. Therefore, City Attorney Dennis Boal, at the request of the council, prepared Ordinance 90-18, which was introduced by Councilman Lunsford at the September 20th meeting, and sponsored by me.

The ordinance read:

Sec. 24-105. Definitions and standard enumerated.

For the purpose of carrying out the intent of this chapter, the following words, phrases and terms shall be deemed to have the meanings ascribed to them and shall be interpreted to have the standards and include the parts, elements and features set forth in this section.

(76.1) "Private" means owned or operated by a non-governmental entity.

(78.1) "Public" means owned or operated by a governmental entity.

Councilman Nelson made a motion to pass Ordinance 90-18 on first reading, seconded by Davis. Motion passed with 6 yes votes, and 1 absent (Wall).

Ordinance 90-18 went on to pass by a unanimous vote on the second and third and final reading, and now there should be no question concerning how to define the words "Private" and "Public."

Also during the meeting, Diane Hodges, Executive Director of the Evanston Chamber of Commerce, reported on the upcoming events for Support Your Community Week, which would begin on October 20th through October 26th. Support Your Community Week was an annual event sponsored jointly by the City of Evanston and the Evanston Chamber of Commerce. This year, 1990, would be the fourth annual event.

Ms Hodges said that October 20th would kick off the week with a parade chaired by First Lady Sandy Ottley. There would also be a Flea Market at Depot Square, and a Super Downtown Garage Sale. Items to be sold off would be provided by the public (private citizens and commercial businesses). There would be "A Taste Of Evanston" on October 21st, and a Senior Citizens Recognition Day luncheon on October 22nd with University of Wyoming President Terry P. Roark as guest speaker.

On October 23rd there would be a fundraising breakfast, sponsored by The Ambassadors of the Evanston Chamber of Commerce and ERA Uinta Realty, Inc., in support of Kristopher Staley. Kris was an Evanston 4-year-old who was badly in need of a liver transplant. Several efforts were made around the Evanston community to raise funds to help alleviate some of the heavy burden put upon his family.

Following the breakfast there would be a Chamber of Commerce mixer that evening at Depot Square.

October 24th would be a full day of Merchants Open House with sidewalk sales, etc., and on October 25th would be the student essay contest with the theme "Evanston the Beautiful." Later that evening would be a special city council meeting to honor the essay winners with special invitations to their families.

October 26th would be the highlight of Support Your Community Week with a dinner honoring senior citizens that were nominated by the public. The featured speaker would be Clay Babbitt of Chevron USA. His topic would be the BEAR Project and community and corporate involvement.

Prior to adjournment, Councilwoman Jerry Wall made a motion approving two street lights at the new Brown Park, and seven additional lights at Depot Square. The motion was seconded with all voting in favor.

The *Uinta County Herald* of October 5th published an article headlined: EVANSTON TO HONOR ITS MILITARY MEN. The article read:

Yellow ribbons are going up all over town.

The ribbons are just a symbol of the hopes, dreams and prayers of everyone going out to local service personnel at this stressful period of time.

Sandy Ottley began her crusade to honor service men and women by placing yellow ribbons on the lights in front of city hall.

Inside, she has used a wall near the council chambers to place the names and branch of service of nearly 45 local armed forces persons.

"I haven't gotten the names of everyone, we are hoping that the families will let us know so we can add their loved ones' names to the streamers," said Ottley.

The idea came to Ottley while she read the Uinta County Herald's edition with the yellow ribbon window placard.

Since that time, the project has mushroomed. She will be placing the ribbons on several of the public buildings and at Depot Square with the hope businesses and private homes will pick up the trend.

The *Herald* concluded: *Oct. 20, John Bowers will spearhead a "Yellow Ribbon" ceremony to be held during Support Your Community Week. The ceremony is scheduled at 10 a.m. at the Uinta County Complex.*

The "Yellow Ribbon" program was initiated to honor those men and women that were called to serve the United States of America during Operation Desert Storm in the Persian Gulf, sometimes referred to as Operation Desert Shield.

YELLOW RIBBONS — Sandy Ottley is starting a "Yellow Ribbon" campaign giving support to all the armed forces personnel from Evanston. She has begun with city hall, but hopes others will pick up the idea. Several other efforts are being made by Davis Middle School and Young Chevrolet. DMS students are writing letters and Young is sponsoring a drive for acceptable items.

Uinta County Herald, October 5, 1990.

It was the war when Dictator of Iraq Saddam Hussein's troops entered the Persian Gulf country of Kuwait, an ally of the U.S.A., to take control of the oil-rich country. The United States could not let this happen to one of its best allies in the Middle East, so President George H. W. Bush sent U.S. troops to defeat Hussein and push his army back across the border into Iraq.

Following the Yellow Ribbon project, others started getting involved: schools, local organizations, and all local government offices including the Post Office under the organized efforts a P.O. employee named Raymond Archuleta, a Vietnam War Veteran. He contacted a number of individuals and businesses to raise funds for postage and for items to put in the packages that were being sent to the troops in the Desert Shield conflict.

City Hall was very busy putting up not only yellow ribbons, but also assembling care packages to be sent to those men and women from the Evanston area who were being called to serve in the service during Desert Shield. In the packages were not only personal stuff, but also some goodies, letters, and so on, but each package had a small American flag along with a Wyoming flag as well.

During this conflict dozens of young men and women from the Evanston area were called to serve, and the City of Evanston got many letters back from the troops thanking us for the packages. One letter stated that those from Wyoming were the only ones getting a state flag, and indicated that people from other states were very jealous of the troops from Wyoming.

As in the past, the City of Evanston was having problems with election signs being placed in the city and state right-of-ways. Therefore, once again, the Community Development Director (City Planner) was directed by the city council to publish a notice in the *Uinta County Herald* stating: "Political Signs Cannot Be In Right-of-ways."

In October, just before the regular city council meeting of October 18th, I was surprised to receive a letter of resignation from our Administrative Assistant to the Mayor, Steve Snyder. I read the letter to the city council during the meeting with a lot of sorrow:

Dear Mayor Ottley:

It is with sadness and regret that I submit this letter, which is to serve as my official notification of resignation from my position with the City of Evanston. The sadness and regret results from my feeling for you and the Evanston community as my family, and I feel that you and the entire community have in effect been my extended family, and I will always be grateful for that. However, my personal circumstances require that now would be as good a time as ever to make a change.

During my time and tenure in Evanston the last 12 years, has provided me with a once-in-a-lifetime experience. Evanston can certainly be proud of its accomplishments, and Evanston has become known statewide for what it has done, and what it is doing. In fact, the Evanston experience is the primary reason that I was even considered for my new position. After my name had been entered into the competition, the District Attorney and Sheriff made an onsite visit and were very favorable and taken with the appearance and sense of community spirit, and were overwhelmed with the progress made in "small town" Wyoming compared to liberal and progressive Nevada.

As I reflect on Evanston, there are two major accomplishments that have occurred during your administration. First and foremost is the infrastructure that has been put in place by taking advantage of the boomtime economy to provide for the downtimes. There is nowhere else in Wyoming that can compare with Evanston's achievements. Secondly, I have felt a tangible sense of community develop over the last four years, and I hope you are able to further that sense during your next four years of administering the City's business. The traditional measure of a community working is the test of "is the community better as a result of my presence?", and although it could be argued, I feel the answer is yes.

Mayor, personally I wish you well in the coming election, and I know that you have the experience and knowledge to handle any challenges that may face you and the City during the next four years after your re-election, and I wish the community well and I will stay in touch both in spirit and with my physical ties to the community.

Sincerely,
Stephen F. Snyder

Although the letter did not have a date of resignation, if I remember right, it was effective immediately or by the end of October.

Following the letter, we all expressed our regrets that Snyder was leaving, because he had been a great asset to the city over the years. I stated that he had been a big help to me, and that he was correct when he asked, *"Is the community better as a result of my presence?"* Because of his efforts in writing grant applications, and being at my side while I visited corporate and state officials, I didn't think that the results would have been as good without his assistance. Steve was a very likeable guy.

Following our comments Councilman Lunsford made a motion to confirm the mayor's acceptance of the resignation of Snyder, seconded by Davis, with all voting in favor.

On October 25th we had the special meeting called for as part of Support Your Community Week.

To start the meeting off and as a special highlight in promoting the Evanston spirit, the Evanston High School Cheerleaders dressed in their classy uniforms performed several cheers to an overflowing crowd in the Council Chambers.

Davis Middle School teacher, Tom Thorpe, introduced his student, Bianca dellaPenta, who was asked to read her poem written on behalf of our troops serving in the Desert Shield conflict. The poem touched many of those present in their heart and soul as she read:

"Soldiers"
By Bianca dellaPenta
We are America, we stand tall.
We want to live in peace and in harmony.
We must work together, together as a team,
we represent our country.
The one in which our President lives.
We live in red, white and blue, all the colors of liberty.
Our soldiers do it for us.
For our mother earth, the earth on which we live,
and the one on which we die. The place of our birth.
We are free unlike some, and our love for one another
continues to follow through.
These are essentials for our tomorrow and yesterday.
We have the Constitution and our laws need to be
obeyed.
Not only do we do it for America, we also protect other
countries.

They get shot in the back and die from hunger.
If we work together we can stop that.
I salute the soldiers of today, and the ones of yesterday.
I am a soldier, and you are a soldier. Together we form
one.

Miss dellaPenta received a standing ovation for the reading of her poem; it was great.

During this meeting, Mr. Terry Privratsky from Amoco Production presented $2,500 to Councilman Craig Nelson and Recreation Director Dennis Poppinga to be used for Sulphur Creek Recreation projects. We all gave our special thanks to Mr. Privratsky.

A plaque was presented by First Lady Sandy Ottley to Jake Jacobs and Dave Alderman, representing Amoco Production, with a special thanks and appreciation to Amoco for sponsoring the Great Endurance Race as a function of the Centennial celebration.

Community Development Director Paul Knopf and Evanston Chamber of Commerce Executive Director Diane Hodges named almost two dozen students who participated in the Pumpkin Carving Contest, and then announced the winners of the contest.

Nelle Gerrard, Chairman of the Evanston Beautification Committee, explained the purpose of her committee, listed some of the projects they had accomplished during the Centennial year and introduced her committee members: Janet Stuglemeyer, Bob Lenz, Archie Willmore, Kevin Murphy, Charlie Maninie, Jim Davis, Jerry Wall, Laurie Quade, Janis Nelson, Debra Bass, Ann Curtis, Paul Knopf and Paula Lind, Secretary.

Ms Gerrard also introduced the winners of the essay contest, and asked each of them to read their winning "Evanston the Beautiful" composition.

Also during the special meeting there were several other presentations made for the completion of various projects, and Paul Knopf stated that approximately 400 students from Davis Middle School were involved in cleanup and painting activities throughout the week.

Ann Bell, Chairman of the Centennial Committee made a presentation and reported on a "time capsule" that was to be placed at Depot Square just in front of the recently rebuilt Joss House. She reported that the capsule would house materials that would enhance the memories of Evanston and the events of this era.

She said that the time capsule was a Centennial year project and was scheduled to be opened in 50 years, on or shortly after July 10, 2040. Everyone was welcome to add their artifacts, letters, articles, and any other items that they felt would give meaning to this time of history.

During the meeting Councilman Craig Nelson introduced Ordinance 90-22, sponsored by me, to require the burial of a time capsule until the Wyoming Sesquicentennial, the one hundred and fifty year celebration. The time capsule would not be unburied, opened or otherwise disturbed prior to July 10, 2040.

A motion to pass Ordinance 90-22 on first reading was made by Councilman Hutchinson, and seconded by Vranish, with all voting in favor. The ordinance was passed by a unanimous vote on both the second and third readings also.

In closing the special meeting I gave a special thanks and appreciation to all those that participated in the Support Your Community Week activities, and reminded everyone of the special honor banquet on Friday, the following evening, and I explained that the time capsule dedication would be sometime in December and that we hoped everyone would participate by putting items in the capsule. We hoped to have something really surprising for the folks in fifty years when they open the capsule.

The next night was the October 26th Annual Honor Banquet to top off, once again, a very successful Support Your Community Week. Those deserving senior citizens that had been so active over the years were honored for their years of voluntary work, showing their love to a community of clean and healthy living, a community where folks would be proud to raise their families.

Those named were longtime residents as follows:

Lois Michelsetter, a high school teacher who said she *came to Evanston from Kansas, planning on staying a couple of years. I learned to love Evanston and its people. I never dreamed I would still be here 47 years later.*

Denice Wheeler, a businesswoman and property owner who stated, *I have had lots of support from people with the same interests. In California there was not that much opportunity to serve. Here, each can do significant things following their own interests. Things were not done only by me, those volunteers that helped me all gave hundreds and hundreds of hours of voluntary work. Those are the ones who really deserve tonight's honor.*

Mary Emerson, who had been involved in many activities, stated "out of all the activities I've been involved in, my favorite was working with the Cub Scouts, I loved it," she emphasized.

And Willis and Marie Barnes, the dynamic husband and wife duo, were honored. Willis was congratulated for his voluntary work and advice in helping to construct a much-needed Sulphur Creek Reservoir and Dam providing Evanston with much cleaner water; and Marie for all the help she had given to the state Centennial projects. Marie told the folks she "she didn't think of it as volunteering, she was just having fun."

Someone once told me that *"Advice is an uncertain gift,"* and I appreciated all the advice that Willis Barnes and others gave me. Some folks who gave advice were older and had much more experience than I did. I didn't always take their advice, but I always listened and gave it a lot of thought.

The banquet concluded with our guest speaker, Clayton Babbit, Quality Improvement Specialist for Chevron USA. "If we want our community strong, we can't sit back waiting for it to happen. Each has to act by supporting our community and its people," Babbit stated. "Evanston's quality of life is something to value," he added.

He explained Chevron's role in the community. "We are proud to be the leading producer of oil and gas and a principal employer in the community," Babbit said.

Babbit had resided in Evanston for about five years and he felt that Chevron would be a long-term employer. He explained, during his talk, how Chevron helped generate several million dollars for the community. He especially recognized the BEAR Project and stated that Chevron was proud to be a part of it by donating $100,000 in support.

During the first meeting of the month on November 1st, a number of Scouts were once again in attendance to fulfill their Citizenship Merit Badge requirements. They were: Pack 23 (Webelos); Leslie Banks, Justin Draper, and Josh Schofield; and Troop 75 were Eric Taylor, Chris Taylor, and Craig Taylor.

We extended a warm welcome to them and also wished them good luck and success in their future endeavors.

Following, Councilman Lunsford inquired about the continuance of the optional one cent sales tax and why it wasn't on the sample ballot recently published in the local paper.

I explained that due to an oversight or misunderstanding of state law, the proposal was not on the absentee or the sample ballots; however, according to the Uinta County Clerk, the proposal to continue the much-needed additional one cent sales tax will be on the ballot at election time.

The General Election was held on November 6th and the continuance of the optional one cent was successfully approved by a 2 to 1 margin, and the 2% excise tax, commonly known as the lodging tax, was also successful, by a 3 to 1 margin.

Governor Mike Sullivan was re-elected and I won my seat as mayor in a very close race against Councilman Tom Hutchinson, who will remain as a member of the council because his council seat was not up for re-election.

During the General Election count I thought I was going to lose because the first two wards that came in were Wards 1 and 3, with me behind by 177 votes, but when the Ward 2 vote came in, I was leading by 244 votes. This gave me the lead with 1581 votes to Hutchinson's 1514. Boy, what a close race, that I won by fewer than 70 votes!

I was very happy about winning, but I felt bad about Tom losing and I called him immediately and congratulated him on such a close race, and thanked him for running an exceptionally clean race. Neither of us campaigned by saying anything negative against one another; we both campaigned on our records as citizens of Evanston.

Tom was one of the cleanest opponents I had ever had in an election and I told him as much.

I don't think I would have felt too bad about it if I had lost because I had a lot of respect for Tom and I think he would have been a good mayor.

The results of Evanston's City Council election were: Ward 1, Will Davis defeated Nelle Gerrard by 620 to 415 votes; Ward 2, Julie Lehman beat Dixie Lynn Trout by 708 to 346 votes; and Ward 3, Craig Nelson was successfully re-elected by a 547 to 422 vote.

We would once again have Julie Lehman, a past member, as a new member of the council this coming January in 1991, and we would be losing one of our city police officers, because Officer Forrest Bright was elected as Uinta County Sheriff, beating out incumbent Leonard Hysell by a vote of 2963 to 2531.

During our second regular meeting on November 15th I introduced another Boy Scout, Rusty Conway, accompanied by Scout Leader Brent Hatch. Rusty reported to the city council that he was working on his Eagle Scout project, which would be a blood drive to take place at the fire hall on December 27th, from 1:00 p.m. to 8:00 p.m. He asked for support from the city administration in his ambitious project.

I thanked Rusty for attending the meeting and told him the city would support his worthwhile project to help make it successful, and wished him luck in completing his Eagle Scout requirements.

During the November 15th meeting Councilman Lunsford made the motion to pass Ordinance 90-22 on third and final reading. This was the ordinance concerning the 50-year time capsule that was not to be disturbed prior to July 10, 2040. The motion was seconded by Vranish with all voting in favor.

Although there had been no set date for the completion and dedication of the time capsule, it was planned for sometime early December.

During the meeting, Ordinance 90-23, authorizing a zone change for real property located in the north part of lot one, block twenty of the original Town of Evanston, was introduced by Councilman

Hutchinson and sponsored by Councilman Nelson. The zone change would be from Low Density Residential to an Office Developing Zone, as requested by Scott and Deborah Smith.

Councilwoman Wall made the motion to pass Ordinance 90-23 on first reading, seconded by Lunsford, but in calling for discussion there was a lot of opposition to the ordinance. This was another controversial zone change that some were claiming was again "spot zoning." Therefore, Councilman Hutchinson requested a definition of spot zoning to be read by City Attorney Boal before the vote, and requested that the definition be spelled out in the minutes as follows:

Spot Zoning:

Spot Zoning is defined as the rezoning of an area into a district which is unrelated to the immediate area or the Comprehensive Plan for the community. Such rezoning may be a special privilege or an inconsistent restriction of one property which is not applicable to other property in the area. Zoning patterns are established to accomplish the purposes of the Comprehensive Plan and to protect those who comply with law. Spot zoning constitutes a disregard for the public welfare and the growth policies and sound planning principles embodied in the Comprehensive Plan. Requested which would result in spot zoning will be denied.

After a lengthy discussion I finally called for the vote, which turned out to be unanimous: there were 7 no votes and the motion to pass Ordinance 90-23 on first reading failed.

After the election the City of Evanston didn't waste any time getting the new 2% excise tax in place; therefore, during our first meeting following the election, Ordinance 90-24 imposing an excise tax on lodging services rendered within the City of Evanston was introduced by Councilman Nelson and sponsored by Councilwoman Wall.

After a short discussion Councilman Davis made a motion to pass Ordinance 90-24 on first reading, seconded by Wall, with all voting in favor. This ordinance went on to be passed on second and third readings prior to the end of the year, with all council members voting in favor.

This ordinance would go into effect immediately upon notification to the Wyoming Department of Taxation and Revenue, which would make the tax effective as of January 1, 1991.

Prior to adjournment of this November 15th meeting, Councilman Nelson made a motion that the City of Evanston call for two special meetings, legally advertised, prior to December 1st. The meetings would be on November 20th and November 29th, both starting at 7:00 p.m., to get Ordinance 90-24 passed on second and third readings, because we would only be having one meeting in December. The motion was seconded by Councilwoman Wall, with all voting in favor.

It was announced also that the Annual Employees Christmas Dinner would be on December 14th at the Elks Club, and that the regular city council meeting for December 6th was rescheduled for December 13th and advertised as such, and it would be the only regular city council meeting in December.

During the Centennial celebration, the Uinta County Centennial Committee (Denice Wheeler, Dorothy Proffit, Melba Amsler, Mary Emerson, Jean Painter Cook, Charlene Parker and Marcie Collins) received a beautiful quilt, stitched by Ruth Graham of Lyman honoring the history of Wyoming during the past 100 years of Wyoming's statehood.

The county's Centennial Committee requested the Uinta County Commissioners' permission to allow them to display the quilt in the Uinta County Courthouse, representing another Lasting Legacy of Wyoming's history.

The committee asked the City of Evanston to allow Gary Bentley, City Carpenter, to build a glass frame and hang it at the courthouse. I approached Bentley on the project and he built a beautiful frame and hung it up. The quilt, to this day, is still in place on the landing of the stairway going to the second floor, and is just as beautiful as ever.

The day after Thanksgiving the City of Evanston, as in the past, kicked off the Christmas season with a torchlight parade, sponsored by Evanston's downtown merchants. The torchlight parade was a fundraising event which cost each participating merchant $2.00 for a space in the parade. Approximately 300 participants joined in the parade, raising over $350.00 to be donated to the Elks Lodge's Christmas Basket for the Needy program. Santa Claus, accompanied by the Evanston Beautification Christmas Elves, would arrive at Depot Square with the torchlight parade, to greet Evanston's children in the new refurbished Evanston Train Depot.

But first the mayor, right after the arrival of the parade, flipped the switch with a "Merry Christmas!" to turn on the Evanston Christmas tree lights. I hoped for a White Christmas (so far this year, there had been very little snow and the ground was bare). The tree was located near the historic Beeman-Cashin Building at Depot Square.

After the lights were lit on the very tall, beautiful Christmas tree everyone was invited to join in singing Christmas carols, and then enjoy themselves with cookies and egg nog in the Beeman-Cashin Building.

The Uinta County Commissioners called for a meeting on November 27th to be held in Mountain View. The meeting was an open meeting and public was invited, but it was a meeting especially for all city, town and county officials of Uinta County to discuss issues that would involve the entire county, such as the various budgets, the passing of the continuance of the optional one-cent sales tax, the Evanston lodging tax, the W.A.M. Convention to be held in Evanston in June, 1991, and other matters of concern.

While I was at the meeting, my wife called with some bad news. My sister, Terry Hutchings, had had a stroke and was in a coma at Evanston Regional Hospital. I had ridden over to Mountain View with other council members and was without a vehicle, but I wanted to get home right away.

With the help of Mountain View Councilwoman Rhea Cox, I obtained help from the Uinta County Sheriff's Department. Deputy Craig Hysell responded to Rhea's call to get me back to Evanston. He picked me up at the meeting and drove me to Leroy Junction, where Deputy Paul Arnell took me on into Evanston and to my home.

I thought to myself, "Only in Uinta County and Wyoming could you get the prompt action that I received from Rhea and the deputies in such distressed times as I had."

When I got home Terry, my sister was still in a coma and never came out of it. She passed away approximately a week later. This was a very big loss to me because Terry and I had always been very close, and I knew I would miss her very much.

During the special city council meeting of November 29th the city council unanimously passed on the third reading of Ordinance 90-24, the excise tax on lodging services.

I read a letter from Forrest Bright, resigning from the Evanston Police Department, because he had been recently elected as the Uinta County Sheriff. Councilman Nelson made a motion to accept his resignation, seconded by Wall, with all voting in favor.

The members of the council and I all expressed our thanks to Officer Bright for his outstanding service to Evanston and wished him well in his new position, and I congratulated him for his successful win in the election.

The City Ditch (sometimes called the Haw Patch Ditch or the Yellow Creek Ditch, which ends up in the Yellow Creek waterway) gets its water from the Bear River and from the overflow of the Evanston Water Treatment Plant located above the "E" Hill. The ditch runs through the Haw Patch area in an open stream above the homes located on Apache Drive in Uinta Meadows Subdivision.

Some folks residing in the Uinta Meadows area attended this special meeting for a hearing on the ditch. Those living on the high side of Apache Drive were claiming that they were getting seepage into their basements from the City Ditch, and had sued the city because of it. Others were there to request that the ditch be covered or fenced or something, because they felt it was a danger for kids that played near it, especially when it was at the high water level.

But some of the folks in attendance that lived near the ditch were against covering the ditch because they were afraid it would kill some of the trees and plant life that grew near there. A lot of the shrubbery along the ditch was Haw Berry bushes; that's where it got the name "Haw Patch."

City Attorney Boal conducted the hearing, but no action was taken at that time. Boal and the city council explained to the folks that the ditch was actually controlled by the ranchers of the Yellow Creek area and that they would have some say in the matter.

One Yellow Creek rancher, Duane Carpenter, was in attendance during the hearing and said that he traveled the ditch on a daily basis during water season. He told the crowd that he had pulled shopping carts, mattresses, refrigerators and all kinds of garbage from the stream, and he thanked the city crews for their efforts in keeping the ditch clean. "But I don't sleep nights worrying that a kid might fall in," he said.

The Yellow Creek ranchers have had the water rights in the ditch dating back as far as 1875, and they were all against covering it or fencing it. Therefore, after a lot of discussion and studies over a period of time, the city decided to leave the ditch as is.

We came to find out that the ditch was not causing the seepage in those homes on Apache Drive. Apparently it was just ground water getting into their basements through foundation cracks and other openings. The lawsuits that had been filed against the city were discontinued.

But the issue didn't stop there; folks continued to try to get the city council to cover the ditch for safety purposes, so the city directed the Engineering Department to get an estimate of the cost to cover the ditch.

Therefore, after more discussion, Councilwoman Lehman made a motion during the city council meeting of March 13, 1991 to pursue the project and direct the City Engineer's department to prepare a grant application to the Wyoming State Farm Loan Board for matching funds to cover the Evanston City Ditch for $626,000. The motion was seconded by Nelson, but failed by a unanimous vote.

There was no more mention of the ditch and it never was covered, and no one, child or adult, has ever fallen into the ditch or gotten harmed in any way.

During our final city council meeting of the year on December 13th I read a letter of resignation from my son Randy Ottley, announcing his resignation from the Evanston Planning and Zoning Commission.

Councilman Hutchinson made a motion to confirm the acceptance of his resignation, seconded by Wall, with all voting in favor.

Councilman Nelson, as representative from the city council to the P & Z Commission, expressed his appreciation and thanks to Randy for his dedicated work. Other council members and I also thanked him and expressed our appreciation for his involvement.

I appointed Ruth Spencer to the Evanston Housing Authority Board with a motion by Councilman Davis to confirm the appointment, seconded by Wall with all voting in favor. I then appointed Claudia Bills to the Urban Renewal Agency with a motion by Councilman Nelson to confirm the appointment, seconded by Davis with all voting in favor.

Ann Bell, Chairperson of the Evanston Centennial Committee announced that the sealing of the time capsule would be at Depot Square on Saturday, December 15th at 3:00 p.m., and there would be a hay ride that same evening at 6:00 p.m.

Ms Bell also presented me with a plaque from the Evanston Chamber of Commerce in appreciation for all the Centennial activities the past year. I returned the plaque to Ann, stating that she was the Chairperson of the Committee and she should have the plaque displayed at a location of her choice.

Other business acted on by the council during the last meeting of the year included Ordinance 90-10, to approve and authorize a zone change as requested by Curtis W. Ellingford and Geraldine Ellingford who owned the lots where Westar Printing is now located. This ordinance had been tabled, and was brought off the table by a motion by Councilman Vranish, seconded by Wall with all voting in favor. Ordinance 90-10 had been passed on first and second readings previously, but after a considerable amount of discussion, it was tabled once again by a 4 yes, 3 no vote until the January 17, 1991 regular city council meeting.

Ordinance 90-27 was introduced by Councilman Nelson and sponsored by Councilwoman Wall to allow professional offices in an established Residential District on property which is adjacent to Regional Business Zones. Councilwoman Wall made the motion to pass Ordinance 90-27 on first reading, seconded by Nelson, with 6 yes votes and 1 no vote (Vranish). Ordinance 90-27 was another controversial issue that would come up for second reading during the first city council meeting in January, 1991.

December 15th was a cold but clear day when Evanston's 50-year time capsule was filled with sealed letters, printed comments and illustrations, news articles, records of interest, artifacts and many other items (personal and professional), all with some significance. This was the final project in celebrating the Wyoming Centennial, and Ann Bell, Chairperson of Evanston's Centennial Committee, began working early in the day to make sure that all of the mementos were wrapped properly, sprayed with sealant and placed in plastic bags and named properly. She filled five boxes, along with a number of name rolls of contributors.

City Engineer Brian Honey packed the first box from the Joss House and placed it on the table, ready to go into the capsule. He and other city employees designed and built the capsule.

A fairly large crowd was on hand to witness the dedication of the time capsule and the placing of all items put into it. But before anything was placed in the capsule, some of the committee members climbed into the capsule to have a picture taken: Ann Bell, Kathy Ball, Sandy Ottley and Eileen Downs-Jacobs. It was quite a sight seeing those four ladies down in that capsule. I jokingly said, *Okay, seal it up.* Everyone seemed to get a big laugh out of it, as the ladies hurriedly climbed out.

Ann Bell spoke a few words during the ceremony, and commented on the "boxes of love" which would be passed on to future generations. She also reminded the folks of the hay ride at 6:00 p.m. that evening.

Following Ann's comments I welcomed everyone there and said, *Today we are placing items, records, other information and messages in this capsule for our descendants. This is our way of leaving to our children and their children the truth of what went on today. This is our way of making it more personal. We want our children to be proud of their heritage. We know that in spite of everything, we have worked very hard in trying to make the world a better place to live.*

On November 15, 1990 the Evanston City Council enacted Ordinance 90-22, officially declaring this time capsule to be sealed and buried in 1990 and not to be removed or opened prior to July 10, 2040, Wyoming's 150th Year of Statehood, Wyoming's Sesquicentennial, I continued.

I also said that a lot of young people present today would be on hand at that time and it would be up to them to see that this time capsule is unsealed and that all the items within the capsule get to the right people and families so that this capsule would give meaning to another Lasting Legacy of the Wyoming Centennial. I then thanked them again for being in attendance and wished them all a very joyous and happy Christmas holiday.

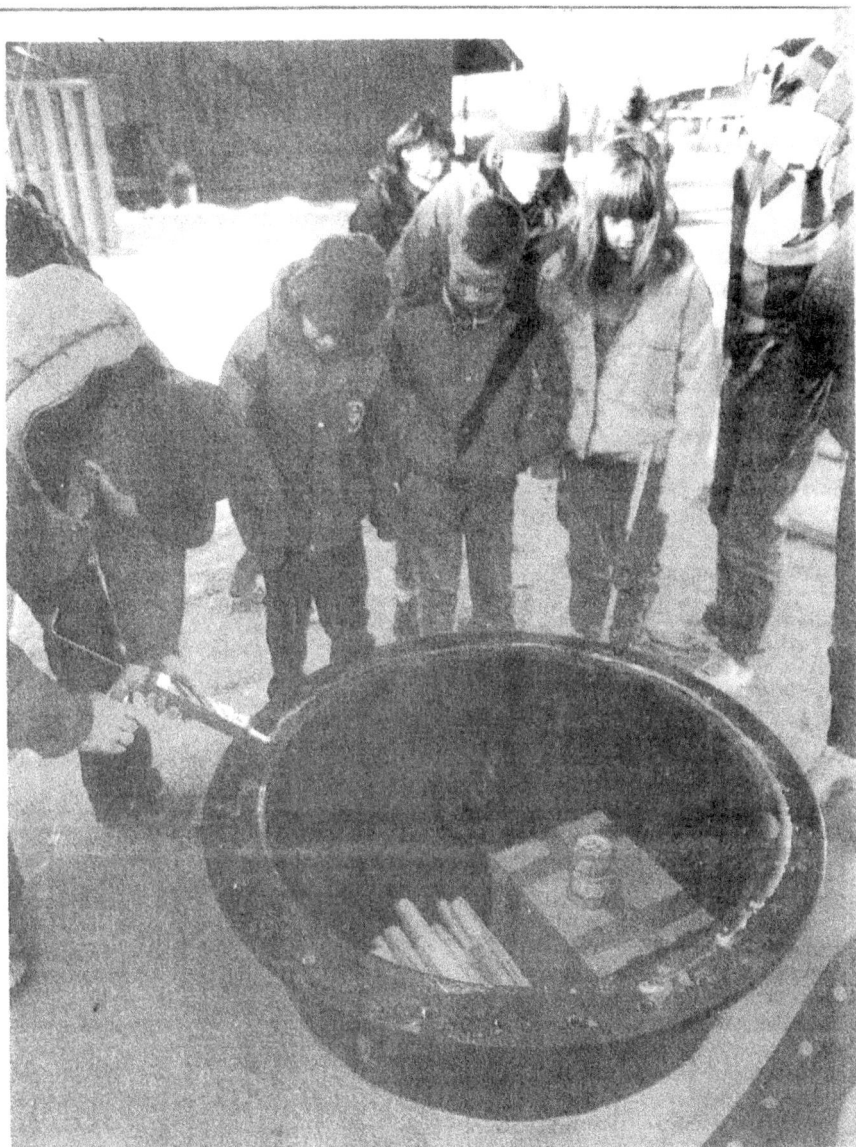

Storing memories

Young people watched closely as Evanston's time capsule was sealed Saturday in Depot Square. Many of them will be alive when the capsule is opened in 50 years. For more on the time capsule ceremony, see page three.

Uinta County Herald, December 18, 1990.

I wrote a long sealed letter, placed in the capsule, addressed to whomever is Mayor of Evanston at the time of the opening of the capsule in 2040. I hope that when he or she receives it, they share it with the public.

Also, a complete list of employee names and their positions in the city was added to the many other items that the city council members and I had placed in the capsule.

Following the ceremony, City Engineer Honey and the city crews sealed the capsule. Honey said a concrete slab with legs, "much like a coffee table," would be placed over the capsule. This slab would contain the city seal and a bronze plaque with instructions for opening the capsule.

The sealing of the capsule was the end of a very productive and busy year for Evanston, and the community and everyone appeared to be ready for the holiday season.

But Evanston was faced with two tragic, fatal accidents that happened just before the Christmas season. The first was a severe traffic accident that happened on Tuesday, December 18th about 13 miles southwest of Evanston on Interstate 80, involving two semi-tractor/trailers and a Greyhound bus. There were seven fatalities and more than 40 injuries. The main cause was poor weather, but there were other factors. Officials did report that there were slick roads and poor visibility, but the first semi-tractor lost control of his vehicle when he attempted to avoid a car that was out of control.

No one from the Evanston area was involved in the wreck, but once again, the folks of Evanston rallied to assist and help make sure that those injured got to the Evanston Regional Hospital and the National Guard Armory, where they received additional medical care and rest. The folks of Evanston also made sure that those uninjured or with minor injuries had a place to rest and that they received proper help.

Denice Wheeler, an Evanston activist, and Kenneth Skalitzky of the Uinta County Division of Public Assistance and Social Services, helped coordinate many of the volunteer activities.

The second tragic accident was also on Tuesday, December 18th. An airplane crashed near Medicine Butte, approximately 10 miles northeast of Evanston, killing a 33-year-old Evanston man, Joel Personne. Personne had been living in Evanston for only about a month and wasn't very well known. He was originally from Grand Junction, Colorado where his body was returned for burial.

According to reports Personne was piloting a Navajo twin-engine cargo plane owned by Alpine Aviation of Provo, Utah, which had been contracted to deliver items for United Parcel Service (UPS).

ACCIDENT SCENE — The eastbound lane of Interstate 80 was littered with processed meat, the contents of one of the semi trucks, following Tuesday's accident. The Greyhound bus is on its side in the background. The accident closed the interstate for several hours.

Uinta County Herald, December 21, 1990.

The cause of the crash, from reports, was apparently strong cross-winds and a snowstorm, but according to Uinta County Sheriff Lou Napoli, it would take several months for investigators to examine the evidence and determine the cause of the crash.

Several days after the accidents I wrote Letters to the Editor to the *Uinta County Herald* and *The Uinta County Pioneer* newspapers. I stated in the letter, *"We all agree that there is no good time for an accident, but when one happens, it's nice to know that a community like Evanston can pull together and organize so quickly to take care of the needs."*

The letter continued, *"Therefore, I would personally like to thank you all for whatever part you may have taken. I have had several phone calls, and many individuals, some who came to our community because of the accidents, tell me what a great community response we had to help those in need. As mayor, it is very heartwarming to hear that about your community.*

Thank you, Evanston, for your warmth, love and kindness, and God bless each of you, hope you all had a good Christmas and will have a safe and prosperous New Year," my letter concluded.

At this time we were all waiting on the completion of Evanston's new Comprehensive Plan. It was in the process of being revised to bring it up to date to meet present problems and concerns. The planning department and commission were both working very hard in trying to complete the plan and have it ready for the city council's approval, with changes if necessary, in a few weeks, and to have it ready to present to the public for their comments and concerns prior to passing it by ordinance.

Evanston's new Comprehensive Plan would be one of the big controversial issues of 1991, but hopefully the city council would adjust the plan where needed, if needed, and successfully create a plan that would not only be fair, but also would be a lot of help in upgrading the present economy.

Through the month of December, the city council and I had received several letters from various businesses and from some local attorneys commenting on the Comprehensive Plan. Some stated in their letters that it was very essential for the city to have a sound and good zoning plan, while some were strictly against any changes in the "outdated" comprehensive plan now in place.

In the month of December, 1990 I received a letter from the Commission on the Bicentennial of the United States Constitution, signed by Jerry W. Browning, Director of Government Affairs. The letter read:

> *Dear Mayor:*
>
> *December 15, 1991 marks the 200th Anniversary of the states' ratification of the Bill of Rights. Throughout 1991, the Commission will be promoting programs and activities commemorating our system of ordered liberties under the Constitution.*
>
> *We have recently published the Commission's 1991 calendar, "The Bill of Rights and Beyond." A copy is being forwarded to you under separate cover. Much work from many individuals went into the creation of this publication, which we hope will prove to be the best in our series of Bicentennial Calendars. Copies have been distributed, courtesy of the United Parcel Service, to the nation's elementary and secondary schools. Copies are also being sent to public, college, and law school libraries.*
>
> *We look forward to your continuing support of the Bicentennial during the final years of commemoration.*
>
> *With all good wishes for the Holidays and the New Year,*
>
> *Yours Sincerely,*
> *Jerry W. Browning*

The Bicentennial of the United States Constitution actually started in 1990, but it continued through 1991. The City of Evanston had already promoted some programs in 1990 celebrating the Bicentennial, and we planned to do the same in 1991.

The Commission was made up of dozens of well-known members of Congress and others. The Chairman of the Commission was the Honorable Warren E. Burger, and included one of our own well-known Wyoming citizens, Lynne V. Cheney, wife of our former Congressman and future Vice President.

We would be having periodic events throughout the year of 1991 for the Bicentennial Bill of Rights. So it looked like the coming year would be another very busy year with many city activities, and all the ordinances and resolutions that would be added to the already-busy agendas of the city council.

Also during the year of 1990, Urban Renewal Director Jim Davis organized a group called The Old-Timers Club of Evanston, aka "The Old-Farts Club." This was a group of Evanston senior citizens that would meet regularly in the conference room of City Hall to discuss and reminisce about the history of Evanston and area, and their experiences living in Evanston for many years.

The group that I remember included Rudger and Thelma Davis, Elmer Danks, Lois Michelstetter, Althena Dallas, Jimmy "Scotty" Anderson, Darla Peterson, Scott Taggart, Archie Willmore, Pat Alexander, Mary Emerson, Marie Hicks and my wife Sandy. I'm sure there were others as time went on, because this group was active for years to come, but I cannot recall all of them.

But the group supplied the City of Evanston and the Urban Renewal Agency with a lot of history of the area. The old-timers who were involved had a lot of fun at their meetings, and the program benefited Evanston by acknowledging senior citizens and, in some cases, motivating them to get involved in other Evanston projects such as the Historic Walking Tour and generating interest in several historic buildings. It was a terrific program and Jim Davis deserves a lot of credit getting it started. I just wish I could remember all those involved.

1990 was a very busy year, but it turned out to be a big success; it was economically progressive, and a year of tremendous volunteerism. It was another year that I would never forget. As the saying goes, *"Great works are performed not only by strength, but by self-perseverance."* And the past year showed just that.

CHAPTER 25

1991....On January 3rd, I called our first city council meeting of the year to order at 7:00 p.m. and welcomed everyone in attendance. Following the pending business of the approval and acceptance of the previous minutes, the revenue and expenditure report, and the payment of all outstanding bills, I gave my State of the City address as follows:

First I would like to thank the people of Evanston for making it possible for me to serve as mayor the past four years and the opportunity to serve you again the next four years.

As I look back through the past years, the City of Evanston has come a long way in improving itself. Four years ago things were looking pretty darn grim and pretty bleak. However, because of close communications, public participation, council and staff cooperation and the ability to plan and dream together, you, as a community have successfully turned things around.

Because of the Wyoming Centennial this past year of 1990, Evanston has probably had one of the busiest years ever in the various community programs and projects. Some of these programs will be ongoing and some will be just a remembrance. But nevertheless, hopefully we can continue to maintain a busy schedule throughout the coming years. This can only benefit our economy.

At this time I would like to acknowledge and thank all of you who have taken part: the city council, the city staff, all of you that served on city boards, commissions and committees, plus the Evanston Chamber of Commerce. I want to thank those officials from Evanston School District No. 1, Uinta County and from the State of Wyoming. Because of close communications and the willingness to understand and listen, we have had a very good relationship with all governmental entities and organizations.

However, we are far from completing some of our goals and projects. We must continue to push on if we expect to maintain the high quality of life in Evanston as we have worked so hard for these past four years. The high quality of life presently in Evanston is something that we can all be proud of and I'm sure that you all are.

That's what it's all about; but to maintain that level of quality we must continue to promote and encourage those projects that we have in the past. These have been healthy and wholesome family-oriented programs. We must continue to build and update our services to meet requirements set by state and federal agencies, and to meet the demands of the public. We must continue to serve the people of Evanston as best we can. We must maintain a good relationship among each other and try to keep the morale and the attitude of the citizens high. We must continue to move forward.

Sure, we've made some mistakes and continuously get reminded of them, but we make them only because we do things and because we are so active. If you don't do anything you're not going to make mistakes, but what mistakes we've made we will learn from.

I later mentioned to the city council, *What isn't tried sure as hell won't work, and any act of increasing growth, including political growth, is the result of risk-taking.*

I continued with my State of the City Address:

What is happening in the Middle East can have a terrific impact on Evanston. Therefore, we can't afford to let up at all. Things could get much worse, but hopefully they don't and our loved ones in the military come home safely. At the present we have Aaron Wall, son of City Councilwoman Wall in the Navy; Eric Vranish, son of Councilman Clarence Vranish in the Army; and Chet Alexander, a member of the Evanston Police Department on leave to serve in the Army. Only hope that they all stay safe.

I don't have to go into priorities or the importance of what's ahead of us. You, members of the council and staff, know what that is. The most important aspect is for the council to work together as a body, and be outspoken, honest, and up-front with me and each other as we plan and build, and as your mayor I promise, as in the past, to continue to do my best to communicate with you. I have and will always be honest and truthful with you, and I would expect no less from any one of you.

I will always welcome those with new and big ideas. I will listen to you and consider what you have to say. After all, America was created and built by those who had the big dreams and unbelievable visions.

Hard work, cheerful persistence and willingness to continue with old ideas and to try new ideas are the trademark of successful citizenship.

I believe we need to keep the public involved as we have in the past. We must work together as a team: the Council, the Staff, and the Public. And as your mayor the next four years, I will continue, with your help, to build this community. I will continue to work towards improving the economy as long as what we do helps maintain that high quality of life we all expect to maintain.

I am looking forward to the next four years. I am looking forward towards a good relationship with you all.

Thank you again and God be with us all...

According to the minutes everyone applauded as I finished my State of the City address.

I also gave special thanks to David Bills for donating his time videotaping the city council meetings the past year, and making sure they were made available to the public through the local television station.

Each council member echoed the sentiment to be honest, open and up-front with each other.

Outgoing Councilman Lunsford stated: "The city government is operating very well, and I feel I can move on to my other responsibilities."

According to him, he decided to run in 1986 because he was dissatisfied with the large city administration of the Martin years. "I felt we were top-heavy," he said.

Although being involved with the projects that have been going on has been very rewarding, he said, being a member of the council does have its drawbacks.

"It takes a lot of time," he said. "I don't think the average citizen has any idea how much time the mayor and council spend. If they put in the time, they should receive the compensation," he added.

I have always felt that Jon Lunsford has been a good and dedicated member of the city council and told him as much. We all thanked him for his service to the city and expressed our appreciation for his participation and dedicated leadership.

And then I, on behalf of the council and myself, presented him with a plaque showing our appreciation, and gave a special thanks for the dedication and service he had given to the City of Evanston as a member of the council for eight years.

At this time Councilman Will Davis called for a few moments of prayerful meditation on behalf of those members from Evanston who are now serving in the armed forces. Following the silent prayer the Oath of Office was administered by City Clerk Don Welling to the newly elected officers: Mayor Dennis Ottley, and City Councilmembers Craig Nelson, Julie Lehman, and Will Davis.

Julie Lehman took her place as a new member of the council in place of outgoing council member Jon Lunsford.

Everyone welcomed Julie back on the council. She had previously served one term in the past, so it wasn't a new venture for her. This would be her second go-around, and would join holdovers Clarence Vranish, Jerry Wall, and Tom Hutchinson, and those re-elected, Will Davis and Craig Nelson.

Next I made my appointments to the following departments: Dennis Harvey, Chief of Police; Paul Knopf, Community Development Director (City Planner); Don U. Welling, City Clerk and Assistant City Treasurer; Steve Widmer, City Treasurer and Assistant City Clerk; Brian Honey, City Engineer; Allen Kennedy, Supervisor of Operations; Dennis Boal, City Attorney; Rick Lavery, Assistant City Attorney; and John Phillips, City Court Judge.

Councilman Vranish made the motion to confirm the above appointments, seconded by Nelson, with all voting in favor.

I then read a letter of resignation from Police Officer Frank Maioran. Motion to accept his resignation was made by Councilman Hutchinson, seconded by Wall, with all voting in favor. We all thanked Maioran for his dedicated service to the community and wished him well in the future.

I appointed the following police officers: Mitchell Allmaras, James R. Dean, Michael L. Johnson, Michael Putman, David Furlong, Jake Williams, Paul Dean, Don Shillcox, Colleen Millburg, Bernard Jones, Russell Dean, Steve Johnson, Eric Dunning, Ralph

Pierce, David Baldwin, Brad Durrant, Ray Varner, Doug Matthews, Victor Matoon, Mike Jaimez, and Chet Alexander.

By ordinance all police officers must be reappointed by the mayor following every mayoral election year. Councilman Nelson made the motion to confirm the appointments of the police officers, seconded by Lehman, with all voting in favor.

Councilman Davis made a motion to accept the Julie Lehman's letter of resignation from the Evanston Urban Renewal Agency, seconded by Nelson, with all voting in favor.

Other appointments included David Bills, Gary Bolger, Tracy Smith and Kendra West to the Evanston Planning and Zoning Commission. Motion was made by Councilwoman Wall to confirm these appointments, seconded by Vranish, with all voting in favor.

I then appointed the following to be on the Police Commission: myself as Police Commissioner, and Councilmen Clarence Vranish and Craig Nelson to serve with me. Motion was made to confirm the appointments and seconded, with all voting in favor.

As required, I appointed a new board to handle the funds received from the new lodging tax. The board would be considered as the Lodging Tax Board. Appointed to serve on the board were Denice Wheeler, Diane Hodges, Bill Alexander, Ranold Phillips, Diane Mills, Jeff Shaffer, and me. Councilman Nelson made the motion to confirm these appointments, seconded by Hutchinson, with all voting in favor.

I stated that terms of the Lodging Tax Board appointments would be determined at a later date.

I appointed the following to the Beautification Committee for an indefinite period of time: Ann Curtis, Janice Nelson, Dianne Hodges, Doug Williams, and Joe Adams. Councilman Davis made a motion to confirm these appointments, seconded by Nelson, with all voting in favor. The Beautification Committee acts under the authority of the Evanston Urban Renewal Agency.

The Liquor Dealers Association, represented by Bill Alexander, requested the following four days to have extended opening hours as set by state law: Sunday, May 26, 1991; Thursday, July 4, 1991;

Sunday, September 1, 1991; and Tuesday, December 31, 1991. Councilwoman Wall made the motion to approve the requested dates of extended hours, seconded by Nelson. The vote was unanimously in favor.

Boy Scout Rusty Conway was in attendance to describe the results of his Eagle Scout project, a blood drive. He reported that over 70 people appeared at the Evanston Fire Hall to donate blood. Sixteen of those people were deferred. He then thanked the many individuals and groups who cooperated with him to promote the drive. It was explained that the last time a project of this type occurred, only eight people showed up. The council and I congratulated him on his successful project and his achievement in receiving his Eagle Scouts badge, and thanked him for his service to the community.

Also during the meeting, Evanston's First Lady Sandy Ottley, Parade Chairperson, requested that the city council approve two parade routes for the Chinese New Year celebration on January 18th and 19th. After Sandy had explained the designated routes and the purpose of the parades, Councilman Davis made the motion to approve both parades and the designated routes, seconded by Vranish, with all voting in favor.

Ordinance 90-27 came up for second reading, amending the zoning ordinance to conditionally allow professional offices in established residential districts on property which is adjacent to regional business zones. Councilman Nelson made the motion to pass Ordinance 90-27 on second reading, seconded by Hutchinson. After a short discussion and comments from Bonnie Pendleton, Debra Smith and Lance Voss, I called for the vote. The results were 5 yes votes, 2 no votes (Vranish and Davis); the motion passed. Ordinance 90-27 would come up for third and final reading during the next city council meeting on January 17th.

During the meeting of January 17th, after the usual business, I appointed Councilman Craig Nelson to the Airport Joint Powers Board to replace former Councilman Lunsford. Motion made by Councilman Vranish to confirm the appointment, seconded by Wall, with all voting in favor.

I then appointed Steve Widmer to the Personnel Board in place of our former Administrative Assistant Steve Snyder, and appointed Jake Williams to replace former Councilman Lunsford also on the Personnel Board. Motion was made by Councilman Nelson to confirm the two appointments, seconded by Davis, with all voting in favor.

I told the city council that I would not be replacing the position of Administrative Assistant at this time. I said, *Steve Snyder was a lot of help to me, but I will not be replacing the position during this term of mayor.* Steve had been the Administrative Assistant for twelve years, covering three terms: two terms under me and one term under Mayor Gene Martin.

I continued: *I hired him during the days of the oil and gas boom, a time when he was badly needed, plus he was a tremendous amount of help to me during the bust period of my previous terms. However, I will, with your assistance as a council board—a board that I feel is very dedicated and willing to serve your community to the best of your ability—although we may not always agree, we will and we must work together to achieve our goals in continuing to improve Evanston's economy. Plus we have a great staff that knows what they are doing and will be a great help. No, we do not need to replace the position of Administrative Assistant,* I concluded.

The next item of business was the election of the President of the Council. I turned the meeting over to the present President of the Council, Tom Hutchinson, to conduct the election.

Hutchinson gave a short speech stating that he had been very pleased with his experience as council president and appreciated the opportunity that the city council had given him. He then called for nominations and stated that the voting would be done by secret ballot, and assigned City Clerk Don Welling to count the votes.

Councilman Hutchinson nominated Will Davis, and Councilwoman Wall nominated Clarence Vranish. After a few minutes Councilman Nelson made a motion that nominations cease, seconded by Lehman. With a unanimous vote, nominations ceased and the ballots were turned over to Welling for the count.

Will Davis had 3 votes, and Clarence Vranish had 4 votes. Councilman Vranish was elected to the position of President of the Council, and would take the place of mayor in my absence.

As the first item of unfinished business, Councilman Davis made a motion to remove Ordinance 90-10, which had been tabled twice, from the table for discussion on third and final reading, seconded by Vranish. Ordinance 90-10 authorized a zone change from Low-Density Residential zone to Regional Business Development as requested by The Store House, M.S. Properties, Curtis W. Ellingford and Geraldine Ellingford.

This ordinance would allow commercial businesses on Seventh Street between Main Street and Center Street across the street from the new Uinta County Library. These businesses were already in place and had been grandfathered in. The only thing the council was trying to do was pass an ordinance to make the zone conform to the present situation. Some folks called this spot zoning, but it didn't really fit the definition of spot zoning because the property being zoned was adjacent to other commercial zones, and the businesses were all active.

Therefore, after another lengthy discussion I called for the vote. The motion passed by a majority with 6 yes votes and 1 no vote (Hutchinson), motion passed by a majority.

Another very controversial ordinance came up for third and final reading. Ordinance 90-27, the ordinance allowing professional offices in an Established Residential District zone that is adjacent to Regional Business zones, would only be allowed under a Conditional Use Permit approved by the Planning and Zoning Commission. Motion was made by Councilman Hutchinson to pass Ordinance 90-27 on third and final reading, seconded by Wall. After another long and lengthy discussion the vote was called for with 5 yes votes, 2 no votes (Davis and Vranish), and the motion passed by a majority.

Under new business, three new ordinances pertaining to the Grass Valley Subdivision came up. Ordinance 91-1, to vacate the Grass Valley Subdivision, was introduced and sponsored by Councilman Vranish. Motion was made by Councilwoman Lehman to pass on first reading, seconded by Davis. Vote was unanimously in favor.

Ordinance 91-2, to vacate a portion of the Grass Valley IV Mobile Home Court, was also introduced and sponsored by Councilman

Vranish. Councilman Davis made a motion to pass Ordinance 91-2 on first reading, seconded by Nelson, with all voting in favor.

Ordinance 91-3, to approve the final plat of the Grass Valley Addition to the City of Evanston, was again introduced and sponsored by Councilman Vranish. This was an amendment to extend the Grass Valley Subdivision by adding part of the Grass Valley Mobile Home Court and was actually meant to clean up a mess started by the Grass Valley owners, but after they realized what we were trying to do, everything turned out for the best. Councilman Davis made the motion to pass Ordinance 91-3 on first reading, seconded by Lehman, and passed unanimously with 6 votes. Ordinances 91-1, 91-2, and 91-3 were all passed and approved by unanimous votes of the council and mayor in the next two meetings.

Councilwoman Wall made a motion to allow a one-day holiday for city employees on a one-time basis on Monday, January 21st to observe Martin Luther King Equality Day, seconded by Lehman, with all voting in favor.

This was a one-time holiday only for this year of 1991. The employees would have to choose between Martin Luther King Day and Columbus Day, but would not be allowed to have both, unless the Employee's Manual was changed, because the manual only allowed 11 holidays to full-time employees at that time. Some employees wanted to give up Columbus Day as a holiday and include Martin Luther King Day in place of it, but most employees preferred to have Columbus Day off because it came up in the fall during the deer and elk hunting season.

However, in months to come the manual was amended to give full-time employees 12 holidays, which always included the Friday after Thanksgiving and either the day just before Christmas or the day after, depending on which day of the week Christmas fell on. Martin Luther King Day was the 12th day which was added to the manual. Therefore, after the manual was amended, employees were allowed both days (Columbus Day and Martin Luther King Day) as a holiday.

Chinese New Year, the Year of the Ram came, with a *Gung Hay Fat Choy* (Happy New Year in Chinese) to everyone from

Chairperson Jerry Wall and Committee. She reported that the annual event was once again a big success. The event started off on Friday evening, January 18th, with the Torch Parade starting at the Uinta County Library and ending at the Joss House at Depot Square. This was followed by the Ball Drop, which was caught by Ken Skalitzky, so he would be the Keeper of the Keys until next year. Other activities were also performed at the Joss House.

The celebration ended on Saturday, January 19th with a food festival at the Beeman-Cashin Building, followed by the Chinese parade. The parade included the Chinese Dragon constructed by Cheryl Lowham's (Knopf) Davis Middle School class and the Chinese Lion Dancers from Salt Lake City, as well as many other entries pertaining to the Chinese heritage. Fireworks donated by Kilburn Porter were fired off during the Ball Drop and other events throughout the program.

Last July, I received a letter from the Chinese Historical Society of America of San Francisco inviting Sandy and me, and other members of the Evanston Chinese New Year Celebration of 1990, to their Annual Chinese Celebration Dinner in San Francisco. I selected Ann Bell, Chairperson of the Evanston Centennial Celebration Committee; Eileen Down-Jacobs, who worked diligently on the new Joss House; Cheryl Lowham; Jerry Wall, Evanston City Councilwoman who was active in all the events of the year; and Jake Jacobs, husband to Eileen had also accompanied the group.

The invitation was in reciprocation for Evanston's invitation of the several members of the society that were present for Evanston's Chinese New Year Celebration in 1990.

Eileen Downs-Jacobs, one of the committee members who attended the San Francisco Annual Chinese Dinner, brought back home a number of Chinese artifacts that she displayed in the new Joss House during Evanston's 1991 Chinese New Year Celebration.

Traditions, rules of etiquette accompany Chinese New Year

The Chinese heritage is rich with tradition and folklore, and several rules of etiquette apply for decorating and participating in the truly authentic Chinese tradition.

—Clean your house thoroughly. Although the project may be started several weeks in advance, wash the front door step, as well as the back door step on the day before New Year's Day.

—Remove all rubbish from the household before New Year's Day, but not on New Year's Day.

—Bring out and hang all ancestral portraits, even if only done once a year.

—Have an abundance of candies, nuts, sweetmeats, and mandarin oranges to display and consume in the festive days ahead.

—Have the choicest sharks' fins, bird's nest, dried fish, Chinese sausage, pressed duck, dried oysters and other delicacies to savor on the first day of the Chinese New Year.

—Bathe in the fragrance of steeped Chinese grapefruit leaves before New Year's Day. If grapefruit leaves are unavailable, bubble bath will do.

—Don't have any old dried plants around. Decorate with fresh blossoming plants — preferably red or pink. Peony stands for good fortune, chrysanthemum for longevity.

—Be pleasant and congenial, wishing all adults good luck; for the children, give them red paper envelopes, containing money and a wish for good fortune.

—Most activities are acceptable. If you follow all the rules, you are certain to have a successful New Year.

FENDING OFF THE DRAGON — Following Chinese tradition, the dragon will be warded away from the Joss House by a group of people following Saturday's parade. If the dragon is allowed into the building, it could mean bad luck during the year.

Uinta County Herald, January 15, 1990.

CHINESE COLLECTION — Eileen Jacobs, one of the organizers of Evanston's Chinese New Year celebration, brought home a number of items from a visit to San Francisco.

The schedule for Evanston's Chinese New Year celebration:
Torchlight parade...
Tonight, 6 p.m.
Library to Joss House
Ball drop...
Tonight, 6:15 p.m.
Joss House
Snow sculpting...
Tomorrow, 11 a.m.-3 p.m.
Depot Square
Food festival...
Tomorrow, 11 a.m.-4 p.m.
Beeman-Cashin Building
Parade...
Tomorrow, noon
Library to Joss House

Uinta County Herald, January 18, 1991.

Fu

福

Good Fortune

Lu

祿

Honor

Hsi

喜

Happiness

Shou

壽

Long Life

FROM THE CITY OF EVANSTON

Although the City of Evanston was already recycling up to a point, there was still room to improve the program, possibly going county-wide. Meetings were held with city and county officials both in attendance to discuss how to come up with ways to help save on the county landfills. The Evanston landfill, now operated by the county, was filling up fast along with the Bridger Valley landfill. Recycling is a major issue for the entire country, and Evanston and Uinta County are no exceptions.

During one meeting I mentioned that solid waste management would be a top priority for the City of Evanston in next few years. "We hope to do the one-man, one-truck system by July 1, 1991," I told them. "Councilman Will Davis will be put in charge of that portion of the city's business," I added.

The *Uinta County Herald* of January 15th reported, *According to* The Economist *magazine, "America has for a long time taken the cheapest option in waste disposal: 90 percent of its rubbish is simply dumped in landfill sites and buried. But landfill sites are filling up; a third have closed since 1980."*

The *Herald's* article continued: *According to Sanitation Director Marvin Munoz, information is being gathered on the pros and cons of the city purchasing one-man garbage trucks.*

City employees at the present time are working on proposals to present to the city council members which could mean the city will begin a recycling program in earnest.

The city already has at least one recycling project going. There are aluminum can drops at approximately seven locations in the city. Profits from some of the bins have been dedicated to local charities. Also being looked at is a community compost heap where residents could deposit lawn clippings, leaves and limbs. These items would be turned and circulated. The results would be used for urban forests by the citizens and the city. Munoz stated that 15 to 20 percent of the total municipal waste is organic material which could be reused and save landfill space, the article continued.

Also during the month of January, the Evanston Chamber of Commerce presented a number of awards. I was presented the Chamber of Commerce's Citizenship Award, on behalf of the City of

Evanston, for the citizens' response to the Greyhound Bus accident. The plaque was presented by John Holderegger and would be displayed at City Hall for all to see.

Awards were given to Tim and Lisa Burridge for Outstanding Service to People With Disabilities, also presented by John Holderegger. And Patsy Madia presented the Pat on the Back award to Lois Michelstetter for her work with the Community Concert and other community projects.

The issue of a Convention Center came up after the Cowboy Casino (formerly Billy's) announced they were selling out. The idea was for the City of Evanston to look into the possibility of purchasing the property for a new center, for indoor Evanston events.

During the February 7th regular city council meeting, because of a lot of local interest in the center, I appointed a committee to look into the feasibility and the need for a proposed Convention Center. Appointed to the committee were: City Councilmembers Will Davis and Julie Lehman; and Citizens Pat Mulhall, Elaine Michalis, John Knopf, Jeff Jewett, Gene Martin, Herb Weston, Gary Ellingford, Judy Bennett, Helen Burns, Sandy Ottley, Ann Curtis and Delia Hansen.

Councilman Nelson made a motion to confirm the appointments, seconded by Vranish, with all voting in favor.

Staff members Paul Knopf and Jim Davis were assigned to work closely with the new committee and give them all the assistance they needed.

I made the appointment of two new police officers, Jon Kirby and Allen Strahl, introduced by Lt. Mitch Allmaras. Motion was made by Councilwoman Lehman to confirm the appointments, seconded by Vranish, with all voting in favor.

In other action at the February 7th meeting, Dennis Farley, Uinta County Planner, made a presentation concerning a matching grant for $20,000 that he successfully in obtained from the Wyoming State Game and Fish Department, to be used on the Bear Project for river bank stabilization. He reported that this was a 50-50 matching grant and the county and city could use a combination of money and in-kind service for their share of the match.

Mr. Farley was thanked for his work and was told that the City of Evanston appreciated the interest that Uinta County had in the BEAR Project.

Resolution 91-3 was introduced by Councilman Nelson to authorize the execution of a contract with the Evanston Chamber of Commerce to provide promotional services.

This resolution provided the Chamber of Commerce with funds not only for their own sponsored programs, but also to funnel funds through the Chamber to assist other non-profit organizations with projects that the city had no contract with. These funds would be based on the amount of funds budgeted each year to the Chamber of Commerce.

After a study was made concerning the new one-man, one-truck solid waste pickup system, Councilman Davis made a motion to allow the Public Works Department to proceed with a bid package for the new one-man garbage trucks and the new garbage containers, seconded by Hutchinson, with all voting in favor.

Because of the request from several property owners in the Uinta Meadows Subdivision to cover the City Ditch (Haw Patch), Councilwoman Lehman made a motion to direct the Engineering Department to prepare a grant application to the Wyoming State Farm Loan Board for funding to cover the ditch, seconded by Councilwoman Wall, but the motion failed by a unanimous vote.

There were several reasons why the ditch was never covered and there never has been any problem with the ditch since the study and investigation determined that the homes in the area were getting water in their basements from ground water runoff from rain storms, and so on, and not because of seepage from the ditch.

During the meeting Community Development Director Paul Knopf gave his report on the recent census that Evanston had disputed. He reported that the official census figures for Evanston were 10,903, or 58% of the county population.

Councilman Hutchinson made a motion to direct the Public Works and Police Department to conduct a traffic survey on County Road and consider added signage and the raising the speed limit from 20 mph to 30 mph, seconded by Wall, with all voting in favor. With no other business to come before the council I called for a work session on March 6th at 5:00 p.m. and then adjourned the meeting of February 7th at 9:10 p.m.

During the second meeting of the month on February 21st, Ordinance 91-4 came up on third and final reading. This ordinance was officially introduced and sponsored a few meetings ago, and passing by a unanimous vote on first and second readings, was now up for the final reading. The ordinance was to once again change the days of the Evanston City Council meetings. The ordinance changed the meeting days from the first and third Thursdays of the month to the second and fourth Wednesdays of each month.

Motion was made by Councilman Nelson, seconded by Lehman, with all voting in favor.

There were City of Evanston employees who were members of the National Guard or in the Reserves, and were subject to being called for active service in the Gulf War, better known as Desert Storm.

The subject came up to allow a portion of their city employment pay to continue while they were serving in active duty for the military. There was a lengthy discussion, with some of those subject to being called in attendance. During the discussion, as a former veteran of the Korean War, I requested that City Attorney Dennis Boal draw up a resolution to take care of this matter.

During this meeting of February 21st, City Attorney Boal had Resolution 91-5 ready for introduction. Introduced by Councilman Clarence Vranish, the resolution read in part:

Section 1: *Section 3-8 (e) of the Personnel Policy Manual of the City of Evanston, Wyoming, is hereby enacted to read as follows:*

Section 3-8 (e). *The City shall pay to any city employee who has been called to active military duty by the National Guard or other reserve military service on hundred percent (100%) of the difference between the employee's gross salary paid by the city and the gross salary paid by the military, for a period of ninety (90) days from the date of activation, provided the city shall not pay any sum to the employee's deferred compensation account pursuant to this provision.*

Section 2: This policy shall take effect immediately upon the passage of this Resolution by the governing body of the City of Evanston, Wyoming, and shall apply to all city employees affected during the 1990-1991 fiscal year and continuing thereafter until the policy is modified or terminated.

Councilwoman Wall made a motion to adopt Resolution 91-5, seconded by Nelson. But Councilman Vranish made a motion to amend the main motion to add in Section 3-8 (e) after the word duty *"for a period exceeding 15 days,"* seconded by Nelson. The motion to amend passed, and the vote on the main motion as amended was passed with all voting in favor.

The speed limit on County Road came up for more discussion after City Engineer Brian Honey gave the report on the Public Works and the Police Department surveys. After discussion Councilman Vranish made a motion to raise the speed limit on County Road to 30 mph, seconded by Wall, but after some more discussion Councilman Nelson made a motion to postpone any action on this motion until the next regular meeting, seconded by Hutchinson, with all voting in favor.

I had spoken against changing the speed limit on County Road because of the pedestrian traffic and the nearby school district, but I would have been in favor of raising it north of Washington Avenue as far as the Highway 89 traffic light.

I also felt that both Nelson and Hutchinson, representing Ward 3, would be against raising the speed limit, but it would come up again during the first meeting in March. When the issue came back on the floor during a March meeting, a petition was presented by Rex Fruits, a resident of County Road, which was signed by a number of folks who lived on County Road, requesting that the speed limit remain at 20 mph.

After a lengthy discussion I called for the vote. The results were 5 votes against raising the speed limit on County Road to 30 mph, and 2 votes in favor (Wall and Vranish). The motion failed.

Thanks for support

Editor's note: The following are letters received by Evanston Mayor Dennis Ottley.

Dear Mayor Ottley:

Thank you so much for the letter, the Evanston pin and the Wyoming flag you sent. I was thrilled with the gifts and overjoyed at the sentiment of love and support for my family and me.

I took the flag to Safwan, Iraq last Saturday on a refugee evacuation mission. I got a picture of me with my Wyoming flag and an American flag there in Iraq with a Scud missile launch site in the background. It was a proud moment for me.

My appreciation to you and the residents of Evanston for the support we felt during Operation Desert Storm. It has been an honor to serve.

Capt. Buckley Condie
APO New York 09762

Dear Mayor Ottley and the City of Evanston:

Thank you very much for the letter of support and the Wyoming mementos. In the military a person gets to meet a wide variety of people from a wide variety of places, so one of the first questions people ask is where are you from. I am always proud to answer that Wyoming is my home state, and being from there almost always lends itself to further questions and discussion about "Big, Wonderful Wyoming."

I am currently serving as a medical platoon leader in an airborne infantry battalion. My unit was not deployed to Desert Storm, but different elements from Alaska were, and we, along with most of the nation, felt a great sense of pride as our military led the way in that multi-national effort.

Thank you all again for the support package. Evanston will always be "home," and here in Alaska we are a long way from home. It's great to hear from you.

"Airborne"
Kennington B. Condie
2LT. Medical Service Corps
Medical Platoon Leader

Show your support

Dear Editor:

In a recent article printed March 12, a reporter called me about my son's homecoming. I told him about the hardships he was enduring, like only being able to take two showers a month (because they are in the desert and there are no public showers). Not that I'd probably ask him to take a bath. My son and all the troops have been through a great ordeal, and I think if he can go without showers, I can surely give him a big hug and kiss him the first time I see him.

My son has been in Saudi Arabia since December and a lot of our sons have been there since Aug. 1. My son has lost a year of his education to serve his country in a foreign land. I don't think a lot of these people in this town know what our sons have been through. None of our sons are home yet! It would be nice if our troops could be recognized for their courage and bravery they so rightly deserve.

Rock Springs showed us overabundant support for our troops, something we haven't received in this town. There are communities all over this great country hanging yellow ribbons, rejoicing for the troops, and planning parades in their honor. As a community and in behalf of the troops, let's honor them in the manner they so rightly deserve. And for the Fourth of July, let's show them a Fourth of July they'll never forget of how proud we all are of our sons and daughters who served in Operation Desert Storm and all wars.

Also, thank you Harrison & Roth for your beautiful display, the mayor for his letters and yellow ribbons, the VFW, Rock Springs, Kemmerer, T-Shirts Galore, Legal Tender and Kemmerer radio station. These are the people and groups that have sponsored us.

Maxine Bye
Mother of U.S. Marine Armando Canales
Evanston

Editor's note: The Herald's story on local families waiting for the return of their relatives serving in the Persian Gulf was in no way intended to make light of the hardships endured by U.S. troops in Operation Desert Storm. In fact, its purpose was to make people aware of the sacrifices made by many service personnel and their families in Uinta County.

Letters to the Editor, *Uinta County Herald*, May, 1991.

Thanks for support

Editor's note: The following letter was received recently by Evanston Mayor Dennis Ottley.

Dear Mayor Ottley:

I received the nice letter and package of Evanston souvenirs from you and the city council. Your thoughtfulness was greatly appreciated. I regard it with great pleasure to be able to call Evanston my home, and to be remembered by the people back home.

I am located with the department of surgery of a hospital at Bad Cannstatt. Bad Cannstatt is realy part of Stuttgardt, the home of Mercedes Benz and Porsche. During WWII the area sustained extensive damage—in fact, there is a fair sized mound out a ways that legend has it was all the rubble of Stuttgardt bulldozed into one big pile and allowed to overgrow. The city is now modern, attractive with many interesting areas to see—and the people very friendly and supportive of our mission.

There are a number of the members of my unit, the 328th General Hospital, located here, but none of the Wyoming people. The European Command took people from units all over the country to fill vacancies created by sending the active duty people to the Persian Gulf. Our mission is to be prepared to treat wounded from Desert Storm. The good news is that we are not busy. Never before has an Army gone into war with the support of such a well trained and experienced medical backup as exists with this operation. I am proud to be a part of it.

I miss home and the people of Evanston. To me this is a small price to pay for the mission at hand. When one is away from home it becomes more apparent just how fortunate we really are and how richly blessed we are with freedom. With this blessing comes responsibility to defend it—fight for it if necessary. I am proud of the way our nation has responded to this threat, and the support of the people back home.

Thank you for your thoughtfulness. Thank you for being home. I really appreciate all the thoughts, prayers and expressions of interest and concern that Marj has received as she goes about her daily tasks. Hopefully this separation will not be prolonged and I shall soon be back home among you.

James A. Morse, M.D.

Home in praise

Dear Editor:
Here is another poem about the war I hope you will print. I hope this poem hits home for the people involved in the war and here in the states. We all have a lot to be thankful for.

Thanks be to God
The lives you did save
By the ending you gave
The prayers we did pray
The war ended today

The thanks we now give
You let most all live
The loved ones we lost
We bury with your cross

World freedom at stake
We did not forsake
You held every hand
As they marched over land

Such strength you gave
So they could not enslave
Our fellow man
In a far-away land

As our forces rang loud
We all stood proud
Our voices we shall raise
As they come home in praise

Michael Wayne Harris

Letters to the Editor, *Uinta County Herald*, May, 1991.

During this meeting Councilwoman Jerry Wall announced that she had been appointed to the National League of Cities' Human Development Steering Committee. Members of the council and I all congratulated her and told her that we knew she would be worthy of the position.

Wall, as Convention Chairman, also gave her report on the upcoming Wyoming Association of Municipalities (W.A.M.) convention to be held in Evanston during the month of June, this year of 1991. In February we received many replies from Uinta County personnel serving in the military during the Desert Storm conflict. These letters thanked the City of Evanston for a program headed by Sandy to send mail and packages to service personnel. The packages included a small Wyoming state flag, City of Evanston lapel pins, state and city maps, and other articles that we felt they could use.

We also received letters from some of the parents of those serving in the military thanking the City of Evanston for remembering their sons and daughters that were serving. It was a great program and Sandy had a great committee assisting her.

I had one letter addressed to me, as mayor, printed in the *Uinta County Herald* on February 18th, from Paul C. LeSarge, U.S. Army, who was expecting to be deployed to the Gulf War shortly. At the end of his letter he said, *"Oh, yeah, I do have one favor if I could please. My mother owns Stuff Shop. It's a store in The Old Post Office. I was wondering if you could just stop in one day and say 'Hi' for you and me? You can't miss her. She is short, blond hair, glasses and the greatest mother in the world! I sure would appreciate this, Mr. O."*

Another letter, dated February 14th, from John A Currie, Chief Warrant Officer-3 of the U.S. Marines said: *"Thank you for the kind letter, maps, flag of Wyoming and pin. It is rewarding to know that so many people back home support us over here. I have several Marines from the Bronx, New York, who didn't know much about Wyoming. The map came in quite handy.*

I know I am one of many from the Evanston area serving in Saudi Arabia but I'm sure all the other service members to whom you sent packets appreciated them as well," Currie's letter continued.

I also received a letter from Mrs. Hera Alexander, Mother of Chet Alexander, a City of Evanston employee. She stated in her letter: *"This is just a quick note to express my thanks and gratitude to you for the nice letter you sent regarding my son, Chet.*

It is good to know that his hometown is supporting him at this particular time in his life. Chet and his family are strong and dedicated people. They understand that our country needs him and they support what he is doing. This helps to make it a little easier to be away from his home for such a long time. Any letters he receives from citizens of Evanston will be greatly appreciated. He looks forward to mail and tries to answer as many letters as possible."

Mrs. Alexander's letter continued: *"On a personal note, I am proud and happy to have a son like Chet. We all miss him and hope he will be home soon.*

"Once again, thank you for taking time out of your busy schedule to recognize and honor Chet. Please bestow my thanks to all of the people in the community."

We received many similar letters, both from those serving in the military and from their parents, thanking the City of Evanston for the packages and the letters that were sent to the military personnel of Evanston and Uinta County that were serving during the Gulf War. I appreciated every one of them and when an answer was called for, I answered them.

We also had letters from Senators Alan Simpson and Malcolm Wallop, and Congressman Craig Thomas, commenting on the Gulf War and mentioning their appreciation for the action and support that the City of Evanston gave our troops that were serving in the military from this area.

The subject of the mayor now receiving $30,000 annual pay came up during the meeting and it was suggested that there should be a job description and set hours that the mayor must be in the office.

During the long discussion, Councilman Tom Hutchinson said he believed the mayor's job needed at least a designated number of work hours. *I'm thinking about the position, I feel we got the cart before the horse when we decided on a full-time mayor,* Hutchinson said.

In the first place, when they voted on the increase of the mayor's and council's salaries, nothing was said about it being a full-time job. It's whatever an elected mayor makes it. With me it has been a full-time job ever since I was elected. $30,000 is not much money for a mayor if the requirements are that he must consider it full-time, especially when there are a dozen positions under the mayor making well over $40,000 a year.

I told the council that as far as I was concerned, although the job does not describe the position as being full-time, it sure in hell has been with me. I told them that I never have the City of Evanston's problems off my mind, and that I probably average 50 to 60 hours a week, including weekends, working for the interest of the City.

"We need to have some kind of guidelines," Hutchinson said.

But Councilman President Clarence Vranish disagreed, saying that other employees have outside employment, and there's nothing saying that the city council members have to put in so many hours.

I spoke up and said, *Whether you make it full time or not is up to the mayor, but if you are going to do the job right it's got to be full time. There are few weeks that I don't get calls 24 hours a day. My telephone number is published, and I am available to talk to anyone,* I said.

I mentioned that I have less support and assistance now that our former Administrative Assistant Steve Snyder had left, and I have no plans to replace him. He was being paid a salary of well over $40,000 a year.

Everything takes more time, more problems, I said. *But, I have a good staff and don't plan on increasing it. There is no way that I can work regular hours and be required to be in my office all that time. Sometimes I need to be out with public works and other departments if I expect to do a good job and keep the city operating as it should,* I continued.

The discussion went on for quite some time and one of the council members requested the city attorney to read the state statute concerning the duties of the mayor. He read the follow:

Wyoming law charges the mayor of cities with the supervision of all officers and affairs of the city or town. The official enforces all ordinances and laws; administers oaths; signs commission and appointments; signs all bonds, contracts and other obligations to be signed in the name of the city or town.

The mayor appoints the clerk, treasurer, marshal, attorney, municipal judge and department heads as specified by ordinance with the consent of the governing body.

Removals can be made by the mayor, without consent of the governing body, unless required by separate statues such as ordinances or resolutions.

The mayor also possesses legislative powers. He presides over all meetings of the governing body according to the rules determined by it for the conduct of its meetings. He has one vote on all matters coming before the governing body except a vote to override a veto.

The mayor can veto any ordinance, order, by-law, resolution award or vote to enter into any contract or the allowance of any claim. His veto can be overridden by a two-thirds vote of all qualified members of council. The mayor does not have a vote in any matter involving the override of a veto.

The mayor also represents the people of his city or town. He is the people's representative, and he spends a good portion of his time in ceremonial functions.

After the reading of the above statute by Boal, discussion went on for a short time, but as I remember nothing more was ever mentioned concerning the duties and the salary of the mayor again. It appeared that the council was satisfied with the Wyoming State Statute and let the issue drop.

Complaints were pouring concerning the problem of skateboarding; the Uinta County Commissioners were getting concerned with skateboarders using the Uinta County Complex and the Uinta County Library properties; the City of Evanston was concerned about increase in numbers of skateboarders using city sidewalks and other city properties, and the endangerment of pedestrians. The concern of liability came up: who is responsible if someone gets hurt from a skateboarder colliding with a person walking? Also, the skaters were causing a lot of damage, especially in the Depot Square and Uinta County Court House areas. There was a lot of damage to the areas that were brick and not concrete.

The problem was getting out of hand, so the City of Evanston requested that Recreation Director Dennis Poppinga Evanston's District Recreation Commission look into the possibility of constructing a skateboard rink, possibly in the area of the tennis courts and baseball fields.

The problem was looked into and a study was completed to determine if there was property that could be made available for a skateboard area. Director Poppinga reported back to the city that a skateboard rink could be constructed in the area between the tennis courts and the baseball fields. The city then directed Poppinga and the commission to continue to look into the construction of the rink and the city would proceed to locate the funding.

Later on the project was completed and the City of Evanston had a new Skateboard Rink open to the public at no charge. It was a good move, because there was no longer a problem with skateboarders using other public properties or sidewalks.

During the month of February, a report came up that Amtrak Passenger Service was coming back to serve the southern route through Wyoming once again starting in June of this year. Amtrak pulled out of Wyoming eight years ago, and now they were talking about bringing it back on a trial basis, serving the south route from Denver, Colorado through Cheyenne to Ogden, Utah—but it might not stop in Evanston.

When the announcement came out there was a lot of wondering: Why not Evanston? Evanston had a lot of support in trying to get Amtrak to stop in Evanston. Lincoln County Commissioners wrote letters, and the Uinta County Commissioners gave a lot of support as well. The Evanston City Council and I wrote letters to everyone that we thought could help in support of Amtrak stopping in Evanston.

The *Uinta County Herald* of March 5th quoted me: *"I'm really excited about the prospect,"* said Ottley. *"I'd like to see it become a rest stop. It would be nice to have people see what we have here."*

The article continued: *The mayor and other city officials say they plan to push for service to Evanston. Ottley commented that the service would make it a lot easier for residents to visit the Legislature, along with basketball and football games on the other side of the state.*

"We could make events without having to fight the snowstorms and being tired when we get there, he said. "Any kind of transportation would

help us. The senior citizens would like taking the train better than taking the bus."

Evanston's train depot was in great condition and would take little work to get it in the condition required by Amtrak to service the passengers. The big addition would be the replacement of the passenger loading platform.

Amtrak officials were "impressed" with the condition of the Evanston Depot on their recent visit to the city, according to Mayor Dennis Ottley and Urban Renewal Director Jim Davis, reported Ann Curtis, in the *Uinta County Herald* of March 22nd.

Curtis went on: *And while the company hasn't officially announced if it plans to provide passenger rail service to the community when it resumes its route through Wyoming this summer, Ottley and Davis said they were given the impression that Evanston will be on Amtrak's list of stops.*

"I think they will definitely come beginning June 1," Davis said. *"Everyone was excited,"* Curtis's article added.

But although Amtrak tried serving Southern Wyoming with passenger service once again, it didn't last long, because after several months they found that it was not feasible to run Amtrak in Wyoming any longer. So it was discontinued again.

During the month of February, the ski area's ten-year lease agreement had come up for discussion and there were concerns about the equipment being old and needing a lot of repairs and upkeep. It was mentioned that the ski lift and the tow ropes were getting to the point where they could be unsafe and the city and the recreation district should be looking at the liability. It was determined that the repairs needed in the near future would be quite costly.

There was talk about closing the area down, but Kilburn Porter, who originally started the project, suggested a survey be conducted to see how the public in the area felt about it. I, for one, knew that there had been a lot of kids and adults who learned to ski at Eagle Rock, and my four sons were among them, so it would be a shame to shut it down. I guess we would just have to see as we proceeded to try to keep it safe.

There was also a lot of talk about relocating the ski area. With the Salt Lake City Winter Olympics coming up in the not-so-far-off future, it would be nice to have an area close by where some of the Olympic participants could come to practice.

However, at the District's Recreation Commission's latest meeting, due to the expense of upgrading the Eagle Rock area, they elected to shut it down, with Director Dennis Poppinga stating that it would be too expensive to open the area up for next year's season.

During the meeting it was said that Evanston would have a downhill ski area one way or another. An area called Rocky Hollow in the Yellow Creek area was mentioned and the area would be looked into, but it was also said that it would take an awful lot of money to get it upgraded to a good usable downhill ski area.

Now the city would be looking at two big projects, an indoor convention center and a new downhill ski area, that would be great for the economy and recreation of Evanston if we could only find the funds to make them a reality.

The annual Agri-Business Banquet would be held on March 14th at Elks Lodge to honor a number of county residents for their voluntary work in various areas.

This year's only nominees for Evanston's Citizen of the Year were Bird "Rip" Bruce and Ann Bell. Both were very active in the community and I'm sure both were very deserving of the honor. The selection of the nominee named as Citizen of the Year was voted on by the Evanston City Council.

After going into a session to determine who the winner was, the Evanston City Council unanimously named Ann Bell as Evanston's Citizen of the Year. Although Rip Bruce was very active helping folks in his neighborhood, being active in the Boy Scouts and very deserving of being mentioned, the city council selected Ann Bell for her hard work in 1990 as Chairperson of Evanston's many programs celebrating the Wyoming Statehood Centennial and for all her help in other projects throughout the year. An award well deserved! Ann did a terrific job on all the Wyoming Centennial projects.

At the regular city council meeting of March 13th, we had more Boy Scouts in attendance. Their leader, Brent Hatch, was invited to introduce the following scouts: Jeremy Jasperson, Derek Haider,

Eric Taylor, Rusty Conway, Ryan Weston, Chad Hughes, and scout leader Kurt Hathaway. The Boy Scouts represented Troop 75 and were filling a requirement for a communication merit badge. Members of the council and I thanked them for being in attendance and wished them all luck in their many requirements.

During the city council meeting of March 27th, Julie Abbot and Joni Loxterman made a presentation and showed a short video on the Walk America program, a March of Dimes program to help stop birth defects.

The program consisted of volunteers doing a walk of 6.2 miles with businesses sponsoring volunteers and pledging so much per mile walked. The event would start on April 27th at Depot Square and the volunteers would walk to North School, over to Uinta Meadows School, and back to Depot Square.

Ms Abbot and Ms Loxterman reported that they already had 58 businesses participating, and as of this date they had 237 pledged walkers.

Councilman Nelson made a motion to approve the *Walk America* route and direct the police department to ensure the route would be safe for the walkers, seconded by Davis with all voting in favor.

During the meeting I introduced more Boy Scouts who were in attendance to fill some requirements for their merit badges. The scouts were Bo Sanders, Pat Adams, Jesse Brazier, Josh Bateman, Lance Widmer, and Brooks Frye.

The council and I thanked them for attending the meeting, and in congratulating them we wished them good luck in their future achievements.

Resolution 91-7 to repeal Resolution 90-46 and re-establish a two-hour parking zone within the downtown area of the city, was introduced by Councilman Craig Nelson during the meeting. It had been established through a survey that the downtown merchants were in favor of it, and after a short discussion Councilman Davis made the motion to adopt Resolution 91-7, seconded by Vranish, with all voting in favor.

Resolution 91-11 was introduced by Councilwoman Wall, to ratify the execution of an agreement with the Wyoming Highway Department to dispose of a parcel of land related to 6th Street, Lombard Street, and Yellow Creek Road.

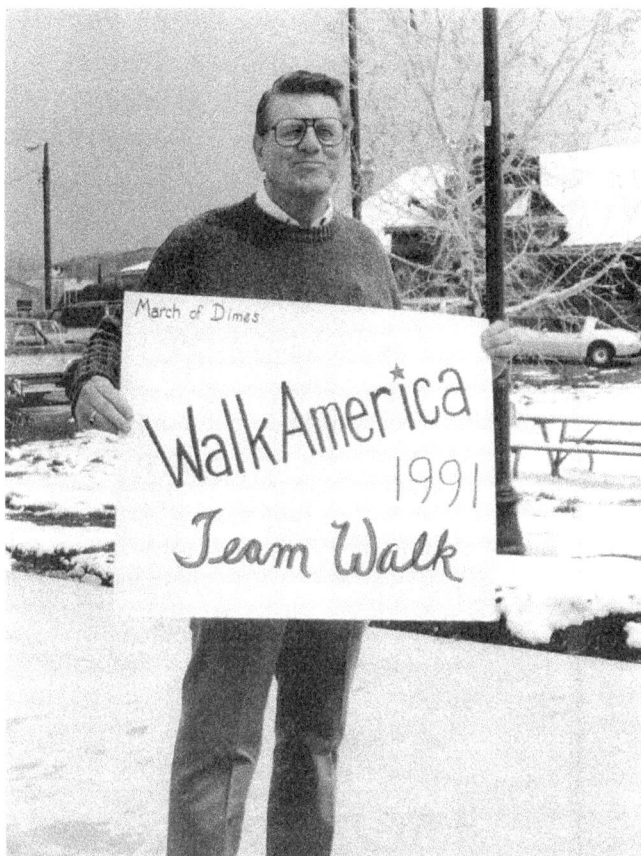

LETTERS TO THE EDITOR
Uinta County Herald
March, 1991

'Walk America' soon

Dear Editor:

Key Bank of Wyoming, along with several other businesses in Evanston, is sponsoring "Walk America" on April 27. We will be walking 6.2 miles in an effort to raise money for healthier babies.

If you have received help or in any way benefitted from the March of Dimes, please contact me at Key Bank, 789-4440.

Thank you.

Julie Abbott
Evanston

Letters to the Editor, *Uinta County Herald,* March, 1991.

This resolution pertained to improvements to the intersection of 6th and Lombard Streets, and Yellow Creek Road. It provided for traffic to enter safely off Lombard Street onto 6th and Yellow Creek, and it provided safe access to some homes as well. This was another project that was constructed at the expense of the Wyoming Highway Department.

The motion to adopt Resolution 91-11 was made by Councilwoman Lehman, and seconded by Nelson with all voting in favor.

Evanston's purchasing agent, Mike Lake, presented the bids to the council that had been received for new sanitation collection trucks and garbage containers. This equipment would make it possible for the city to change to the one-man, one-truck system, which would be a much safer and faster system for the employees and the public. The new system would not affect the sanitation pickup employees, except that they would be transferred to other departments with no drop in pay.

Lake named the bids, announcing that H & K Truck Equipment was the lowest bid and met all bid specifications. The bid included two GMC white operational trucks and 3,850 bins for a total price of $526,171. Councilwoman Lehman made a motion to accept the low bid of H & K Truck Equipment, seconded by Davis, with all voting in favor.

Ann Curtis wrote in the *Uinta County Herald* of March 29th: *By the end of summer, the City of Evanston will be sporting two new one-man garbage trucks 3,200 new garbage receptacles.*

Curtis went on to report: *The new trucks will be operated by one driver. From the cab, he will be able to operate the arm, which reaches out and grasps the large wheeled containers. The container is then automatically raised, dumped and returned to its original resting place.*

Evanston's new residential trash receptacles can be maneuvered by just about everyone, as shown by the Munoz family. Above, City Sanitation Supervisor Marvin Munoz stands in one of the containers, along with his parents, Helen and Valentine. At right, the elder Munoz moves the container with his son inside. The new system is scheduled to be demonstrated at Smith's Food King from 10 a.m. to 5 p.m. today and at Wal-Mart from 10 a.m. to 3 p.m. on Saturday. A video on the new system is being shown daily from noon to 3 p.m. on Century Cable Channel 12.

Uinta County Herald, May 3, 1991.

According to manufacturers, the wheeled containers can be maneuvered by anyone.

The city sanitation department now employs nine staff members. When the trucks are put online, four staff members will be required.

City officials say the additional five staff members will be relocated into other departments within the city crews, Curtis reported.

Before the Evanston City Council voted to go with the new garbage system of one-truck, one-man operation, there was a public discussion on whether or not the new system would be good for Evanston. Those in attendance were more or less in favor of the changeover, but as I recall, Lance Voss, a former City Council member under the Martin administration, spoke against the system, stating that they tried to make the same changeover during their administration and it didn't work.

My response to Mr. Voss was, *You people just didn't try hard enough; you gave up too easily, but we will make the change and it will work.*

I have always been told that that in cases where there is no easy way to do something, if you don't at least give it all you can, you won't get anything to work. *"A will finds a way,"* said a famous American writer, Orison Swett Marden.

Mr. Voss wrote a Letter to the Editor that was published in the *Uinta County Herald* of April 2nd titled, *"Don't Change System."* His letter ended with, *"I believe this is a classic example of 'It may not be broke but I am going to fix it'."*

Well, Mr. Voss, the system may not be broken, but there were a hell of a lot of employees that ended up with back problems from lifting those cans, sometimes half full of frozen ice in the wintertime. And as of this writing, the new system is still operating, over 26 years, as we expected.

Public meetings to gather input from Evanston residents regarding the updating of the city's new Comprehensive Plan will begin on April 1st, according to Planning and Zoning Director Paul Knopf, reported Ann Curtis of the *Uinta County Herald* on March 19th.

The city has been divided into seven areas, each of which will have a residential leader who picks a committee to work on their area and make recommendations for the Comprehensive Plan Committee, Ms Curtis reported.

The seven leaders will then join Knopf, Planning and Zoning Chairman Dan Yates, City Council liaison Will Davis and City Attorney Dennis Boal to work on the plan.

Knopf said the seven team leaders will serve as "conduits" for their neighborhoods.

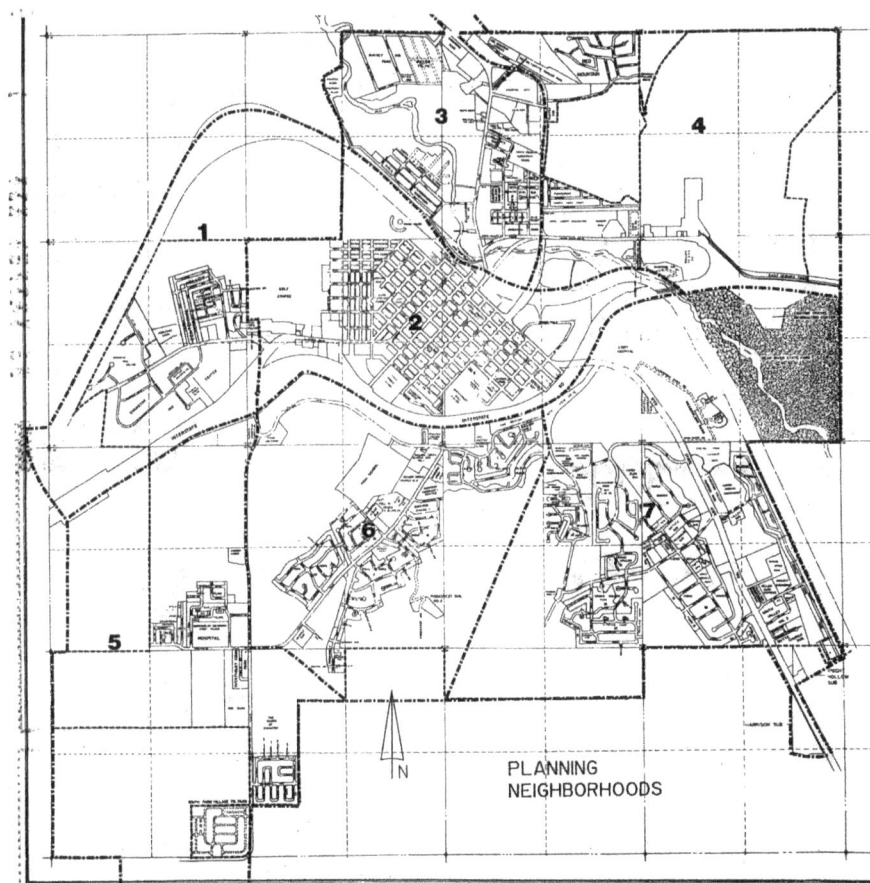

Evanston has been divided into seven areas which will be used in updating the city's comprehensive and master plan. Resident are encouraged to participate in discussion on their particular areas during a series of meetings that begins April 1. Each area wi have its own committee, and those committees will make recommendations to a special city task force.

Uinta County Herald, March 19, 1991.

"During these brainstorming sessions, the group is to discuss what they want to see in their neighborhood, the future direction of the area and identify the problems," Knopf said. "They then need to summarize those thoughts into a written report," Curtis's article continued.

Knopf will coordinate the process based on his professional knowledge of the subject. "We need citizens' input to make this work," he said, Curtis's article concluded.

The city council's thoughts and mine were that the Comprehensive Plan was going to take quite some time, because seven teams had to meet and come up with a plan for each neighborhood, but we thought by having the public involved there would be a lot of input that would be helpful and realistic.

The council and I also thought that it best that none of us attend the meetings, with the exception of Councilman Davis who had been assigned as liaison between the P & Z Commission and the city council. The team meetings should be attended only by those named as team members, Knopf, P & Z Chairman Yates, and City Attorney Boal.

After the teams presented their ideas to the P & Z Commission and with recommendations from the commission, the plan would be presented to the Evanston City Council for final approval. Those involved needed to realize that there could be some changes by the council.

During the city council meeting of April 10th I once again recognized several Boy Scouts and requested they introduce themselves.

From Troop 40, we had Ben Cox , Randon Kennedy, and Lance Widmer; from Troop 2 we had Rusty Linford and Justin Linford; and from Troop 9 we had Casey Cummings.

The council and I thanked them for being in attendance and wished them success in their future achievements.

Also during the meeting, Lt. Mitch Allmaras of the Evanston Police Department introduced Steve Smith as a new member of the police department, and I made the appointment of Steve Smith to the police department. Motion was made by Councilman Nelson to confirm the appointment, seconded by Vranish, with all voting in favor.

Resolution 91-13, to execute an agreement with H & K Truck Equipment to furnish the City of Evanston with automated refuse collection trucks and containers, was introduced by Councilwoman Lehman. Councilman Hutchinson made a motion to adopt Resolution 91-13, seconded by Vranish.

Several folks in attendance were interested in the sanitation change-over, so I opened the floor for discussion. During the discussion it appeared that some folks were opposed to the new system so Councilman Hutchinson made a new motion to postpone any action on Resolution 91-13 for 30 days, but the motion died from a lack of a second.

I then ended any more discussion and called for the vote on the motion to adopt Resolution 91-13 with 6 voting in favor and 1 vote against (Hutchinson). Motion passed and the City of Evanston would soon be changing their garbage pickup to the one-truck, one-man system.

With all the questions and concerns of what the speed limit should be on the streets within the City of Evanston, City Attorney presented Ordinance 91-7 which was introduced and sponsored by Councilman Hutchinson. This ordinance would amend certain sections of the Evanston City Code to provide that the speed limit within the City would be 25 miles per hour unless otherwise posted and to provide the governing body with the authority to set speed limits based on Engineering and Traffic Investigations.

After a bit of discussion Councilman Davis made a motion to pass Ordinance 91-7 on first reading, seconded by Lehman with all voting unanimously.

Ordinance 91-7 passed on second reading also, but was amended by a motion by Councilwoman Wall, seconded by Lehman, to change the speed limit named in the title of the ordinance from 25 mph to 30 mph, which passed by 4 votes in favor and 2 votes against (Nelson and Davis), and 1 absent (Hutchinson). On the third reading the ordinance as amended was again passed by 4 votes in favor, 2 votes against (Nelson and Davis) and 1 absent (Lehman).

Ordinance 91-7 passed all three readings making it law, but I don't know why Nelson and Davis voted against it on the second and third readings, unless it was because of the change in the speed limit, because they did vote in favor of it on first reading.

During the city council meeting on April 24th a public hearing was opened by City Attorney Dennis Boal to hear an application for a catering permit for serving alcohol from Spirits of Red Mountain during the Wyoming Association of Municipalities (W.A.M.) Convention to be held in Evanston from June 5th to June 7th of this year.

Councilwoman Jerry Wall, Chairperson of the W.A.M. Convention Committee spoke in favor of the catering permit application, and since there was no opposition during the public hearing, City Attorney Boal closed the hearing.

Councilman Davis made a motion approving Spirits of Red Mountain's application for a catering permit, seconded by Lehman with all voting in favor.

During this meeting I appointed Rick Lavery to the Evanston Housing Authority Board for a 4-year term. Appointment was confirmed by a motion from Councilman Nelson, seconded by Davis, with all voting in favor.

I read a letter of resignation from another police officer, Ralph Pierce. Motion was made by Councilwoman Wall to accept the resignation of Officer Pierce, seconded by Nelson, with all voting in favor. I stated that Officer Pierce had been a good officer and thanked him for his service to the community and wished him well in his new position with the Uinta County Sheriff's Department.

Resolution 91-14 allowing the City of Evanston to set forth and offer a one-time early retirement incentive program to city employees age 54 and older was brought on the floor and introduced by Councilman Nelson. The resolution read:

Section 1: *The City of Evanston shall offer to all of its full time employees, who are 54 years and older as of the date of this resolution, an early retirement incentive program pursuant to the following terms and conditions:*

a. Any qualified employee who accepts this offer shall receive the payment of One Thousand Dollars ($1,000) for each complete year of full time employment service provided to the City of Evanston by that employee. The effective date of retirement for all employees accepting this offer will be August 1, 1991, unless a sooner date is requested by the employee and approved by the governing body of the City of Evanston.

b. To receive the benefits of this offer, all qualified employees must submit a signed, written acceptance of the early retirement incentive program to the City Personnel Officer no later than May 15, 1991.

Section 2: The administration is hereby authorized to take all steps which are necessary to inform the City employees of this offer and to implement the program for all qualified City employees.

This was an incentive program to permit any employee 54 or older to accept early retirement in order for the City of Evanston to reduce employment to a number of employees actually needed to operate the city efficiently. Since the changeover of the new sanitation department and other adjustments, the Evanston City Council and I felt the city was operating with too many employees, and we felt that rather than laying anyone off, it would be a good incentive program for those close to retirement age to take retirement early.

Councilman Davis made the motion to adopt Resolution 91-14, seconded by Lehman. After a short discussion, the motion passed with 5 yes votes, 1 no vote (Vranish), and 1 absent (Hutchinson).

If I recall right, four employees from the Public Works Department were the only ones out of ten who were eligible, to take advantage of the program. One of the employees who took advantage was Public Works Superintendent Allen Kennedy, who began working for the city in 1951 (40 years). Kennedy was going to be hard to replace.

"The mayor and council were really fair with the guys, especially with the new garbage system coming in, Kennedy stated according to the May 24th edition of the Uinta County Herald. The four (4) employees' last day will be July 31, 1991. "We want to have the new (garbage) system set up before that time," Kennedy added. The adoption of Resolution 91-14 turned out to be a good program giving the employees their choice of early retirement. The City of Evanston never had to lay any employee off because of the new garbage pickup program.

Before adjournment I announced that there would be a public meeting at City Hall on May 13th at 7:00 p.m. to discuss a Capital Facilities tax and how it may be utilized for a multi-events center and other facilities.

The *Uinta County Herald* issue of April 9th ran an article titled, "ASSESSMENT TEAM" TO VISIT COMMUNITY. The article read: *An "Assessment Team" organized by the Wyoming Department of Commerce is scheduled to be in Evanston next week to look at the city.*

"They'll be looking us over, spotting our weaknesses, strengths—good and bad points," Community Director Paul Knopf said.

The team, scheduled to be here April 16-18, will consist of Reba Massey, State Historic Preservation Office; Don Johnson, Hot Springs Economic Development Council; Doug Black, Wyoming Arts Council; Margaret Hunt, Utah Power and Light; Joe Evans, team leader and business development officer; Sharon Kelsey, governor's office; and Rick Hunnicut, community economic development specialist.

"They will be interviewing commercial, industrial and public sectors for the three days gathering information," said Knopf.

At the end of the interviews, the group will give a public presentation of its findings on Thursday, April 18th, at 3 p.m. at city hall, the *Herald* continued.

On April 23rd Ann Curtis, reporter for the *Uinta County Herald*, published an article titled EVANSTON A "PLEASANT SURPRISE" TO STATE TEAM. Her article read, *Evanston was hailed as a "pleasant surprise" by the community assessment team, put together by Gov. Mike Sullivan, which evaluated the community and its facilities last week.*

Evanston is the 22nd community to be evaluated by the assessment team since 1989, the article continued.

Joe Evans, team leader and business development officer, stressed that the community is fortunate to have an airport, river, interstate, and access to a major airport. He called the location of the city "excellent." He said the oil and gas industry provides an excellent tax base and provides good jobs. Some of the pluses also included a diversity of jobs, good infrastructure, adequate space, good suppliers and an active economic development organization.

Curtis's article continued: *The community's economic development efforts had some negatives, too. He felt too much emphasis is placed on recruitment of new industry. Evans feels the emphasis should be placed on the retention of local businesses. A need for financial business advice locally is an essential, he said.*

Don Jackson of the Hot Springs Economic Development Council said that how the citizens feel about their government was a pleasant surprise. "They feel the government of the city is very involved, progressive and very well coordinated in efforts between city and county," he said. "They feel there are excellent basic services such as police, fire and water."

He praised the "whopper" of an infrastructure and he congratulated officials in being able to budget to maintain it. He also spoke about the Comprehensive Plan, and stressed continuing to use it and not put it on the shelf, Curtis's article concluded.

After the report was presented to me, the council and the public during the April 18th meeting, in discussion, there was a good feeling from most everyone in attendance about the group's report. The city council and I both felt that it was something that the city should take very seriously.

We thanked the governor's group for all the information they had provided us and assured them that it would not be taken unnoticed.

During the regular city council meeting of May 8th I again recognized and welcomed another group of Boy Scouts. Scout Leader Ned Cutler of Troop 200, who was in attendance with the scouts, stated that the boys were there to earn points towards their merit badges. I then asked Leader Cutler to introduce the boys. He introduced them as Ryan Staley, Darren Linford, Joshua Davis, Brandon Platt, Daniel Fields, Sterling Pierce, Ben Platt, Scott Jensen, and Ryan Linford.

During the meeting Operations Superintendent Allen Kennedy awarded a plaque to all the operators of the Water Treatment Plant. This was a housekeeping award from the Wyoming Water Quality and Pollution Control Association.

Butch Whitaker, Plant Superintendent, and Barry Constantine were in attendance to receive the plaque. I expressed my appreciation to all the operators, Whitaker, Constantine, Bud Eastman and Jeff Martin for their extra effort in having the cleanest plant in the State of Wyoming.

Patty Bates was in attendance to make a presentation and request permission for a route to hold a Great Strides Walk for Cystic Fibrosis on May 18th at 9:00 a.m. using the same route as the March of Dimes Walk.

Councilman Davis made a motion to approve the Great Strides Walk as requested and to make the Evanston Police Department aware of the walk, seconded by Wall, with all voting in favor.

It was time for the City of Evanston to be audited for the fiscal years ending in June of 1991, 1992, and 1993. Therefore, Councilman Nelson introduced Resolution 91-16 authorizing the City of Evanston to execute a letter agreement with Porter, Miurhead, Cornia and Howard of Casper, Wyoming to provide the city with the General Audit Services for those fiscal years.

This group had been doing Evanston's audits for quite some time and had always been very prompt and up-front with the audits. They are well qualified and we have always felt good about them. Councilman Nelson made the motion to adopt Resolution 91-16, seconded by Hutchinson, with all voting in favor.

During a previous meeting, Councilman Nelson had made a motion directing me to authorize Uinta Engineering and Surveying, Inc. (UESI) to survey 3.0 acres of the Red Mountain Subdivision to provide the residents with a neighborhood park.

During this meeting of May 8th, UESI had the survey completed and the city attorney had prepared Resolution 91-19 authorizing the City of Evanston to purchase the 3.0 acres of the Red Mountain Subdivision surveyed by UESI for a neighborhood park.

Councilman Nelson introduced Resolution 91-19, and Councilman Hutchinson made a motion to it, seconded by Wall, with all voting in favor.

During the meeting Police Chief Dennis Harvey displayed a plaque given to the Evanston Police Department from Adjutant General Charles J. Wing, Wyoming National Guard, to show appreciation for local support of the armed services during the Gulf War.

I also announced that I had received a "Certificate of Appreciation to Mayor Dennis Ottley," from the United States Department of Defense's National Committee for Employer Support of the Guard and Reserve for distinguished contributions to the National Defense, signed by the Unit Commander and State Chairman.

These awards were presented to us because of the way we treated our employees that were called to active duty during Desert Storm.

Prior to adjournment Councilman Nelson made a motion to assign me as the voting delegate, with Nelson as the alternate delegate, for the W.A.M. Convention in June, seconded by Davis with all voting in favor.

The Convention Center Advisory Committee completed their feasibility study to determine whether or not a multi-events center would be a net benefit to the Evanston community, and if any of the existing buildings could be renovated enough to serve the purpose or a new structure would be more practical. The City of Evanston was first attracted to the Cowboy Casino building (presently the Evanston Alliance Church), which was owned by the Key Bank of Wyoming, but after reading the feasibility study, it appeared that the best and most practical location to build a new Indoor Convention Center would be at the Uinta County Fairgrounds.

Therefore, the committee dropped the idea of purchasing the Cowboy Casino building and worked towards a plan to build the Convention Center at the fairgrounds. The feasibility study indicated that the Casino building would not be large enough for certain events. The cost wouldn't be much different since the fairground is already owned by the City of Evanston and leased to Uinta County for a never-ending lease agreement.

The committee then turned their interest towards the fairgrounds, but needed to approach the Uinta County Commissioners first. As none of them opposed the idea, the committee continued to draw up plans for the Center at the fairgrounds and hoped to have something completed by the 1992 elections to add to other projects that would be voted on through the one percent Capital Facility Tax.

During this month the Uinta County Commissioners requested that Evanston either sell or donate the old single-lane Bear River Bridge off Holland Drive. The Wyoming Highway Department had donated and installed one of their old two-lane bridges on Holland Drive to replace the single-lane bridge. This was done a few years ago when the highway department rerouted Wyoming State Highway 89 North and replaced the highway river bridge with a new one.

The Commissioners wanted to install the old Holland Drive Bridge on a location at River Bend Drive on the Smith's Fork River in Mountain View. The City of Evanston had kept the old bridge in storage these past few years. So during one of the regular council meetings a motion was made by one of the council members to donate the bridge to the county and was seconded, but it would have to be done at the county's expense. The motion passed with all voting in favor.

Another project that would be on the ballot in November, 1992 was the new downhill ski area which a committee had been working on with Evanston Recreation District Director Dennis Poppinga.

In Poppinga's report he stated that Rocky Hollow, just off Yellow Creek Road, the area planned for a new ski run, was owned by sisters, Kathy Urroz Seale and Mary Urroz Lindley of the Urroz Ranch. After meeting with them, he stated that they would be willing to give the City of Evanston a lease under similar conditions that existed with the Eagle Rock lease. He said that they agreed verbally to lease the property on a long-term basis for 15% of the annual gross lift sales.

Poppinga also reported that he met with Mike Pexton and Scott Hansen to discuss access to the site through the Ranches of Evanston subdivision on Sundance Street, which would provide access to the Rocky Hollow site. But using Sundance Street as an access would create high traffic through the developed residential area, and the street is not a direct route to the area that would be used for parking.

Mr. Pexton stated that he would be willing to sell property for an access along a proposed street that was designated in the subdivision master plan. Poppinga reported that this would be the most direct route to the ski area site.

The ski hill project was still being considered and hopefully the recreation commission and their committee would come up with something more definite in time to be added to the Capital Facilities Tax projects by election time.

On May 13th a Multi-Event Center Advisory Board and concerned citizens meeting was held with dozens of citizens from Evanston and Bridger Valley, including me, Evanston council members and employees, mayors and council members from Lyman and Mountain View, and Uinta County Commissioners and state legislators. It appeared that the entire County of Uinta was pretty much covered.

I opened the meeting and introduced the Chairman of the Advisory Board, Jeff Jewett. He explained to the group the Multi-Event Center Board's purpose and displayed the drawings that the Board had put together.

Mary Keating-Scott and Kirchner Moore spoke to the group regarding the Capital Facilities Tax. She had pamphlets on facilities tax information that included counties in Wyoming where the voters approved the tax.

After her presentation there were follow-up questions. The group then decided to list the projects that each community would like to include in the Capital Facilities Tax monies.

The projects submitted from county entities were:

Lyman: Urie Connector Road – .8 million; Recreation (outdoor) bike trails, cross country skiing, and 9 hole golf course, etc. – 1.2 million.

Fort Bridger: Mary Aimone – Ground for Rendezvous – $350,000.

Mountain View: Senior Center improvements, sewer improvements, and bridge improvements.

Evanston: Multi-Event Center & Indoor Arena (entire county), BEAR Project and Senior Citizens Center.

Evanston Parks & Recreation District: Downhill Ski Area and Outdoor Recreation improvements at Sulphur Creek Reservoir.

The estimated cost of all the projects listed above would be approximately 12 to 14 million dollars.

I mentioned to the group that the next step would be to have the mayors of each community and the Uinta County Commissioners select a small group from all areas to study the different projects, and contact Mary Crosby with the Lincoln Uinta Association of Government (LUAG) about the possibility of getting a feasibility study done on the various projects.

This meeting was taped and would be available at the Evanston City. I felt the likelihood of these projects being approved was not good. When we first started talking about the Capital Facilities Tax, I felt the event center and the ski hill could possibly be approved, but the above slate of projects seemed to be quite a load for the folks to think about. I did not feel good about putting that many projects up for vote, and before next year there could be more.

During the regular city council meeting of May 22nd, a public hearing was held concerning budgetary adjustments to the 1990-1991 fiscal year and the use of some unanticipated income the city had received. City Attorney Dennis Boal acted as the hearing officer, and the hearing would be recorded and would be on file at City Hall.

City Treasurer Steve Widmer gave explanations and answered questions from the city council. There was no one in attendance who was opposed or had comments about the adjustments that the treasurer's department recommended.

Boal closed the hearing and Councilman Vranish introduced Resolution 91-20.

RESOLUTION 91-20
A RESOLUTION AUTHORIZING ADJUSTMENTS TO
CITY FUNDS OF THE CITY OF EVANSTON FISCAL YEAR
1990-1991 BUDGET AND ALLOCATING SUCH FUNDS
AND EXPENDITURES AMONG THE FUNDS/DEPART-
MENTS AS SPECIFIED HEREIN AND AUTHORIZING
A LOAN FROM THE GENERAL FUND FOR THE PUR-
CHASE OF AUTOMATED GARBAGE COLLECTION SYS-
TEM.

The resolution gave the city full authority to adjust and transfer funds needed, not only in other areas, but also to purchase the necessary equipment to get the new automated (one-truck/one-man) system started and in operation by July 1st. Councilman Hutchinson made a motion to adopt Resolution 91-20, seconded by Lehman, but the resolution was amended with a word correction. The motion was passed to adopt the resolution as amended by a unanimous vote.

The Evanston Lions Club requested a catering permit to allow the Veranda Bar to serve alcohol during the 9th Annual Renewal Ball on June 1st, which was another very successful event. The Lions Club request was approved by the city council unanimously. Other events discussed during the May 22nd meeting were the Evanston Lions Club's Annual Rib-O-Rama fundraiser to be held on May 27th. The council approved a malt beverage permit by motion, with all voting in favor.

A malt beverage permit was approved unanimously for the V.F.W. for their Softball Tournament to be held during the first two weekends in June.

Evanston's First Lady Sandy Ottley made her report on the upcoming 2nd Annual Endurance Horse Race from Evanston to Fort Bridger and back. She reported that the event would take place during the Memorial Day weekend, May 25th and 26th.

Sandy reported at that time they had 18 entries and the event appeared that it would be successful again because there was a lot of interest in the race, but the challenge of the event is all the tough requirements of the Environmental Protection Agency (E.P.A.) and all the ranchers that were getting a bit tough to deal with.

Sandy reported that this year would be a little different because there would be a mule named "Trapper" taking part in the race, entered and ridden by owner Mike Davis. This would be the first time a mule had been entered.

The race this year was successful. Darrel Nielson of Fort Bridger, last year's winner, won the again this year. Mike Davis and his mule Trapper finished the race with no problems.

However, there was an unfortunate accident with one of the riders and his horse. During the return run back to Evanston, Travis Eskelson of Evanston and his Appaloosa horse named Jake had entered the race and appeared to be going along fine. It even looked like they had a chance of winning, until on the return trip, when he reached the Piedmont area, Travis and Jake got into a marshy area where the horse got bogged down.

Travis was very upset with himself but safely got out of the mess. He tried to get Jake out of the marsh, but the horse wasn't cooperating much. The more Travis, some of the committee members and a few area ranchers tried to rope and get Jake out of the mess, the more the horse sank in, until it finally lay down and there was nothing else to do except put the horse down. Travis was very upset with himself and the situation, and hated losing a good horse like Jake, but there wasn't any other alternative but to put the horse down rather than see him lie there and slowly die.

Some of the ranchers in the Piedmont area arranged to take care of burying the horse. It didn't make Travis or any of us feel any better, except it was a big job that had to be done and everyone appreciated it. It was a sad tragedy and everyone seemed to feel the pain that Travis and his folks were feeling.

Not because of Travis's accident, but because of all the red tape with the government agencies and ranchers, unfortunately the committee voted this would be the last year for the race, and it would not become an annual event.

During the May 22nd city council meeting Joni Loxterman and Julie Abbot presented me with a plaque of appreciation and expressed their thanks for the support given to the March of Dimes Team Walk by the City of Evanston. They reported that there were over 400 walkers, and approximately $12,000 was raised. The program was a big success, beyond what they had imagined.

The plaque was displayed in City Hall where it could be seen by everyone. The city council and I congratulated their committee for a successful event and thanked them for the honorable presentation of the plaque.

Councilman Hutchinson made a motion for the council to go into executive session to discuss a personnel matter, seconded by Davis, with all voting in favor. This was in regard to a possible new position in the Police Department, and who would fill that position.

After the executive session I called meeting back to order and the following resolution was introduced by Councilman Nelson:

RESOLUTION 91-22
RESOLUTION OF THE CITY OF EVANSTON, WYO-
MING AUTHORIZING THE CREATION OF THE POSI-
TION OF LIEUTENANT IN CHARGE OF LAB AND CRIME
SCENE INVESTIGATION WITHIN THE CITY OF EVAN-
STON POLICE DEPARTMENT.

A job description was attached to the resolution and the administration was directed and authorized to implement the new position within the Evanston Police Department. Motion was made by Councilman Davis to adopt Resolution 91-22, seconded by Wall, with all voting in favor.

Detective Russ Dean, who had formerly been head of detectives, was appointed by me to the new position as Lieutenant in Charge of Lab and Crime Scene Investigation. A motion was formally made by the council and seconded, with all voting in favor.

Accordingly to the job description, Dean would perform professional law enforcement work dealing with crime scene investigations and the gathering and safeguarding of evidence. He would also be responsible for the operation and maintenance of the evidence lab.

Dean had been on medical leave from the department since earlier this year. A reorganization of the department changed his position from head of detectives to the crime scene lab, and he would assume his new position on June 3rd.

After reminding everyone of the upcoming W.A.M. Convention on June 5th, 6th, and 7th, I adjourned the meeting at 9:05 p.m.

During the month of May, Pam Rankin of the Wyoming Parks and Cultural Resources Commission came to my office and presented me with a check in the amount of $25,000 to be used on the Better Environmental and River (BEAR) Project. The funds were from the federal Land and Water Conversation Fund Program, and would be used for site improvements, pathways and trails, and planning and engineering of the BEAR Project.

Also in the month of May, the Urban Renewal Agency moved their office into the newly remodeled home of Evanston's first Mayor, Dr. Francis H. Harrison. The home is located at 236 Ninth Street, and it would also be used as a meeting place for several Evanston Commissions, Boards and Committees. However, Urban Renewal Director Jim Davis would retain his office in one corner of City Hall.

The 36th annual W.A.M. Convention, held during the first week in June, was another big success with approximately 350 city and town officials from throughout the State of Wyoming, and several special guests such as Fort Worth, Texas Mayor Bob Bolen, past president of the National League of Cities, who gave the keynote address on Thursday morning on the subject of "American Cities – Where We Are Going."

Also in attendance were Governor Mike Sullivan and Wyoming's First Lady Ann Sullivan. The Governor spoke on Friday evening, winding up the W.A.M. Convention, commending the Evanston community on what it had accomplished "during boom and bust to make something happen." He added that the theme of the Convention, "Back to Basics"—helping local officials accomplish everyday tasks—takes Wyoming from the "me" generation to the "we" generation.

Other dignitaries that attended the Convention included Wyoming Senators Jim Geringer (Platte County) and Kelly Mader (Campbell County), and Wyoming State Representative Ron Micheli from Uinta County, who would meet and discuss legislative issues of interest to municipalities from the point of view of the state legislature.

The following comments are taken from the June 7th issue of the *Uinta County Herald*: *During the legislative steering committee discussion, Evanston City Councilwoman and Convention Chairperson Jerry Wall stated that the cities and state are a partnership and dependent upon one another, but she didn't want to be lumped with the state agencies for funding.*

Representative Ron Micheli brought a round of applause from the city leaders when he stated that it was his opinion "the system of funding cities and counties is upside-down. It is humiliating and degrading to go begging for money which is actually yours," he said.

During my comments at the banquet on the last day of the convention thanking everyone for their attendance and thanking W.A.M. for giving the City of Evanston the opportunity to host the 36th Annual W.A.M. Convention, I called on Evanston City Council President Clarence Vranish to present to Convention Chairperson Jerry Wall a plaque and a gift for her outstanding hard work and what she had accomplished in making the W.A.M. Convention such an outstanding and successful program. Jerry and her committee had done a terrific job and the presentation from the city was well deserved.

The City of Evanston received several letters from Wyoming mayors and city officials, but one that was sent to the *Uinta County Herald* Letters to the Editor column from City of Buffalo Mayor Jim Hicks read:

> *Dear Editor:*
>
> *It's been too many years since I've had the opportunity to visit Evanston. But because of the recent WAM convention, I did have the opportunity to spend a few days in your community.*

New look

The historic Harrison House, which is headquarters for the Urban Renewal Ball Committee, has received a face lift. The Evanston City Council and the Renewal Ball Committee have each provided $1,500 in matching money to paint the exterior of the structure, and the work was finished this week.

Uinta County Herald, August 16, 1991.

Evanston may have been one of Wyoming's better kept secrets, but no more. The exposure afforded during the WAM meetings opened a lot of eyes.

Everyone in the community should take a great deal of pride in what Evanston has accomplished. The business community and others responsible for the restoration of the downtown area have done a great job.

Evanston is a bright spot in Wyoming! Congratulations.

I thought it was a great letter and, I, for one, was very appreciative of Mayor Hicks's comments.

Other successful projects that came off in June included: the Ambassadors Horseman's Steak Fry at Depot Square on June 10th; the 9th Annual Chili Cookoff on June 15th; the High Uintas Classic Bike Race from Kamas, Utah to Evanston the weekend of June 22nd and 23rd; and Krazy Days in Evanston on June 28th and 29th. All were very successful.

On Thursday, June 13th Amtrak returned to Evanston and was greeted with a mock train robbery, a hanging, and speeches beginning at 10:30 a.m. at Depot Square.

This was a big day for Evanston. The city had been chosen as one of the regular stops for Amtrak as they returned to passenger service across southern Wyoming after an eight-year absence.

On this special inaugural run, an Amtrak passenger train would be coming from Salt Lake City that Thursday morning. Passengers from S.L.C. would get off in Evanston and then be bused back to S.L.C. Approximately 150 citizens of Uinta County were invited to board the train to Rock Springs to be bused back to Evanston later. The official run of the passenger service of Amtrak would not start until the following Monday.

During the trip to Rock Springs everyone enjoyed the short Amtrak train trip. I know Sandy and I enjoyed it very much and I was especially happy that they had decided to include Evanston as one of their regular stops. For some of the young folks who rode the train that day, it may have been the first time they had ever been on a passenger train, and for a lot of the folks it could be the last time for them.

During my welcome back speech that morning I said, "We have all missed Amtrak passenger service in the time that it has been absent from Wyoming....We are proud to offer the Depot as a waiting facility for rail passengers....There is no finer passenger service facility in the state."

Uinta County Herald, June, 1991.

Mayor Dennis Ottley giving welcome speech on June 13, 1991 to the arrival of Amtrak Passenger Service.

Several hundred people turned out to welcome the inaugural run of Amtrak's Pioneer Line at Evanston's Depot Square Thursday morning, and the occasion was a festive one. Representatives of the passenger rail service, which is returning to Wyoming after an eight-year absence, praised the city's Depot restoration efforts, while local officials hailed Amtrak's return. Some 150 local people boarded the train and went on to Rock Springs, where they were scheduled to get off. Regular passenger service is scheduled to begin on Monday.

Photo by Chad Baldwin

Uinta County Herald, June, 1991.

I continued, "Evanston is a community on the move. Amtrak is a corporation on the move. Evanston is a proud, spirited community. Amtrak provides exciting spirited service. Evanston and Amtrak – partners in the people business, partners in the entertainment business, partners in promoting community and state unity and pride. Thank you Amtrak, and I hope you all enjoy the trip to Rock Springs."

During the regular city council meeting held on June 12th, Resolution 91-21, approving a Charter which would create the Evanston Youth Government, was introduced by Councilman Davis. The Evanston Youth Government would provide services to the youth of the community by informing the city government and the school board of their needs and wishes, and aid in the planning and implementing of social, educational, cultural, athletic and recreation-al activities for the youth.

The Charter supporting the youth program would be attached and incorporated within the resolution, and made a part of it.

Councilman Will Davis, who had been working on this program with the school district since October of 1990 stated in his memo to the city council, *"...This is one step up from our current Student Govern-ment Day. It has some exciting possibilities and may help us prepare leaders to take our places throughout our country"*.

His memo continued, *"It is by no means an original idea of mine. I have received information from several other communities who have similar programs and then put them together to fit our own particular needs."*

The structure defined by the Charter consisted of a Mayor and six City Council members who will be required to meet once a month to conduct business. They would be elected by the youth of the community at a general election. Their requirements will be very similar to the City of Evanston, and they would work directly with corresponding Evanston City Council representatives and the May-or of Evanston. Following some additional discussion, Councilman Hutchinson made a motion to adopt Resolution 91-21, seconded by Lehman, with 6 votes in favor and 1 absent (me). I was out of town on city business visiting the Gowen Field National Guard Base in Boise, Idaho with other Wyoming groups for the day. The meeting was conducted by Council President Vranish.

During the meeting Councilwoman Wall gave her final report on the W.A.M. Convention, and expressed her appreciation to all those who assisted and supported her in making the 36th Annual W.A.M. Convention a great success.

Prior to adjourning, Council President Vranish reminded everyone of the upcoming budget hearing on Tuesday, June 18th at 8:00 p.m.

During the month of June, our local Cowboy Joe Club coor-dinator Pat Mulhall met with me to declare June 17th to June 21st as Cowboy Joe Week. During this week the club would raise funds through a number of programs, including the 1991 Evanston Cow-boy Joe Scramble golf tournament at the Purple Sage Golf Course.

On June 18th, a special city council meeting was called for the public hearing on the budget for the 1991-1992 fiscal year. Wyoming state law requires that a public hearing for the budget for cities must be held on the third Tuesday of June at 8:00 p.m. each year, prior to the city council's acceptance of the fiscal year budget.

City Attorney Dennis Boal conducted the hearing, and City Treasurer Steve Widmer presented the proposed budget for fiscal year 1991-1992 and explained aspects of the budget. He indicated that the 1991-1992 budget would be about 2.2 percent more than the previous year.

There was no one present, except city officials and staff, to express concerns or questions pertaining to the proposed budget that had been published in the local newspaper as required by state law.

City Attorney Boal then closed the hearing and Councilman Craig Nelson introduced the following resolution:

RESOLUTION 91-24
A RESOLUTION PROVIDING INCOME NECESSARY
TO FINANCE THE BUDGET AND PROVIDE FOR AND
AUTHORIZE ANNUAL APPROPRIATION OF FUNDS FOR
THE FISCAL YEAR 1991-1992.

Following the reading of the title of the 8.4 million dollar budget resolution by City Attorney Boal, Councilwoman Lehman made a motion to adopt Resolution 91-24, seconded by Wall.

But after a lengthy discussion Councilwoman Wall made a motion to amend the resolution on page 11 and insert $7.00, following the wording: "Additional Residential Service Containers," seconded by Nelson, with a unanimous vote.

Vote on the main motion to adopt Resolution 91-24 as amended also passed by a unanimous vote.

During the regular city council meeting on June 26th, and due to the recent resignation of John Phillips from the city judge position, I appointed Attorneys Greg Phillips and Bruce Barnard to serve as part time municipal judges. Motion was made by Councilman Nelson to confirm the appointment, seconded by Wall, with all voting in favor.

I appointed DeWayne Moore to serve on the Public Service Advisory Board for a three-year term, and appointed Kevin Smith and Duane Bruce to serve on the Parks and Recreation Board, each for a three-year term. Motions were made by members of the city council to confirm the appointments and second them, with all voting in favor.

Operations Supervisor Allen Kennedy presented certificates to Rick Lunsford, qualifying as a Level 1 System Operator, and to Barry Constantine, qualifying as a Level 2 Water Treatment Plant Operator. The city council and I congratulated the two employees and thanked them for taking such a great interest in their work, and for their service to the community.

A catering permit to serve alcohol during the All Alumni Red Devil Class Reunion, requested by Veranda Bar, to be used at the Depot Square on July 6th, was unanimously approved by the council. The Reunion is an annual event and is held on the weekend nearest to the July 4th celebration.

Also approved were malt beverage applications requested by the V.F.W. for the Proud To Be An American celebration at Depot Square on July 4th, Independence Day, from 12:00 noon to 12:00 midnight, and one requested by Dev Fry representing the Ellis Ranch softball team for the Softball Tournament on June 29th and 30th from 10:00 a.m. to 10:00 p.m. at the Overthrust Ball Fields. Both malt beverage applications were approved by a motion from the city council and seconded with all voting in favor.

Sandy Ottley, Parade Chairman, requested permission to clear the route and hold a parade on July 4th to kick off the Proud To Be An American program. The parade would start at the Uinta County Fairgrounds, proceed over the Overpass, down Front Street to Harrison Drive to Main Street, ending at the War Memorial area of the courthouse yard to start off the celebration.

Motion was made by Councilman Nelson to authorize the parade and the parade route on July 4th, seconded by Wall, with all voting in favor.

Josephine "Joy" Walton requested permission to have a noisy parade on July 6th for the All Alumni Class Reunion, from the Uinta County Library parking lot down Main Street to Harrison Drive, over to Front Street and to Depot Square. Motion was made by Councilman Davis to authorize the parade, seconded by Lehman, with all voting in favor.

The City of Evanston had purchased additional property adjacent to the city shop property on Allegiance Circle with access off Patriot Court, where the city would locate and construct a new Animal Control Shelter.

The new animal shelter would be a 20-pen facility, fenced, with parking for customers and a waiting room and office. It would be a first-class shelter and would cost approximately $77,000.

Before adjourning, Community Development Director Paul Knopf reported that the High Uintas Bike Race had another successful year. He reported that there were 179 bike riders, and the event went off with no problems.

Councilwoman Julie Lehman reported that the Bridger Valley Conservation District donated $18,000 to the BEAR Project.

On June 28th I received a letter from Evanston High School thanking the City of Evanston for supporting The Engineering Experience '91 high school project. The letter read:

Dear Mayor Ottley,

We just recently completed our excellent summer program, The Engineering Experience '91, and would like to extend our sincere thanks to you, the Evanston City Council, your water facilities staffs, and your City Engineering Department for your contribution to the program.

The letter went on with more comments and was signed by Evanston High's Engineering Experience Instructional Staff: teachers Jim Williams, Bob Lancaster, and Todd Nixon.

I read the letter to the city council and staff during a meeting and they all appreciated the comments and indicated that the program was very enjoyable and that they were happy to be involved.

During the June 26th meeting, Community Development Director and City Planner Paul Knopf suggested that the city be broken up into seven neighborhood teams to meet and furnish Evanston's 2000 Review Committee with input for the new Evanston Comprehensive Plan.

"These people will serve as representatives of their neighborhoods. They will solicit input and bring it back to the committee," said Planning and Zoning Director Paul Knopf, as reported by the *Uinta County Herald* on July 5th.

Knopf presented a list of names that he suggested be appointed to the neighborhood teams, and said he had talked to many of them and they had agreed to serve. Those named to serve on the teams were:

NEIGHBORHOOD #1: Rick Schuler, Lin Adkins, Scott Siemers, and Dusty Lym representing the Centennial Valley area and Wasatch Drive.

NEIGHBORHOOD #2: Wayne Bell, Blaine Sanders, Lloyd Lanning, Diane Mills, Rick Sather, and Chris Bauman representing the area covering downtown, 1st Street to 19th Street, and Front Street to Wasatch Drive.

NEIGHBORHOOD #3: Kathy Defa, Claude Smith, Willis Barnes, Bill Aaron, Bob Stocking, and Kirk Ellingford representing Front Street to Highway 89 and north of Bear River Drive to Red Mountain Road.

NEIGHBORHOOD #4: Terry Prete, Jim Jackson, Betty Thornhill, Ruth Dahlman, and Ranold Phillips representing Red Mountain, Fair Meadows and Bear River Drive east of Highway 89.

NEIGHBORHOOD #5: Neal Lesmeister, Cyndie Nordwall, Traci Gomez, and Dave Datteri representing Overthrust Meadows and Ranch Estates.

NEIGHBORHOOD #6: Bill and Marlene Deeter, Ursula Morris, Robert Child, Mike Green, Mary Ann Anderson, and Louise Angwin representing all of the Twin Ridge area and Uinta Meadows to City View Drive.

NEIGHBORHOOD #7: Clyde Pruitt, Randy Ottley, Larry Krantz, Robert Gavin, Julie Cowan, Lance Voss, Naomi Parkin, and Susan Winfield representing the Wyoming State Hospital, all areas east of Highway 150, and all areas between Highway 150 and City View Drive, including Aspen Groves, Southridge and Crestview.

Councilwoman Julie Lehman made the motion to allow the neighborhood teams to be formed and to appoint those named by Director Knopf to serve on the teams and assist the Evanston 2000 Review Committee by offering their input, seconded by Davis, with all voting in favor.

Knopf stated that the new committee members would be brought up to speed on the work previously done before beginning their work. He had indicated that the first meeting of the group will probably be sometime during the first part of August.

Knopf projected that the revamping of the comprehensive plan should be finished by the end of 1992 or the beginning of 1993.

During the latter part of June, the Purple Sage Golf Course called the city about sewage backing up onto the course. When the city crew arrived, they found that one of the manholes had sewage coming out the top of the cover and running into a rough area of the golf course.

The city also got a call from a resident on West Sage Street who had sewage backing up into their furnished basement, causing a lot of damage.

The city checked three or four manholes in the area and found the sewer running fine, but after pulling the cover off of the manhole closest to the resident that with the flooded basement, they found the manhole full of sewage.

After pumping the sewage out of the manhole they found several sticks and large boards. The largest board was a 2″ x 4″ board that was four feet long. When they got the proper equipment to enter the manhole and cleaned out all of the boards the flow was fine. They retrieved 5 or 6 boards that were all 2 feet long or longer, but never found out exactly how they got there. The boards apparently blocked off the flow of the sewer line and caused it to back up in various areas.

At this time the Evanston Lodging Tax Board was going strong and had started putting out notices that those groups or committees working on promotional programs should be applying for funding assistance. They said that so far the board had received $11,500 from the 2 percent lodging tax that was voted on by the people of Evanston last election.

During this July 4th celebration the Evanston community had chosen to honor all of its military veterans—those from Operation Desert Storm, as well as from previous conflicts—with a special observance titled Proud to be an American. The Proud to be an American celebration had a special meaning to millions of Americans. The United States had an extremely successful military operation in the Persian Gulf, and that success had prompted a nationwide resurgence in patriotism that was reflected in July 4th activities. It was a festive, meaningful occasion for everyone. The program was a big success with amazing attendance and participation.

The day started off with the dedication of a recently installed 115-foot flagpole with a 25-foot American flag, "Old Glory," waving at the top, and what beautiful sight. This 115-foot flagpole was installed at the Bear River State Park Information Center. The flag and pole and their installation were donated by John Winfield in honor of his brother, who had recently been killed in an industrial accident. This was a tremendous gesture by Mr. Winfield.

I, as mayor, suggested to John that we put a memorable plate at the bottom of the pole in memory of his brother, but John, for some reason or other, did not want that. I told him that the City of Evanston would be more than happy to pay for it, but he made me promise that the city would not do this.

I was told that he and his brother were very close, but for some reason he just didn't want a plaque or any type of notice attached to the flagpole. He just wanted to get the pole up and see the Stars and Stripes flying at the state park.

What was ironic and very unfortunate was that many years later, John also was killed in an industrial accident. Two brothers, very close, both now gone. It was years apart, but such a waste, and a loss to Evanston of two good young men who worked so hard to build a successful business.

I don't know about anyone else, but every time I go by that park and see that big wonderful flag flying I think of the two Winfield brothers.

During the first city council meeting of the month on July 10th, Councilman Craig Nelson made a motion to approve the application of a malt beverage permit requested by the Evanston Cowboy Days Committee for August 31st through September 2nd for all events during the three day celebration, seconded by Davis, with all voting in favor.

I then re-appointed Marvin Munoz and Roberta Dean to the Public Service Advisory Board for three-year terms. A motion was made by Councilman Davis to confirm these appointments, seconded by Hutchinson, with all voting in favor.

There was also a request from Alvin R. Lundgren to rezone some property that he was leasing, from Agricultural Zone to Industrial Zone. Ordinance 91-8 to do so was introduced by Councilman Hutchinson and sponsored by Councilman Nelson. But during discussion City Attorney Dennis Boal told the city council that the property was only being leased by Mr. Lundgren, and that he was not the owner of the property described in Ordinance 91-8. City Attorney Boal stated that, by law, only a property owner could request any type of change in property. Therefore, a motion was made and seconded that Ordinance 91-8 be tabled until the owner was made aware of the ordinance and application was properly made. The motion passed unanimously.

Various ordinances were acted on that did not coincide with Wyoming state law pertaining to people under 21 consuming alcohol, the use and sale of tobacco to minors, fraudulent checks, helmets required for minors riding motorcycles, requirements for emergency vehicles, disturbing the peace, and traffic violations. These were ordinances that were passed on all three readings to bring local code up to date with state laws.

We passed an ordinance on all three readings removing the words "metered parking" from the Evanston code pertaining to parking.

Since we no longer had parking meters, there was no reason to leave the wording in the ordinance.

Most of this meeting was what I called "house cleaning": cleaning up and correcting portions of ordinances no longer needed and making sure that the City of Evanston's ordinances were brought up to date with state law.

All three incorporated communities, Evanston, Lyman and Mountain View, voted for the Capital Facility Tax proposition to be on the ballot for the general election in 1992.

During the meeting of July 10th Councilman Will Davis introduced the following resolution:

RESOLUTION 91-31
RESOLUTION OF THE CITY COUNCIL FOR THE CITY OF EVANSTON, WYOMING REQUESTING THE COUNTY COMMISSIONERS FOR UINTA COUNTY TO ESTABLISH A CITIZENS' COMMITTEE FOR THE PURPOSE OF RECEIVING PUBLIC INPUT AND PROVIDING A RECOMMENDATION REGARDING THE SUBMISSION OF A PROPOSITION TO THE VOTERS OF UINTA COUNTY TO IMPOSE AN EXCISE TAX FOR THE PURPOSE OF CONSTRUCTING CAPITAL FACILITIES.

The capital facility projects included a Urie connector road, an outdoor recreation facility and nine-hole golf course in Lyman, additional grounds for the Fort Bridger Rendezvous, sewer and bridge improvements in Mountain View, a multi-event center in Evanston to be constructed at the Uinta County Fairgrounds, Senior Citizens Center improvements in Evanston and Mountain View, additional money for the BEAR Project, a new downhill ski area at Rocky Hollow in Evanston, and recreation facilities at Sulphur Creek Reservoir.

I had to admit that this was quite a bundle of projects for the citizens of Uinta County to swallow, but both of the other communities, Lyman and Mountain View, adopted a similar resolution.

Motion was made by Councilwoman Lehman to adopt Resolution 91-31, seconded by Davis. The motion passed by a unanimous vote.

In the resolution I as mayor was directed to submit a copy of the Resolution to the County Commissioners, as the other communities also did. I immediately sent a letter to Commissioner K. Casey Davis, who was at the time Chairman of the Commission, with a copy of Resolution 91-31 attached. For the proposition to be placed on the ballot, it required support of two-thirds of the municipalities in the county and the consent of the county commissioners.

The three county commissioners voted in favor of putting the proposition on the ballot after receiving copies of the Resolutions from each community. When meeting with the commissioners, I said to them, "We just would like to get it on the ballot for the people to vote on it." At that point the commissioners agreed, but stated they thought it was a large agenda for the folks to consider. I agreed, but I said, "Hopefully it will pass for the sake of the economy. This agenda, no matter how big it is, will give the county a chance to complete some of the projects that have been needed for quite some time, and with the Winter Olympics coming to Salt Lake City in the near future, a ski hill will be an asset to the county, and an indoor arena will make it possible to utilize the fairgrounds year 'round, which will help the county's economy considerably."

If the proposition got on the ballot and passed, it would increase the County's sales tax from 5 percent to 6 percent which is not too bad, considering that when folks go to shop in Utah, they pay a 7 percent sales tax and don't bat an eye or bicker about it.

Also during the July 10th meeting, Councilwoman Wall made a motion to authorize a survey on the Union Pacific Land Resources (Upland Industries) property that was west and northwest across the tracks. This was the former Union Pacific Roundhouse. The cost for the survey would come from the Council's budget line item 5401, with a limit not to exceed $7,000. The motion was seconded by Hutchinson, with all voting in favor.

The property to be surveyed was the property that I had been talking about for quite some time with George Peters, District

Supervisor of the U.P. Land Resources, but the U.P. had not come up with a price for the 300+ acre property. However, I would be getting in touch with Mr. Peters again for permission to do the survey.

There were approximately 265 acres of the property that lay southwest of the tracks and approximately 75 acres that lay northwest of the tracks. The negotiations with U.P. was still in the hands of Mr. Peters, and the City of Evanston indicated that they would be interested in purchasing all, or at least 100 acres of the property, but it had to be adjacent to the city property which Union Tank Car Company was leasing.

Our main concern was to get enough property to be used by U.T.C.C. so they wouldn't move out of Evanston to somewhere in Utah, where at this time they were looking to relocate, because they had such a tough time getting a long-term lease from the City of Evanston, and now had given up on it.

A large number of Evanston folks, including some of the city council members, would rather retain the roundhouse and other railroad buildings on the city-owned property for historic preservation. They didn't care as much about the soft economy Evanston was experiencing or the 40 or 50 jobs that the tank car company provided. Rather than loose the company it inspired me to negotiate with George Peters and U.P. Land Resources to purchase all or some of the 300+ acres west of the roundhouse property.

After thanking everyone for their assistance and support in the July 4th celebration of Proud to be an American, and with no other business the meeting was adjourned at 10:15 p.m.

Uinta County Herald

50¢ Per Copy

| Volume 57, Number 59 | Friday, July 26, 1991 | Save $18.50 Home Delivered |

City working on deal to acquire railroad property

■ Land would be transferred to Union Tank Car Co. for expanded facility, leaving roundhouse to city for historic preservation.

By ANN CURTIS
Herald Reporter

Evanston city officials are negotiating a proposed deal that could result in the city acquiring more than 300 acres of land from the Union Pacific Railroad, part of which would be sold to Union Tank Car Co. for the company to build a new, expanded facility.

Mayor Dennis Ottley and other members of the administration and staff have been negotiating with Union Pacific Resources Co. and Union Tank Car for some time about the property and expansion. And although the proposed deal is far from being completed, city officials say they're excited about its potential

benefits for the community.

The property involved lies between the present Union Pacific Roundhouse east to the Purple Sage Golf Course. Some of the land being negotiated for would be on both sides of the railroad tracks. Included would be the old Union Pacific dump site which is being cleaned up this summer.

During Wednesday's city council meeting, engineer/surveyor Kevin Jones was given a contract not to exceed $7,000 to determine the boundaries of the property.

Ottley received a letter from Charles Perczok, vice president of shop operations for Union Tank Car, stating a preliminary inspection by a

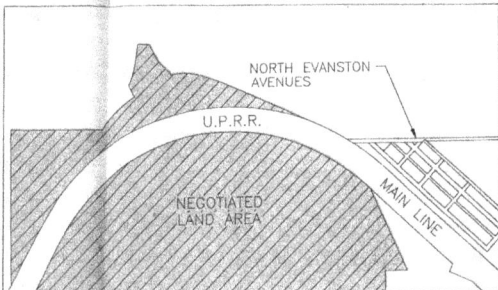

NORTH EVANSTON AVENUES
U.P.R.R.
NEGOTIATED LAND AREA
MAIN LINE

Propery currently under negotitiation covers more than 300 acres along the railroad tracks in Evanston.

consultant for the company found no obvious items of concern on the property.

Plant engineering staff members for Union Tank Car have also completed initial estimates to prepare the property for construction costs.

A shop strategy team has confirmed the proposed new facility

would likely contain a new repair area, cleaning area, flare stack, blast and paint facility, storage yard and adequate land for future construction of an interior coating facility.

The company is hoping to purchase the property at a token fee from the city. Approximately 12 acres of the land and trackage currently leased

by the company would be included in the transaction. It is used, at this time, for storage and switching.

The company proposes that after the new shop is operational, the old roundhouse, machine shop and adjacent property would be returned to

See Deal on page 13

At this time the Evanston Parks and Recreation District Board was in the process of drawing up plans for a neighborhood park in the Centennial Valley area. When the subdivision was approved it was in the county, and at the time, the county had no provision or requirement to demand a portion of land for public use or payment in lieu of the land. Therefore, the city had to provide a park or playground for the area, which the folks in the subdivision well deserved. The closest playground or park for them to have a family picnic or where their children could play and enjoy themselves was the Clark School area.

But there were funds allocated to construct a neighborhood park in the area of Centennial Valley in the 1991-1992 budget and the park would become a reality sometime during the summer of 1992.

During the regular city council meeting dated July 24th, the Evanston Lions Club requested malt beverage permits for two events. They were sponsoring the Small Town Toy Club Show to be held at Hamblin Park between 9:00 a.m. and 9:00 p.m. on July 27th, as well as a dinner and dance at the Beeman–Cashin Building from 7:00 p.m.

to 12:30 a.m., also on July 27th. The permits were approved with all voting in favor.

Community Development Director Paul Knopf and Ken Decaria, representing the BEAR Project, presented a conceptual illustration of the project. They showed the proposed locations of various items of interest. Decaria reported that many hours of work had been contributed to further the development of the project. Knopf stated that this plan, when completed, would be incorporated into the city's Master Plan.

Due to the resignation of Councilman Will Davis from the Uinta County Economic Development Board, Councilwoman Julie Lehman was appointed to replace Davis. Motions were made by the council to accept the resignation of Davis and also to appoint Lehman to the board. The motions were seconded, with all voting in favor.

Judd Redden, representing Lincoln Uinta Association of Governments (LUAG) presented the council with a preliminary proposal to form a Joint Powers Board to manage the Community Development Block Grant (C.D.B.G.) program.

The council and I thanked Mr. Redden for the information and said that we would take his proposal under advisement and get back to him.

During the meeting, several resolutions pertaining to ongoing work projects, executing agreements with various engineering firms, and agreeing to complete a geological survey related to the Bear River were all acted on and adopted by motion and seconded with all voting in favor.

Allen Kennedy, who recently held the position of Superintendent of Operations but had retired as of August 1st, introduced Allan "Oop" Hansen, who was recently approved by the council as the new Superintendent of Operations. Kennedy expressed his thanks to me, members of the council and the staff for the association he had with each. This would be his last city council meeting. He had been with the city for 40 years and received a standing ovation. In my mind he will be hard to replace because he knew so much about the workings of city.

In wishing Allen Kennedy the best and thanking him for his outstanding service over the many years, the city council and I also congratulated Oop Hansen on his new position and wished him the best in taking over such an important position.

Prior to adjourning the July 24th meeting, I reported that I had been informed that the Evanston Youth Government Council, sponsored by the City of Evanston and the Uinta County School District No. 1, received a grant from the State of Wyoming. I then appointed city council members Will Davis and Julie Lehman, and city treasurer Steve Widmer to serve on a committee as representatives to the Youth Council. Motion was made by Councilwoman Wall to confirm the appointments, seconded by Vranish, with all voting in favor.

I announced that the Annual City Picnic would be held at Hamblin Park on August 16th.

During a special meeting that was called by the city council to begin at 5:00 p.m. on August 7th to bring Ordinance 91-8, in which Mr. Alvin R. Lundgren, who was only leasing the property, had requested a zone change, off the table. The ordinance was tabled because only the owner of a property could request a zoning change.

However, a new ordinance numbered 91-17 was submitted to replace Ordinance 91-8, sponsored by Councilwoman Lehman and introduced by Councilman Nelson, was the only business to take place at this meeting.

Ordinance 91-17 was very similar to the previous Ordinance 91-8, but was corrected by having the names of the property owners, Fred and Joyce Tammany, as the parties requesting the zone change.

The property named in the ordinance was located south of the city just off Wyoming State Highway 150 South. It was outside of the boundaries of the City of Evanston, but within one-half mile of the city limits, giving the City of Evanston jurisdiction to determine what the zone would be. The ordinance requested the City of Evanston to change the zone from Agricultural to Highway Business.

Motion was made by Councilman Nelson to pass Ordinance 91-17 on first reading, seconded by Lehman. There was no one in opposition to the motion, but there were folks living in the area in favor of

the ordinance. Therefore, I called for the vote. There were 4 in favor
and 3 absent (Wall, Davis and Hutchinson). Motion passed.

The special meeting adjourned at 5:20 p.m., and Ordinance 91-17
was passed during the next two meetings on second and third readings by a unanimous vote.

When meeting with the Uinta County Commissioners concerning the three communities' request to form a county-wide committee
to form a Proposition to be put on a ballot for a vote for the Capital Facilities Tax for the upcoming election, the Commissioners declined. They declined to even take the lead on any proposed projects.

According to the *Uinta County Herald* issue of August 9th, *If communities in Uinta County want to place a 1 percent capital facilities tax proposal on the ballot, they'll have to put together a package of projects without
direct participation from the county commission.*

*"We don't want to lend the political clout of the county commission to any
community's project this early," Commissioner Chairman Casey Davis said.
"We'd like to see the local entities sell their projects to their own people before
we become involved."*

The *Herald* article continued: *Evanston Mayor Dennis Ottley, who
presented the request to the commissioners, said such a committee is needed to
assure that all areas of the county receive benefits from the proposed tax so that
the proposal would be acceptable to each of the local governments and to voters.*

*But Davis and Commissioner Pat Mulhall said it's not the commission's
role to provide anything more than "technical help" in developing a facilities
tax package.*

*"I think it's most appropriate for the city to form its own committee and
work with the other communities," Davis said. "Then, once you go through
that process and have a proposal to bring to us, I don't think you'll see us fight
it or veto it."*

The article continued: *Ottley said after the meeting that he now in-
tends to contact the other communities to see if they want to form a committee
on their own. But he told the commissioners that they should be involved from
the start because many of the suggested projects involve county facilities.*

*Ottley admitted the communities have "a long way to go" before they'll
be ready to present a proposal to voters, but he said the capital facilities tax is*

"a terrific way" to generate money for community projects. *By using the op-tional tax, the communities would be able to accomplish projects they can't undertake by themselves, he said.*

At this point I could see that the proposed projects were going to be a lot of work and it would be very tough to sell the idea to the folks of Uinta County, but I was quite sure we would be successful in getting the proposition on the ballot, even without the county commissioners approval, but I wasn't too confident that the proposition would pass in the election. There was already large group of folks in the county that were actively trying to defeat it.

In the *Uinta County Herald* of August 13th, Chad R. Baldwin wrote an Editorial titled PUZZLING ATTITUDE. His editorial stated:

The Uinta County Commissioners last week gave the county's three municipalities a clear message: Don't expect any help from us to bring a 1 percent capital facilities tax proposal before county voters.

What they were really saying, however, was that they're not particularly interested in seeing the facilities tax effort get off the ground, and they don't want to do anything to assist that effort.

The commissioners' attitude is puzzling. No one was asking them to endorse the additional sales tax at this point; the communities were simply looking for a way to assure that a tax proposal benefits and is acceptable to people from all areas of the county.

What is particularly puzzling about the commissioners' position is that they have committed to develop a new senior citizens center in Evanston and expand the senior center in Mountain View. And unless they have some secret funding mechanism of which we're not aware, the capital facilities tax may be the only way to pay for the senior center projects.

Perhaps the commissioners are hesitant to form a facilities tax committee because they believe a majority of county residents is opposed to the idea. That may indeed be the case. But the only way we can know for sure is to give them an opportunity to vote on the issue, and the commission's cooperation is necessary to give them that chance.

We believe that with the proper leadership, the capital facilities tax could be an excellent tool to maintain and improve Uinta County's quality of life.

It's unfortunate that leadership must come from the individual communities, rather than from the people we elected to lead the county, Chad Baldwin's editorial concluded.

When the Downtown Improvement District was put together to guarantee that the new United States Post Office would remain downtown area, there were some properties excluded from the improvement district that maybe should have been included. One of those additional buildings was the former Federal Credit Building on the corner of 10th and Center Streets. This building, in 1991, was in the process of being sold to a group called Center Street Partnership.

During the regular city council meeting on August 14th the council held a public hearing concerning the Federal Credit Building property and why the property was omitted from the Downtown Improvement District Assessments, which was formed during former Mayor Gene Martin's administration in 1986. Local Attorney Robert Morton, representing Center Street Partnership, made a presentation for the partnership requesting that the property, at this late date, not be included in the assessment district.

According to a news article in the *Uinta County Herald* of August 16th, *Local Attorney Bob Morton, representing the company [Center Street Partnership], stressed that the building had originally not been affirmed on the assessment role.*

He claimed the property had been recorded at the Uinta County Clerk's office in 1986 as having no assessment, claiming now council was trying to "change horses in mid-stream."

"If not assessing the property was a mistake, who is to bear the brunt of the mistake, the new buyers or the council?" he asked.

The *Herald* article continued: *Councilwoman Julie Lehman inquired if the new owners had been told the additional assessment might occur.*

City Attorney Dennis Boal stated he had spoken with personnel at Uinta Title about the charge. He claimed he was told money would be placed in escrow in case the council decided to include the building, the *Herald* added.

Later in the meeting, after the public hearing had been heard and closed, Ordinance 91-18 was sponsored by Councilman Vranish and introduced by Councilman Hutchinson.

ORDINANCE 91-18
AN ORDINANCE OF THE CITY OF EVANSTON, UINTA COUNTY, WYOMING, ASSESSING REAL PROPERTY PREVIOUSLY OMITTED FROM THE ASSESSMENT ROLL OF THE DOWNTOWN IMPROVEMENT DISTRICT, SAID REAL PROPERTY BEING MORE PARTICULARLY DESCRIBED HEREIN.

Section 1: The following described real property shall hereafter be assessed and included in the assessment roll of the Downtown Improvement District, to wit:

Lot 1, Block 23, of the Original Town of Evanston, Uinta County, State of Wyoming.

After the title of the ordinance was read by City Attorney Boal, Councilwoman Lehman made a motion to pass Ordinance 91-18 on first reading, seconded by Nelson, with 6 votes in favor and 1 vote against (Wall). Motion passed.

At a later meeting, Councilman Nelson made the motion to pass Ordinance 91-18 on second reading, seconded by Lehman with completely different results. The results were 4 no votes and 3 yes votes (me, Vranish and Lehman). The motion failed. Therefore the ordinance did not go to a third reading.

All though I voted in favor of the ordinance I had no problem with it failing, except after requiring Rick Sather to pay for the assessment on the old post office building, I didn't quite feel that it was being fair to Sather. However, when the assessment district was formed, I don't believe the Federal Credit Building had been built and the property was still considered residential. I believe that is why it was kept off the assessment district roll, but the new owners, Center Street Partnership, were very happy with the results.

During a previous Evanston Planning and Zoning meeting, Kern River Gas Transmission Company, the company constructing a natural gas pipeline from Opal, Wyoming to southern California, better known as the Kern River Pipeline, requested that helicopter landing areas be allowed in Industrial Zones.

The *Uinta County Herald* of August 8th reported: *Jon Germyn, pipeline design manager for Kern River, said a helicopter pad at the [Kern River's] Evanston base would "be a matter of convenience" during normal operations, but would increase efficiency and "cut down response time" in emergencies.*

Time would be lost if the base used Evanston Airport facilities to respond to emergencies because it would have to fly a contracted helicopter to the accident site, determine necessary equipment and transport those tools from the base to the airport, he said.

"And timing is really of the essence in some of these things. In an emergency, you need to know continually what the situation is," he said. "Response to emergencies can vary and changes from time to time."

The pad would comply with all Federal Aviation Administration regulations, the Herald continued.

The helicopter pad would be located at the Kern River base at 126 Commerce Dr. in Evanston, and the company had requested a text amendment to the city code which would conditionally allow helicopter landing areas in industrial zones.

The helicopter pad would facilitate aerial inspection of 850 miles of pipeline along the interstate, which must be conducted at least 26 times a year as well as increase efficiency during emergency situations, representative Dick Yeaman said.

But the P & Z Commission recommended against allowing helicopter take-off and landing sites in industrial zones. The issue would now go before the Evanston City Council.

The P & Z Commission had questions about the Kern River request from a number of citizens from the nearby residential area. The closest residential zone would be less than one-half mile from the helicopter pad's proposed location.

J. D. Kindler, who was present at the P & Z meeting, was concerned about his daughter's horses, which were kept in a pasture near the proposed helicopter pad site. He was concerned about helicopters passing overhead frightening the animals.

Quinton Bonner, also present at the meeting, who lives at 122 Colonial Avenue, said he is not worried about the noise but does not want a precedent set allowing companies to land helicopters within city limits.

"If it's just an emergency kind of thing, and they'd only come in every two weeks [the noise] wouldn't be a problem," Bonner said. *"Primarily my opposition was, I didn't want a precedent established. If we allow one company in, it opens the door for other companies,"* the *Herald* reported.

Mr. Quinton Bonner didn't understand, or it wasn't explained to him, that if another company came to the P & Z Commission for another helicopter pad they would have to apply for a conditional use permit, which would require hearings by the commission and city council before it was approved. This would give those concerned citizens plenty of time and the opportunity to offer any pros or cons they may have at that time.

It seemed that most times when an issue of controversy came up someone would make the comment, "We do not want to set precedent." When I hear that I always try to explain that when an issue is approved you only set precedent if you allow the action taken on the issue to set precedent. It is up to the hearing group to look at all issues separately.

I tell them that every case should be judged on its own merits and benefits. Just because you approved a similar situation for one person or company doesn't mean you should approve it for another person. There are no two situations exactly alike – maybe similar, but not alike.

As in a courtroom the judge, hopefully, doesn't announce his decision based on other cases, no matter how similar they are, but judges each case on its own merits. Oh, maybe he will look at similar former cases, but for informational purposes only. As I say, "There are no two cases alike," and "There are no two persons alike."

Therefore, when the issue came up during the August 14th meeting, Councilman Nelson introduced Ordinance 91-19, and Councilwoman Lehman sponsored the ordinance to put it on the floor.

ORDINANCE 91-19
AN ORDINANCE AMENDING SECTION 24-15 (c) (12)
TO CONDITIONALLY ALLOW HELICOPTER AREAS IN
AN INDUSTRIAL ZONE.

Notice the word *"Conditionally"*. That means any application would have to apply for a "Conditional Use Permit," requiring all applications to be heard.

Following the introduction of the ordinance and City Attorney Dennis Boal reading the title, Councilman Vranish made the motion to pass Ordinance 91-19 on first reading, seconded by Nelson. I then opened the floor up for discussion and the city council heard comments from those concerned citizens that were in attendance.

After a motion to amend the ordinance was made to correct some wording and was seconded for approval, I asked for the vote on the main motion to pass Ordinance 91-19 on first reading as amended, with 7 votes in favor and no votes against.

In the next two meetings Ordinance 91-19 as amended was brought up on the floor for second and third readings, with a unanimous vote in favor on both. Ordinance 91-19 was now law and Kern River was allowed to have a helicopter landing and take-off pad. This was one of the few times that the Evanston City Council overruled the Evanston Planning and Zoning Commission.

During the meeting more bids were opened on street and sewer projects, and resolutions were adopted authorizing the city to enter into agreements with those construction companies receiving the bids.

Resolution 91-41 was introduced by Councilman Nelson, authorizing the City of Evanston to apply to the Wyoming Game and Fish Department for a grant of $55,000 for construction of the Ice Ponds and Water Diversion Structure for the BEAR Project. Motion was made by Councilwoman Lehman to adopt Resolution 91-41, seconded by Davis, with all voting in favor.

Purchasing Agent Mike Lake presented bids for a medium-size car to be used for executive purposes. The low bidder was Young

Chevrolet (presently Castle Rock) with a 1992 Lumina Chevrolet for $15,792.43.

Councilman Hutchinson made a motion to accept the low bid, seconded by Lehman, with 6 votes in favor and 1 vote against (Wall). I don't know why Jerry voted against it, but I'm sure she had her reasons.

Before adjourning I once again reminded the council and staff of the city picnic on Friday, August 16th at 6:00 p.m. at Hamblin Park, and I also reminded them of the work session at City Hall at 5:00 p.m. on August 21st, and that there would be a meeting at the Mountain View Town Hall, with the three county municipalities, to discuss the Capital Facility Tax on August 22nd at 7:30 p.m.

Tours of Depot Square had been started and Urban Renewal Agency Director Jim Davis announced that Carol Broadbent and Clinton Schroeder had been hired by the agency to conduct tours through the summer months, seven (7) days a week, between the hours of 7:00 a.m. to 10:00 a.m. and 1:00 p.m. to 8:00 p.m.

The second regular city council meeting for the month of August was held on August 28th and was a meeting to remember. Evanston's First Lady approached the city council about allowing a "Cattle Drive" on August 31st, the first day of the Evanston Cowboy Days celebration during Labor Day weekend on August 31st, September 1st and 2nd.

She told the council that several local cowboys had approached her to meet with the city council and request permission to promote a cattle drive to kick off the Cowboy Days celebration on August 31st. The drive would be a couple dozen head of stock and cattle trucks would drop off the herd at City Hall's parking lot where the drive would begin. They would be herded down Front Street to 9th Street, east under the underpass to Highway 89, then north into the Uinta County Fairground using the gate by Evanston Fire Hall #2.

After some concerns and questions pertaining to the control of the cattle, property and public safety, and liability by City Attorney Boal and Police Chief Harvey, Sandy told them and the council that there shouldn't be any problems because there would be experienced cowboys handling the drive, and she was very confident that the cowboys knew what they were doing.

After it appeared that everyone felt pretty good about the drive, Councilwoman Wall made a motion to approve the Cattle Drive and the route, with the police department's assistance, seconded by Nelson, with all voting in favor.

However, it didn't turn out the way we expected. By the time the cowboys got to 10th Street, they lost control of some of the herd, and cattle ended up in places like the golf course, the gravel pit just west of the roundhouse, out by the Yellow Creek Center, and some in Depot Square, causing damage to some of the flowers. Thank God there was no real damage and thank God the cowboys were successful in rounding up the entire herd and finally getting them to the fairgrounds.

When Sandy asked the cowboys what happened, one cowboy told her that the problem was that this herd was a bunch of range cows that weren't used to being herded. He said they should have had cattle that had been penned up for a while. They would have been much easier to handle.

Sandy was worried about the outcome and hoped there wouldn't be too much damage or injury. The chief of police and the city attorney, who also were going nuts worrying about the outcome of the event, suggested that she forget any more cattle drives through downtown in the future. Although there were no complaints from any citizens claiming damages, or anyone hurt, the city attorney suggested, "No more," and there weren't.

The *Uinta County Herald* of September 3rd reported:

The early-morning cattle drive through downtown Evanston took some unusual detours, as the herd occasionally decided to travel its own trail. However, the cowboys tracked down the cattle and led them to their pens at the Uinta County Fairgrounds. The cattle drive was part of the Evanston Cowboy Days activities Saturday morning.

In the Evanston Chamber of Commerce column published in the *Uinta County Herald* of September 6th, Executive Director of the Evanston Chamber of Commerce Dianne Hodges wrote:

Evanston really had a great Labor Day weekend! All of our tourists really seemed to enjoy all of our events.

I enjoyed all of the events, but the funniest one was the cattle drive down Front Street! The cattle weren't quite sure where they wanted to go. They definitely have a mind of their own – when one decides to leave the group, they all follow. The cowboys did a great job in trying to keep them all together. Sandy Ottley was in charge of this event. I wonder what she'll come up with next.

Dianne went on with her column announcing the various events coming up, such as the Chili Cookoff.

During the city council meeting of August 28th I gave a verbal pat on the back to honor Dianne Hodges for her efforts in scheduling and hosting a tour group with representatives from four countries. I don't recall all four of the nations, but I do remember that there were representatives from Japan and the Philippines.

I announced that the new recycling committee would start having their meetings on Tuesday and Thursday evenings to lay the groundwork for upgrading the recycling program.

I also mentioned that The Pines apartments were for sale and that I wanted to make sure the council was aware that the Wyoming Community Development Administration (W.C.D.A.) office in Casper might be looking into buying it. I told them that I didn't know whether it was a good idea or not, taking the rental business out of the private business sector and putting it into the public sector, but we would just have to wait and see what came up.

Prior to the meeting of August 28th, Safeway Stores Incorporated (at that time known as Safeway Inc.), had requested that the City of Evanston sponsor Industrial Development Revenue Bonds not to exceed $3,700,000 to construct a new grocery and pharmacy store on Front Street (which is where Jubilee Super Shopping Center is located at the present). The Safeway Store was previously located where the new Uinta County Library parking lot is now. When the county purchased that entire block, Safeway Stores had to relocate.

Ordinance 91-20, to approve the issuance and sale of Evanston, Wyoming Industrial Development Revenue Bonds not to exceed

$3,700,000 as requested by Safeway Inc., was sponsored by Councilman Hutchinson and introduced by Councilwoman Lehman to bring the ordinance on the floor.

After the reading of the title by the city attorney, Councilman Davis made a motion to pass Ordinance 91-20 on first reading. After a short discussion I asked for the vote, which was 6 yes and 1 no (Vranish). The motion passed on first reading.

This had been one of the very few requests for Industrial Development Revenue Bonds since Evanston's boom period had ended, and maybe that was the reason Vranish voted against the motion: there were other means created since the boom period that could lend money to companies for new industrial or commercial construction. However, I felt that I.D.R. Bonds were a great way to go because the City of Evanston had no obligation whatsoever to pay them back and the city gained money for sponsorship. I know they sure helped the city through the boom.

During the next two regular meetings of the city council Ordinance 91-20 passed on second and third readings, with all voting in favor except Vranish, approving the bonding for Safeway Inc.

Towards the end of the August 28th meeting, Councilwoman Lehman made a motion to go into executive session to discuss making an offer on the 300+ acres of the Union Pacific Land Resources property located west of the Roundhouse. The motion was seconded by Nelson with all voting in favor.

Since the survey had been completed and the city now had something to make an offer on it was decided that I, as mayor, would be directed to make an undisclosed offer to the U.P.L.R.

Coming out of executive session, Councilwoman Lehman made a motion to authorize the mayor to extend an offer to purchase real property from U.P.L.R. in an amount discussed in executive session, seconded by Davis and passing unanimously in favor.

Therefore, my next step was to contact George Peters, the U.P.L.R. District Supervisor of the area, and who I had been negotiating with all along, but this time I had something to negotiate with. Of course the offer would be subject to the U.P. cleaning up the polluted areas and a guarantee that there would be no toxic materials left on the property. The property would need to be clean of all garbage and other materials.

Prior to adjourning the meeting of August 28th, I also announced that the Second Annual Mayor's Invitational Golf Tournament would be held at the Purple Sage Golf Course on September 13th, and it would be an 18-hole four-man scramble. A brunch would be served at the clubhouse after the 9th hole.

During the regular city council meeting of September 11th, a public hearing was held concerning the renewal of all liquor licenses held within the city limits of Evanston, as it is every year, conducted by the city attorney. Most years we had citizens in attendance questioning a license or a number of licenses that had caused problems in some areas, or as reported by the police when one or more license holders were not upholding the law or they were not controlling their patrons.

However, this year there was no one in attendance that expressed any opposition or questioned any liquor license holder during the hearing. Therefore, the city attorney closed the hearing and I called for a motion to renew all liquor licenses, including full licenses, limited licenses, and restaurant licenses.

Councilman Nelson made a motion to approve the renewal of all liquor licenses held in Evanston as they were listed in the minutes, seconded by Wall, with all 7 voting in favor.

Mr. George Barker, Chairman of the Uinta County School Board District No. 1, Mr. Norman Gaines, Superintendent, Mr. Harold Shockley, Assistant Superintendent, and Mr. Bob Fry, Director of Lifelong Learning Center were all in attendance for the September 11th meeting. They were there to make a presentation, to answer questions and request the city's support concerning the 5 mill levy that was proposed to be on the ballot during a special election on October 8, involving all the citizens residing within the area of U.C.S.D. #1. After everyone was satisfied with discussion, Councilman Hutchinson made a motion for the Evanston City Council to go on record in support of the 5 mill levy as it was proposed to appear on the ballot on October 8. The motion was seconded by Wall, with 5 yes votes and 2 no votes (Vranish and Davis).

The *Uinta County Herald* of September 13th reported Councilman Vranish stating, *It was not the council's "place" to "give its blessing" or lend support to a measure that would soon be decided by voters.*

Davis said he was opposed to the district's purchase of a $286,000 warehouse and questioned board members about wasted school supplies.

He said he had seen several unopened cases of glue while touring the warehouse, and he asked why his children were required to bring their own glue to school if the district had plenty.

"To my way of thinking, I am spending my money twice," he said.

Assistant Superintendent Harold Shockley responded that a committee had been formed to solve inventory problems, the *Herald* reported.

On October 8th the 5 mill levy for Uinta County School District No. 1 was voted on in the special election. The folks in District No. 1 voted in favor of the levy by a large margin.

During this city council meeting of September 11th, Mr. Carl Classen, Director of the Wyoming Association of Governments (W.A.M.) from Cheyenne was in attendance. He was there to express his appreciation and gratitude, on behalf of W.A.M., for the outstanding job Evanston had done on the recent W.A.M. convention in June.

Classen explained some of the functions of W.A.M. and why it was important that all municipalities should be a member, and he gave a special expression of appreciation to Councilwoman Jerry Wall for her outstanding work in making the convention such a big success.

Carl Classen was relatively new to his position as Director of the W.A.M. association. He had recently replaced Bob Cantine, who had been Director of W.A.M. for a number of years, until he retired. I felt that Cantine had done a terrific job as director, and I, among many, really hated to see him go, but after getting to know Mr. Classen during the convention, I felt that he was going to be just fine.

Also during the meeting Councilman Vranish introduced Resolution 91-49. This resolution was for the City of Evanston to authorize the Revolving Loan Fund to be administered by the Lincoln–Uinta Association of Governments (LUAG) instead of the City of Evanston. The city had been administering these low-interest economic development loans for the purpose of financing training and counseling to promote economic development within Lincoln and Uinta Counties.

After some discussion Councilman Davis made the motion to adopt Resolution 91-49, seconded by Nelson, with all voting in favor. The Evanston City Council members voted to transfer responsibility for the program because they felt that the city's system for analyzing loan requests was not mature enough.

The Lincoln–Uinta Revolving Loan Fund is a pool of money created to help eligible businesses create or retain jobs in Lincoln and Uinta Counties. It is intended to bridge the gap created by shortfalls in conventional financing. Funds are repaid into the program and then recycled to other qualified businesses. Each application is based on its own merits and may request up to 40 percent of the total project costs, not to exceed $100,000.

During the regular city council meeting of September 25th I appointed Evanston Treasurer Steve Widmer to the 12-member LUAG Revolving Loan Fund Joint Powers Board with the confirmation of the council. City Councilman Vranish was assigned as the council's representative to the board and was required to attend all LUAG meetings and report back to the council.

The new garbage pickup system was now in full service and the City of Evanston was getting many people writing letters, notes, and even commenting during the meetings about how much they appreciate the new system and how well it was working out. There were many changes that had to be made, but after working out all the bugs in the new system it was working much better than the previous system.

The *Uinta County Herald* of October 1st quoted City Engineer Brian Honey: *"An initial concern was that the [new] trucks would not be able to negotiate the alleys, so in the last week we have been working on that. We are now picking up many of the cans in the alleys,"* he said. *"I would really like to thank folks for their patience in this."*

If the homes are located without alley access, Honey added, the city sanitation department asks that homeowners put their cans about four feet into the street with their wheels against the back of the curb, the *Herald* added.

The project was working out fine and there were very few complaints. Some folks were against the change of systems, including some former city council members, but this proved to me, once again, that the old saying *"Where there's a will, there's always a way,"* was always the way to go. I know it sure made a difference in the attitude of our employees; no employee previously liked working on the back end of the garbage truck.

Once again Sandy approached the city council during the September 25th meeting to have a parade for Support Your Community Week on October 19th as a kick-off for the annual event. She said they would again start at the library parking lot and proceed down Main Street to Harrison Drive (11th Street), over to Front Street, to the lot adjacent to the 6th Street overpass. A motion was made by Councilman Hutchinson to authorize the parade and inform the police department to prepare for it, seconded by Nelson, with all voting in favor.

❧

In October, 1991 Sandy and I finally gave up our home because of our foreclosure. Harry Palmer, President of the Pioneer Bank (presently Wells Fargo) gave us an opportunity to save our home, but the payments were so high we just couldn't afford them any longer, so we signed a "deed in lieu of foreclosure" with the bank and gave up our home that we had built in 1960. We moved into a two-story rental unit of the Grandview Townhouses located south of town on Fox Point Loop Road.

We rented for several years until we got back on our feet financially, and by improving our credit, we then were in a position to get a mortgage to purchase the unit.

❧

The Evanston City Council had been working with the Wyoming Highway Department on a proposed construction project for the improvement of Park Road. This project had been suggested by the Highway Department and approved by the Evanston City Council. The construction of this project would be through the highway department with the assistance and some guidance by the city engineer, and would be financed by highway funds.

In early October the Evanston City Council got final word that the proposed Park Road project would get underway as soon as weather permitted. The project would entail reconstruction of curbing, sidewalks, storm drainage, new surfacing and widening, plus a change in routing of access to Park Road and Cedar Street off Bear River Drive. It would definitely be a change for the better and hopefully they would begin the construction at least by spring of 1992.

During the October 9th city council meeting the issue came up of the Wyoming Community Development Authority (W.C.D.A.) purchasing the Pines of Yellow Creek, an apartment complex with over 70 units. W.C.D.A.'s interest in the project was to turn it into a low- and moderate-income housing complex.

When it came on the floor for a vote Councilman Vranish introduced Resolution 91-43, pledging the support of the City of Evanston for the W.C.D.A. purchase of the Pines of Yellow Creek. Councilman Vranish made the motion to adopt Resolution 91-43, seconded by Lehman.

A lengthy discussion followed the motion. Mr. George Axlund, Director of the W.C.D.A. from Casper was in attendance to answer any questions or concerns that the council and the public may have.

There were a number of concerned citizens in attendance, mostly those who owned, rented, or were in the property management business, but there were a few neighbors concerned that the project may have a negative effect on the value of their property.

The Pines of Yellow Creek was already available for low-income rentals approved by the U.S. Department of Housing and Urban Development (HUD), and I thought that it would be nice to have the units remodeled into condominiums and sold to moderate- to low-income families, which W.C.D.A. proposed to do, and

I thought it would help the economy through the construction period by creating jobs.

Also, I knew that Gary Bolger, Director of the Evanston Housing Authority, wanted the housing authority to purchase them to add to the already 60-plus units they were renting out to senior citizens and low-income folks, for which the housing authority was formed during the high-rental period of the boom. I felt that the Housing Authority had enough units and didn't want to see them get into the property management business in competition with the private sector.

However, after ending discussion I called for the vote, which was 5 against and 2 in favor (Vranish and me). The motion failed and Mr. Axlund said that without the support of the city the W.C.D.A. would no longer pursue the issue, and thanked the city council for giving him the opportunity to at least try.

The Union Tank Car Company marked their 100th anniversary of being in business this year. They celebrated at their Evanston plant, expressing their desire to still expand their operations in Evanston, but the idea remained up in the air. I assured them that we were working really hard to get the Union Pacific Land Resources to sell all or part of the property west of the roundhouse to the City of Evanston.

The city had made their offer but had heard nothing from the U.P. since. If the city is successful in obtaining the property, there is a good chance that U.T.C.C. would remain in Evanston and build a new facility on part of the land purchased by the city.

There was no question that the U.T.C.C. was still looking in the Utah area, because they were determined to have a plant in the western states. I kept in touch with Mr. George Peters, District Supervisor for U.P.L.R., waiting for a reply from him on the U.P.'s decision, but I found out over the years that big corporations do not act very fast.

A news article by *Herald* reporter Ann Curtis was published, titled OFFICIALS PREPARING "EVANSTON 2000" PLAN: *The community meetings and brainstorming sessions are over, and Evanston city officials are now preparing the document which will guide development in the city for the next decade.*

Planning and Zoning Director Paul Knopf said the new comprehensive plan – called "Evanston 2000: A Community Vision" – will be issued in approximately six weeks.

Knopf had conducted the meetings with members of each neighborhood to determine their priorities and wants. At those first meetings, some 40 residents were asked to circulate in their areas and speak with residents about their ideas. Further meetings were conducted to refine the ideas, and they were placed on a map, Curtis added.

Support Your Community Week began on Saturday, October 19th with the Volunteer Parade kicking off the event first thing Saturday morning. The parade was to honor volunteers in the community.

Uinta County Herald reporter Ann Curtis stated in the issue of October 18th, *According to parade organizer Sandy Ottley, the event is to honor all those volunteers who help bring about the many community events. The theme of the parade is "A Thousand Points of Light."*

Other events on Saturday would be the Flea Market, the Pumpkin Carving Contest, the Pumpkin Seed Spit, the Cow Chip Toss, Railroad History, and a showing of the Endurance Race video.

On Sunday, in addition to the promotional week, was the Octoberfest – A Taste of Evanston, and Historic Railroad Photo Exhibit & Displays at Depot Square. The Mayor's Prayer Breakfast was held Monday morning at Lotty's Family Restaurant with Pastor Richard O. Meyer of the Trinity Lutheran Church as main speaker.

LETTERS TO THE EDITOR

Happy experience

Editor's note: This letter was received by Evanston Mayor Dennis Ottley.

Dear Mayor:

I had the pleasure a few weeks ago of visiting your city and found it to be a very happy experience. Everywhere I went I found the people so very friendly.

My sister-in-law, Mildred Beckwith, made the trip with me. We are the sole survivors of the John A. Beckwith family. The grandfather, A.C. Beckwith, was one of the pioneer settlers of Evanston. We were gathering history for our children and grandchildren.

Upon visiting the museum, we met Clint Schroeder, who was so very helpful in spending his time looking up documents, finding old buildings and helping us find graves in the cemetery.

We went to the old Beckwith home, and Mr. and Mrs. Bert Slavens were so very kind in giving us a tour of the home. We were so happy to see the restoration being done.

We were so delighted to meet a young man who showed such enthusiasm for pioneer history and feel he is well qualified to be in this Renewal Agency.

I only wish our small town here had had more foresight in keeping and restoring our old buildings. Our railroad depot was sold for one dollar and moved from its former site. Also, the city hall and first school house were moved several miles.

I am looking forward to making another trip with my daughter, who is John Beckwith's granddaughter.

We enjoyed our stay in the old Quinn home, now the Pine Gables, and Mr. and Mrs. Monroe were so helpful in making copies of old documents they had.

I am looking forward to our next visit with them.

Irena Beckwith Parks
McCall, Idaho

Uinta County Herald, October 25, 1991.

On Wednesday was the Essay Winners' Pizza Luncheon, and that evening was the regular city council meeting when the Evanston High School Cheerleaders once again entered the Council Chambers and gave a number of cheers to help celebrate Support Your Community Week. During the meeting, Essay Contest winners of what "Evanston Means to Me," were in attendance. There were approximately 36 placed winners from the four Evanston Elementary Schools.

Bruce Hudson and Bob Addy had been introduced as administrators of the schools involved in the essay contest, and several teachers from the various schools were also in attendance, appearing to be very proud of their students.

The city council and I expressed our thanks and appreciation to all the students and teachers for being so supportive and involved in the week-long program, for their fine essays and for their attendance at the council meeting.

Thursday was Senior Recognition Day Lunch at the Weston Plaza, and the Support Your Community Week Mixer sponsored by the Evanston Chamber of Commerce and hosted by the Evanston Motor Company at their new location.

To top the week off was the Support Your Community Week Banquet at the Legal Tender with Secretary of State Kathy Karpan as the featured speaker, who gave a great speech on "Community Volunteerism." In her speech she said, "*I am sure your service to Evanston and your fellowship with each other would lead you to agree with Cotton Mather who, over 250 years ago, wrote 'Doing good is a sound policy, an honor, a privilege, an incomparable pleasure and a reward in itself',*" Karpan said.

During the banquet, those nominated and chosen to be honored for their outstanding service to the City of Evanston over the many years were Rudger and Thema Davis, Jean Painter Cook, Norwood "Sutt" Sutton, and Athena Dallas, folks who were loved by everyone and well deserving of the honor.

Support Your Community Week, once again, was a great success, involving many citizen volunteers showing plenty of GRIT.

During the city council meeting of October 23rd, the regular meeting during the Support Your Community Week, I presented the "Pat on the Back Award" from the Evanston Chamber of Commerce to David Bills for his continuous service to the community. I also presented a Certificate of Appreciation from the City of Evanston and the Beautification Committee to Les Banks for his efforts in getting the old U.P.R.R. dump cleaned up, and I presented a plaque to the Overthrust Chili Cookoff Committee from the City of Evanston in appreciation for their service to the community. Committee Chairman Steve B. Norman accepted the award and introduced his committee members: Jean Stevens, Tracy Smith, Sue Spring, Craig Spring, Fred Martinez, Craig Hillcrest, Dwayne Plschefsky, Esther Gattif, Chris Bauman, Sheila Albrecht, Dick Damron, Keith Cerny, Claudia Blackwell, Betty Mathson, Paul Barnard, Joe McInnis, Julie McInnis, Ralph Page, Dawna Rae Page, Les Banks, Kathy Edwards, Tim Lynch, and Angelo Aimone, who were, to my knowledge, all in attendance.

I explained to those at the meeting that the award to the Chili Cookoff Committee was in appreciation for ten years of service to the community, and that each year the Chili Cookoff event became bigger and better in bringing people to Evanston from all over the country. *In ten years of service, this committee has raised over $140,000 that had been distributed to local charitable organizations,* I added.

Offerings on access property items the city had allowed the public to bid on were brought up by Purchasing Agent Mike Lake. He announced that most of the items had been bid on, but there were some that had not received a bid offer. He said a couple of doors and 15 bicycles had not had any bid.

A motion was made by Councilman Davis to honor those bids as received, seconded by Lehman, with all voting in favor.

The bicycles that were being bid on were bikes that the Evanston Police Department had gathered up over many, many years and had never been claimed.

I announced that the Elks Club had mentioned that they would like to bid on the leftover bikes to fix up and give them out at Christmas time. Therefore, Councilwoman Wall made a motion to award the 15 remaining bikes to the Elks Club for a total price of $1.00 to be used for their Christmas package program, seconded by Hutchinson, with all voting in favor.

During the month's first meeting on November 13th, an updated report was given by Eric Heltzel from the Recycling Committee that their plans to upgrade the recycling program had been completed and the public appeared to accept their idea of adding more bins in additional areas in the community and issuing information to the public about what it means to the life of the landfill and other benefits of recycling.

The city council and I thanked Mr. Heltzel and the Recycling Committee for their service and time given to the City of Evanston in assisting with the city's recycling program.

During the meeting I once again recognized a group of Boy Scouts who were in attendance to gain points toward their merit badges. The scouts were of Troop 23 with Greg Duerden, Scoutmaster accompanying them. Scoutmaster Duerden introduced the scouts as follows: Jason Hartley, Nathan Hartley, Jason Privett, Gary Duerden, Bryant Voss, and Ward McCombie. Applause followed their introduction and I thanked Scoutmaster Duerden and his scouts for being present and wished them all the best in achieving their goals for their merit badges.

Next I made a new appointment to the Evanston Police Department, Wayne Weston. Chief Dennis Harvey introduced him, and Councilman Vranish made a motion to confirm the appointment, seconded by Nelson, with all voting in favor. We all welcomed Weston to the department and wished him luck and success in his new position.

During the meeting Patricia Henry, past president of the Urban Renewal Ball Committee, introduced new president Carol McKinley, and Lori Alexander, Treasurer of the Committee, presented a check for $25,000 to Urban Renewal Agency Director Jim Davis.

I expressed the city's appreciation to all who had helped with the Renewal Ball and especially those who had been working on improving the Historic Depot Square.

Mr. Larry Matthews, Student Council Advisor, introduced the new student leaders who were elected to serve as Youth Government

Leaders. In the recent student school election, Bryan Moore was elected Mayor. Other members of the student council elected were as follows: Ryan Berger, Scott Jensen and Jeff Honey – Ward l; Lori Hanks, Jennifer Boehme and Brandon Wagstaff – Ward ll; and Dave Revelli and Dreama Brizendine – Ward lll. All were in attendance.

Adult advisors from the city included City Treasurer Steve Widmer and council members Julie Lehman and Will Davis.

I removed myself from the podium and shook hands with each successful candidate and congratulated them and thanked them, presenting each with a pin of the official City of Evanston Seal and the Fresh Air, Freedom and Fun pin. I also thanked Widmer, Councilwoman Lehman and Councilman Davis for their guidance and involvement in the Student Government Program.

During this November meeting Resolution 91-63 was introduced by Councilman Nelson, designating Evanston's City Hall, police department building and public works building as smoke-free facilities.

Motion was made by Councilman Vranish to adopt Resolution 91-63, seconded by Hutchinson with all voting in favor.

Motion was made by Councilwoman Wall to hold only one meeting during the month of December, because of the holiday season. The one meeting would be on December 18th at 7:00 p.m. The motion was seconded by Lehman with all voting in favor.

The city employees had recently taken a poll of all city employees concerning which holiday they would take off this coming year. The poll was between the Martin Luther King Day and Columbus Day. The poll showed that a large majority of the employees selected Columbus Day. Probably one of the big reasons was because Columbus Day was always during the fall hunting season.

The personnel manual only gave the employees so many holidays and had never been changed to add Martin Luther King Day, but that would be changed in the next year or so where they would get both days off.

Before adjournment of the November 13th meeting, I announced that there would be a work session on November 20th at 7:00 p.m., and I reminded everyone of the annual Christmas Dinner on December 13th, given in honor of the employees every December thanking them for their past year's work.

Winter had arrived early this particular year. It started snowing in late October and had not stopped for quite some time. Evanston had plenty of snow before Thanksgiving. Normally snow doesn't start accumulating until around Thanksgiving, but this year it started much sooner and the snow was falling so fast it was causing public work crews to be called out much earlier than usual.

Citizens complained that the streets were not getting plowed early enough and when the city did get to their streets, like other years, the city would plow in their driveways and folks would get upset. Not all, because most citizens understood that the city could not take the time to clean everyone's driveways. But they do try to be as careful as they can to avoid plowing in driveways too much. This year the snow not only started early, it kept snowing heavily for weeks, causing the city crews to have problems keeping up.

With so many complaints from citizens, I directed the city engineer to put an article in the local newspaper, the Uinta County Herald, and explain to the citizens the city's procedure in snow plowing. The Herald came out with an article on November 1st titled CITY REVIEWS ITS SNOW PLOW RULES. The article mentioned City Engineer Brian Honey explaining that the level of snow plowing service is adjusted to match the rate and accumulation of snowfall, wind velocity, temperature, storm duration and time of day.

The Herald reported: According to City Engineer Honey, the order of priority for snow removal is: first, access to the IHC Evanston Regional Hospital, the fire stations and arterial streets; second, collector streets, school bus routes and signalized intersections; third, the central business district and residential streets; and fourth, the city parking lots. According to Honey, the property owner owns the snow that falls on his (or her) land, including driveways, sidewalks and to the center of the city street.

He asked that snow be removed from sidewalks within 24 hours.

Honey also stated that snow plowed by city equipment to clear streets should not be pushed, thrown or otherwise moved back into the street.

The *Herald* article continued: *Honey advises those with trailers and seldom-used vehicles to remove them from the streets. If that is not possible, those, along with "on-street parkers," should expect that their vehicles may be "plowed in," he said.*

"It is not feasible for the city plowing equipment to clear the streets and also leave your personal driveway open and clear," Honey stated. Depending on the accumulation of snow, it may take more than one or two passes with the plow to clear the street, the Herald article concluded.

During the November 27th regular city council meeting Urban Renewal Agency Director Jim Davis requested a permit to have the Torch Light Parade on November 30th following Thanksgiving Day, and the Teddy Bear Parade on December 14th. Councilman Nelson made the motion to permit the two parades and to make the police department aware of it, seconded by Davis, with all voting in favor.

Resolution 91-61 was introduced by Councilman Vranish, a resolution authorizing the City of Evanston to purchase certain property from the Evanston Industrial Center Partnership. This was property adjacent to the public works operation and the new animal control building.

This property would be an asset to the city for more storage area, and due to the fact that it was listed by Uinta Realty, Inc. and I was the sales agent that had it listed, I did make a commission from the sale of the property to the city. This was the only time in my period as a mayor or member of the council that I ever made a commission from any property the city purchased or sold.

Although I was accused of making money off properties that the city had purchased during my terms as mayor many times, I can honestly say that this particular time was a first and would be the last and only time I had ever benefited through the purchase or sale of any property that the city was involved in.

Motion was made by Councilman Nelson for the adoption of Resolution 91-61, seconded by Davis. The motion passed with 5 yes votes, 1 abstaining (me), and 1 absent (Hutchinson).

I received a very nice letter on November 14th that I would like to mention and make the readers aware of from Willis and Marie Barnes, which read as follows:

> *Dear Mayor Ottley,*
>
> *Thank you for your sweet letter expressing our appreciation to us for attending all the activities during Support Your Community Week. They all were a lot of fun and some educational too!*
> *We realize you, Sandy and the Chamber of Commerce members and probably others, have worked arduous hours to put this on for us to enjoy. So I think it is our place to thank all of you.*
> *Our children were all born and graduated from High School in Evanston; when coming home for a visit, they enjoy the various activities and say our city is a lively, fun place to bring their families.*
> *We owe our gratitude to all of you who meet and plan unique activities and follow-through for Evanston and all visitors to enjoy.*
>
> *Our <u>best</u> to you,*
> *Willis and Marie Barnes*

Will and Marie had been nominees honored at a previous Support Your Community Week Honor Banquet and had become very good friends to Sandy and me.

During the November city council meeting I read the letter to the council and the visitors. They all seemed to accept the letter as an appreciation to the city, and several made some good comments and thanked the Barneses for acknowledging Evanston's activities. The letter made me feel good, and that what we were doing was helping the economy and making Evanston a fun and respectful community to reside in.

During the last regular city council meeting of the year on December 18th, Mr. Jerry Troshynski, the Public Health Nurse presented me, as mayor, a certificate of commendation for declaring City

Hall and other city facilities smoke-free work areas. Mr. Troshynski was thanked for his presentation, and appreciation was shown by the city council members and me.

Parks and Recreation Director Dennis Poppinga also made a presentation concerning the Eagle Rock ski area and its discontinuance as a safe ski area, and he introduced Mr. Beat "Bayot" vonAllman who presented his feasibility study of the new location, called Rocky Hollow.

With several concerned Evanston citizens in attendance a lengthy discussion. Some spoke very much in favor of the study, while others questioned the cost.

I told those in attendance that the capital facilities tax committee will be looking at a number of projects, for which proposals must be submitted by April. The group will then decide which projects will be presented and how they could be placed on the ballot.

During the year's final meeting I also introduced Boy Scout David Bennett, who was in attendance to earn points toward his merit badge. I welcomed him to the meeting and thanked him for his attendance, and the council and I wished him the best of luck and success in his scout achievements.

I read a memo that the City of Evanston received from the Town of Mountain View, stating that they were declining to participate in the one cent proposed Capital Facilities Tax Proposition on the upcoming election in November. They also sent a copy to the Town of Lyman.

I told the city council that this was a very disappointing letter and was going to make it much harder to sell the proposed projects to the people within the county. The memo stated that one reason was that the ranching community was concerned that large farm equipment would cost more. That's okay, I can respect their concern, but I have been told that most of the ranchers go to Utah to purchase their equipment, costing them almost seven percent in sales tax. However, everyone to their own personal beliefs.

I also told the council that if Lyman also decides to pull out that we would probably have a hard time convincing the County Commissioners to allow the proposition on the ballot.

The *Uinta County Herald* of December 31st quoted County Commission Paul Barnard: *"The County has no money at all,"* Barnard said. *"The capital facilities tax is easier, better, and a tax the voters have direct control over."*

Barnard also said he was disappointed at the Mountain View officials' decision. *"I am totally in favor of the capital facilities tax,"* Barnard said. *"But the town council is entitled to their opinion."*

"It's an ideal tax," he said.

Before the meeting adjourned I gave a short speech on how much the City of Evanston had accomplished this past year. I said, "It appears to me that Evanston has had another great year. Economically, Evanston is looking good."

I mentioned that we had accomplished all basic service projects that had been proposed for the year, and our streets were all in great shape. The downtown tree planting project and the new street lighting made the downtown area much more attractive.

I stated, "Evanston's economy has been on an upward trend for the past few years and seems to be getting stronger each year. We must, and will keep this trend going through the efforts of all of us working together."

I ended by thanking all those involved throughout the year in making Evanston a better place to live, and wished all a Merry Christmas and a Happy, Safe and Prosperous New Year in 1992.

It seems like the years go by so fast there just doesn't seem to be enough time to get done what you would like to get done. Somebody once said *"Time sneaks up on you like a windshield on a bug,"* and I think they were right, but we would be looking at another big year in 1992—another election year and the big program we will be looking at is the new Comprehensive Plan that a committee of many citizens have been involved with during this past year.

CHAPTER 26

1992....At this point I knew the City of Evanston would be looking at another very busy and very controversial year. Two big goals for this election year of 1992 would be first, to complete the very controversial Evanston-2000 Comprehensive Plan, which was nearly ready for the Evanston City Council to make the final decision and approval; and second, the additional one cent Capital Facilities Tax Proposition that hopefully would be on the ballot at election time. Two of the three Uinta County incorporated communities and the Uinta County Commissioners had to approve the proposition to get it on the ballot. With the number of projects that the three communities were requesting it was going to take a lot of work to sell it to the citizens of the county.

We also had all the ongoing annual projects to keep in mind, while at the same time the city council and I would be reorganizing the city staff with the assistance of the appointing officials: City Engineer Brian Honey, City Clerk Don Welling, and Chief of Police Dennis Harvey. Reorganizing would place the right people in the right positions with fair wages and determine whether or not we are overstaffed or not. We would like to have this completed prior to the next fiscal year's budgeting.

To start off the first city council meeting of the year on January 8th, following the usual business of approving the minutes and paying of the outstanding bills, I recognized and welcomed more Boy Scouts. Ms Bobby Lou Fruits, troop committee member, introduced her son, J. R. Fruits of Troop 911, and Dennis Poppinga, Parks and Recreation Director, introduced his two sons, Brady and Casey Poppinga of Troop 30.

The Boy Scouts were in attendance as part of their requirements towards earning their merit badges. The council and I thanked them for their attendance and wished them the best in completing their requirements and earning their merit badges.

I then delivered my State of the City Address by speaking of all of the city's goals and accomplishments in the past year. I spoke of the budget, the completion of the street projects, and mentioned that it was another great year, busy, but we got a lot accomplished. *"But,"* I said, *"probably the most costly and difficult project of the year was the implementation of the one-man system in solid waste. This change has been a long time coming; however, it's going to be a change that will benefit the people of Evanston a great deal, not only in service but also in tax dollars. We are still having a few problems but most of the wrinkles have been pretty well ironed out."*

Other accomplishment I spoke of was the continuance of the improvements in Historic Downtown Evanston, Depot Square, the BEAR Project, and the improvements of Hamblin and Brown Parks. I also spoke of the completed plans of the Centennial Park and the new ski hill at Rocky Hollow.

I mentioned how much work the Planning and Zoning Commission and the volunteers had done to get the Comprehensive Plan completed, and all the work and planning the new Evanston Tourism Promotion Board went through to promote the Evanston area.

I mentioned the city's success in hosting the W.A.M. convention and all the hard work Councilwoman and Chairperson Jerry Wall and her committees put in to it to make it such a success.

I congratulated and thanked all the members of the council, the city staff, the members of all the boards and commissions, all committee members and all those who assisted in any programs helping make Evanston a great community.

The *Uinta County Herald* of January 10th quoted me: *"I believe very strongly that if government only deals in basic services and doesn't show a concern for the community's future, eventually there may be no need for basic services."*

I was trying to point out that the city needs to encourage citizens to get involved and promote Evanston, and that the city government needs to assist in the programs and projects that are taking place in the area, especially those that help with the economy. All city officials, employees and citizens need to stay active in the community, and at the same time, they must all decide whether they want a community that provides jobs and opportunities for good and healthy living, or if they want to just sit back and hope good things will happen. I have always believed that a person has got to help make things happen if they want things better. They must, at least, keep themselves informed of what is going on in their community.

After applause from those in attendance, each council member expressed their desire to serve the community and appreciation that they had the opportunity to do so. They each expressed their wish for the council to be united and to work as a team, with a special interest expressed in human services, and then each thanked me, as mayor, and gave a special thanks to the news media for their time and dedication.

I thanked the council members for their desire to serve together, and I thanked David Bills for operating the video camera and taping all the city council meetings.

I then made my appointments as follows: Chief of Police, Dennis Harvey; Community Development Director, City Planner, Paul Knopf; City Clerk, Don Welling; City Treasurer, Steve Widmer; City Engineer, Brian Honey; Assistant City Court Judge, John Phillips; Assistant City Court Judge, Bruce Barnard; City Attorney, Dennis Boal; and Assistant City Attorney, Rick Lavery, and I also announced that Allan "Oop" Hansen would remain as General Supervisor over Public Works. Councilwoman Wall made the motion to confirm the appointments, seconded by Nelson, with all voting in favor.

I then appointed all members of the Evanston Police Department employed under Chief Harvey, including patrolmen, detectives, animal control officers and the parking officer. The motion was made by Councilman Hutchinson to confirm the appointments to the Evanston Police Department, seconded by Davis, with all voting in favor.

I made the following appointments to the various boards and commissions: Evanston Planning And Zoning Commission and Board of Adjustments, both 3-year terms; John Thomas, Dan Yates, and Kevin Kallas, Evanston Tourism Promotion Board, 3-year term; Ran Phillips and Councilwoman Jerry Wall, Evanston Housing Authority, 4-year term; Marie Hicks, Police Commission, 1-year term; me as Commissioner, Councilmen Craig Nelson, and Clarence Vranish; Councilman Craig Nelson, Airport Joint Powers Board, 3-year term; Personnel Board, 1-year term, Councilmembers Clarence Vranish and Julie Lehman, City Treasurer Steve Widmer, Public Works Employee Arvel "Bud" Eastman, and Police Training Sergeant Jake Williams; Uinta County Emergency Management, 1-year term: Don Bodine as Coordinator and City Planner Paul Knopf.

Councilman Nelson made a motion to confirm all of the above appointments, seconded by Lehman, with all voting in favor.

Miles Alexander, representing the Evanston Liquor Dealers, requested the four days in 1992 for extended hours of operation as allowed by law: May 24th, July 4th, September 6th, and December 31st. Motion was made by Councilwoman Wall to approve the requested dates, seconded by Vranish, with all voting in favor.

Resolution 92-1 was introduced by Councilwoman Lehman to authorize the City of Evanston to approve and adopt the final Master Plan of the BEAR Project for the preparation, development and improvement of outdoor recreation for the citizens of Evanston and Uinta County. After a short discussion, Councilwoman Wall made the motion to adopt Resolution 92-1, seconded by Nelson. With 7 yes votes the motion passed unanimously.

Councilman Hutchinson introduced Resolution 92-2, authorizing the execution of the Highway Safety Grant Agreement with the Wyoming Transportation Department to conduct an Urban High Hazard Location Study for the Evanston area with a 100% grant in the amount of $16,000.

According to the *Uinta County Herald* of January 10th, Councilman Vranish said, *"In the olden days, the Greeks built a wooden horse. I worry, when the federal government is giving money, what strings are attached."*

I couldn't understand where he was coming from because the City of Evanston had been receiving federal money for various projects for years. But the *Herald* also reported: *Mayor Dennis Ottley urged the council to keep in mind who they are serving. If there is a traffic problem which could be hazardous to the citizens, they should be aware of it, he said.*

After a short discussion I called for the motion to adopt Resolution 92-2, which was made by Councilman Davis and seconded by Hutchinson. More discussion continued until I called for the vote. The vote was 5 in favor and 2 opposed (Davis and Vranish). The motion passed by a majority.

I couldn't understand why anyone would vote against a safety study like the one in the agreement, because it would be paid for with a grant from the State of Wyoming and could only help the city by identifying areas in Evanston where the traffic could be unsafe. I don't recall just what problems Clarence and Will had with the resolution, or what their objections could possibly be, but the resolution was adopted.

The issue of the American National Bank going under came up. The City of Evanston had funds in the bank therefore, Councilman Vranish made a motion that the City of Evanston accepts the bank's offer of $30,000, which was a little more than what we had deposited but less than what it should have been including interest. This closed the city's account that was outstanding at the time the bank shut their doors. The motion was seconded by Davis, with all voting in favor.

The American National Bank was a new bank to Evanston that had only been in operation fewer than 10 years; therefore the City of Evanston never had much of a deposit in that bank. The bank was on the corner of Yellow Creek Road and Cheyenne Drive in what is presently the Trinity Lutheran Church. It was built about the time the big oil and gas boom had come to an end, when the area went into a bust period.

Prior to adjourning, I reported that there would be a Capital Facilities Tax Committee meeting at City Hall on January 13th at 7:30 p.m. City Councilmembers Jerry Wall, Craig Nelson and Julie Lehman each gave their report on the recent National League of Cities conference, and I called for a work session to be held at City Hall on January 15th at 5:00 p.m.

At the next city council meeting on January 22nd all department heads were required to be present to give an update on their department's present and future plans. They weren't only requested to give an oral report during the meeting, but were also required to submit a written report to each council member and myself. After hearing each report and looking over their written reports, it appeared that the city was in for another big year of improvements in every department. I then, along with the council, thanked them all for such thorough reports, and I said to them that, "If the city completes all that they have in their reports, Evanston will have another busy and outstanding year."

During this meeting I appointed Mark Harris and Scott Rasmussen to the Urban Renewal Agency with a motion by Councilwoman Wall to confirm the appointments, seconded by Lehman, with all voting in favor.

Sandy Ottley, representing the Chinese New Year Committee, requested a single parade route to be used on two occasions, on February 7th and 8th, for the Chinese New Year celebration. She said both days of the parade would begin at the Uinta County Library parking lot entering Main Street, to Harrison Drive (11th Street), then up Front Street to Depot Square and the Joss House. She said the Torch Parade on February 7th would begin at 6:00 p.m., and the parade on February 8th would begin at 12:00 noon.

Sandy had chaired so many parades over the years that folks started kidding her about being "Evanston's Queen of Parades." It seemed like every time a committee wanted to have a parade they would come and ask Sandy to be the parade chairperson. Her adopted title got to be quite popular and a lot of folks had a lot of fun with it.

The *Uinta County Herald* of January 24th quoted Councilman Clarence Vranish saying, *"If Sandy ever leaves town, we're not going to have fun anymore."*

Councilman Nelson made the motion to approve Sandy's request for the parades and to notify the Police Department of the routes and days, seconded by Davis, with all voting in favor.

Ordinances 92-1, 92-2, 92-4, 92-5, 92-6 and 92-7 came up, all pertaining to zone changes: definitions of day care centers, zoning for home occupation childcare, and amending the city code concerning the requirements for home occupations. All of these ordinances passed unanimously on all three readings and were entered into the Evanston Book of Codes and made law.

However, issues arose concerning Ordinance 92-3, sponsored by Councilwoman Lehman and introduced by Councilman Nelson titled as follows:

ORDINANCE 92-3
AN ORDINANCE AMENDING SECTION 24-94.(e)(1)b, AND f. OF THE EVANSTON CITY CODE TO INCREASE THE DISTANCES BETWEEN OFF-PREMISE SIGNS AND ENACTING SECTION 24-94.(g) AND SECTION 24-94.(h), TO REQUIRE A SINGLE POLE STRUCTURE FOR OFF-PREMISE SIGNS AND TO LIMIT THEIR HEIGHTS.

<u>Section 1.</u> Section 24-94. (e)(1)b, f, g and h of the Evanston City Code are hereby amended and re-enacted to read as follows:

b. No portion of any off-premises advertising sign shall be closer than 1,000 feet to any other off-premise advertising.

f. No off-premise sign shall be erected in or within 1,000 feet of the boundary of a residential or public zoning district.

g. No off-premise sign, except freeway oriented signs, shall exceed 50 feet in height unless a conditional use permit is obtained.

h. All off-premise signs shall be single pole structures.

The city council was split on this ordinance. There was a lengthy discussion during the last work session as well as during this regular meeting of January 22nd. The big issue, if I remember right, was the 1,000-foot distance and the single pole structures. There were some business owners who felt the ordinance was too extreme and requested that it be less restrictive.

But after more discussion, Councilwoman Wall made the motion to pass Ordinance 92-3 on the first reading, seconded by Hutchinson, with a vote of 4 in favor (me, Wall, Nelson and Lehman), and 3 against (Vranish, Hutchinson and Davis). Motion passed by a majority on first reading. However, despite all the time and discussion this Ordinance 92-3 had taken, after Councilwoman Wall's motion to pass on second reading, seconded by Nelson, the motion failed with 1 vote in favor (Wall), and 6 votes against including mine. This ordinance was now dead.

Towards the end of the meeting Councilman Davis announced that the Renewal Ball Committee would be holding their Kick-off Meeting at City Hall on January 30th at 7:00 p.m. and that all members of the city council were invited.

Prior to adjournment, I announced that the Utah Boat and Travel Show would be held at the Salt Palace in Salt Lake City on January 29th through February 2nd; that the Evanston Chamber of Commerce would have a booth once again this year to help promote Evanston, and that the Agri-Business Banquet would be held on February 25th at 6:00 p.m. in Fort Bridger at the American Legion Hall; and that nominations for Evanston's Citizen of the Year must be in no later than 5:00 p.m. on February 10th.

I called for a city council work session to be held at City Hall on February 5th at 5:00 p.m.

On January 13th there was also an arena meeting concerning the new proposed convention center to be located on or near the Uinta County fairgrounds. In attendance were Uinta County personnel, Kim Martin, Di Henniger, Sam Hatch and Sallie Waters, as well as Evanston City Council members and me.

Plans were discussed concerning the location and the idea of purchasing additional property such as the Sunset Motel with 4-5 acres adjacent to Hamblin Park for $190,000 (purchased by the city several years later for historic purposes), and the New Motel and Western Motel, owned by Kurt Nelson, with 3.5 acres located on the west side of Highway 89, for $290,000 (Lincoln Self Reliance, Inc. at present).

Several committee members had recently made trips to Ogden, Utah to look at the new 21,000-square-foot Golden Spike Arena at the Weber County, Utah Fairgrounds, and to Rock Springs to look at their new 20,000-square-foot fairgrounds exhibit hall. These trips to get an idea of what Evanston would need for an indoor arena. There was also a lot of discussion about the utility of an indoor center and the possibility of locating it within the present fairgrounds by relocating some of the buildings and structures already in place, but parking was a big concern.

The issue of the Martin Luther King Jr. holiday came up again, and was reported in the Uinta County Herald of January 17th in an article titled, VFW WILL DISPLAY FLAGS THIS YEAR. The Veterans of Foreign Wars Post 4280 had refused to fly the Stars and Stripes on that particular holiday until this year. According to the Herald issue of January 17th the V.F.W. stated they will fly the flag on that day this year, but sort of under protest. They were concerned calling it "Martin Luther King Jr. Day," because they didn't feel King deserved it, and that the State of Wyoming never had the opportunity to vote on the issue separately. A lot of folks in Wyoming felt the same way.

The article quoted Commander Dennis Sundberg saying, "We will be flying the flag that day, but won't be calling it that, it's Wyoming Equality Day."

Sundberg said the group wouldn't recognize the holiday because it was not voted on by Wyoming citizens. The VFW's refusal to fly the flags was criticized by Evanston Mayor Dennis Ottley and others, the article read.

The article continued: *As the occasion approached this year, Ottley wrote a letter to Sundberg [Post Commander], asking him to once again consider the flag to mark the day.*

"I hope that we all can look at this as a day of equal rights for everyone and not as a day of racism," Ottley's letter read.

Ottley, a longtime member of the VFW, has donated $2,000 of city money over the past four years to support the flag program, the Herald read.

"It's not the organization, it's just a couple of soreheads," Ottley said about the VFW's choice not to recognize the holiday last year.

"I don't want to get involved, they're doing such a great job with the program," he added. *"I'd like them to realize what that flag means, to all of us...I don't want to stop paying them."*

"I'm not saying I don't have a prejudiced bone in my body," Ottley continued. *"But I had two blacks in my tank in Korea and they were both good men, and we all drank from the same whiskey bottle. I try to base the person by his or her character, not color.*

When asked why the VFW chose to fly the flag this year, Sundberg said, "personal reasons, nobody's business," and chose not to elaborate, the news article concluded.

At first when the Martin Luther King Jr. Day was named by Congress (only because it was considered "Politically Correct," which I thought was very cowardly), I also had a few problems. I didn't mind declaring the day as an equal-rights day, but I would rather that they named it "Equality Day" or something similar. I'm not trying to take anything away from Martin Luther King, Jr.; he was a great man, and deserved recognition, and I believed that many folks in Wyoming felt the same way. But Presidents George Washington and Abraham Lincoln were also great men, and it really bothered me to omit their birthdays from the calendar and make it a one-day holiday called Presidents' Day. The new MLK holiday was the only day of the year named after someone in particular with the exception of Columbus Day and Christmas. This bothered me, but I got over it.

My decision to send $2,000 per year to the V.F.W. for their flag program was because I had requested that they place flags at City Hall and all other city buildings in the downtown area, and I requested flags at Depot Square and on each street light going over the new viaduct on the westerly side.

During the time I was mayor I had always paid the V.F.W. for their flag service out of the Mayor's Contingency Fund, but I don't know what the city has done since I left office. The funds the city paid the V.F.W. were legal, because the City of Evanston was receiving a service, so it was not just a donation.

I felt that it was worth every penny to help the V.F.W. continue their flag program. I felt it was one of the most patriotic and proud annual programs the City of Evanston had. It not only reminded folks to recognize each and every holiday, but when a person traveling around Evanston saw so many flags waving, it had to make folks mighty proud of our community. I know it did me.

To this day the Veterans of Foreign Wars Post 4280 have continued their flag program, and I can only say, "You've got to take your hats off to one of Evanston's finest service clubs, V.F.W. Post 4280, and to all those veteran members who have giving their time serving Evanston, as well as serving our Great Nation, the United States of America. Real heroes!"

During the month of January the City of Evanston had two bomb threats. They were about two weeks apart, but it wasn't ever determined whether both threats were from the same person. The *Uinta County Herald* of January 14th reported: *At about 8:30 a.m. Monday, two downtown Evanston locations received calls from a female who stated "there is a big bomb on your block" and then hung up.*

This is the second such threat in recent weeks. The first was received by the Uinta County Herald, the article continued.

According to Evanston Police Department spokesman Jake Williams, the caller stated there was a "mega bomb" on the block. According to Uinta County Attorney Anderson, terrorist threats were a felony and those caught and convicted could be sentenced to up to three years in the Wyoming State Penitentiary, fined $10,000, or both.

"I hope the person doing these adolescent pranks realizes it's serious business. If they are apprehended, the prosecuting attorney's office will not hesitate to do just that [charge them with a felony]," Anderson said.

No bombs were found either time, even after a thorough search of the downtown area. It appeared to be a prank, but after the news article came out the threats seemed to stop. I don't think they ever found out who was behind the calls.

The Evanston City Council, the Uinta County Commissioners and the Uinta County School Districts were starting to get concerned with the shortfall of tax revenues due to the slow-moving, but improving, economy. When the economy declines as it did after the boom period, it takes time for tax revenues to catch up with the needs of a community. In other words, when the economy is down and starts improving, the city infrastructure and other necessities are seriously in need of funds, but it may be one or two years before the tax revenues catch up.

Therefore, at this time, all Uinta County officials were looking to cut where possible. Uinta County Commission Chairman Patrick P. Mulhall put out a memo on January 24th to all Uinta County elected officials, directors and department heads indicating that the county budget was in trouble. The county's reserve fund of $1,000,000 had been depleted because they had to use it for present budgetary purposes. He also requested that all county employees cut costs wherever possible.

This memo was also a warning to all levels of county government because if there was a shortfall in county revenues there would be one in other government entities as well.

This caused Evanston to also start thinking early about the budget for fiscal year 1992-1993. We requested that all department heads start working on their goals and budget for the next year immediately. We also requested that they be very conservative on their budget requests. Through good budgeting and being conservative, the City of Evanston was financially sound, with a fair-sized reserve that could be used if necessary, though we tried very hard not to dip into it if we didn't have to. But the way revenues were coming in we still had to be careful.

One major reason that everyone was concerned about revenues was legislation recently passed by the United States Congress declaring that all public buildings had to be altered to be accessible to the disabled. The legislation was called the Americans with Disabilities Act (ADA). It declared that all public buildings have open access and are set up to accommodate the handicapped. This would be a big budgetary concern, because most public buildings would need more funds to meets those requirements.

Evanston got working on the ADA requirements immediately by directing the city inspector to assess every building that the City of Evanston utilizes for public services and get back to the mayor and council as soon as possible with a list of the necessary improvements.

During the first regular city council meeting of the month on February 12th, I appointed Councilman Tom Hutchinson to the Human Services Joint Powers Board for a three-year term. Motion was made by Councilman Davis to confirm the appointment, seconded Nelson, with all voting in favor.

The city council then heard a report from Eric Heltzel, Chairman of the Recycling Committee, assisted by committee members Jackie Skog and Neil Lesmeister. They reported the need to upgrade the existing program and the support everyone had given them towards an upgraded recycling program. The committee's written proposal was attached and included as part of the upcoming resolution.

City Treasurer Widmer also reported on a recycling meeting that he attended at the Evanston High School and spoke of their enthusiasm and plans for recycling.

The council and I gave special thanks to all of them for the time and interest they gave the recycling program, and I told them that a new resolution, pertaining to their proposal, was the next item of business and that the Evanston City Council was ready to act on it.

Following, Councilwoman Wall introduce Resolution 92-7, a resolution reading:

THE CITY OF EVANSTON, WYOMING ACKNOWLEDGING AND ACCEPTING THE RECYCLING PROPOSAL FOR THE EVANSTON RECYCLING PROGRAM.

The proposed recycling program presented by the committee was made as an attachment and created a very exclusive recycling plan for Evanston. We already had the building which was being used to store the recycling material until it could be sold, and we already had bins placed throughout the city for recycling some materials, but not all. The committee's plan would make recycling much more thorough. Employee Barry Constantine had been appointed as the supervisor over recycling prior to the adoption of this resolution.

Motion was made by Councilman Hutchinson for the adoption of Resolution 92-7, seconded by Wall, with all voting in favor.

The Evanston City Council acted on Ordinance 91-22 which came up on the third and final reading, an ordinance to repeal, amend and re-enact the improvement of the city code regarding animals and fowl, to provide for an upgraded system of licensing, controlling and impounding animals and fowl within the City of Evanston.

This ordinance had been passed on first and second readings as amended, with all voting in favor of it both times. The motion to pass Ordinance 91-22 as amended on third and final reading was made by Councilman Vranish and seconded by Nelson, once again with 7 votes in favor. The motion passed unanimously.

Ordinance 91-22 was a very lengthy ordinance, and because of so many amendments and the lengthy discussions, and having tabled it once for folks to get more information, City Clerk Don Welling was directed by the council to publish this ordinance in full in the Uinta County Herald. Animal Control Officer Tim Purcell stated that the changes in the ordinance would be much fairer to pet owners and other citizens that don't own pets.

During the February 12th meeting, Resolution 92-9 was introduced by Councilman Vranish authorizing the City of Evanston to enter into a memorandum of understanding with the Evanston Parks and Recreation District for the development and implementation of a fitness program for the employees of the City of Evanston.

This fitness program would give city employees a break on membership fees and daily fees to encourage them to utilize the recreation center and use its equipment to help keep them fit. A copy of the agreement was attached. The motion to adopt Resolution 92-9 was made by Councilman Davis, seconded by Wall, with all voting in favor.

District Parks and Recreation Director Dennis Poppinga reported that the Wyoming Parks and Recreation Annual Convention would be held in Evanston on February 26th, 27th and 28th. He also reported that the Evanston District Parks and Recreation Board had worked very hard the past several months to get the convention in Evanston and had a good program lined up for the three-day event.

The city council members and I thanked Poppinga and his board for their success getting the convention to Evanston and wished them the best for an exciting and successful convention.

I also expressed the city's appreciation to Councilwoman Jerry Wall for her and her committee's hard work in making the 1992 Chinese New Year Celebration, once again, a big success.

Prior to adjournment of the meeting, I announced that I had received three nominations for Evanston's Citizen of the Year honors and gave each council member a copy of the nominations, which included Evanston's First Lady Sandy Ottley, Uinta County School Board, District No. 1 member Kendra West and Attorney Mark Harris.

I mentioned that all were well deserving of such an honor and that the city council would vote on it. I made it a point to mention that Sandy was nominated by Ann Bell who chaired the Joss House Project and received the honors of Evanston's Citizen of the year in 1991.

On January 24th the *Uinta County Herald* came out with an article titled, RESIDENT CHASTISES CITY COUNCIL.

The article by Ann Curtis read: *An Evanston resident accused the Evanston City Council Wednesday of "dragging their feet" in complying with the new Americans with Disabilities Act (ADA).*

"We are all just a half second away from being disabled," David Heinse said. "You're dragging your feet and waiting until the last minute to begin bringing the city into compliance. You should provide a package of information about the act with business licenses issued by the city."

The article continued: *"The city building inspector has been looking at city buildings; the Wyoming Association of Municipalities (WAM), Blue Cross and Blue Shields have been looking at the personnel policy; and the Evanston Police Department is looking at their procedures," City Attorney Dennis Boal said. "It's like the question 'How do you eat an elephant?—one bite at a time'," he said. "The new federal law requires public and private entities to make facilities accessible to disabled people, to make sure their personnel policies are not discriminatory and to make changes,"* the article added.

Boal explained some city buildings have small problems, while some problems are bigger.

"The ADA is not intended to put people out of business," Heinse said. *"It's nothing to be afraid of and can be valuable to us all."*

The council members agreed to a resolution appointing the city treasurer to delegate tasks regarding the law, the news article concluded.

The second city council meeting of the month came up on February 26th, at which time I appointed Keith Cerny to the Uinta County Economic Development Board. Motion was made by Councilman Davis to confirm the appointment, seconded by Lehman, with all voting in favor.

Ruth Nickerson from the Public Health Office was in attendance. She made a presentation about the program now available at the Lifelong Learning Center (at the present is called Uinta BOCES #1 Education Center) to train nurse's aides, nursing assistants and home health aides. She reported that by 1993 only certified aides would be hired for health care.

After a short question and answer period I congratulated Ms Nickerson on the work that had been done in finding the funds to make the nursing program available at the Learning Center and wished her the best for a successful program.

Councilman Nelson introduced Resolution 92-13, the resolution that Mr. David Heinse had been waiting for, came on the floor.

RESOLUTION 92-13
RESOLUTION OF THE CITY OF EVANSTON, WYOMING ESTABLISHING A DISABLED AMERICAN ACCESS BOARD

This resolution required the City of Evanston to comply with the Americans with Disabilities Act (ADA), and establish a citizens committee to aid and assist the city in complying with the act. Councilman Davis made the motion to adopt Resolution 92-13, seconded by Lehman, with the vote being unanimous.

As mayor, I made the following recommended appointments to the newly created DAA Board: Tom Huddleston, Marcia Salmela, Nina Gutierez, Wayne Knopf, Kathryn Devaney, Gary Parker, David

A. Kimball, Joyce Morrow and Tim Beppler. These appointments had all either been recommended by city council members, by some interested parties, or some just volunteered. The board, according to the resolution, had to be made up of at least five and not more than nine members. Councilwoman Lehman made a motion to confirm the appointments, seconded by Davis, with all voting in favor.

The City of Evanston had never adopted an official flag, so, with the assistance of the city council members, we designed an Evanston flag that we could all accept and be proud of. Councilwoman Lehman introduced Resolution 92-14 as follows:

RESOLUTION 92-14
RESOLUTION OF THE CITY OF EVANSTON AUTHO-
RIZING AND ADOPTING AN OFFICIAL CITY FLAG.

Section 1: The governing body of the City of Evanston, Wyoming hereby adopts an official flag for the City of Evanston.

Section 2: A facsimile of the official flag shall be attached hereto by the City Clerk.

Councilman Hutchinson made the motion to adopt Resolution 92-14, seconded by Nelson. The motion passed unanimously.

The flag would be white with the Wyoming bucking horse and Evanston's official seal in gold in the center of the bucking horse, and Evanston's promotional logo, "Fresh Air, Freedom and Fun" next to the horse, all in red, white and blue with the gold-colored city seal. It would be a beautiful flag with a lot of class and everyone was very proud that Evanston, Wyoming would finally fly their own flag right along with Wyoming's State Flag and the good old Stars and Stripes of the United States of America. However, it would probably be late in the year before the flag was completed and available.

Resolution 92-16 was introduced by Councilwoman Wall and read in full to the council by City Attorney Boal, to direct Evanston's public works directors, City Engineer Brian Honey and Superintendent of Public Works Allan "Oop" Hansen, to prepare a new reorganization/layoff plan for public works and apply it to the personnel manual. This resolution was necessary to update and amend the personnel manual because of the new garbage system. Motion was made by Councilwoman Lehman to adopt Resolution 92-16, seconded by Nelson, with all voting in favor.

City Engineer Honey and Superintendent of Public Works Hansen, with the assistance of their lead department heads, put together a great plan that was very acceptable to the employees and the city council.

At this time, before acting on the plan presented by City Engineer Honey, Councilman Hutchinson made a motion that the city council go into an executive session to discuss personnel matters and the reorganization/layoff plan for the Public Works Department, seconded by Davis, with all voting in favor.

The city council and I excused ourselves, along with Honey and Hansen, from the council chambers and held the executive session in the small meeting room next to the council chambers and discussed the new reorganizational plan.

After closing the executive session, we all re-entered the council chambers to reconvene the council meeting, at which time I took action on the new plan by asking for a motion to implement the plan as discussed in the executive session. Motion was made by Councilman Vranish that we implement the plan, and that the plan go into effect upon notification, in writing, to all public works employees. The motion was seconded by Wall. I then asked if there was any more discussion.

Councilman Hutchinson stated that he would be voting against the resolution because although he was appointed to serve on the committee, he ended up being sick and unable to make the meetings, and not having had an opportunity to give any input, he didn't feel good about the plan as presented in the executive session.

The discussion was quite lengthy and before calling for the vote I said, "The only thing I would like to say is, you know there is a reason for this and we all know that one reason is because we have an abundance of employees in some of the departments in Public Works that we need to recognize because of budgetary purposes and it is not because we are trying to hurt anybody in any way....I know it's going to affect some people, but at the same time I think the council has got to be realistic and be responsible. I would hope that the council would favor this plan."

Councilwoman Wall made the statement that she "would just like to say, that those of you who worked on the committee, I think did a good job."

I called for the vote on the motion. There were 6 in favor and 1 against (Hutchinson). The motion passed by a majority.

I was very thankful that this issue was over, because it had been dragging on for quite some time and it was essential that the resolution be adopted. The surprising thing about it all was it had very little effect on anyone and, if I remember right, no one was laid off. There were some adjustments but no lay-offs.

Also during the meeting I reported that Evanston had received a $25,000 grant from the Wyoming Department of Commerce to be used to help improve the BEAR Project.

I announced there would be a Blood Drive on February 27th at the Evanston LDS South Stake Center from 3:00 p.m. to 8:00 p.m. This drive had been organized through the efforts of Boy Scout K. C. Cummings as part of earning his Eagle Scout Badge. K. C. had worked hard to make the Blood Drive a success by getting the information out to the Evanston folks, setting up the officials to help conduct the drive and taking care of those giving blood. I hoped K. C. was proud.

The Agri-Business banquet had been held in Fort Bridger on February 25th. The nominee receiving Evanston's Citizen of the Year was Mark Harris and during this meeting I offered my congratulations to Mark and thanked him for the volunteer service that he had given to Evanston over the years.

Each year they rotate having the Agri-Business event in one of the communities (Evanston, Lyman, Mountain View or Fort Bridger) in Uinta County to honor county folks in many categories for their outstanding service to their communities, and each year nominees for Evanston's Citizen of the Year were nominated by the public and then voted on by members of the city council and the mayor.

The *Uinta County Herald* news article of November 14th was titled: COUNTY ASKS CITY FOR $500,000. This article was based on a recent work session of the Evanston City Council and the Uinta County Commissioners. The article by Ann Curtis read:

According to commissioners, the city is being asked to contribute $175,000 for fire department services, $50,000 for ambulance services, $175,000 for landfill fees, $20,000 for mosquito abatement, $40,000 for dispatch, radio and communications, and $40,000 for booking fees at the jail.

Currently the city contributes $40,000 annually for the use of the jail plus an additional $50,000 for the fire department. The city also pays some dumping fees for special materials at the landfill.

During the work session, Commission Chairman Pat Mulhall told the city council that the county-assessed valuation dropped from $946 million in 1985 to $517 million at present, and as a result the county had depleted its $8 million cash reserve to $900,000 in the last several years.

"We need to maintain services. We realize this is a significant amount of money, but we wanted to give you some figures to work with," said Mulhall. He stated the commissioners would also be speaking with both the Mountain View and Lyman town councils about contributions.

"The city works on their budget earlier than the county—see what you can do for us," he said. "Based on what you do here, we'll work on our budget and hope the valuation goes up."

County officials reminded the city officials that they had taken over the expenses of the fire department and landfill when the city finances were down.

But to counter that, the city representatives reminded them that Evanston had footed the bill for the fire department and the landfill for many years before the boom. The city still owns the building in which the fire department is housed.

According to 1990 census figures, Uinta County's population is approximately 18,000, with about 11,000 of those people living in the city of Evanston.

County Special Projects Director Marion Malnar stated the county had paid $186,000 for landfill permits alone during the past year. "That's one that's not going to go down. We have to stay in compliance with DEQ. We *don't want to have the landfill close," Mulhall said. "The contract (for the landfill operation) is up."*

Evanston Mayor Dennis Ottley asked if the city might bid on the job, stating that if the city is being asked to pay $175,000, it might be worth looking into.

Ottley reminded the county officials that the city is making an attempt to recycle in order to reduce the amount of waste which would be going into the landfill.

City Councilman Clarence Vranish asked if the city would have any input regarding the operation of the fire department, jail and landfill if it were to pay the $500,000.

Mulhall stated the county officials would "welcome the city's input just as we do any other citizen."

Ottley reminded the county representatives that the city has seen decreased revenues also.

"We're OK this year, but we don't know for next year," he said. "We don't have any assessments. All we can do is raise rates [on water, sewer, garbage]."

According to Commissioner Casey Davis, last year the county asked for $150,000 from Evanston, $6,000 from Lyman, and $3,000 from Mountain View.

He admitted that even though the commissioners had asked for the contribution, the county had not followed up on getting any money from the two Bridger Valley municipalities, the article concluded.

The County Commissioners also were requesting $52,000 from the Town of Lyman and $33,000 from the Town of Mountain View. My question was, Will the commissioners be fortunate enough to receive any funds from the two towns for this coming fiscal year? Because, according to Commissioner Davis, the two towns just ignored their request from the past year and didn't pay anything.

The meeting ended with good feelings, but the city never made any bids on the operation of the landfill. We told the commissioners that this would be a priority and we would look at what we could do when we started getting serious about next year's budget.

According to all reports, the city and county were not the only ones concerned about revenues for the next budget period. The area newspapers reported that all of the Uinta County School Districts and the State of Wyoming were also having shortfalls. It was looking like everyone in the state was going to have problems trying to balance their budget this coming fiscal year, but Evanston would have a balanced budget one way or the other.

At the first city council meeting of the month on March 11th, Councilmembers Jerry Wall, Craig Nelson and I were out of town on city business. We were all excused from the meeting. Therefore the meeting was conducted by Council President Clarence Vranish with Councilmembers Tom Hutchinson, Julie Lehman, and Will Davis all present, which made a quorum.

Council President Vranish called the meeting to order at 7:00 p.m. After the usual business was taken care of he introduced Boy Scout Ryan Weston who was requesting the city for their approval of an Eagle Scout project. Ryan wanted to paint house numbers on the curb in front of each house in the Twin Ridge Subdivision area to make it easier to locate the homes. The paint would be luminous so it would reflect even at night.

After a short discussion Councilman Davis made a motion to allow the proposed project, seconded by Hutchinson, with all voting in favor. Council President Vranish complimented Ryan on his proposed Eagle Scout project and wished him well in achieving it.

Roy Wall made a request for the Webelo Scouts to use the city property across the street from the Super 8 Motel (presently America's Best Value Inn & Suites) for a campout on June 26th from 4:00 p.m. to 9:00 a.m. on June 27th.

Councilwoman Lehman made a motion to allow this campout at the requested location with the possibility of moving the camping site to the rear location of Hamblin Park if arrangements could be made with the Parks and Recreation Department. The motion was seconded by Davis, with all voting in favor.

With no other business Council President asked for comments from the staff and council.

Councilwoman Lehman questioned the cable TV franchise and reported she had received many telephone calls from dissatisfied customers. This information was passed on to the cable company to get straightened out.

City Attorney Boal stated he would review the present Franchise Ordinance and outline all the terms and procedures for review and report on it at the next council meeting.

The meeting was a short one, adjourning at 7:50 p.m.

The second regular city council meeting of the month was held on March 25th with all members present. After the usual business was taken care of, City Attorney Dennis Boal held a public hearing on an application for a transfer of a liquor license from County Road Building Properties, Inc. (Jolly Rogers Restaurant and Lounge), as requested by James B. Merzon, Inc. With no opposition or objections to the requested transfer, Boal closed the hearing.

Following the public hearing Councilman Nelson made a motion to authorize the transfer of the liquor license from the present owners of the Jolly Rogers to James B. Merzon, Inc. The motion was seconded by Wall, and after a short discussion I called for the vote, which was unanimously in favor.

Community Development Director and City Planner Paul Knopf, and Urban Renewal Director Jim Davis followed with a presentation to Hugh Duffy of the National Park Service for his expertise and assistance in formulating a master plan for the BEAR Project. Mr. Duffy thanked the city for the recognition and expressed his pleasure for the opportunity to work on the plans, and mentioned how nice it was to see a group of people working so well together to achieve such a beautiful project.

Prior to adjournment of the March 26th city council meeting, and after hearing City Attorney Boal's comments concerning the cable TV franchise, Councilman Vranish made a motion to initiate a performance evaluation of Century Cable TV, seconded by Lehman with all voting in favor.

City Attorney Boal then stated that the public evaluation had been set up for June 17th, which would include representatives from the cable company, and it would be an open meeting to the public.

City Treasurer Steve Widmer, City Planner Paul Knopf, and Chief of Police Dennis Harvey each gave their report on a Risk Management Seminar they recently attended in Salt Lake City sponsored by Olympus Insurance Company. They all indicated that the seminar was well worth their time and said that they would be looking to implementing some safety programs from the seminar after they had time to do some planning.

I reported on the Capital Facilities Tax meeting that Councilwoman Jerry Wall and I had attended in Lyman on March 24th. I, as committee chairman, reported that the meeting was a good meeting. I stated that although the meeting was an open meeting and there were folks in attendance besides the committee members, I was still able to hold the meeting to those items on the agenda. But the slate of projects that had been requested to be put on the ballot was growing and I felt that, because of so many projects, it would cause folks to think twice before voting in favor of any of the projects, even if they were on the ballot as separate propositions.

A request to extend the project deadline was mentioned, and the committee voted to extend it from April 1st to April 6th.

I said to the council, *Every time we have a Capital Facilities Tax meeting, it seems like someone requests another project, and it worries me.* I also said that the next Facilities Tax meeting had been set for April 6th at the Evanston City Hall, and there will be an American with Disabilities (ADA) meeting on March 31st, also at City Hall.

The *Uinta County Herald* of April 3rd posted a photo of me recognizing and congratulating two Clark Elementary School students, Ryan Williams and Steve McCombs, who were honored as the Grand Prize Winners in the recent Clark School Science Fair. Other students were also recognized for their achievements in Young Authors, Reflections, Spelling Bee and Continental Mathematics League.

I met with them in the Mayor's office and congratulated all of them and told them that they were the future of this nation, and I told them that I knew they all would be looking at a great and successful future.

Uinta County Commissioner Chairman Pat Mulhall put out a memo early in April to all county department heads stating that the county's assessed valuation had decreased by $7 million dollars, making the valuation approximately $510 million. He said in the memo that the county had taken $1.1 million from its reserve fund last July to balance last year's budget. There is no question, revenues will be significantly reduced this year, he stated.

Therefore, his memo read, each department is instructed to begin their budget worksheet based on dollar figures from the 1991-1992 budget, less 10%.

After obtaining a copy of the county commissioner's memo, I presented it to the city council and the department heads during a work session and requested that they pay attention to the county assessment because this would have a big effect on the 8 mill levy that the city receives. I knew that the 8 mills the city receives isn't the city's largest revenue, but it helps, and the county valuation would also have an effect on other special mill levies such as the Uinta County Fire Department, the District Parks and Recreation Commission and others that we have been asked to help in funding.

UINTA COUNTY HERALD   April 3, 1992

Mayor greets Clark students

Evanston Mayor Dennis Ottley congratulated Clark Elementary students at a recent awards program. Ottley is shown with Ryan Williams and Steve McCombs, who were honored as grand prize winners in the Clark science fair. Students were also recognized for achievements in Young Authors, Reflections, Spelling Bee and Continental Mathematics League.

Uinta County Herald, April 21, 1992.

I pointed out that we all need to take the budget very seriously this year. I know we have always taken it seriously, I said, but this year, with all the projects we have on the agenda we need to find ways to cut spending. We know the assessed valuation is down and we also know the economy is still pretty soft. I said, "I'm not asking you to cut a certain percentage, but I am asking you to be as conservative as you possibly can, and when your request comes in for the council to look at we'll have an idea just where we are going at that time."

I also mentioned that we do have an amount in our reserve fund that we can use if needed, but I would rather not touch that unless we really had to.

I reminded them that the sooner they get their proposed budgets in the better, because we must meet the deadlines for advertising the public budget hearing. The council members also made a few comments, mostly agreeing with me, and they were aware that they should also be involved in the budget of the department(s) they represented.

There was a big concern about air pollution and global warming at that time, and the Environment Protection Agency (E.P.A.) was starting to push naturally operated vehicles. Therefore, since Evanston was located in the Overthrust Belt and we had natural gas producing plants in the area, the city council started thinking about running city vehicles on natural gas.

Early in the month of April, Evanston City Council members and I were given a demonstration by Mountain Fuel Supply Company's representatives on their natural gas-operated vehicles. We were told the vehicles could be adapted to run on both natural gas as well as gasoline.

This started the city council talking seriously about trying to maybe change over one or two vehicles and see how well natural gas would perform against gasoline. It was mentioned that since the area produces so much natural gas, if folks would go to natural gas in their vehicles it could boost the economy.

Later on the Evanston City Council approved an application for a Conditional Use Permit to Dave Madia, owner and operator of the

Hillcrest Chevron convenience store, for the right to add a natural gas pump for the convenience of the people who were already using natural gas as fuel for their vehicles.

At that time we were told that Mountain Fuel Supply (presently Dominion Energy) was using natural gas in all their vehicles, but the city never did change over. One reason was the cost, and there were very few vehicles on the road that used natural gas for very long. Eventually the pump at Hillcrest Chevron was removed.

During the first regular meeting of the city council on April 8th, we had a public hearing to consider an application for a new restaurant liquor license by Chico's at 909 Front Street, applied for by Le Anne J. Trosper, and another public hearing concerning an application for renewal of a Gaming/Pull-Tabs License applied for by the Wyoming State Liquor Association with Mr. J. D. Kindler representing them. Both hearings were conducted by City Attorney Dennis Boal, and both applications were approved by a motion and second with the vote unanimously in favor.

Julie Abbot and Joni Loxterman once again made a presentation and requested a Walk-a-thon for the March of Dimes Walk America program using the same six-mile route that was used the previous year. Councilwoman Wall made the motion to support the Walk America program and approve the route as presented, seconded by Nelson, with all voting in favor.

Mr. Jim Jackson, a resident of the Red Mountain Subdivision, requested sidewalks to be installed along Red Mountain Road for the safety of children and other pedestrians that walk in the road.

City Engineer Brian Honey responded that sidewalks along the south side of Red Mountain Road from Highway 89 to the Red Mountain Apartments were already being planned as a budget item for the upcoming fiscal year, provided that funds can be made available. The council members and I thanked Mr. Jackson for his interest and told him that the Red Mountain sidewalk would be one item of high priority for next spring.

Under new business, Councilwoman Lehman introduced the following resolution:

RESOLUTION 91-19
RESOLUTION OF THE CITY OF EVANSTON, WYO-
MING DECLARING THE CITY'S SUPPORT FOR THE WY-
OMING POW-MIA ASSOCIATION AND ESPECIALLY PVT.
LLOYD G. ROGERS.

Section 1: *The City Council of the City of Evanston, Wyoming hereby symbolically adopts and declares honorary city citizenship on Pvt. Lloyd G. Rogers, a POW-MIA from the Korean War.*

Section 2: *The City will honor Pvt. Rogers by recognizing the anniversaries of his birthday, the date of his loss, and other dates that the City may deem significant to the cause of POW-MIAs.*

Section 3: *The City expresses its support for the Wyoming Forget-Me-Not Association, Inc. in their many efforts to obtain a full accounting of all POW-MIAs from all military conflicts in which United States military personnel were called to serve, and especially an accounting of Pvt. Rogers.*

Councilman Davis made a motion to adopt Resolution 92-19, seconded by Vranish. After Mr. Michael Ferrin, representing the POW-MIA organization that requested the resolution, explained the organization's plans, I called for the vote on the motion to adopt resolution, with all voting in favor.

It was announced that the 1992 W.A.M. Convention would be held in Cheyenne on June 3rd, 4th, and 5th. Councilman Nelson followed up with a motion to appoint me, as mayor, to be the voting delegate for the 1992 W.A.M. Convention, with Councilwoman Jerry Wall as alternate. The motion was seconded by Vranish with all 7 votes in favor.

Prior to adjournment of the April 8th meeting I announced that there would be a luncheon held on April 16th at 11:30 a.m. with representatives from Union Pacific Resources Company to discuss their property northwest of the city.

I also reported on a recent Capital Facilities Tax meeting and enumerated some of the proposed projects to be funded if it is passed by the committee.

And I asked City Engineer Brian Honey to offer our congratulations to Wastewater Plant Supervisor Randy Roper for getting the Water and Wastewater Quality Convention to be held in Evanston.

As announced, the luncheon with the Union Pacific Resources Company (UPRC) was held at 11:30 a.m. on April 16th at the newly remodeled depot at Depot Square.

During the luncheon UPRC Vice President Dale Bossert made the announcement that they were donating 73 acres of property located west of the old Roundhouse to the City of Evanston. He also hinted that an additional land donation beyond the 73 acres might be coming in the future.

The April 17th issue of the *Uinta County Herald* headlined: CITY RECEIVES 73-ACRE GIFT.

The article went on: *At a Thursday afternoon donation ceremony and press conference Union Pacific Resources Company donated a 73-acre tract of land to the City of Evanston to expand its industrial land base.*

Evanston's Mayor Dennis Ottley stated, "We are very excited to have this land transfer completed and to have the opportunity to work with the Union Pacific Resources Company on this donation. We certainly thank Resources for their cooperation and generosity. We also appreciate the help that Governor Mike Sullivan gave this project."

He noted the expansion of the tank car company should create new jobs and will also boost the local economy.

"This will be the first real break that Evanston and Uinta County have had in a long time to help diversify their economies. We're anxious to get online with the expansion because this is a big opportunity to expand our local industries and to attract new industry to our area," he explained.

UPRC officials thanked the city, county and state officials for their work and cooperation in making the land donation a reality. "We especially appreciate Mayor Ottley's hard work on this project," said Dale Bossert, Vice President for UPRC. He stated, "It's our hope that this donation will enable the city to prosper in the future. We look forward to a long and friendly relationship with the city and the people of Uinta County."

Mayor Ottley said Union Tank Car Corporation has strongly indicated they would be expanding, with the possibility of creating 60 additional jobs.

"It took a lot of effort and we will continue to work with UPRC in giving the city an additional 195 acres, which will be used to entice other businesses to the city and expand ones that are already here," Ottley said.

He also mentioned that the Purple Sage Golf Club members were hoping to expand the golf course to 18 holes. This was in the plans if we could talk UPRC into giving the city the additional land.

The second regular city council meeting of the month was held on April 22nd, and the first order of business under public participation was an introduction by local Attorney Mark Harris. He introduced representatives from UPRC, Ed Gladish, Dennis Earhart, Karl Nesselrode, Jim G. Neuner, and Pete Straub. Mr. Straub made a presentation of the Wahsatch Gathering System and described their plans to gather the gas by pipeline to be processed at the Whitney Canyon Processing Plant. Straub also stated that he would be moving to Evanston with his family and would be the District Superintendent for the Wahsatch System for the area.

After a lengthy question and answer period I thanked the representatives of UPRC for their interest in Evanston and, once again, for the generous contribution they had already made to the local economy by donating the 73 acres of property to the city; and I welcomed Mr. Straub and his family to Evanston as new residents.

More presentations were made on the BEAR and Ski Evanston projects by the committee members, and Councilwoman Wall made the two motions to recommend the projects to go on the ballot as propositions to be voted on in the November election. The motions were seconded by Vranish and Nelson, with all voting in favor.

Professional Secretaries Week
April 19 - 25, 1992

City of Evanston
1200 Main Street
789-9690

EVANSTON'S FINEST--Secretaries serving the City of Evanston include, front from left, Jo Roesler, Lee Mayhew, Sharon Constantine; back, Nancy Stevenson, Kathy Defa, Cindy Hutchinson, Shanda Thomas, Sandy Douglas. not pictured are Linda Eastman, Paula Lind and Sue Norman.

Uinta County Herald, April 21, 1992.

New garbage collection system in place

The City of Evanston began its new and innovative one-man-one-truck garbage system last fall.

"The system is working well," says its manager Alan "Oop" Hansen.

Mayor Dennis Ottley is spearheading an effort to initiate a recycling system for the city which will reduce the amount of waste going to the landfill. He encourages citizens to use the green aluminum recycling bins placed at high traffic areas around the city.

Evanston initiated a new garbage system earlier this year. The one-man-one truck system is considered state of the art. The system is working well and citizens are enjoying the new efficient, easy to use rolling cans.

Uinta County Herald, April 28, 1992.

At this time Councilwoman Wall and City Attorney Boal were excused from the rest of the meeting so they could travel to Casper to attend a cable TV seminar the next day.

The first readings of some new ordinances came up, pertaining to new subdivision plats, with all passing unanimously. Councilman Davis introduced Resolution 92-20 authorizing the city to enter into an agreement with X-It Construction as the contractor to implement and complete the Centennial Park Phase I Project. The motion was made by Councilman Hutchinson to adopt Resolution 92-20, seconded by Lehman, with all voting in favor.

This action was a long time coming, and it was finally going to give the folks of Centennial Valley a park where they could have family gatherings and a playground for their children within their neighborhood.

Prior to adjourning the meeting of April 22nd I announced that there would be a Capital Facilities Tax meeting the next Monday evening, April 27th. I stated that it would be an open meeting and encouraged everyone to attend.

During the first regular city council meeting of the month on May 13th I read a letter from Claudia Bills resigning from the Urban Renewal Agency. She mentioned that she was moving to Laramie to further her education. Motion was made by Councilwoman Wall to accept Mrs. Bills's resignation, seconded by Davis, with all voting in favor.

I thanked Claudia for her many services to the City of Evanston and wished her the best in the future.

David Nees, Director of Pioneer Counseling, and Gary Bolger, Director of the Evanston Housing Authority, made a presentation for a mental health group home and explained the need for a new structure to house the Pioneer Counseling residential services. They requested that the City of Evanston transfer a portion of the Housing Authority property to allow a new home to be constructed for the service.

This would be part of the 40 acres that the City of Evanston had pledged to be used for elderly and low-income housing. The new structure would be just off Uinta View Drive (presently known as City View Drive) just south of the Youth Alternative Home (YAHA) and right across from Human Services.

Director Nees stated that a minimum of seven new jobs would be created with this new facility, and that the Evanston Housing Authority would be responsible for the maintenance contract.

Councilwoman Jerry Wall said, *This adds to the human services delivery system here, and it is already … a model throughout the state.* Director Bolger stated that this would be the first such group home in the state. In fact, he said, *the state felt so strongly about this that $220,000 was approved in this last session of the legislature for the project.*

After a lengthy discussion, Councilwoman Lehman made a motion to direct City Attorney Boal to prepare a Resolution and a deed for the property needed for the Pioneer Counseling residential services, seconded by Wall, with all voting in favor.

Boal stated that he would have the Resolution ready for the next meeting, but the quitclaim deed would have to wait until a clear description was prepared and made available to him. Also, the deed wouldn't be valid unless the Resolution was adopted. But he said that he would get on both right away if the city engineer could get him the description as soon as possible.

Councilwoman Wall made the motion to award a contract in the amount of $39,379 to the low bidder, TJG Corporation, for the landscaping, including the sprinkler system and sidewalks at Depot Square. The motion was seconded by Lehman, with all voting in favor.

Resolution 92-28 was introduced by Councilman Hutchinson to authorize the City of Evanston to enter into a contract agreement with TJG Corp. as the contractor for the Depot Square landscaping, sprinkler system and sidewalks.

Motion was made by Councilwoman Wall to adopt Resolution 92-28, seconded by Nelson with all voting in favor.

There had been many complaints and concerns and problems with Century T.V.'s system and it was taking too much time to extend cable TV to other parts of the Evanston area. Therefore it had been previously suggested to the City attorney to draw up a Resolution to authorize the appointment of a Cable Television Evaluation Committee to conduct a periodic evaluation of the city's cable TV provider, pursuant to the Franchise Ordinance.

Resolution 92-25, authorizing to the Cable TV evaluation committee, was introduced by Councilman Nelson. And after some additional discussion and a few comments by the Century Cable T.V. manager, motion was made by Councilman Vranish to adopt Resolution 92-25, seconded by Davis, with all voting in favor.

Resolution 92-27 was introduced by Councilman Hutchinson to enter into an agreement with Vista Landscaping, the low bidder, as contractor for landscaping at the intersection of 6th Street, Lombard and Yellow Creek Road after the highway department finished improvements to the intersection for right and left turns and access for some of the residents in the area. Motion was made by Councilman Nelson to adopt Resolution 92-27, seconded by Wall, with all voting in favor.

Towards the end of the meeting we rejected all bids on the Animal Control Building because they didn't meet specs, and Councilman Nelson made a motion to direct City Engineer Brian Honey to call for new bids on the building, seconded by Lehman. The motion passed with 6 votes in favor and 1 abstaining (Hutchinson). The reason Hutchinson abstained was that he had some kind of connection with one of the bidding companies and felt that he had a conflict of interest.

City Clerk Don Welling announced that filing forms to run for election of municipal offices were available at City Hall, and that filing dates were from May 14th to June 5th with a $10.00 filing fee.

Councilman Clarence Vranish then announced that he would be running for re-election for the position of Councilman representing Ward 1.

I reported on the last Capital Facilities Tax meeting held in Lyman on May 13th, and listed the proposed projects to be put on the ballot as follows:

- **Question 1.** *Senior Centers in Mountain View and Evanston, estimated at $2,264,031, and the Lyman Connector Road estimated at $725,000.*
- **Question 2.** *Phase 1 of each: the BEAR Project in Evanston estimated at $1,897,093 and the Lyman Recreation Project estimated at $1,780,000; and*
- **Question 3.** *The Evanston Ski Project estimated at $2,543,184. A total of 5 projects amounting to $9,209,308.*

The projects removed were the Indoor Arena Convention Center at the Uinta County Fair Grounds, Fort Bridger's Recreation Project, and the Bridger Valley Child Development Center.

I said that the committee had made arrangements to meet with the County Commission during their regular meeting on Tuesday, May 19th to discuss these proposed questions, because the measures require the approval of the County Commission to be put on the ballot. I named the 11 member Capital Facilities Tax Committee as follows: Jim Hissong, LaVerle Simmons and Norman Bates of Mountain View; Gary Poore and Marvin Lee Wickel of Lyman; Mary Aimoni of Fort Bridger; and Ruth Spencer, Diane Hennigar, Jerry Wall and me of Evanston, and County Commissioner Paul Barnard. Lyman Mayor Marvin Lee Wickel, Lyman Councilman Gary Poore, Senior Citizen Representative Ruth Spencer and I would be in attendance to represent the committee at the commission meeting.

Councilwoman Lehman made a motion supporting Question 2, and requested that the BEAR Project and the Lyman Recreation Project be in the same proposition on the ballot in the November election. The motion was seconded by Wall with 6 voting in favor and 1 against (Vranish). Why he voted against it I don't recall.

Just before adjournment I expressed concerns about the Wahsatch Gathering System and reported that Chevron Production Supervisor Gordon Park and I had discussed having an independent safety firm make a study or look into safety issues to insure that all is being done that needs to be done.

Following a short discussion, Councilwoman Lehman made a motion to authorize the mayor to look further into the safety matters concerning the Gathering System, seconded by Hutchinson, with all voting in favor.

In the *Uinta County Herald* of May 15th reporter Ann Curtis's article titled, CITY WANTS UNBIASED SAFETY STUDY CONDUCTED ON PROPOSED U.P. PIPELINE read:

Evanston's Mayor Dennis Ottley received the go-ahead from the city council Wednesday night to approach the Uinta County Commissioners and the Wahsatch Gathering System (WGS) personnel about safety concerns.

WGS is planning to construct a 40-mile pipeline which ties in several sour gas wells and delivers the product to Whitney Canyon Processing Plant north of town.

Several of the wells are located near or within city limits and have been capped since the 1980s.

Ottley said he wants a disinterested party to conduct a study to see if all safety precautions are being taken with the opening of several sour gas wells near the city. He said he had several "oil and gas people" approach him saying it would be prudent for the city, county and the company to invest in this private, neutrally done study.

Estimates on the costs for the information are $50,000 to $80,000.

"I am concerned about the uncapping of the well heads, leaks around the wells and making sure the proper valves are used," he said.

He stressed that he didn't think the Union Pacific Resources Company (UPRC), owner of WGS, was doing anything wrong, but he is worried about the city's liability.

"We certainly don't want to stop the project, but we want to be prudent," Ottley said.

Ottley appointed Clarence Vranish, Will Davis, Ken Klinker and Tom Hutchinson to accompany him Tuesday when he addresses the County Commission about the study.

Currently, no money has been allocated for the study, Curtis's article concluded.

During the second monthly regular city council meeting on May 27, two liquor license applications were heard, with Attorney

Dennis Boal conducting the hearings. The first application was by TJG Corp. of Prairie Inn Amoco (at present Jody's Diner), and the second application was by Four Star Enterprises, Texaco Truck Stop (Motel 6). Motions for approval of both applications were made and seconded by the council members, with both motions failing by a majority vote.

I read a letter from David Bills that he was resigning from the Planning and Zoning Commission and would no longer be able to operate the video camera, because he was moving to Laramie with his wife, Claudia. Motion was made by Councilwoman Lehman to accept Bills's resignation and release him from his agreement to run the video camera, seconded by Wall, with all voting in favor.

The council members and I all thanked him for his service on the P & Z Commission, and for his time running the video camera so that the meetings could be shown on the local TV channel. We also extended our best wishes to him and Claudia in their new endeavors.

Kayne Pyatt, representing Evanston High School's All Alumni Annual Reunion requested permission to have a parade on July 4th during the reunion at 10:00 a.m. After Ms Pyatt explained the routing of the parade, Councilman Nelson made a motion to permit the parade and to make the Evanston Police Department aware, seconded by Wall, with all voting in favor.

Jennifer Boehme was in attendance representing the Youth Student Government. She made a presentation concerning the Y.S.G. Leaders' plans to unite all students in middle school and high school through a Resolution designed to coordinate all their activities.

Miss Boehme also announced that she would be a Rotary International Exchange Student to Finland for her entire junior year of high school. She was thanked for her time and activity in Youth Student Government and we all wished her well during her school year in Finland.

Resolution 92-31 came up and was introduced by Councilman Nelson, to authorize the City of Evanston to execute a quitclaim deed to the Pioneer Counseling Residential Services, a Wyoming nonprofit corporation, to enable the construction and operation of housing facilities specially designed to meet the physical, social and psychological needs of low-income, handicapped persons. Councilwoman Wall made a motion to adopt Resolution 92-31, seconded by Lehman, with all voting in favor.

To make the recycling head position official, Councilwoman Wall made a motion to approve the position of Recycling Coordinator, and to hire staff member Barry Constantine, who was already on board. The position would be effective July 1, 1992. The motion was seconded by Nelson with 5 votes in favor, 1 vote against (Vranish), and 1 absent (Davis). The motion passed with a majority, but why Vranish voted against the motion I don't recall.

The developer and owner of property within the Red Mountain Subdivision offered to sell 3.8285 acres of property to the City of Evanston for a neighborhood park in the Red Mountain area.

After a lengthy discussion Councilwoman Wall made a motion for the mayor to be given authority to make an offer for the property at a purchase price of $7,000.00 with no requirement for street improvements or laid dedication imposed on the owner, seconded by Nelson. The motion carried with 6 votes in favor and 1 absent (Davis).

On May 22nd, *Uinta County Herald* Reporter Ann Curtis came out with an article titled EVANSTON PLANNER HELPS INNER-CITY KIDS PLAN FOR LIFE GOALS.

Curtis's article read: *Evanston's own City Planner Paul Knopf taught and entertained Washington D.C. inner-city middle school children while attending a National Planner Association meeting recently.*

This is the second year that Knopf has participated in the NPA program, which gives the children an idea about what a city planner does and why the job is important.

According to Knopf, most of the students came from a low-income background.

To get the students warmed up to the ideas Knopf wanted to express, he prepared and performed a "rap song" about his job.

In return, a part of the assignment for the class was for the middle school children to return the favor – and prepare a "rap" for Knopf.

"It was interesting and sad, their songs were about poverty, crime, drugs and brother killing," Knopf said.

"I was amazed at the horrible blight just across the street from the White House," he said.

The students talked about citizen input, neighborhood coalitions and how it takes people working together to get things done.

In the latter half of the class he played a slide show about Evanston and Wyoming.

"There were slides of deer and moose in the BEAR Project," Knopf said laughing.

At first the youngsters didn't know what the animals were and couldn't believe they could be seen in an urban setting.

They were also amazed at the wide open spaces in the state.

Evanston City Planner Paul Knopf teaches middle school children in Washington D.C. about his profession and "sells" Wyoming with slides and fun.

Uinta County Herald, May 22, 1992.

Knopf said he explained that even though Wyoming has fewer people, it still has some of the same problems to contend with in the future such as un-employment, pollution, etc.

He said the teachers of the schools appraised what he and 48 other plan-ners from around the country were accomplishing with the program, saying it broadened the children's horizon to what the rest of the country had to offer.

This is the fourth year that the NPA's public affairs office has offered the program.

Previously the organization (NPA) members had gone into schools in New Orleans, Denver and Atlanta, Curtis's article concluded.

For the regular city council meeting of June 10th, Stanton Wid-mer, son of City Treasurer Steve Widmer, operated the video camera. Stanton was a high school student who volunteered to take over the job after Dave Bills quit and moved to Laramie. He was only going to operate the camera until the start of the school year.

After the usual business was taken care of, I made appointments to the new Cable TV Evaluation Committee that would work with Bob George, Manager of the Century Cable T.V. Company (presently known as Allwest Communications), and assist him with suggestions and ideas to satisfy the public's many complaints and to encourage the cable company to expand their service in areas that were still on the UHF system.

My appointments to the new committee were: Attorney Paul Skog, Businessman Mike Ringer, Schoolteacher Kerri Ottley, City Councilwoman Jerry Wall, City Councilmen Clarence Vranish and Tom Hutchinson, and city staff members Dennis Boal, Steve Widmer, and Gary Bardsley.

Councilwoman Lehman made a motion to confirm the appointments to the TV committee, seconded by Nelson, with all voting in favor.

Councilwoman Wall presented Scott Smith, Chairman of the BEAR Project, with a plaque stating that the BEAR Project master plan had been named the Wyoming State Planning Association Project of the Year. The plaque had been presented to the City of Evanston by the Association at their annual meeting.

I offered my congratulations and thanks to City Planner Paul Knopf for submitting the project to the State Planning Association and to Chairman Scott Smith and his committee for all the work and dedication they had given to the project.

Councilwoman Wall also announced that Evanston City Planner Paul Knopf had been elected President of the Wyoming State Planning Association at their annual meeting. I again offered my congratulations to Paul for being elected president of the association, and stated that any city employee that becomes involved in community and state affairs to that magnitude is bound to enhance his employment.

During the June meeting, bids for the new Animal Control Building were opened. The apparent low bidder was Davis Construction Company in the amount of $89,000 with all specifications being in order, according to City Engineer Brian Honey. After a short discussion Councilwoman Wall made a motion to accept the bid offered by Davis Construction, seconded by Lehman. The vote was 5 yes votes, 1 no vote (Davis) and 1 abstaining. Councilman Hutchinson abstained because he felt he had a conflict of interest. Why Davis voted no, I don't recall.

However, after the present animal control shelter was deemed inadequate, I was glad that we were finally going to have a decent shelter: a shelter that had been a long time coming, and that the public should definitely approve of and the city should be proud of.

Following Wall's motion that was passed by a majority, she also introduced a resolution to enter into an agreement with Davis Construction for the construction of the animal control building.

RESOLUTION 92-34
RESOLUTION AUTHORIZING THE CITY OF EVAN-
STON, WYOMING TO ENTER INTO AN AGREEMENT
BETWEEN THE CITY OF EVANSTON, AS OWNER, AND
DAVIS CONSTRUCTION, AS CONTRACTOR, FOR THE
CONSTRUCTION OF THE ANIMAL CONTROL SHELTER
FOR THE CITY OF EVANSTON.

After City Attorney Dennis Boal read the title, Councilman Vranish made a motion for the adoption of Resolution 92-34, seconded by Nelson, with the same vote: 5 in favor, 1 opposed, and 1 abstaining. The resolution was adopted by a majority.

Councilman Nelson made a motion for the temporary closure of the downtown streets, as in the past, on Sunday June 21st from 11:30 a.m. to 5:30 p.m. for the in-town bike race during the weekend of the Uinta Classic Bike Race from Kamas, Utah to Evanston. The motion was seconded by Davis, with all voting in favor.

I then, as always, polled the city council members and the staff for any comments and announcements prior to adjournment.

District Parks and Recreation Director Dennis Poppinga reported that there were some folks requesting to have concessions at the Sulphur Creek Reservoir area. But it was noted that approval should be up to the district, not the city. However, it was stated that the city would have no objections as long as the area and the lake were kept clean from garbage.

I reported that it appeared the Renewal Ball was the largest ever and was again a big success. Funds would be distributed to the various nonprofit organizations as always. I thanked the committee for all their hard work and planning to make the event another great and successful program in Evanston.

Councilwoman Wall gave a report on the W.A.M. Convention in Cheyenne, and reported that the President of W.A.M., Max Debolt, had a heart attack on the Thursday night of the convention. However, she reported, because of the miracle of modern medicine he was recovering satisfactorily.

Finally, I reminded everyone that the public hearing on the next fiscal year budget would be on June 16th at 8:00 p.m. in the council chambers of City Hall, and that there would be a public hearing concerning the cable TV issue on June 17th at 7:00 p.m., also at City Hall.

Evanston Cowboy Days was late in applying for a malt beverage permit, so I called for a special city council meeting to be held on June 12th at 5:00 p.m. to take care of only the two items: first a motion to waive the required three-day advance notice in applying for a malt beverage permit, and second a motion to approve the application for the permit.

Besides myself, there were only Councilmembers Clarence Vanish, Craig Nelson and Will Davis in attendance (we had a quorum), as well as City Clerk Don Welling and City Attorney Dennis Boal.

First item of business: Councilman Davis made a motion to waive the three-day requirement for applying for a malt beverage permit, seconded by Nelson, with all 4 voting in favor, including me.

Second item of business: Councilman Nelson made a motion to approve the application presented by Chairman Tom Marshall of the Evanston Cowboy Days Committee for a malt beverage permit for June 12th and 13th, from 6:00 p.m. to 11:00 p.m. each night of the event, at the Uinta County Fairgrounds rodeo arena, called Battle of the Bulls (a fundraising event put on by the Evanston Cowboy Days Committee). The motion was seconded by Vranish and passed with 4 votes in favor.

This short meeting adjourned at 5:12 p.m.

On June 16th the special meeting was held at 8:00 p.m. for a public hearing for the fiscal year of 1992-1993, with all members of the city council present, except for Councilman Will Davis, who was excused.

I called the meeting to order at 8:00 p.m. and welcomed everyone present, stating that this was the largest group of people I had ever seen in attendance at a budget hearing, and told them that it was great to see that much interest in the budget.

I called for City Attorney Dennis Boal to conduct the hearing and stated that the hearing would be recorded and tape would be on file at City Hall for public's use.

After declaring the hearing open, Attorney Boal called on City Treasurer Steve Widmer to give an explanation concerning the proposed budget.

Presentations and questions were made by Charlotte Fry, Jim Jackson, Terry Prete, David Heinse, and Director of Urban Renewal Jim Davis, each representing special groups.

After City Attorney Boal closed the hearing Resolution 92-36 was introduced by Councilman Craig Nelson.

RESOLUTION 92-36
A RESOLUTION PROVIDING INCOME NECESSARY
TO FINANCE THE BUDGET AND PROVIDE FOR AND
AUTHORIZE ANNUAL APPROPRIATION OF FUNDS FOR
FISCAL YEAR 1992-1993.

There were no amendments and very few adjustments to the proposed 12.9 million dollar plus budget; therefore Councilwoman Wall made the motion to adopt Resolution 92-36, seconded by Vranish. The motion passed with 6 votes in favor and 1 absent (Davis).

Councilman Hutchinson thanked the budget committee and City Treasurer Widmer for all the work they did on their success in coming up with a balanced budget. Councilman Vranish expressed his thanks to the budget committee and his appreciation to me, as mayor, for making the budget process available to any member of the council who wanted to be on the budget committee.

I was very pleased with the budget being approved with no amendments and no real opposition from those in attendance. The City of Evanston had a carryover of cash on hand in the amount of $2,911,670 and was able to maintain a cash reserve of $900,000. We also were able to give all employees a 3% pay increase, and still maintain a balanced budget. It was very satisfying to be able to come up with a balanced budget with approximately an 8% decrease from the fiscal year's budget for 1991-1992.

The second regular city council meeting of the month was held on June 24th, and following the usual business, a number of applications for malt beverage permits and catering permits to serve off-premises liquor came up.

Applications for a malt beverage permit were presented as follows: the Police Benevolent Association for their Annual Mudd Bogg event to be held on July 18th and 19th at the fairgrounds rodeo arena; the Evanston Lions Club for a Rib-O-Rama to be held on July 4th at Depot Square; and the Ellis Ranch Psychos for their Annual Softball Tournament on July 27th and 28th.

Applications for catering permits were as follows: Veranda Bar for the Uinta County Employees Picnic at the fairgrounds on July 9th; and Veranda Bar for Railroad Days at the Beeman-Cashin Building on July 12th.

All applications were approved by motions by the council members and seconded, and all passed unanimously.

I then read a letter from Brian Patterson stating that he was resigning from the Evanston Planning and Zoning Commission. Councilman Nelson offered a motion to accept Patterson's letter, seconded by Hutchinson, with all voting in favor. The members of the city council and I all thanked Patterson for his service and involvement in the community and wished him the best in the future. I also expressed the city's appreciation to both Mr. and Mrs. Patterson, for their involvement as committee members of the Renewal Ball and the BEAR Project.

I followed up by appointing Dale Gardner to serve on the P & Z Commission to fill the vacancy created by David Bills. A motion was made by Councilman Nelson to confirm the appointment of Gardner to the P & Z Commission, seconded by Wall, with all voting in favor.

I then reappointed Craig Nelson to serve on the District Parks and Recreation Commission, and appointed Roger Cazin to serve on the Urban Renewal Agency to fill the vacancy of Claudia Bills. Both appointments were confirmed by the city council.

Diana Hennigar made a written request for a parade route for the Uinta County Fair Parade on August 1st at 10:00 a.m. The route would start at Evanston Middle School, proceed down 4th Street to Front Street, continue up Harrison Drive to Main Street, turn left on Main and continue back to 4th Street to Evanston Middle School. Councilman Hutchinson made a motion to approve both the parade and the route, and to notify the Evanston Police Department, seconded by Wall, with all voting in favor.

A request was made by the Railroad Days Committee for Front Street from Martin Park to 12th Street, 12th Street to Main Street, and Main Street from 12th to 15th Street to be closed to all but local traffic on July 11th and 12th for the purpose of having miniature train rides on Main Street from 12th to 15th Streets.

Councilman Nelson made a motion to allow the closure of these streets as requested by the Railroad Days Committee on July 11th and 12th, seconded by Hutchinson, with all voting in favor.

Railroad Days is a new event which will keep Evanston residents and visitors busy July 11 and 12. Visitors will enjoy the grand opening of the "baggage room" at Depot Square. It is now used as a waiting room for Amtrak users. A number of events are planned such as style shows, miniature railroad, railroad history, films, etc.

Uinta County Herald, April 28, 1992.

July 17, 1992   UINTA COUNTY HERALD

Depot dedication

Evanston's Red Carpet Committee officially cut the ribbon on the new Amtrak waiting room during the "Historic Railroad Days" celebration. Representing the city were Mayor Dennis Ottley and Urban Renewal Director Jim Davis.

During the meeting Councilwoman Lehman introduced the following resolution:

RESOLUTION 92-39
RESOLUTION AUTHORIZING THE CITY OF EVANSTON, WYOMING TO EXECUTE ALL DOCUMENTS NECESSARY TO COMPLETE THE PURCHASE OF REAL PROPERTY IN THE RED MOUNTAIN MESA VI PARK SUBDIVISION.

With this resolution the city would be able to complete the offer of $7,000 for the 3.8285 acres for which the city had previously made an offer, in order to give the residents of Red Mountain a neighborhood park. The motion was made by Councilman Hutchinson to adopt Resolution 92-39, seconded by Nelson, with all voting in favor.

When asked for comments from staff and council prior to adjournment, Parks and Recreation District Director Dennis Poppinga invited everyone to the dedication of the new Brown School Park on the corner of 1st Avenue and B Avenue on Saturday, June 27th at 11:00 a.m.

Community Development Director and City Planner Paul Knopf expressed his thanks and appreciation to everyone who had any affiliation with the High Uinta Classic Bike Race held June 20th. He stated that 215 bikers participated in the annual event this year, making it the largest classic held in this area so far.

He also expressed his appreciation to all the volunteers that helped on Sunday, June 21st with the in-town bike race, and stated that the bikers said they would return for next year's event and they were amazed at how attractive a community Evanston was.

Poppinga also mentioned that the State Little League Baseball Tournament was to be held in Evanston July 18th to July 24th, and that anyone who wished to volunteer would be very much appreciated.

I then offered my congratulations and thanks to several public works employees for completing another level of certification: Dan Martin, Rick Lunsford, David Albrecht, Lon Richardson, Randy Roper and Kevin Dean.

I complimented Urban Renewal Agency Director Jim Davis for his efforts in pulling together several communities in the Union Pacific Railroad Corridor across Southern Wyoming. He stated that other communities across the state that were interested seemed to be looking at Evanston for leadership in forming the corridor and obtaining the railroad history of Southern Wyoming.

Jim Davis was also thanked for all his work in preserving the history of Evanston and for forming the Old Timers Group, better known as The Old Farts Club, of senior citizens that met often and discussed past events and the history of the area.

I reminded the council members that they were all invited to attend dinner with Carl Classen, Executive Director of W.A.M. at 6:00 p.m. on Monday, June 29th at Sorella's Restaurant.

During the past few meetings, the city council had been going into executive session to discuss a personnel matter concerning a former member of the Evanston Police Department who was discharged for insubordination and misconduct of service. The officer did not feel that he had been discharged fairly. He didn't think his discharge met the procedure of Evanston's Police Personnel Manual and had decided to file suit against the City of Evanston. This lawsuit went on for over a year before settlement, but never got to the courts.

At this time, prior to adjourning the city council meeting, we needed to go into executive session to discuss the matter. Therefore, Councilwoman Lehman made the motion for the city council to go into executive session to further discuss the personnel matter once again. The motion was seconded by Nelson with 6 votes in favor and 1 absent (Davis). The motion passed unanimously.

Other than members of the city council and me, City Attorney Dennis Boal and Chief of Police Dennis Harvey were permitted to attend the executive session.

This lawsuit ended up being settled several months later, early in 1993, with the City of Evanston paying the employee in question, an undisclosed amount to settle the matter rather than go through the courts, which would have been very costly for the city whether they won or not. At the city attorney's and my suggestion, though against my better judgment, the city council elected to pay the settlement, rather than go through the court process.

The dedication of the new Brown School Park was held on June 27th with remarkable attendance. This park was constructed on property where the Old Brown School, housing grades first through third, was located until the new North Elementary School was constructed.

The Parks and Recreation District Commission welcomed everyone to the dedication by giving a little history of the park, followed by comments from me as mayor, and City Councilmen Tom Hutchinson and Craig Nelson, both representing Ward 3. Other speakers were George Barker, Chairman of the Uinta County School District No. 1 Board of Trustees and Dorothy Proffit, a long-time former teacher at Brown School.

The following comments and quotes were from an article written by Ann Curtis, Reporter for the *Uinta County Herald* for the issue of June 30th:

The school was built in 1902, according to residents, and was named for James Brown, Sr. Brown was a renowned citizen who was a judge, LDS Stake President and member of the school board during the time.

Dorothy Proffit, a teacher at the school for several years, spoke of the teachers' innovative ways to compensate for the problems of the outdated building. She taught at the school until she was transferred to the school district's newest building, the new Clark School.

According to George Barker, School Board Chairman, the district had several businesses offering to purchase the property, but the board decided to give the property to the city for a park for the neighborhood.

Barker spoke of the "old fashioned teachers" who cared for the children in the facilities.

"They were truly dedicated. They were willing to work seven days a week, 12 hours a day in spite of salary," he claimed.

"This park is a memorial to all those hundreds and hundreds of students and teachers who have gone through this school," he said.

Director Poppinga requested that if there were anyone in the crowd who would like to speak of their experiences while attending school at Brown, "Please feel free to come to the mike and tell us of your experiences," he said.

My wife Sandy was one of several folks to tell a story. She said that she had gone to school at Brown in first and second grades, and both of her oldest sons, Randy and Dave, had also started school at Brown until we moved to the Clark School district.

She told a story about Dave, our second son, who had been going to first grade at Brown. The first grade would let out a few minutes earlier than the second and third grades, and Sandy had told Dave to always wait for his older brother before crossing the street to come home.

One particular cold day in the middle of the winter, when the first bell rang Dave left his class. While he was waiting on the school porch for his brother to get out of school, for some reason other, Dave did something very stupid. He licked the school door knob, causing his tongue to freeze to the knob. Why he did this we had no idea, Sandy said.

When the second bell rang and Dave heard all the kids running down the hall to leave school, he didn't know what to do. Then all of a sudden someone opened the door. With his tongue still stuck to the knob, it pulled a good part of the flesh off of his tongue, leaving Dave with a big painful wound.

Randy grabbed him and ran home with him to have me look at it, Sandy continued. It looked pretty bad and Randy was worried that he would be blamed for it, but I started doctoring his tongue to help relieve the pain. *I don't think he ever did that again,* she added.

After the program I, as mayor, officially dedicated the park as Brown School Park and gave out door prizes and refreshments for everyone. The rest of the afternoon the folks enjoyed themselves by just visiting and getting acquainted with their neighbors. It was a nice day for the dedication and turned out to be very successful.

During our first city council meeting of the month held on July 8th, I read a letter of resignation from Lieutenant Russell Dean. He stated that his resignation would be effective July 10th due to the immediate circumstances of his new employment. Councilman Nelson made the motion to accept Lt. Dean's resignation as requested, seconded by Vranish, with all voting in favor. Each member of the city council expressed their thanks to Dean for his many years of service to Evanston, and I also voiced my appreciation to him as well.

Toni Albrecht made a request for a parade to be held for the State All-Star Baseball Teams that would be in Evanston for the State Little League Tournament on July 18th through 24th. She reported that the parade would be held on July 18th at 6:30 p.m. and would start at City Hall, go up Main Street to 6th Street, turn right on 6th, and end at the Overthrust Baseball Field Complex.

Councilwoman Lehman made a motion to approve the parade and to notify the police department of the route, seconded by Davis, with all voting in favor.

Next Councilman Hutchinson introduced Resolution 92-45 as follows:

RESOLUTION 92-45
RESOLUTION OF THE CITY OF EVANSTON, WYOMING AUTHORIZING THE CITY TO ENTER INTO A JOINT FUNDING AGREEMENT WITH THE GEOLOGICAL SURVEY, UNITED STATES DEPARTMENT OF THE INTERIOR FOR THE OPERATION OF A STREAM GAUGING STATION ON THE BEAR RIVER AT EVANSTON, WYOMING.

Section 1: The Mayor is hereby authorized to sign, and the City Clerk attest the execution, of the Joint Funding Agreement, No. WY92055300, a copy of which is attached hereto and incorporated herein, with the Geological Survey, United States Department of Interior, for the purpose of continuing the operation of the stream gauging station on the Bear River at Evanston, Wyoming.

I believe this was the first gauging station located on the Bear River and it was placed near County Road Bridge. The purpose was for the Geological Survey Group and the City of Evanston Public Works to keep tabs on the flow of the river at different times of the year, especially through the high water season to help prevent flooding and keep control of the new Sulphur Creek Dam.

Flooding had been a serious concern every spring for Evanston and the downstream areas such as Almy and the town of Bear River. Through the recommendations of City Engineer Brian Honey and Community Development Director and Planner Paul Knopf, the city council also agreed, especially after meeting with representatives from the Geological Survey Group.

After Resolution 92-45 was introduced, a motion was made by Councilwoman Wall to adopt the resolution, seconded by Nelson. During discussion it was pointed out that the Department of Interior would not approve the project unless the city and/or the county would fund at least half of the cost. The City of Evanston agreed to the funding, because we felt it was well worth it, but for some reason or other the Uinta County Commissioners refused to be a part of it.

Just before calling for the vote on the resolution, Councilwoman Wall made a request that City Clerk Welling put in the minutes that the Uinta County Commissioners refused to participate in the program. I then ended discussion and called for the vote, which was unanimous, all voting in favor.

My understanding is that, as of this writing, there are still several stream gauging stations in various locations on the Bear River where it flows within Uinta County, and that the U.S. Department of Interior had been paying 100%, as per agreement, of the funding and is monitored by the U.S. Geological Survey .

During this time, late June and early July, Uinta County was doing some repairs on the courthouse and library parking lot, causing an inconvenient parking situation for their employees. So the Uinta County Commissioners approached me on the possibility of waiving the two-hour parking restrictions on the courthouse side of Main Street and Center Street from 7th to 9th Streets, because there was no other place for the county employees to park.

I told them that I would have to get city council approval, but I also told them to go ahead, that I would notify the Evanston Police Department and tell them that the two-hour parking limit had been waived on the two streets on the courthouse side. I also said that I would bring it up in the next city council meeting to have my actions ratified.

Therefore, during our July 8th regular city council meeting I had added it to the agenda, and late in the meeting Councilman Nelson made a motion to ratify and approve the action that the mayor took in waiving the two-hour parking requirement on the courthouse side of Main and Center Streets while the county parking lot was being repaired, seconded by Vranish, with all voting in favor.

Just before adjournment Urban Renewal Agency Director Jim Davis expressed his thanks to everyone who helped make the recent Evanston High School Alumni Celebration a big success once again; and I reported on several other items: I told them that I had met with George Peters of the Union Pacific Land Resources and that everything was still on track for their donation to the city of the land west of the roundhouse; and I had some bad news, that the Oxbow (sometimes called the Golden Eagle) Refinery east of Evanston was shutting down. I told them I didn't know why except that maybe production was down; finally, I told them that the Red Mountain Park project was moving right along.

I then called for a work session to be held on July 15th to discuss several projects that were ongoing and adjourned the July 8th city council meeting at 7:45 p.m.

In June, the Uinta County School District No. 1 Board had started working on the school district budget, knowing that tax revenues were going to be down. The school board talked about items such as reduction in medical benefits, freezing salaries of all district employees including teachers, plus other cuts in benefits, long before any definite decision was made on finalizing the budget. Folks in Evanston, especially those with a connection to the teachers, such as family and friends, got overexcited, and Letters to the Editor and threats to community and school board members got unnecessarily out of hand.

The *Uinta County Herald* of June 2nd ran an article by Reporter Andre Marcus Vospette titled, TEACHER QUESTIONNAIRE SEEN AS THREAT TO LOCAL BUSINESS OWNER. The article started out:

A questionnaire circulated to teachers by the Evanston Education Association has upset at least one local merchant, but the association president said the list is only a rough draft.

Well, if it was only a rough draft, how the hell did it get into the hands of the press? Good question.

The article continued: *The survey, titled "Our Answer to Meet and Confer Results," lists 25 responses to the Board of Trustees' decision to freeze salaries and cut insurance benefits for certified staff. The survey was handed out to district staff last week and their choices were tabulated Monday.*

"We're asking the school board to meet our proposal, which is not unreasonable," said association president Larry Uhling. The association asked the board to grant a step increase on the salary schedule and either retain vision insurance [apparently this was the area where the board was going to cut on the insurance] or use the $55,000 budgeted to pay for a $100 across-the-board raise.

Other options included in the survey but not chosen by the board were: refusing to accept calls for parents or students after contracted hours, holding report cards, pulling summer paychecks out of Evanston banks, boycotting businesses with board connections, walking out, or refusing to coach athletics.

Vospette's article continued: *Uhling called the survey an "option list," and said although most teachers would not support the more "radical" options the association chose to put them to a vote.*

"We don't want to have a negative effect on the community," Uhling said. "Some of the things on the list are things people wouldn't want to do. We'll let everybody decide what we'll be doing."

When I read that news article and noticed the questionnaire mentioning "pulling paychecks out of Evanston banks" and the word "boycotting businesses" I really got upset. I couldn't believe a bunch of educators would suggest something like boycotting the local people who were paying the taxes so that they can receive a paycheck.

All my life I have believed that the teacher's first interest was the children, but after checking in on that questionnaire, whether it was just a "rough draft" or not, my opinion of teachers really dropped. My daughter-in-law was a teacher in the district, but I know she would never have gone for that questionnaire.

The people running the teachers union of the local board, Evanston Educators Association, were supposed to be well educated people, but putting out a questionnaire like that showed that they were just a bunch of idiots.

I don't know much about the school budget, but I do know that almost all of their funds come from the 25 mill school levy paid by the property owners within the school district, and other special mill levies. These tax dollars come from local businesses and pay school employees' salaries. I do honestly believe that a very large percentage of the educators of Evanston would be opposed to any kind of boycott in the school district.

FRESH AIR FREEDOM AND FUN! EVANSTON - WY

We Salute The Businesses That Make Up The
Economic Base of Our Community

Uinta County Herald, April 28, 1992.

I don't normally write letters to the editor, but when I do it's gen-
erally just an editorial, but with all these Letters to the Editor in the
paper, I thought I had better say something about the questionnaire.
Some of those items would negatively affect the City of Evanston if
they were implemented, and I didn't feel that the questionnaire was
fair to the teachers or the public.

So I wrote and I sent the following Letter to the Editor of the
Uinta County Herald:

Dear Editor;

*Upon reading the Uinta County Herald last week, mainly the
Letters to the Editor and the editorial, as Mayor of Evanston I became
quite concerned with what is happening in the Uinta County School
District #1. Normally, I do not get too involved with what goes on
in other governmental entities. I am familiar with what it takes to
run government and unless you are active and know all sides of every
issue it is unfair and almost impossible to criticize, but when I read
about the rebellious list of suggestions put out in the form of a questionnaire by the Evanston Education Association I felt that the City
of Evanston and its citizens should be concerned. And apparently
they are.*

*When people start talking about boycotting their own commu-
nity and doing things that adversely affect the economy, then they
are affecting their own pocketbooks. Educators, administrators, and
school staff all receive their pay through tax revenues. Revenues de-
rived through property taxes that even commercial establishments pay
no matter who is affiliated with that business, school board members
or whomever. I am glad to hear that a large majority of the educators
were in opposition to most of the suggestions printed, especially those
that would have an effect on Evanston's economy.*

*Evanston appreciates the employees of the district, and realizes
that Uinta County School District #1 is one of the largest payrolls
in the area and it is certainly appreciated and needed to help our community prosper.*

Therefore, I sincerely hope that the school board takes everything into consideration in the possibility of making things better for our educators. They deserve to be treated with honesty and with utmost respect. Educators are a necessary force toward our youth's education. However, I also believe that the board and administration have a job to do and I feel they will make the right decisions where possible.

On behalf of the people of Evanston I want you to know that you all are truly an important part of this community. You are vital to the economy and extremely appreciated.

I signed the letter and sent it to the *Uinta County Herald*. After the issue came out I received nothing but good comments from citizens who called me, some school employees, folks meeting me in my office, and some just running into me on the streets and stopping me to talk about the letter.

During the second monthly city council meeting of the month on July 22nd I appointed Ruth Dahlman, who was introduced by City Planner Paul Knopf, to serve on the Evanston Planning and Zoning Commission for a three-year term. The motion was made by Councilwoman Wall to confirm the appointment, seconded by Vranish. The motion passed unanimously.

Motions were made by council members to approve two applications for a malt beverage permit: The Evanston Lions Club applied for a permit for the Small Town Toys Car Club to be held at Hamblin Park on July 25th from 8:00 a.m. to 6:00 p.m. Bill Alexander was in attendance representing the Lions Club; and the V.F.W. Post 4280 applied for a permit to be used also on July 25th for the Small Town Toys Car Club dance and banquet at the Beeman-Cashin Building from 3:00 p.m. to 1:00 a.m. of July 26th. V.F.W. Commander Dennis Sundberg was in attendance representing the Vets.

Both motions were seconded, and the two applications for malt beverage permits were approved and passed with all voting in favor.

Following that action I read a letter of resignation from Officer Brad Durrant of the Evanston Police Department. The reason Durrant was resigning was unknown, but Councilman Nelson made a motion to accept Officer Durrant's letter of resignation, seconded by Hutchinson, with all voting in favor.

The council members and I all thanked Durrant for his past services to Evanston and wished him well in his new ventures.

At this time I opened the floor for discussion on the letter the city had received from County Commissioner Chairman Pat Mulhall concerning the charges they were requesting from the city for dispatch services.

On July 7th Uinta County Commissioner Pat Mulhall, Chairman sent a letter addressed to the mayor and the city council mentioning that due to the shortfall in revenues the county was going to be charging the City of Evanston $135,920 through the next fiscal year for dispatch services, which is far above what the city had previously paid.

He stated in his letter: *The Commissioners believe it is not only fair but also very necessary to charge the City of Evanston for the cost of at least one dispatcher. The cost for one 24-hour-per-day Evanston Police dispatcher is $135,920 per year. To ease the impact to the City Budget when we go into the 92-93 budget year, we would be willing to bill the City on a quarterly basis.*

The invoice will be in the amount of $34,000 per quarter. We would propose that the first quarter (July, August and September) would be done free of charge. The second quarter (October, November and December) would be invoiced at the end of December. Each quarter thereafter an invoice for $34,000 would be sent, Mulhall's letter concluded.

During a short discussion with the council the following question was brought up: Why wasn't this request presented to us prior to the adoption of the city budget in June? It was suggested that if we agree to pay their requested amount, that they may have to wait until the next fiscal year before getting paid in full. Our budget had been heard by the public and was approved by the city council in June. At this time there was no way we could meet their request until the fiscal year of 1992-1993. The council suggested that I write a letter to the Commissioners explaining our position. I wrote the letter the next morning.

Prior to adjourning the July 22nd meeting I asked for reports:

- Police Lieutenant Mitch Allmaras gave a report on the Mudd Bogg and stated that it had a good crowd both days;
- Recreation Director Dennis Poppinga gave a short report on the State Little League Tournament that was going to be held in Evanston;
- City Attorney Dennis Boal gave his updated report on Century Cable T.V. Company. He indicated that the TV company was being very cooperative;
- Evanston Community Development Director and Planner Paul Knopf reported on the Comprehensive Plan. He stated that it was coming along with great interest and should be almost ready for mayor and council action soon;
- It was reported that the annual Railroad Days In Evanston held on July 11th and 12th was another big success. The attendance was outstanding with many folks from out of town participating. The annual Chili Cookoff also had another successful year.

All these programs were helping the economy by getting local folks involved and bringing them out to enjoy themselves, and the programs also enticed a lot of out-of-town folks to Evanston to enjoy the "Fresh Air, Freedom and Fun" Evanston had to offer.

City Engineer Brian Honey brought up the request by the school district asking for painted cross walks and flashing lights at some of the elementary school locations. But no action was taken at this time.

After all reports I called for a work session to be held at City Hall on August 5th at 5:00 p.m. The July 22nd meeting adjourned at 8:00 p.m.

I wrote my letter the next day, dated July 23rd, to Chairman Pat Mulhall and the County Commissioners in regard to "County User Fees For Dispatch Service" as follows:

Dear Commissioner Mulhall:

I have informally discussed with the City Council your letter dated July 7th, 1992, which I received on July 15, 1992. We were a bit surprised by it. As you know, the City had concluded its budget process for the fiscal year some time ago and that would have been the appropriate time to consider your letter. Besides, the local newspaper just recently reported that county services would be maintained at their current level for at least another year because county employees had done a good job of eliminating unnecessary expenditures from your budget.

At any rate, the City Council needs more information before it can decide what action it will take in response to your letter. First, please clarify whether your letter of July 7, 1992, is a request for the City's assistance to fund the dispatch service or is it a demand? Second, if the City is unable or unwilling to pay the fees, will dispatch service be denied to Evanston citizens and other people who happen to be in our city when they need help? Finally, if the City pays your request of $135,920 for dispatch services, what steps will the Commission implement to make sure the City has input in and some control over the policies, procedures and costs of the dispatch service? Will the Commission create a Joint Powers Board for this purpose?

Please provide this information as soon as possible so the City can take appropriate action. Any changes in the city budget will require the City Council hold a public hearing after providing notice to our citizens. In the meantime, we will notify several agencies, (by mailing a copy of this letter and your correspondence), that the City may not be able to honor its budget commitments because the funds may be needed to pay fees to the Commission for dispatch service.

Finally, be advised the City Council would be glad to meet with the Commission to discuss this matter, if you think such a meeting would be useful.

Sincerely, Dennis J. Ottley (signed)
Mayor

cc: County Commissioners; Casey Davis, Paul R. Barnard; Evanston City Council Members; Uinta County Human Resources Board;

Evanston Child Development Center; Evanston Ministerial Association; SAFV; UCRC, Pioneer Counseling Services; Uinta Senior Citizens, Inc.; Western Wyoming Family Planning; YAHA; Uinta County Sheriff; Evanston Chamber of Commerce; Evanston Urban Renewal Agency; Evanston Parks and Recreation District; and Uinta County Fire department.

In writing the letter and sending out copies to all of the above I certainly wasn't trying to upset the commissioners, but I wanted to get their attention and meet. I felt that this would be a good time to talk about city and county problems. Meeting with the County Commissioners never happened often enough as far as I was concerned. I have always believed in good and close communications by all entities.

I did receive a letter from Commissioner Mulhall prior to our next meeting on August 12th and read the letter to the council. The letter was dated July 31st and read as follows:

Mayor and Members of the City Council:

In order to clarify your questions concerning user fees for county dispatch services per your letter dated July 23, 1992 we submit the following:

Our letter of July 7, 1992 was a notice to the City of Evanston that they will be required to pay for dispatch services provided by Uinta County to the City of Evanston. We assume that the City is able and willing to pay for this service. We also assume that the dispatch service is a high priority to the City and that the proposed fees are a reasonable expense.

City input into the operation of any County run program is always welcome as any user of our services is. If you have further questions please let us know.

Sincerely yours,
Patrick P. Mulhall, Chairman (signed)
Uinta County Commission

cc: James Anderson, Uinta County Attorney; Lynne Fox, Uinta County Clerk; Terry Brimhall, Uinta County Treasurer; Commissioners Paul Barnard and Casey Davis.

The letter had no mention of a meeting in it. There was some concern about the word *required,* and after a short discussion Councilman Nelson made a motion to authorize me to write another letter to the commissioners in response to their last letter, seconded by Davis, with all voting in favor except for Lehman, who abstained. Why? I don't know, unless it was because of her connections with the county through her work.

The next day I got a hold of Commissioner Mulhall and told him how the city council felt and that we had better set up a date for the County Commissioners and the city council to meet, and we did. The date was set for Tuesday, September 1st at 3:00 p.m. at the County Courthouse, which was the commissioners' regular monthly meeting.

During our council meeting, Councilman Nelson made a motion to approve the Cowboy Days Committee's application for a malt beverage permit for September 4th, 5th, 6th, and 7th. The motion was seconded and approved unanimously. Dan Lunsford, Chairman of the committee thanked the council and spoke briefly on the event.

I read a letter from Debby Smith resigning from the Evanston Housing Authority. Her husband and former County Attorney Scott Smith had been assigned to a State of Wyoming judgeship and the family was leaving Evanston. Councilwoman Wall made the motion to accept Debby's letter, seconded by Lehman, with all voting in favor.

On behalf of the city council, I expressed appreciation and a big thank you for her service as well as Scott's, because they both had been very active in the community. I wished them well in the future.

I also read a letter of resignation from Officer Ray Varner of the Police Department. Motion was made by Councilwoman Wall to accept his letter, seconded by Nelson with all voting in favor.

We thanked Ray for his service to the city and wished him well in his new position with the Uinta County Sheriff's Department.

I appointed Sue Norman to serve on the Evanston Housing Authority. Councilman Davis made the motion to confirm, seconded by Lehman, with all voting in favor.

I then left the podium to present Scott Smith a plaque of thanks and appreciation for his guidance, work getting the BEAR Project started and keeping it going to be successful.

All BEAR Project board members were in attendance and all came to the front when Urban Renewal Agency Director Jim Davis presented to Scott Smith a picture of Red Bridge, taken in 1918. Red Bridge was well known. It had a history behind it, and it was where a lot of local young kids went swimming (sometimes skinny-dipping). The restoration of Red Bridge was part of the BEAR Project.

Ron Barnard, Chairman of the Bear River Stabilization Committee, made a presentation and showed a video of the possibilities for erosion control and channel stabilization on the Bear River as it ran from the I-80 overpass to County Road Bridge.

I expressed the city's appreciation for the work that was being accomplished on the Green Belt Area along the Bear River, part of the BEAR Project, and how it would make Evanston more attractive.

Several citizens who resided on or near 19th Street were in attendance to express their concerns about the excessive speed of traffic driving down 19th Street. This had been a problem since the entire road had been paved and was getting worse. Lieutenant Mitch Allmaras from traffic control of the Police Department was in attendance and he said that they were aware of the problem and would monitor the area more closely, but that it would be a big help if and when people saw this happening, they should try to get a license number or any information on the offending vehicle, call the police department, and sign a complaint.

I assured folks that if they were willing to call and give the police whatever information they might have, even if they requested to stay anonymous, the police would still look into the matter and put a close watch on that particular vehicle. Lt. Allmaras agreed.

We had previously requested bids for slurry-sealing the Evanston streets where needed. During this meeting City Engineer Brian Honey presented the only bid received. He said the bid was from Intermountain Slurry Seal Inc. and met all specifications. After a short discussion Councilwoman Lehman made a motion to award the bid to the low and only bidder and direct City Attorney Boal to prepare a resolution and contract with Intermountain Slurry Seal Inc. The motion was seconded by Nelson and the vote was unanimous in favor.

City Engineer Honey also presented the only bid submitted, which was from Shaker Paving, for the street overlay project. Upon Honey's recommendation, Councilman Hutchinson made a motion to award the bid on the street overlay project to the only bidder, and also directed the city attorney to prepare a resolution and contract, seconded by Davis, with all voting in favor.

Uinta County School District No. 1 Superintendent Norman Gaines was in attendance to request crosswalks, signs and flashing lights on County Road for North Elementary School, and on Washakie Drive and Aspen Grove Drive for Aspen Elementary School.

Gaines said that it was a safety matter to protect the children going and coming from school. After a short discussion, Councilwoman Lehman made a motion to authorize these crosswalks, signs and flashing lights per the district's request, seconded by Davis.

But during discussion it was pointed out that the total cost would be approximately $35,000 and that this was another item that was not in the budget and that we had to wait to commit to the flashing lights until we had a chance to look at the budget.

Therefore, Councilwoman Wall made a motion to amend the main motion to temporarily eliminate the flashing lights until the budget can be examined and monies found, but to paint the crosswalks and install signs immediately. A report on the budget would be scheduled for the next regular council meeting. The motion to amend passed unanimously as did the main motion as amended.

After examining the budget during the next meeting, I suggested that we use monies from the emergency reserve fund to pay for the flashing lights, because there were enough funds in that budget line item to pay for them. Therefore, the council made a motion and seconded that we approve the flashing lights as well, with all voting in favor.

On August 28th Superintendent Norman Gaines wrote a letter addressed to the Mayor and Council thanking us, on behalf of the School District's Board of Trustees, the staff, and most importantly, he said, "our students and parents" for the crosswalks, school zone signs and flashing lights.

Urban Renewal Director Jim Davis reported that the Southern Wyoming Railroad Corridor Committee said that work had been done to pull all communities along the corridor together to help the committee prepare historic information to promote tourism in Wyoming.

Jim Davis was chairman of this committee made up of folks from communities across southern Wyoming that had been involved from the beginning with the construction of the Union Pacific Railroad in the state. It was turning into a great project and everyone involved was excited about it. During the report Councilwoman Wall announced that the Corridor Committee had adopted a name of distinction, *Tracks Across Wyoming*, as the official title of the program.

Meetings had been held in the Cheyenne train depot and rail yards, in Medicine Bow at the Virginian Hotel, visiting their old depot and at other places of railroad interest.

We also met one time in Reliance, an old mining and railroad town several miles north of Rock Springs that has since been annexed into the City of Rock Springs. As a point of interest, Western Wyoming College originated at the old Reliance High School building. At one time, Reliance High School was in the same athletic conference with Evanston, Superior, Rock Springs and other major high schools in Southwest Wyoming.

I thanked Jim and the Urban Renewal Agency for taking the lead for such an enormous project that would promote Southern Wyoming in a big way.

City Attorney Boal reported on the TV Evaluation Committee and stated that they were meeting often and getting a lot of information, hoping to get things finalized very soon. He said that Bob George of the TV company was being very cooperative.

I then reminded everyone of the Annual City Picnic on August 18th at 6:00 p.m. and called for a work session on August 19th at 5:00 p.m. at City Hall. We adjourned at 9:30 p.m.

On August 25th the *Uinta County Herald* ran an article titled, CITY OF EVANSTON RECEIVES $934,762 OVER SIX YEARS FOR ROAD IMPROVEMENT PROJECTS. This was great news which we had been expecting, but now it was a reality.

The article went on: *Over the next six years the City of Evanston will receive $934,762 from the Intermodal Surface Transportation Efficiency Act of 1991, which can be used to construct new roadways, repair or upgrade connector and arterial roads in the city.*

ISTEA is a federally funded program for communities with greater population than 5,000. The monies are given to the state then filtered down to the cities. Evanston will be receiving $153,000 for the next six years for a variety of projects.

The *Herald* article continued: *According to City Engineer Brian Honey, this program is a continuation of a similar Urban Systems Program which Evanston still had money invested in. That additional money will be put in with the new program, therefore, extending the life of ISTEA an additional two years.*

"The city can use the money for anything pertaining to collector or major arterial streets based on the 1984 classification map," Honey said.

The ISTEA officials are asking that Honey update the map to fit the new criteria. The older map had Evanston listed with too many major collector roads for the population base. The next hurdle will be to prioritize projects that the city council wishes to attempt.

Once the project is determined, the city will have to prove its ability to provide its share of the expenses.

ISTEA is a 90½ percent funding match. The city will be required to show its ability to provide the 9.5 percent to complete the project. For a $153,000 project, Evanston will provide $14,535.

The *Herald* article concluded: *On the drawing board for next year will be a street project on Park Road. That project will connect into the new*

Bear River Drive planned for next year's construction. Evanston recently received a $186,000, 50-50 grant from the Farm Loan Board to complete that $398,000 road system.

The ISTEA funding would be a big help in keeping our streets in good shape. These were funds that we could definitely depend on as revenues for the street department, and as we planned our budget over the next several years, it would free up other funds that we could budget for other necessary items. During our second regular meeting of the month on August 26th, Clint Schroeder, a high school student representing the Future Leaders of America, was in attendance to express his appreciation for the opportunity to work for the city through the summer months and for the experience he gained by doing so.

I thanked Clint for being a good employee and working hard for the city, and wished him success in the future, whichever path he may take.

Sergeant Paul Dean and Sergeant Doug Matthews of the Evanston Police Department were in attendance to give a verbal report about their recent trip to Toronto, Canada where they were requested to narrate and assist in the production of a segment for the TV program, *Top Cops.*

Top Cops was a popular television program at the time, about heroic police stories of actual events that happened to police officers while in dangerous situations.

Dean and Matthews stated that they used Canadian actors to portray the incident that happened in Evanston four years ago, regarding the shooting of Phil Mensing and seriously wounding his brother, Steve at the Evanston landfill. Stefanick was the shooter and was chased and cornered near the courthouse by local officers who were under fire. Sgt. Dean was the officer who advanced on Stefanick firing the fatal shot that took the shooter down.

The incident got back to the *Top Cop* producers and they called the Evanston Police Department wanting to make it one of a story of their TV series. The trip to Canada for Dean and Matthews was paid for by the producer.

Following the officers' report, the council and I congratulated them and thanked them for their outstanding and heroic services in protecting the citizens of Evanston, and for representing Evanston so well while visiting Canada.

Jake Williams, Evanston Police Department Training Officer, presented a plaque to me on behalf of the Police Benevolent Association, thanking the city, the mayor and the council for their approval and assistance in supporting their fundraising project, the Mudd Bogg.

I expressed our thanks and appreciation to the Police Benevolent Association for their hard work and contribution to the economy of Evanston by supporting another very successful program that brought local folks out and drew others to our community.

After other old business, including the unanimous passage of several pending non-controversial ordinances on second and third readings, we addressed new business.

Councilwoman Julie Lehman introduced Resolution 92-53 as follows:

RESOLUTION 92-53
RESOLUTION OF THE CITY OF EVANSTON,
WYOMING AUTHORIZING THE SUBMISSION OF A
GRANT APPLICATION TO THE WYOMING COMMUNI-
TY RECYCLING GRANT FUND FOR A SEVENTY-FIVE
PERCENT (75%), TO ENABLE THE CITY TO OBTAIN
A CHIPPER.

This ordinance was to get grant monies to purchase a chipping machine for our recycling program to chip old trees and brush that had been gotten rid of and to dispose of old Christmas trees, etc. The motion was made by Councilwoman Lehman to adopt Resolution 92-53, seconded by Davis, with all voting in favor.

The application would go out immediately for the 75% matching grant money and, if the application was approved, we would then call for bids on the chipper with specifications.

Councilwoman Wall made a motion to transfer title of a city-owned van, at no cost, to the Uinta County Joint Powers Human Services Board and to direct City Attorney Boal to prepare an ordinance setting up a Transportation Board to regulate how to use the buses that had been given to the city by the School Board District No. 1. The motion was seconded by Nelson, with all voting in favor.

The U.C.S.D. No. 1 had given a couple of their used buses to the city for outings and other activities sponsored by the recreation district and the human services board.

After a short recess and calling the meeting back to order, I called on Chief of Police Harvey to request the city council to approve the sale of all city-owned shotguns to the officers who had been using them. These shotguns were outdated for police work and had been replaced by more up-to-date weapons. City Attorney Boal intervened and said that he had better research state law concerning this type of matter. Therefore, no other action was taken at this time.

A motion was made by Councilwoman Wall to hold a special meeting on September 2nd at 7:00 p.m. and to advertise it, following the already scheduled work session that had been called for 5:00 p.m. The special meeting would only be to consider a new resolution, No. 92-54. The motion was seconded by Lehman, with all voting in favor.

Prior to adjourning, I requested as many city council members as possible to attend the Uinta County Commissioners meeting on Tuesday, September 1st at 3:00 p.m.

At the meeting of the county commissioners, they agreed to permit the propositions pertaining to the Capital Facilities Tax to be on the ballot for the November election.

We held a special city council meeting on September 2nd for one item only: to introduce a resolution approving the optional one cent sales tax increase.

Councilman Clarence Vranish introduced Resolution 92-54, which read as follows:

RESOLUTION 92-54
RESOLUTION OF THE CITY OF EVANSTON, WYO-
MING APROVING THE IMPOSITION OF THE ADDITION-
AL ONE CENT ($0.01) SALES TAX PURSUANT TO W.S.
39-6-412 (K) SPECIFYING THE PROCEDURE FOR
QUALIFICATION OF THE BALLOT QUESTION, SPECIFY-
ING HOW EXCESSIVE FUNDS ARE SPENT AND
SPECIFYING THE PROJECTS OF THE CITY TO BE
FUNDED BY SUCH.

Section 1: The City of Evanston shall present to the voters of
Uinta County the following projects with the respective costs, the
total costs, including to the extent allowable by law, debt service, of
which shall not exceed $10,606,103.84, each project to be individu-
ally approved by the voters, to be funded by the additional County
One Cent ($0.01) Sales Tax authorized by W.S. 39-6-412 (k), in con-
junction with the County and the other incorporated municipalities
within the County:

- Senior Citizens Projects $2,964,031.00
- Urie Connector Road $ 882,900.00
- Lyman Recreation Project
  and the B.E.A.R. Project $3,986,230.28
- Evanston Ski Area $2,772,942.56

Motion was made by Councilman Nelson to adopt Resolution
92-54, seconded by Wall, with all 7 votes in favor.

The Town of Lyman adopted a similar resolution and the Uinta
County Commissioners approved the four questions to go on the
ballot in the upcoming election as Propositions 1, 2, 3, and 4.

The opposition to the tax was getting hot and plentiful for all four
propositions, and I was getting worried that none of them would pass,
especially since the town of Mountain View pulled their projects out
and the town council went on record as being opposed to all of the
questions.

Mountain View and many folks residing in the Bridger Valley area indicated that they were opposed to all propositions and put out a lot of adverse information through Letters to the Editor in the *Uinta County Herald* and the *Bridger Valley Pioneer*, the two county-wide newspapers.

However, there were a lot of folks sending letters and placing editorials in the newspapers indicating that they were very much in favor of the propositions.

On September 8th the *Uinta County Herald* ran an article by Ann Curtis titled, CAPITAL TAX MEASURE GETS GREEN LIGHT FROM CITIES AND COUNTY.

The article read: *The Evanston City Council, the Lyman Town Council and the Uinta County Commissioners gave the green light to placing the Capital Facilities tax question on the November ballot.*

Information on the projects will be presented to voters to help them decide on the projects.

Voters can accept none, one or all the projects on the Capital Facilities Tax question.

The *Herald* article continued: *Last Tuesday, the Uinta County Commission gave its approval to place the measure on the November ballot. At a brief special council meeting Wednesday evening, the Evanston City Council also voted unanimously to place the measure before the public.*

The Lyman Town Council reached its decision with three members voting in favor, one against and one abstaining.

Voting in favor was Gary Poore, Sam Johnston and Lee Wickle. R. Dan Neilson voted against the measure and Michael Vercimak abstained from the vote.

If all the projects are accepted by voters then the sales tax will be dropped in about 4½ years when the projects are expected to be paid off, the *Herald* article concluded.

During the first city council meeting of the month on September 8th, following the completion of the usual business, Julie Abbott and Donna VanRiper announced that Key Bank (presently known as The Bank of the West) would close their doors at noon September 16th and all Key Bank employees in the State of Wyoming would donate one half day to community service. The Key Bank employees in

Evanston would be picking up trash, making paths and putting wire around the base of trees for the BEAR Project.

In the afternoon of September 16th there would be a fundraiser that would be a Rubber Duck Race in the river at the BEAR Project. Donna VanRiper challenged the city council to sponsor one of the ducks for $25.00. Councilwoman Julie Lehman made a motion for the council to accept the challenge and sponsor one of the ducks, seconded by Wall, with all voting in favor. Ron Barnard, member of the BEAR Project, stated that there would be a barbecue after the race and invited everyone to attend.

I expressed the City's appreciation to Key Bank for their community involvement and interest in keeping Evanston clean.

Charlotte Fry, representing several residents of the Red Mountain areas, was in attendance to request that the city council would give the Red Mountain sidewalk project a high priority among the projects to be constructed by the funds received through the Intermodal Surface Transportation Efficiency Act of 1991 (ISTEA). The sidewalk project would run along the Red Mountain Road from Wyoming State Highway 89 to Mountain Village Drive, but would only be on one side on the road.

I told the group that I hesitated to put the Red Mountain Road sidewalk project into the ISTEA program. I said, *I feel, because of the amount of money involved, the project could be done faster if it was financed out of the general budget next year. I think it would be faster to use an $8,000 budget line item earmarked for Red Mountain and begin engineering this fall so construction could begin next spring. ISTEA money would not be available until 1994.*

Under the ISTEA program, the city could ask that the Park Road and Red Mountain sidewalk projects be engineered at the same time, but there wouldn't be enough money to complete both projects simultaneously, and the Red Mountain project would be postponed until money was available.

Jim Jackson and Terry Prete expressed concerns about people walking along Red Mountain Road. I said, *I agree that folks should not be made to walk in the street and that the city would do all they we can to put the project on high priority for next spring, plus we will be looking at the speed limit for safety purposes.*

City Attorney Boal reported that the state law pertaining to the sale of the Police Department shotguns, as requested by Training Officer Jake Williams during the last council meeting, was perfectly legal, but he suggested that we place a minimum price on each. Therefore, Councilman Nelson made a motion to authorize the sale of the shotguns with $100.00 being set as the minimum price on each weapon, seconded by Vranish. The motion passed with 6 yes votes and 1 no vote (Hutchinson). Why he was not being in favor I have no idea or I just don't recall, but I'm sure he had his reasons.

Prior to adjournment the speed limit on Red Mountain Road, which at this time was 35 mph, was brought up for discussion. The council felt that with no sidewalks the speed limit was too high; therefore, after a short discussion, Councilman Nelson made a motion to lower the speed limit on Red Mountain Road to 25 mph, seconded by Lehman, with all voting in favor.

Meeting adjourned at 10:00 p.m.

On Tuesday, September 22nd the *Uinta County Herald* ran an article by Reporter Ann Curtis titled, AIRPORT MANAGER DIES IN CRASH...Two-day search ends in discovery of plane wreckage east of Evanston.

Information taken from Curtis's article indicated that Terry Schaefer, 44 years old, manager of the Evanston Municipal and Bridger Valley Municipal airports, was killed in an airplane crash Friday evening. The cause of the accident is unknown at this time.

According to reports received by the Uinta County Sheriff's Department, they received the call on Saturday that contact had not been received by Schaefer, and a search immediately was organized following Schaefer's flight plan path.

The article stated, *On Saturday, 11 aircraft were involved, Sunday saw an additional four planes join the search. A call went out for local ranchers, landowners, hunters and gas plant employees for help with any unusual occurrences such as low flying planes being heard, explosions, grass and brush fires to call the incident into headquarters.*

The wreckage was found a few miles east of Evanston and it appeared that Schaeffer died instantly in the crash. This was another big loss to Uinta County, because Terry was managing both county airports and was doing a great job. He was also well liked in the community and I knew he was going to be hard to replace. It was another sad time for the Evanston area and all our thoughts went out to his family.

The second city council meeting of the month was held on September 23rd, but when opening the meeting and before any business I asked for a moment of silence and prayer for Terry Schaeffer and his family.

After taking care of all usual business, we went into public participation. Community Development Director and City Planner Paul Knopf, representing First Lady and Parade Chairman Sandy Ottley, Paul requested a parade and parade route for Support Your Community Week. The parade would be held on Saturday, October 17th at 1:00 p.m. to kick off the week's program.

Paul said the parade would start at the City Hall parking lot, go down Main Street to 6th Street, over to Front Street, and back to the City Hall parking lot. A motion was made by Councilwoman Wall to approve the time and route of the parade and to notify the Police Department, seconded by Davis, with all voting in favor.

Ruth Ruiz made a request for a Bike-a-thon to be held October 3rd at 10:00 a.m., which would start at Rips parking lot on County Road and then go north on County Road to Wyoming State Highway 89, then south on Highway 89 to Park Road, and finish at Rips. This would be a fundraising program, and the money raised would be used by St. Jude Children's Hospital for research. Motion was made by Councilman Hutchinson to authorize the Bike-a-thon and have the Police Department notified to oversee the route, seconded by Wall, with all voting in favor.

After some other business was acted upon, Councilwoman Wall made a motion to direct City Attorney Boal to prepare, for the next regularly scheduled meeting, a resolution to approve a contract with the Evanston Child Development Center (E.C.D.C.) to provide an after-school pick-up service upon receiving the 1981 van from the City of Evanston, seconded by Lehman with all voting in favor.

A few weeks ago we had officially donated the van to the E.C.D.C. to transport the children under their care. Marie Bluemel represented E.C.D.C. at this meeting and after the motion had passed expressed their appreciation for the opportunity to provide this service.

On October 1st Debra Hansen, Service Unit Manager and Brownie Leader, approached me with a group of Girl Scouts to purchase the first official box of Girl Scout Cookies on Cookie Delivery Kick-Off Day at City Hall. Girl Scout cookie deliveries would be going on through the month of November, and cookie booths would be set up in front of Walmart for easy purchase during the weekend of Saturday, November 21st.

During the first city council meeting of October, Resolution 92-67 was introduced by Councilwoman Jerry Wall as follows:

RESOLUTION 92-67
RESOLUTION OF THE CITY OF EVANSTON, WYOMING, AUTHORIZING THE EXECUTION OF A CONTRACT WITH THE EVANSTON CHILD DEVELOPMENT CENTER TO ENABLE AND FACILITATE THE EVANSTON CHILD DEVELOPMENT CENTER TO PROVIDE TRANSPORTATION SERVICES TO CHILDREN UNDER ITS CARE.

Motion was made by Councilman Hutchinson, seconded by Wall, with all voting in favor.

On May 15, 1987, Councilman Tom Hutchinson had held the dedication of Bear River State Park and Information Center. Months before the opening, the Wyoming State Tourism Board, who was the agency running the state parks, asked for bids and resumes from anyone interested in operating and managing Bear River Park and Information Center.

The Tourism Board announced that whomever received the bid would be required to enter into a contractual five-year agreement with the Wyoming Tourism Board. Tom Hutchinson was the board's choice and he got the opportunity to open the park and manage and operate it for the next five years.

However, just recently, Tom Hutchinson got the word that the Bear River State Park and Information Center would no longer be under the jurisdiction of the Wyoming Tourism Board, but instead would be controlled by the Wyoming Parks and Recreation Commission, of which Al Pilch of Evanston had been a member for many years.

This was a notice to Hutchinson that after his 5-year contract was up in 1992 the state would be turning the park and center over to a park superintendent and would not renew his contract once it terminated.

Mayor receives first box of Girl Scout Cookies

Debra Hansen, service unit manager and Brownie leader together with Cadet Amanda McFadden, 12, Junior Jeri Hansen, 11, Brownie Katie Hansen, 8, and Daisy Jessica Bond, 5, present Mayor Dennis Ottley with the first box of Girl Scout Cookies.

Mayor Dennis Ottley received the first official box of Girl Scout Cookies on the Cookie Delivery Kick-Off day Oct. 1 at City Hall.

Girl Scout cookie deliveries will be going on through the month of November.

Cookie booths will be set up in front of Wal-Mart for easy purchase during the weekend of Saturday, Nov. 21.

The six varieties sell for $2.50 per box. Girl Scouts sell cookies to raise money for camping, leadership training, educational programs, scholarships for girls, troop camp equipment, newsletter service and badge and insignia supply service. Each troop earns .40 cents from each box.

Uinta County Herald, October 2, 1992.

In mid-1992 the state announced they would be hiring someone on a short-term contract to operate and manage the park and center. When official notice got to the public there was a lot of interest and the State Commission received several applications. My wife Sandy applied for the position along with several others, including Jerry Wall, who was a member of the Evanston City Council at the time.

After several weeks of interviewing and checking the applicants' resumes, they called Sandy and told her that they wanted her for the position. Sandy was quite surprised because they hadn't even called her for an interview. She asked them if she had to come to Cheyenne for an interview or whether they were coming to Evanston. They surprised her again when they told her that they had read her resume and heard enough high recommendations that the Commission didn't think it was necessary to interview her.

Apparently the Commission had received recommendations in favor of Sandy from State Representative Ron Micheli, Former State Senators John Fanos and Janice Bodine, and from former State Senator and County Commissioner Hight Proffit and his wife Dorothy and other high-level government folks.

This made some of the applicants pretty upset and some made statements like, *The only reason she got the job was because she was the mayor's wife,* or *There must have been a lot of politics involved,* and so on.

Well I can tell the world that Sandy did not need any so-called clout from me or anyone else. She had an outstanding resume and the reputation of doing a good job wherever she worked, including the Wyoming State Hospital, where she worked for almost 20 years. She had been a terrific First Lady for Evanston and most Wyoming State officials knew that. She didn't need any help from me. No one ever called or talked to me about her application; I was just as dumbfounded as she was when they called her.

She was initially hired under a contract with the state and started the job under the new superintendent from Wyoming Hot Springs State Park in Thermopolis, Allen Cowardin.

At first when she started working under Cowardin, he had gotten the word that she was the mayor's wife and he was a little worried that he would get into problems with City of Evanston politics. But she surprised him and he ended up really appreciating her work. She never ever mentioned that she should receive any preferential treatment; she just did her job and did it well.

She was working under a contract for about two years before they decided, with the recommendation of Cowardin, to put her on as a full-time employee and give her full benefits like other state employees receive.

We were damn glad that she got the job because it sure helped pull us out of a bad financial situation.

⚜

After opening the first city council meeting of the month on October 14th, and following the usual business of approving minutes, payment of outstanding bills and approving department reports, I read a letter submitted by George McKinley that he wished to resign from the Urban Renewal Agency. Motion was made by Councilwoman Lehman to accept Mr. McKinley's resignation, seconded by Wall, with motion passing by 5 yes votes and 2 absent (Davis and Nelson).

I expressed the city's appreciation to Mr. McKinley and thanked him for the voluntary service he had given to the City of Evanston and wished him well.

I appointed Mark Hansen to the Urban Renewal Agency, and I appointed Lori Alexander and Kathy Edwards as ex-officio members. Councilman Vranish made a motion to confirm all of the above appointments, seconded by Lehman, with all those present voting in favor.

I appointed Richard McMurray, introduced by Patrol Lieutenant Mitch Allmaras, as an officer of the Evanston Police Department. Motion was made by Councilwoman Wall to confirm the appointment, seconded by Vranish with motion passed by all. I welcomed Officer McMurray to the department and wished him well in his service.

Colleen Gilmore, representing the Uinta Investment Corporation (known as the Pink Elephant Bar and Lounge located on Front

Street), had applied for a malt beverage permit for the Support Your Community Week Octoberfest to be held at the Beeman-Cashin Building on October 19th from 6:00 p.m. to 10:00 p.m.

Councilman Hutchinson made a motion to approve the application, seconded by Lehman, with all voting in favor with two absent.

Town Councilman Gary Poore from the Town of Lyman was in attendance to give a presentation on the Lyman Recreation Project that would be on the November election ballot jointly with Evanston's BEAR Project as Proposition #3. He made an excellent presentation of the project, which I also felt would be a real asset to the entire county.

Lyman Town Councilman Poore stated that the funding would only be available if the Capital Facilities Tax proposition passes in November. "It would not only help the Town of Lyman, but would be a great addition for the entire County," he said.

I agreed with him and stated that the Capital Facilities Tax, if it passes, would enable all projects to be paid off in less than five years. I hoped that the folks of Lyman understood the benefits that it would bring to their community.

As the first item under new business during the meeting, Councilman Vranish sponsored Ordinance 92-17, introduced by Councilman Hutchinson:

ORDINANCE 92-17
AN ORDINANCE AMENDING SECTION 4-38 (b) OF ARTICLE 4 OF THE EVANSTON CITY CODE TO MAKE IT A CRIME FOR PEOPLE UNDER THE AGE OF 21 YEARS TO CONSUME ALCOHOL.

This was another ordinance that the City of Evanston was required to act on to conform to the changes in the State of Wyoming laws.

After a short discussion with no one objecting, Councilman Vranish made the motion to pass Ordinance 92-17 on first reading, seconded by Hutchinson. The motion passed with 5 votes in favor and 2 absent (Nelson and Davis).

Ordinance 92-17 came up for second reading during the next regular meeting of October 28th and passed again by 5 votes with 2 absent (Nelson and Lehman). On third and final reading the ordinance passed unanimously (7 votes) during the first city council meeting in November making our code in agreement with state law.

Councilwoman Wall made a motion to change the city council meeting dates of November and December. November regular meetings would be held November 4th and November 18th, the 1st and 3rd Wednesdays; and we would hold only one meeting in December on the 9th. The motion was seconded by Lehman with 5 votes in favor and 2 absent (Davis and Nelson).

I had signed a proclamation declaring October 17th through 23rd as Support Your Community Week jointly with the Evanston Chamber of Commerce. I also wrote an article in the guest column of the *Uinta County Herald* of October 16th titled, TAKE PRIDE AND HELP CELEBRATE SUPPORT YOUR COMMUNITY WEEK.

My article read: *Support Your Community Week is once again upon us. Sponsored jointly by the City of Evanston and the Evanston Chamber of Commerce, the week of Oct. 17, 1992 through Oct. 23, 1992 has been proclaimed as the 6th Annual Support Your Community Week. This is a week of enjoyment to be had by all. The agenda starts with a parade in downtown Evanston to begin at City Hall at 1 p.m. on Saturday, Oct. 17, 1992 and ends with a banquet on Friday, Oct. 23, 1992 with many fun activities and events in between. Everyone is welcome to any and all events.*

Support Your Community Week was first started in 1987 for the purpose of building a stronger, more vibrant community, and to build morale and improve the attitude of all.

We do this; first by encouraging CITIZEN PARTICIPATION (informed citizens through participation builds better relationships); second by building good COMMUNITY LEADERSHIP (making citizens more knowledgeable builds better leaders); third by showing honest GOVERNMENT PERFORMANCE (making local government more professional and competent); and fourth by encouraging VOLUNTEERISM AND

PHILANTHROPY (building for a much stronger foundation through communications, education and sharing information for better ideas).

This all adds up to CIVIC EXCELLENCE, and that means continually strengthening the civic infrastructure of our community just as we must maintain a strong physical infrastructure. This is vitally important to our future.

Support Your Community Week the past five years has been very instrumental in building and maintaining the HIGH QUALITY OF LIFE, we are presently accustomed to. The City of Evanston and The Evanston Chamber of Commerce hopes to continue doing this.

Therefore, we wish to personally invite every citizen to take part in this next week's activities. TRY IT, YOU'LL ENJOY IT.

Thank you and please watch for schedules of events in this newspaper or call the Evanston City Hall or the Evanston Chamber of Commerce.

Dennis J. Ottley, Evanston Mayor

Therefore, a motion was made by Councilman Vranish to hold a special meeting on October 21st at 7:00 p.m. for Support Your Community Week. The meeting would feature the Student Essay Program "Why Evanston is Beautiful to Me?" and the Evanston High School cheerleaders would perform a few cheers for Evanston. Also during the meeting there would be some unfinished business of the City of Evanston to get completed during the year because we would be having only one meeting in December. The motion was seconded by Hutchinson with all those present voting in favor.

Prior to adjournment I reported that if the City of Evanston was interested in putting in a bid for the 1995 W.A.M. Annual Convention, those bids must be presented by December 15, 1992. I also suggested that everyone become acquainted with the full schedule of the many events planned for Support Your Community Week, beginning on Saturday, October 17th and running through Friday, October 23rd.

This would be a great week, starting off with the parade followed by a flea market at Depot Square, and for the young at heart there would be a pumpkin carving contest, a seed spitting contest, a cow chip throw, and a paper plane launch.

The BEAR Project Committee would be providing food for a noon luncheon and there would be hay rides during the day.

On October 18th there would be an ice cream social at the Beeman-Cashin Building. Ice cream cones and chamber music would be featured from 1:00 p.m. to 4:00 p.m.

On October 19th there would be guided tours by the Old Timers' Club of the Evanston Design Committee, better known as "The Old Farts Club," throughout the historic areas of Evanston, followed the next day with "A Taste of Evanston" and the *Oktoberfest* at Depot Square with a favorite group from Utah's Snowbird called the "Bavarians." They would be playing German music.

Also the Uinta County Search and Rescue members would be honored during the intermission of the Oktoberfest.

On October 20th the Evanston Beautification Committee would host a pizza luncheon for the participants of the Essay Contest and name the winners at Depot Square, followed by an After Hours Business Mixer from 5:00 p.m. to 7:00 p.m.

A special city council meeting would be held the evening of October 21st, honoring the winners of the Essay Contest, and the Evanston High School Cheerleaders would be giving a few cheers for the city.

October 22nd the Mayor's Prayer Breakfast would be held at Lotty's Family Restaurant with guest speaker Third Judicial District Court Judge John Troughton, a great judge who gave a great speech. I was told I would never be able to get Judge Troughton to speak at my prayer breakfast, but I did and he gave a terrific speech on fellowship.

At noon on the 22nd the Senior Citizen's Luncheon would be held at the Weston Plaza (now known as the Days Inn). The goal was for everyone to bring their favorite elderly person(s) and treat them to a lunch. I always invited two or three of my favorite folks to the luncheon, as other folks did as well.

On Friday, October 23rd Governor Mike Sullivan was planning to be in Evanston to dedicate the new Port of Entry near the Utah-Wyoming State Line.

Since we knew ahead of time that he was going to be here that particular day, we asked him to attend Friday night's Support Your Community Week Honor Banquet and if he would agree to be our guest speaker. He agreed to do that which was a great honor and one of the highlights of the banquet.

Page 6   UINTA COUNTY HERALD   October 23, 1992

Judge tells crowd Fellowship is 'communion of spirit'

By ANN CURTIS
Herald Reporter

"I'm not an expert on fellowship— but I am an expert on non-fellowship. If everyone practiced fellowship, they wouldn't need me," said Third District Court Judge John Troughton at the Mayor's Prayer Breakfast held at Lotty's Thursday morning. About 100 people attended the breakfast.

"If there was fellowship there would be no need for the proliferation of lawyers we have. In this country, I see non-fellowship in my court day after day and it is a burden on the soul," he said.

Troughton was introduced by City Attorney Dennis Boal who thanked him for his work in cleaning up the corruption in the Attorney General's office, Troughton's previous position.

Troughton was visibly touched by the tribute.

He jokingly called Mayor Dennis Ottley, "sneaky and manipulative" saying that Ottley had made an appointment to come to his office and speak to him. He thought it was something to do with his court and the community.

The pair had coffee, discussed Evanston as it once was, common acquaintances—"then when I was completely off guard he said he wanted me to speak at the prayer breakfast. There was no way out and here I am today," he said.

Troughton explained he had once received a "plain speaking award". His wife Barbara had reminded him the award was not for his eloquence—but for his profanity. She also warned him that he had a case of "foot-in-

Judge John Troughton

mouth" disease.

He urged the audience to read the works on "Fellowship" on their program.

It included, "Fellowship is more than giving of presents or material considerations. Neither is fellowship a one-sided affair. It is a mutual sharing of enjoyment, or possibly, worthwhile study or work. It is a communion of interests and a communion of spirit."

He explained that in the dictionary, the words community and fellowship are synonymous.

"It is only appropriate that during 'Support Your Community Week' we dedicate ourselves to practicing fellowship," he said.

He explained that 11 years ago he had "gotten a belly full of politics" and vowed not to make any more of

these speeches because it made him a target of jealousy, envy and ambition. "I don't want those (people) to see me as a competitive threat," he said.

In his courtroom, Troughton said he sees people everyday who have fallen away from fellowship.

The bright spot where he sees "a community of interest and a community spirit" is during adoption hearings.

But he contrasted that with the divorce rate which occurs in two-out-of-three marriages.

"The reason why it occurs is that there is too much attention to the absorption of self. Far less attention is given to the other guy. It is painful to see good decent men and women where non-fellowship causes them to use their children to hurt the other

person," he said.

Troughton said he'd rather see parents use community spirit in making their decisions about the fate of their children and "not leave it to Judge Troughton when they can do it better."

He asked the audience to "lay aside envy, jealousy, ambition and other baser human qualities in the spirit of the Golden Rule of treating others as you would have other treat you.

"We need to dedicate ourselves to fellowship and support of our community, nation, neighbors and most of all our children," he said "God help us in this country if we don't turn back to the spirit of fellowship. If not, we will be leaving our children, grandchildren and great grandchildren a life no where near as luxurious as the one we live today."

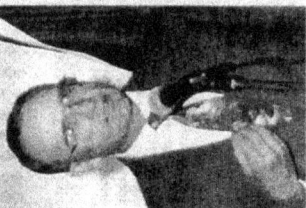

Gov. Mike Sullivan and Evanston Mayor Dennis Ottley congratulate longtime volunteers honored during Support Your Community Week. From left to right are: Elmer Danks, Melba Amsler, Gov. Mike Sullivan, Ann Pennington, Pat Alexander, Leonard Wold and Mayor Dennis Ottley.

Uinta County Herald, October 27, 1992.

The seniors that were honored that night were Ann Pennington, who had been very active in many ways in the community and had written a number of poems, some pertaining to our wonderful community; Melba Amsler, also very active in the community, and a coordinator and volunteer for the Lord's Food Pantry, a nondenominational means of providing food for people in difficult situations; Captain Leonard Wold, retiree of the Wyoming Highway Patrol and a WWII veteran who had also been active in many city functions, including serving as City Judge for a short term and being involved for 25 years with the Boy Scouts of America; Pat Alexander, who had been a member of the Urban Renewal Agency and the Old Farts Club, was active in the Evanston improvement and beautification projects, and had helped make costumes for the Christmas season productions of "The Nutcracker"; and Elmer Danks who had also always been very active as a volunteer for Evanston. He was also a member of the Old Farts Club, and was on the Evanston Downtown Design Committee. Elmer was a great guy and a lot of fun to be around.

Following Governor Mike Sullivan's inspiring speech, I presented him with the first official Evanston flag that had been adopted by the city council earlier this year.

Like other years, after the Honor Banquet of 1992, I received several letters from Seniors that had been honored in past Support Your Community Week Honor Banquets. Those letters came from seniors like Mary Emerson, Athena Dallas, and others commenting on how much the week-long program does in bringing our community together, and thanking First Lady Sandy and me for the time and effort we put into our community and in making Evanston a great place to live.

The special city council meeting of October 21st was called especially to honor the winners of the Essay Contest sponsored by the Evanston Beautification Committee and the Evanston Chamber of Commerce during Support Your Community Week. The essay theme was "Why is Evanston beautiful to me?"

Paul Knopf, representing the Beautification Committee, and Diane Hodges, Director of the Evanston Chamber of Commerce, presented participation awards and an Evanston promotional pin to each of the top three winners, plus a T-shirt to the 1st place winners in each category.

Also during this meeting, Ron Barnard, Chairman of the BEAR Committee, gave a presentation on Proposition #3 concerning the BEAR Project and Lyman's Recreation project. He explained how the two projects would benefit the entire county and how especially how they would benefit the two communities.

Art winners

These young artists were named winners in the Depot Square Art Contest, held during Support Your Community Week. In the front row, Tim Fountain won $15 and took third place at Davis Middle School; Lindsey Lester won $15 and took fourth place at DMS; Catherine Kennedy won $15 and took second place at Clark School; Jordan Thomas won $25 and first place; Danielle Long won $15 and took first place at Clark; Joshua Jett won $10 and took third place at Clark. In the back row are Kevin Murphy, Mike Fulks, Koby Ward, who won $20 and second place at DMS, Cecilia Fulks, Ann Bell and Mike Wilson, who won $25 and took first from DMS.

Uinta County Herald, October 27, 1992.

City colors

Evanston Mayor Dennis Ottley presents Gov. Mike Sullivan with the first official City of Evanston flag at the volunteers banquet Friday as part of Support Your Community Week.

Uinta County Herald, October 27, 1992.

Page 8   UINTA COUNTY HERALD   October 23, 1992

Youngsters give Evanston leaders fresh view of city through their eyes

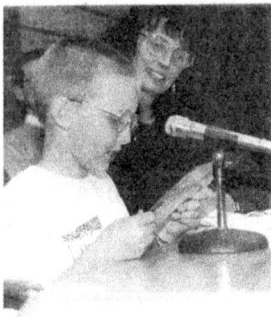

By ANN CURTIS
Herald Reporter

A special city council meeting highlighting the works of Evanston school children reading their essays on "Why Evanston Is Beautiful To Me" gave the parents, teachers, spectators and council members a fresh view of the city.

The comments ranged from "smiles on the surrounding mountains" to "there would be less alcoholism if there weren't so many bars."

According to Mayor Dennis Ottley, it gave him "a new view of the city through youngster's eyes."

Clark Second Grade winners were: first, Jacob Skog; second, Lindsey Woodward and third, Danielle Long. The teachers are Mrs. Miller and Mr. Sisson.

Uinta Meadows Second Grade winners were: first, Kaile Myrick; second Clara Laird; third, Michelle Klements and honorable mention went to April George. Teachers are Mrs. Myers and Mrs. Deen.

Aspen Groves third grade winners were J.C. Snyder; second, David Lym; third, Sean Lavery. Their Teachers is Mrs. Walton.

Clark third grade winners were: Keli Jo Schroeder; second, Angie Garza and third, Tristyn Staley. Their teachers are Mrs. Fickert and Mrs. Carlson. Amanda Dunklef was the first place winner at Uinta Meadows third grade. Taking second was Kristin Fuller and third, Tony Rawhouser. The teacher is Mrs. Trosper.

Mrs. Freuchte's third grade class at Clark Elementary received an honorable mention for their poster they submitted. Fourth grade winners from Uinta Meadows was Rachel Heath, first; Angela Thorpe, second and Molly McGee, third. Mrs. Clements is the teacher.

EHS cheerleaders do a cheer in front of the Evanston City Council to show their community spirit.

Aspen School winners were McKenzie French, first; Guy DiBartolo, second and Christal Deiber, third. The fourth grade teachers are Mrs. Uhling and Mr. Douglass.

Clark fourth grade winners are Mark McCoy, first and Ketlen George, second. They are in Mr. Reynolds class.

Amy Murray was the only winner from Uinta Meadow's fifth grade. Her teacher is Mr. Sibbett.

Mrs. Way, Davis sixth grade teacher had a first place winner in Mikaill Silcox.

Ms. Lowham and Mrs. Ottley's seventh grade class at Davis had four winners with first going to Alyson Wilde; second, Robbie Nickel; third, Wendy Bowen and honorable mention going to Austin Moon.

Evanston Middle School's eighth grade winners are April Adams, first; Teresa Martinez, second and Kaili Murray, third. The teacher is Mr. Ball.

Winning essay on "Why Evanston is Beautiful"

Clark Elementary second grade student Jacob Skog reads his essay on "Why Evanston is Beautiful to Me" at Wednesday's special City Council meeting. Skog won first place for his class. He received a T-shirt an "I Love Evanston" button and a pen.

Next, Kilburn Porter, a supporter of projects that would benefit the youth of Uinta County, made a presentation on Proposition #4, the Ski Evanston Project and how it would draw folks to the area for skiing, especially with the Salt Lake City Winter Olympics coming up in the next few years, and also how a local ski area had given the young folks of Uinta County the opportunity to learn to ski without having to pay a lot of money. He stated that very few of our youth have the opportunity to go to the Utah ski resorts, because they are so expensive.

He said that while the Eagle Rock Ski Area was open, they always had a lot of kids and their families taking advantage of the area on weekends. And, he stated, a good share of those kids and their parents were from Bridger Valley. *Eagle Rock was affordable for our young people to ski on weekends, so they could enjoy the winter months,* he added.

This was a Presidential election year and the Legal Tender had applied for a catering permit, which came up during the meeting, for their use at a political rally to be held October 23rd at the Bee-man-Cashin Building from 8:00 p.m. to 12:00 p.m. Motion was made by Councilman Nelson to approve the Legal Tenders application for a catering permit, seconded by Wall with 5 votes in favor and 2 absent (Lehman and Davis).

Following some additional business that was acted on, City Engineer Brian Honey reported that the school crosswalks, the signage, and the flashing lights had been installed at the areas requested by the school district.

Councilwoman Wall reported that 38 people went on the bus tour of the city facilities as one of the activities available during Support Your Community Week.

The Evanston Rotary Club was chartered on October 23, 1982 and at that time I was a charter member, but due to being very busy as mayor, I was not able to attend enough meetings, so I was ousted and no longer a member of the Club. The Rotary Club had a very strict rule: if you miss three or more meetings in a row you are automatically ejected, and that's what happened to me and my administrative assistant Steve Snyder.

However, the Evanston Rotary Club had requested that I be their guest speaker at their 10th Anniversary Dinner on October 27th. I was very honored to have this opportunity to speak at such an elite club.

As this was a special anniversary dinner the turnout was great, and after being introduced by Rotary President Larry Meyer, I started my talk. My talk was based on "What is Economic Development and why we need to set Economic Policies?"

I started my speech: *"Like the weather, it seems like everyone speaks of the economy and everyone seems to be concerned. Yet, unlike the weather, many do actually try to improve it. Despite all efforts put forth to try to improve it, there are those who offer nothing but criticism. No solutions, only criticism.*

Economy is the art of making the most of life. The love of economy is the source of all progress. It appears progress is wronged more by the greedy than it is loved by the selfless.

I continued: *Education, Sound Judgment, and Statesmanship are the antidotes for ignorance, ideology, and self-interest groups. They are therefore the three critical ingredients for economic success in any community.*

Former President John F. Kennedy once stated, "Economic growth without social progress lets the great majority of the people remain in poverty, while a privileged few reap the benefits of rising abundance."

Building the quality of life for everyone is a sure way of improving the frugality of a community. Sometimes we, the taxpayers, must sacrifice to make this happen. We may elect to impose additional taxes to make things better. If so, we would consider such a tax as a progressive tax, that is, if we all use sound judgment.

There are many ways to build towards a better economy and a better way of life, I continued. *Some of these are:*

- *Revitalization of our downtown area and other deteriorating and blighted areas.*
- *As a group, set the goals for a successful community.*
- *Encourage expansion of existing businesses and make them aware of the advantages and available finances.*
- *Offer business and marketing seminars and workshops to small businesses.*
- *Make affordable education and recreation available to all citizens. Sometimes this takes more tax dollars.*
- *Spend locally and support your community where possible. This includes government spending as well as public spending.*

Building your community in this manner will help encourage new business and industry to locate in your area. Most business (industry) will choose to locate in an area with a high quality of family life and a community of much volunteerism. Everyone must be progressive in building a community. This is the only way the economy will survive for all.

I ended my speech with: *"Let's work together".*

MIKE SULLIVAN

GOVERNOR
OF
WYOMING

November 2, 1992

Dennis M. Ottley, Mayor
City of Evanston
1200 Main Street
Evanston, WY 82930

Dear Dennis:

Just a quick note to thank you for
your kind hospitality during my visit to Evanston as well as the great pin and flag.   I
enjoyed the afternoon and hope I can get back
your way soon.

With best regards, I am

Very truly yours,

Mike Sullivan
Governor

MS:smp

Following my talk I received a grand applause, indicating that it went over very well. It was a great and enjoyable evening.

The second regular city council meeting of the month was held on October 28th, and after all the opening business was acted on we had two public hearings: the first concerned vacating a portion of South Park Village Mobile Home Court located on Yellow Creek Road; the second concerned vacating a utility easement in Twin Ridge Subdivision #1. Both hearings were conducted by City Attorney Dennis Boal, and were taped. The tapes would be on file at City Hall.

City Attorney Boal stated that both hearings had been properly advertised and no written protests had been received by the city clerk's office. Also there were no protests during or following the hearings from anyone in attendance. Therefore, I told everyone that action on these two hearings would take place later in the evening, as two ordinances had been prepared and would be considered under new business.

A public hearing was held to consider an application to transfer the retail liquor license of Lloyd's Liquor Store to John and Kathleen Edwards, doing business as Kate's.

Again, City Attorney Boal was directed to be the hearing office and stated that the hearing will be taped, and the tape would be on file at City Hall. Mr. John Edwards was in attendance to represent Kate's.

There were no protests; therefore, Boal closed the hearing and turned the meeting back to me. I then asked for a motion from the council to approve the Edwards's application.

Councilman Wall made a motion to approve the transfer of the liquor license, seconded by Hutchinson. Motion passed with 5 votes in favor and 2 absent (Lehman and Nelson).

Bill Wolfe and John Thomas addressed the need for a new regulation-size baseball field and that there was space available on the Evanston High School grounds.

Dennis Poppinga, Director of the District Parks and Recreation Board, also spoke in favor of Mr. Wolfe's and Mr. Thomas's suggestion. He told the council that there were approximately 130 young people interested in playing Babe Ruth Baseball and only one regulation field to practice on.

I asked for comments from the city council, and after a short discussion, Councilwoman Wall made a motion to direct Director Poppinga to meet with the school district and approach them concerning the additional ground, mentioned by Wolfe and Thomas, for a new regulation baseball field, seconded by Vranish. The motion passed by 5 votes in favor and 2 absent.

Under new business, action was taken on the two hearings that were conducted earlier in the meeting. First Ordinance 92-20 was sponsored by Councilman Hutchinson and introduced by Councilman Davis, to vacate a portion of the South Park Village Mobile Home Park Subdivision; and second, Ordinance 92-21 was introduced to vacate a utility easement located on Lot 74 of the Twin Ridge Subdivision #1.

During this meeting of October 28th, both Ordinance 92-20 and Ordinance 92-21 passed unanimously by the city council on the first reading, and during the next two regular council meetings both ordinances passed unanimously on second and third readings.

After all agenda items had been addressed, I polled the staff and council, as I always do prior to adjourning, for their comments and announcements. General Superintendent of Public Works Allan "Oop" Hansen offered his congratulations to five public works employees who took some certification exams on September 7th and passed: Jeff Martin – Class III Water Treatment; Paul Vozakis – Class III Wastewater; Bruce Hartzell – Class 1 Wastewater System; Frank Sheets – Operator in Training Water System; and Deb Wagstaff – Operator in Training Water Treatment.

Following Hansen's announcement, I expressed my appreciation to those employees for spending the many hours to study and prepare themselves to better serve the City of Evanston in their respective fields of employment.

Councilwoman Wall followed up with a report on the Tracks Across Wyoming committee and announced that their next meeting would be in Laramie on November 19th and 20th.

Tracks Across Wyoming, spearheaded by Evanston's Urban Renewal Director Jim Davis, was getting a lot of attention from all of the communities that had been part of the construction of the Union Pacific Railroad along Southern Wyoming during the mid-1860s. Most of these communities started out as tent cities and ended up being a very important part of Wyoming history.

Councilman Hutchinson then recognized and introduced Carl Classen, Executive Director of W.A.M., who spoke a few words on the future of W.A.M. and the possibility of Evanston bidding on the 1995 W.A.M. Annual Convention. A short discussion followed with questions and concerns by the city council.

In closing the meeting I thanked everyone for their cooperation and involvement given during the Support Your Community Week activities and stated that it was another very successful event, and I called for a work session to be held at City Hall on Wednesday, November 4th at 6:00 p.m., one hour before the next regular city council meeting on the same date.

Well, it was now November and the elections were over with almost 88 percent of the 7,932 registered voters casting ballots. It was one of the largest voter turnouts ever to cast their ballots in a Uinta County election.

America was getting a new President and Vice President: President George H. W. Bush and Vice President Dan Quail were defeated by Bill Clinton and his running mate Al Gore.

Craig Thomas of Casper was re-elected as Wyoming's only United States Representative; and Attorney Gregory A. Phillips of Evanston was elected as State Senator, representing District 15 (which Evanston is in); and Gordon L. Park was elected as State Representative of District 49 (which Evanston is also in).

John Fanos from Bridger Valley, who had given up his State Senate seat to run for County Commissioner of Uinta County once again won easily. Fanos had been County Commissioner through the Uinta County boom period and had been a very active commissioner and helped me, as mayor at the time, a great deal with all the problems that were created for Evanston through a rough boom period.

Evanston City Council incumbents Clarence Vranish of Ward 1, Jerry Wall of Ward 2, and Tom Hutchinson of Ward 3 were all re-elected to their positions as council members.

I was disappointed but not surprised that all four propositions concerning the one-cent increase of the Capital Facilities Tax were defeated. Some of the propositions were defeated by a very close vote, but defeated nonetheless.

It was no surprise, since the Town of Mountain View pulled completely out of the Capital Facilities Tax projects, and went on record as being opposed to all four propositions. I have no idea why they pulled out except one of their town council members was leading a crusade in opposition to the projects and he was able to sway the mayor and town council members of Mountain View to act in opposition of the proposals.

Uinta County was experiencing a very soft economy at the time and Evanston and the county needed something to get the economy moving even if it took a few dollars out of our pockets. Wyoming already had a low sales tax rate at four percent, much lower than most states, and Wyoming was one of the few states without an income tax. Utah, one of our neighboring states had a sales tax of almost seven percent plus an income tax.

The best part of the additional one-cent Capital Facilities Tax was that all those projects would have been paid for in less than five years.

The communities of Evanston and Lyman were concerned with creating programs that would benefit our local citizens and create some tourist traffic, but some folks think that government should only fund the infrastructure of the communities and police and fire protection. But, in order to give our locals the opportunity to learn to ski and play golf at a reasonable cost, and have a nice affordable recreation center, plus a nice place for our senior citizens to gather without increasing the budget seemed like a good way to go.

It is too costly for most folks, young and old, to go to Utah to ski and play golf because most golf courses are privately owned, and only available for the elite. It's the same with health and recreation centers.

It's almost like having to be a member of a private club, because most of them have very high membership dues.

As I said before, *"I believe very strongly that if government only deals in basic services and doesn't show a concern for the community's future, eventually there may be no need for basic services."*

After the study by City Attorney Dennis Boal concerning the Century Cable T.V. franchise, the *Uinta County Herald* of October 30th ran an article by Reporter Ann Curtis that read, *A draft report solicited by the City of Evanston to determine if Century Cable TV is living up to its franchise contract has been delivered to the city. And what the report indicates is bad news for Century Cable TV.*

The article was titled, CONSULTANT'S REPORT INDICATES CENTURY CABLE TV FAILED TO LIVE UP TO CONTRACT, and went on to read: *According to the report, adequate service has not been provided and there are a number of problems with technical, financial and customer service.*

City Attorney Dennis Boal said he will begin to circulate the report this week to all participants in the hearing conducted by the city, including Century Cable TV, the city council and all those who request to see the document.

"The city will give everyone who wishes a period of time to comment and give information, then if there is new information a public hearing may be scheduled by the city council," he said. *But the hearing is not required,* the *Herald* article continued.

Evanston's consultant, Gary L. Bardsley of Boulder, Colorado, after several months of gathering comments, records and interviews suggests that the local franchise is not receiving adequate support and guidance from Century Communications. He said given its size, the company seems oddly non-professional or deliberately non-cooperative in dealing with the city and the local entity.

According to the report, revenues to Century have increased dramatically despite claims to the contrary. Given the many changes in structure, service tiers, and price levels, it was difficult to identify the "real" increase, the report showed.

"Clearly, this demonstrates a substantially increased financial burden for a relatively fixed audience of subscribers," the report showed.

After the *Herald* article came out, City Attorney Boal announced, by giving everyone a chance to do their homework and giving Century Cable TV time to get their company structure and errors straightened out, that there probably would not be another meeting by the committee until February of next year.

In the meantime, the cable company was working on getting straightened out and catching up on their delinquent franchise fees and other items in their franchise agreement that they needed to take care of.

The day after the election, the first city council meeting of the month was held on November 4th. I opened the meeting, stating that I was very disappointed, but not surprised, that not one of the four propositions passed election. I stated that I thought that at least Propositions #1 and #2 might have had a good chance of passing, but none of them made it. Too bad!

I congratulated the three incumbent city council members, Clarence Vranish, Jerry Wall, and Tom Hutchinson for their success in their re-election to the city council.

Following those statements and the usual business of approving the minutes of previous meetings, paying outstanding bills and accepting staff and committee reports, I read a letter from City Councilwoman Julie Lehman. In her letter she stated that she would be resigning from her position as a member of the council, plus from all boards and committees she is presently serving on, effective November 16th.

Councilwoman Wall made the motion to accept all resignations in Ms Lehman's letter as of the date specified, seconded by Davis, with all voting in favor. Yolanda Gavin, who was in attendance representing the BEAR Project Committee, made a presentation on behalf of the committee to Julie for her involvement and the assistance she had given to the committee. Ms Gavin presented her with an old-time picture of Red Bridge.

I then presented Julie with a plaque and a statuette on behalf of the City of Evanston, and thanked her for all her service and the time she had given to the city and wished her well in her future endeavors.

A verbal response was made by each City Council member expressing their good wishes to Julie and each stated that, *You will be missed.*

Urban Renewal Director Jim Davis expressed his thanks to Julie for her services and assistance to both the BEAR Project and the Renewal Ball.

Julie responded by expressing her appreciation to everyone for their patience, tolerance and love of community.

I then read a letter from Councilman Tom Hutchinson that he was resigning immediately from the Evanston/Uinta County Human Services Joint Powers Board because he felt that it was time for someone else to serve. Councilman Nelson made a motion to accept the resignation of Tom Hutchinson, seconded by Davis, with all voting in favor.

I took time to express the City's appreciation to Councilman Tom for his long-time service to the Human Services Board.

I then appointed Councilman Nelson to serve on the Uinta County Economic Development Commission, with a motion from Councilman Davis confirming the appointment, seconded by Lehman, with all voting in favor.

The Evanston Chamber of Commerce was sponsoring a "Slosh 'n' Nosh" event on November 13th. Chamber representatives were in attendance requesting a catering permit, through Spirits of Red Mountain Liquor Store, to be used for the event located at 225 9th Street (the courthouse).

Councilman Hutchinson made a motion to approve the catering permit by the Spirits of Red Mountain, seconded by Wall. The motion passed.

Urban Renewal Director Jim Davis requested permission to have the 4th Annual Torch Light Parade in downtown Evanston on November 27th. Motion was made by Councilman Davis to allow the Torch Light Parade and to make the Police Department aware of it, seconded by Nelson. The motion passed.

I then recognized and introduced Mr. Vaughn Hutchinson and had him introduce his two Boy Scout sons from Troop #42, Brett and Kevin Hutchinson, who were in attendance to earn their *Citizenship in the Community* merit badges. After their introduction I thanked them for coming to one of the city's meetings and wished them the best in earning their badges.

A discussion was held concerning the vacancy that would exist on the Evanston City Council when Councilwoman Lehman left on November 16th, her date of resignation.

After City Attorney Dennis Boal explained, on an earlier occasion that by state law, the city council must pass an ordinance stating procedures concerning how to declare a vacancy. Councilwoman Wall had made a motion to direct the city attorney to prepare an ordinance that would outline the proper procedures to follow when a vacancy occurred on the city council, seconded by Nelson, with the motion passing unanimously.

Before adjourning, I expressed a special thanks to Community Development Director and City Planner Paul Knopf, Urban Renewal Director Jim Davis, and District Parks and Recreation Director Dennis Poppinga for their hard work on getting the BEAR Project and Ski Hill Project on the ballots for the election, and sending an important message to citizens concerning the Capital Facilities Tax proposals.

The second regular city council meeting was held on November 18th, and in attendance was a group of Boy Scouts from three different Scout Troops: David Staley, Scout Leader of Troop 200 introduced his scouts, Cullen Pace, Brandon Platt, D. Ryan Staley, Dan Faddis, Josh Davis, Bret McCoy and Eric McCoy; Robin Conk, Leader of Troop 30 introduced his scouts, Jeremy Conk and Dustin Conk; and Kyle Lowham, leader of Troop 42 introduced his scouts, Courtney Lowham and Kode Martin.

The scouts were in attendance to gain merits for their Citizenship Badges, and I welcomed them and thanked them all for coming to the city council meeting. I also expressed my best wishes to them in achieving their required merits in receiving their badges.

As we now had a vacancy caused by Julie Lehman's resignation from the city council and the city attorney had been instructed to draw up an ordinance setting in place the procedure to replace a mayor or council member if the seat should become vacant.

Therefore, Ordinance 92-23, sponsored by me and introduced by Councilman Hutchinson, came up for consideration as follows:

ORDINANCE 92-23
AN ORDINANCE CREATING SECTION 13.2. A VACAN-
CY IN MAYOR AND COUNCIL MEMBER OFFICES; SET-
TING FORTH THE CIRCUMSTANCES WHICH CREATE
A VACANCY IN THE OFFICE OF MAYOR OR COUNCIL
MEMBER; THE PROCEDURE FOR DECLARING A VA-
CANCY AND A PROCEDURE TO FILL THE VACANCY.

The procedures were spelled out in the ordinance and Council-man Nelson made a motion to pass Ordinance 92-23 on first reading, seconded by Wall. The motion passed unanimously.

Councilwoman Wall then followed up with a motion to direct City Clerk Welling to begin advertising to fill the council vacancy and to accept applications in written form, attached with résumés, with a deadline of December 4th at 5:00 p.m. The motion was sec-onded by Nelson, with all voting in favor.

Of course we were all aware of the fact that we could not ap-point anyone until Ordinance 92-23 was passed on third and final reading; therefore later in the November 18th meeting Council-man Nelson made a motion to hold a special city council meet-ing on November 25th for the single purpose of acting on Ordi-nances 92-23 and Ordinance 92-24. During that special meeting both ordinances passed on second reading, unanimously, and then passed on third and final readings during the city council meet-ing on December 9th meeting, the last meeting of the year by a unanimous vote.

During the special city council meeting, after the called-for busi-ness was taken care of and before adjournment, I reminded everyone of the Torchlight Parade on Friday night November 27th, and the Annual City Employees' Christmas Dinner on December 11th.

The final regular city council meeting for the year of 1992 was held on December 9th. After roll was called and City Clerk Don Welling declared that there was a quorum I recognized another group of Boy Scouts in attendance to fill the requirements for their citizenship badges.

I first introduced Scout Leader Robert Blakeman, and he had each scout introduce himself as follows: Matt Blakeman, Garland Pierce and Wes Bryant from Troop 200; and Ryan Bodine and Jake Schroeder from Troop 23. I thanked the scouts for their attendance and wished them luck and success in achieving their merit badges, and I told them all that they were very welcome to attend future meetings anytime.

I then left the podium to make a presentation to Evanston Chief of Police R. Dennis Harvey in the form of a framed certificate commending him as the longest serving Chief of Police in the State of Wyoming. At that time he had been Chief of Police for 15 years and was Chief until the year 2002.

He had served as Chief of Police under four mayors; Dan South, me, Gene Martin and Will Davis. He was Chief during some hard and fast times, the boom period, and he was chief through soft economic times, the bust period. He was very consistent and kept a low-key department during a period when it was needed and, at the same time, kept crime down to a minimum.

During the meeting I also introduced and appointed Mary Hyde to serve on the Human Services Joint Powers Board. Motion was made by Councilwoman Wall to confirm the appointment, seconded by Nelson. The motion passed unanimously by the members of the city council.

I then read a letter from Ruth Dahlman resigning from the Evanston Planning and Zoning Commission. Motion was made by Councilman Davis to accept Mrs. Dahlman's letter of resignation, seconded by Vranish with all voting in favor.

Under public participation, Ann Curtis, Reporter of the *Uinta County Herald* introduced the new Publisher of the *Herald*, Mike Jensen.

We all welcomed him to Evanston and thanked Ann for bringing him to the meeting. We also wished him well in his new position and told him he was more than welcome to attend any of our meetings, and I told him that we had always appreciated Ann's attendance at all our meetings.

I reported that Wyoming State Representative Janice Bodine had been instrumental in receiving an award for the City of Evanston from the Associated General Contractors. This award would be presented in Cheyenne, and Janice and I would be there to receive it. However, Representative Bodine, as a special guest at the Annual City Christmas Dinner, made the official presentation to the City of Evanston that evening.

During the meeting of December 9th, Resolution 92-73 was introduced by Councilman Davis as follows:

RESOLUTION 92-73
RESOLUTION AUTHORIZING THE CITY OF EVANSTON, WYOMING TO ENTER INTO A MEMORANDUM OF UNDERSTANDING WITH THE EVANSTON PARKS AND RECREATION DISTRICT FOR THE DEVELOPMENT AND IMPLEMENTATION OF A FITNESS PROGRAM FOR THE EMPLOYEES OF THE CITY OF EVANSTON.

This would be an agreement that employees could use the recreation center at no cost, and also by their own choosing and at their own time. This program was requested by city personnel, and since the City of Evanston supplements funding for Parks and Recreation the District, the council also agreed to the program.

Motion was made by Councilman Vranish, seconded by Nelson, with all voting in favor.

The City of Evanston audit report was presented by City Treasurer Steve Widmer for the fiscal year of 1991-1992, and after a short discussion and finding no problems with the report, Councilman Hutchinson made a motion to accept the audit report, seconded by Nelson, with all voting in favor.

For the vacancy left on the city council by the resignation of Julie Lehman, the city had received nine applications. They were all good and qualified applicants and it was going to be a tough choice to choose just one person out of the nine who applied.

The applicants were as follows: Kevin Smith, Shelly Horne, Glenda Krejci, Lance Voss, Bruce Barnard, Randy Royer, Ronald Barnard, Gale Curtis and Joy Walton, all very active in the community.

Councilman Vranish made a motion that the council interview each of the nine applicants on Thursday, December 17th beginning at 3:00 p.m., and that each interview be no longer than 20 minutes. The motion was seconded by Nelson, passing unanimously.

I told the council that I would like all of the council members present at the interviews.

Prior to adjournment, I announced that a special meeting had been called at 7:00 p.m. on December 21st only to name the successful candidate for the council vacancy, and to have that person sworn in to immediately serve out the remaining two years of Ms Lehman's term, and I reminded the council that there would be a work session on January 6, 1993.

During the special meeting of December 21st, after a short discussion, Councilwoman Wall made a motion to appoint Mr. Ronald Barnard to fill the vacancy left on the city council by Ms Lehman, seconded by Vranish. The motion passed with 5 votes in favor and 1 absent (Nelson).

I, as mayor, then administered the Oath of Office to Mr. Barnard and welcomed him to the council.

I pointed out that the decision of which applicant would fill the vacancy was very difficult, because all the applicants were well qualified, and any one of them would have been a good choice. But the city council voted for Mr. Ron Barnard, who had been chairman of the BEAR Project and very active in other programs, plus he had shown a lot of interest in the problems confronting the city.

We all congratulated Ron and looked forward to working with him as a city official.

Looking back over the past year, I noted that it had been another very busy year. Some disappointments, some sad times, but most of the projects had been very successful and the City of Evanston once again came through with an overall good year.

I mentioned that the animal control facility was up and looking good, and that the recycling program was complete, with the building and bins located throughout the city. I mentioned that the new one-man, one-truck solid waste pick-up was working out very well, and I mentioned the two new parks in Centennial Valley and Red Mountain. I mentioned the accomplishments by the beautification committee and the work they had done, the additional Sternberg lights in downtown Evanston, and the additional trees and the landscaping at the underpass. I also mentioned several other projects that we needed to continue working on: the BEAR Project, the recreation area at Sulphur Creek Reservoir, Depot Square. I mentioned the improvements at the cemetery and the Hamblin Park restrooms. I also mentioned that one important item was the need to complete the Comprehensive Plan. We needed to get it done and make our final decision on which way we wanted this city to go.

I also mentioned the many improvements we had made to Evanston's infrastructure: street improvements, the extension of Washington Avenue and upgrades in our water and sewer systems, and the Hazardous Intersection Study that we would be implementing this coming year. I mentioned the upgrades at City Hall, especially the computer system, and updating some of our ordinances.

One big accomplishment was obtaining the deed from the Union Pacific Resources Company to the 70-plus acres adjacent to already-owned city property. This could help Evanston retain the Union Tank Car Company, since they would have the room to expand and construct a new facility. If the U.T.C.C. decided to stay in Evanston and relocate to the new property, this would give the City of Evanston the opportunity to get the Roundhouse back for historic preservation purposes.

I stated my concern about the economy. I said that the economy was still pretty soft and we needed to put a lot of focus on that. I also emphasized the need to be concerned with job retention and job expansion, and to do whatever we could to keep the locals active and enthusiastic. This all helps the economy.

But, I added, addressing the council members and the city staff, *I do look forward to another busy and successful year in 1993, and hope we can all work together and get things done. We must work together and communicate with each other with ideas to do the right thing. Someone once told me, 'There is no right way to do the wrong thing'; therefore, close communication is very important in getting the right things completed.*

In adjourning the special meeting I wished everyone a very Merry Christmas and a happy and prosperous New Year, and I once again said that I was looking forward to another good year for the city.

ACKNOWLEDGEMENTS

This book would never have been written if it hadn't been for a number of people who had assisted me in remembering some of the events and occurrences mentioned in the book, and making minutes of meetings and other materials available to me. In showing my appreciation I wish to name those folks.

First of all, I would like to thank my wife Sandy for all her support and encouragement she gave me to help me through this book. There were many times when I was ready to quit, but with her encouragement and her editing, I was able to get it finished.

I also wish to thank Maryl Thompson, Receptionist and Administrative Assistant of my real estate agency, Uinta Realty, Inc., for all the assistance she gave me in using my computer. When I had a computer problem, she was always on hand to help me through it, as did Tonya Dennis, Associate Broker in the office, who also assisted me on the computer when necessary.

Also, I want to thank the Executive Assistant to the Mayor of Evanston and Deputy City Clerk Nancy Stevenson for her time and hard work in providing me with 16 years of copies of the minutes of all the official meetings of the Evanston City Council during my tenure as Mayor of Evanston, 1979-1983 and 1987-1995, plus the term of Mayor Gene Martin, 1983-1987.

Other folks I wish to thank and show appreciation to are Shelly and Deann Horne of Creative Ink Images for their assistance in preparing the book cover; and Former City Engineer Brian Honey for information he provided me concerning the Sulphur Creek Dam Project and many other projects that were constructed during my term as Mayor. Brian was City Engineer under me for my last eight years in office. Thanks are also due to City Attorney Dennis Boal for straightening me out on a few matters. Dennis was my City Attorney also during my final eight years of my term as mayor. Thanks also to retired Urban Renewal Agency Director Jim Davis for providing me with information for my book; and former City Councilmember Tom Hutchinson for the information and input that he provided me. Other city employees that I wish to thank are Paul Knopf, former city planner, Public Works Superintendent Allan "Oop" Hansen and Engineering Tech Bob Liechty for their input to my story.

I also want to thank the Uinta County Library in Evanston for the use of their equipment, the Uinta County Museum in Evanston and the Evanston Chamber of Commerce for materials provided me to be used in my book; and the *Uinta County Herald* for giving me the opportunity to look through many of their old newspapers.

I appreciate all those named above for the completion of this book *"Evanston, Wyoming...Boom-Bust-Politics"*.

However, I want to let you, the reader, know that almost all of the material used in this story was from my personal collection of photos, newspaper clippings, letters, etc., and from the actual minutes of the Evanston meetings during the period from 1967 to 1995. But some material is also from my own memory and from talking to some of those folks I mentioned above.

Thank You...
April 25, 2018

ABOUT THE AUTHOR

Born January 28, 1932 in Salt Lake City, Utah, Dennis ended up in Evanston, Wyoming. He quit high school and joined the 141st Tank Battalion of the Wyoming National Guard.

When the Korean War started in 1950, his unit was called to active duty in September, but he and his wife, Sandy got married on July 26, 1950 before he left for active duty, and to serve time in Korea.

Dennis and Sandy settled in Evanston, where he served three 4-year terms as a member of the Evanston city council and three 4-year terms as mayor. Dennis retired at the age of 81 from his real estate agency, and after raising four sons and over 68 years of marriage, he and his wife Sandy still reside in Evanston.

Be sure to look for
Volume 5 of Evanston Wyoming

www.ingramcontent.com/pod-product-compliance
Lightning Source LLC
Chambersburg PA
CBHW030409100426
42812CB00028B/2886/J